Physical Education for Children

Physical Education for Children

A Developmental Program

ELIZABETH HALSEY

Professor Emeritus of Physical Education
The State University of Iowa

LORENA PORTER

Professor of Physical Education
Northern Illinois University

With a Foreword by
Dr. Paul J. Misner

HOLT, RINEHART AND WINSTON

New York · Chicago · San Francisco · Toronto · London

PICTURE CREDITS

Grateful acknowledgment is made to the following institutions, publishers, and individuals for permission to reproduce their photographs. Numbers following the names refer to the pages in this book on which such reproductions appear.

Baltimore, Maryland, Department of Education, 157

Children, Campus School, State University College at Cortland, Irving Miller, photographer, 181

The Christian Science Monitor, Gordon N. Converse, photographer, 136 and cover

Cincinnati, Ohio, Public Schools, Division of Health and Hygiene, Marsh Photographers, 70, 71, 147

City of Denver, Colorado, Department of Parks and Recreation, 34, 119, 127, 145, 194 (bottom), 195 (bottom), 390, 392

Denver, Colorado, Public Schools, Department of Health Education, 194 (top)

Denver *Post*, 99, 195 (top), 258 (top)

Duluth, Minnesota, Board of Education, and Duluth *News Tribune*, 48, 65, 141, 251

Exeter, New Hampshire, Public Schools, 9

Glencoe, Illinois, Public Schools, E. C. Bonhivert, photographer, 158 (top); James Sternig, photographer, 158 (bottom)

Kondreck Studio, Belleville, New Jersey, 127

Lincoln, Nebraska, Public Schools, Audio-Visual Department, 29, 418

Ministry of Education and Central Office of Education, Physical Education in the Primary School, Part One: Moving and Growing, Part Two: Planning the Programme (London, Her Majesty's Stationery Office, 1952–1958), by permission of the Controller of Her Britannic Majesty's Stationery Office, 7, 37, 53, 186, 265, 389

Monkmeyer Press Photo Service, 2, 14, 96

Muller Studio, ii, 274 and cover

Northern Illinois University, Audio-Visual Department, Harold Williams, photographer, 220, 221

Oregon State College Nursery Schools, Mary Alice Russell, photographer, 20, 55 (top)

RCA Educational Services, 362

St. Mary's School, Iowa City, Iowa, James Kent, photographer, 5, 170, 183, 264

School District of Philadelphia, Pennsylvania, Division of Visual Education, 55 (bottom), 72

Sioux City, Iowa, Public Schools, Department of Instruction, 63, 142

State University of Iowa, University Elementary School, James Kent, photographer, 116 and cover, 130, 143, 144, 154, 218, 243, 244, 245, 246, 250, 254, 255, 256, 258 (bottom, right), 259, 261, 262

Upton County Primary School, Bexleyheath, Kent, England, 85, 89, 173, 258 (bottom, left)

Winona State College, Workshop for Elementary Teachers, The Durfey Studios of Photography, 248, 281

Wyalusing Valley Joint School, Pennsylvania, 76

Foreword

The authors of *Physical Education for Children* are to be commended for the preparation of a revised edition of this excellent publication. Since the appearance of the first edition there has continued to be widespread public interest in and concern for the physical fitness of children and youth. Like President Eisenhower, President Kennedy has attached high priority to physical fitness and has furnished aggressive leadership in efforts to improve programs and practices throughout the nation.

Most appropriately, the schools of the nation are expected to assume a major share of responsibility for the improvement of facilities and programs in health and physical education. School administrators have an inescapable responsibility to exercise creative leadership in this vitally important area of educational improvement. The effectiveness of their leadership will be reflected in the extent to which budget appropriations make provision for adequate facilities, personnel, and services, and to the extent that health and physical education are recognized as integral phases of the total instructional program.

Physical Education for Children will continue to be enthusiastically received by all individuals concerned with the planning and improvement of programs in health and physical education. It will be helpful to specializing students and to those who are preparing to teach in the elementary school. It will, of course, be an extremely valuable resource for all individuals, both teachers and specialists, who are concerned with the daily provision of appropriate learning experiences for children.

A unique contribution of *Physical Education for Children* stems from the fact that it is based upon sound principles of child

v

growth and development. I predict wide acceptance of this distinctively new approach to the teaching of health and physical education. I predict also that the use of the text will result in significantly improved programs in schools throughout the nation.

Paul J. Misner

Glencoe, Illinois
February 1963

Preface

In revising the first edition of *Physical Education for Children*, the authors have been guided by the results of recent study and experience, their own as well as that of others. In addition the junior author has conducted workshops on movement exploration and conferences on elementary education that have been productive of ideas, materials, and new emphases.

In this revised edition, movement exploration has been emphasized as an effective method of developing all activity skills and understandings, as well as a challenge to the ingenuity and inventiveness of children and teachers in specific problems. Additional suggestions have been included to help teachers in presenting movement exploration and in integrating this material with the rest of the physical education program.

National concern for the fitness of children and youth makes it advisable to call attention to some of the basic contributions of the text as well as certain additions in this revision. Methods of evaluating fitness have been expanded to include recent testing programs and guides to the use of fitness tests and the evaluation of results. The purpose of total fitness, including the morale that improves endurance, is made more clear. Such methods of class organization as preplanning and self-direction allow greater activity from a class by reducing the time children spend in waiting and listening to the teacher. Solving problems in movement gives meaning as well as exercise in "work sessions" preliminary to the main content of the lesson. In these work sessions each child may work at his individual problems under his own volition.

The organization of the book is designed to assist in many ways the teacher who is using it as a text. The first two chapters will give background material orienting the students so they may understand reasons for later procedures. In the third and fourth chapters they will come to practical planning of program and lessons. In this work, of course, they will use the last four chapters as resource material. Here actual descriptions of movement problems, stunts and apparatus, games, and dance will familiarize students with activities that form the content of programs and lessons. Most course teachers will interpose laboratory periods here so the students (teachers-in-training) will actually participate in activities and thus experience them firsthand, rediscovering fun, exercise, skill, and strategy at their own more mature level. Teachers-in-training and older teachers as well seem to find enjoyment in working out the problems of movement exploration, and they appreciate the educational possibilities of this material.

Chapter 5, "The Teacher," readily integrates with beginning experience in laboratory teaching, and should be studied with care in preparation for it, as should Chapters 6, 7, and 8. Teachers-in-service as well as teachers-in-training find it very helpful to have resource material in activities easy to find; therefore Chapters 9, 10, 11, and 12 have been grouped together toward the end of the book. Chapter 9, "Movement Exploration," is the first of the group since many of these problems relate to the other activities.

The authors have found the suggestions made by teachers and students using the text very helpful. Every one was carefully considered; many were adopted and are gratefully acknowledged here. We are grateful also for help from other countries. Three of the English authorities whose work was mentioned in the first edition attended the International Congress on Physical Education held in Washington in August 1961. In addition to their papers on movement presented at that congress, suggestions were received by the senior author from Ruth Foster, Marie Crabbe, and Muriel Webster, who read some of the revised material in process at that time. In 1960 the junior author gained insight and inspiration from the observation of classes taught by Sheila Stanley, Physical Education Lecturer, Toronto Teachers' College, and Rose Hill, University of Toronto. Visits to public schools under the direction of Mary Lidell, Supervisor of Physical Education, Township of Etobicoke, Ontario, Canada, and Nora Chatwin, Physical Education Inspector, Department of Education, Ontario, Canada, were equally enlightening. While it is impossible to mention all others who have contributed useful suggestions for revision, the authors would like to acknowledge the help of Dr. Mildred Doster, Joan Tillotson, Jane Fink, Lela Trager, Jane Perry, and other colleagues of the junior author at Northern Illinois University.

E. H.
L. P.

February 1963

Contents

Physical Education for Children

CHAPTER 1

Introduction

As THE YOUNG CHILD goes about his busy day, the adult with him begins to believe again in perpetual motion. Moving about and exploring whatever he finds that is new is, of course, the child's way of learning. Through exploration he develops his ideas of the world around him, and extends his control over the things he can control. As he develops in size, in strength, and in manipulatory skill, he also develops in understanding of things and people. This many-sided development of childhood is the process of adaptation, through which the child learns to fit into the complicated way of life we call civilization. And although each change is a new marvel to new parents, the child is following an orderly sequence common to all children. True, he establishes his own rate, and sets a pattern of development unique to him. He may walk earlier or later than other children of his own age, have fewer or more teeth than they. But he crawls, hitches, or creeps before he walks, and gets his front teeth before his molars, just like any other baby.[1]

[1] According to Dr. Howard V. Meredith, nine out of ten children develop teeth in this sequence. (Unpublished data.)

The child's growth limits, or his growth potential, may be a matter of genes. His actual day-by-day development, however, is determined by the interplay of his growth potential with environmental experiences. Just as a plant needs sunlight, so the child develops best in the favorable social climate of love and acceptance. Neither plant nor child can grow without proper food and nutrition. The child is distinguished from the plant in many ways, but especially by the fact that he is capable of conscious and voluntary movement. The quality of his movement experience does much to determine the nature of his total development.

What Is Physical Education?

In a sense the whole process of development may be regarded as education. In another sense, it may all be regarded as *physical* education, because the child's moving organism, his body, is also his feeling and thinking organism. It is customary, however, to reserve the term *education* for what is learned in school, and to talk about *physical education* as one important part of this school experience.

The school today is society's means of giving all children and youth experiences that will help each one to develop to the limits of his capacity. Education, then, may be defined as *planned developmental experience* for all children and youth. *Physical education is the use of vigorous movement as planned developmental experience for all children and youth.* Physical education is the only part of the educational program in which the child is not merely encouraged to move, but is taught to move effectively. Effectiveness of movement depends on its purpose, which may differ at different times. The child may run as fast as he can to win a race or to tag another player. He may move slowly and with strength to show how a large and powerful giant moves. He may climb up on apparatus and jump down to prove to himself that he can master an obstacle. In each case, achievement of his purpose is important to his general development. In each case, instruction is an aid to achievement. Through physical education we make sure that a child's movements are the most suitable ones for his stage of development.

". . . to show how a large and powerful giant moves."

Why Is Physical Education Important?

Physical education is important, first, because the child is built for movement. The power of muscles, the leverage of bones, the mobility of joints are geared for this function of movement. Since such a structure must be used if it is to be kept in good condition, the child's movement fulfills a biological law, often stated as "structure demands function." Bones, muscles, and joints move the body, and vigorous movement helps to make bone, muscle, and joint stronger. Because other functions of the body are also well geared with movement, they, too, improve as movement becomes more vigorous. The heart pumps more blood, which is more quickly distributed throughout the complex and far-reaching system of arteries, capillaries, and veins. Breathing becomes more rapid. Internal ventilation improves; the body heats up as internal fuel is burned for energy, and cools off as thermostatic controls bring more blood to the surface, turning on the skin water bath less elegantly known as sweat. The various organs that function to produce these responses develop as they work, and proper organic development is, of course, basic to the child's present and future health.

There is much more to the picture, however. Physical education is important because the child's movement leads him into experiences that promote other lines of development in addition to organic growth. As he learns to climb up and over obstacles and apparatus and to jump down, his skill gives him new confidence. Learning new skills of movement helps him to overcome fear and to avoid frustration. It helps, therefore, in his emotional development. Another contribution becomes apparent whenever children are guided in playing games. Here, there is the process of the common enterprise, the rules which all observe so that the game may go on, the discipline of the self in the interest of belonging to the group. Sometimes this is the small child's first experience with self-discipline, which then becomes a step in his social adjustment. Social adjustment, including the indispensable ability to get along with other persons, is one of the most important lines of development to which physical education makes a significant contribution.

To summarize, physical education is essential to the best development of the child along the lines of physical and organic growth, motor skill, emotional maturity, and social adjustment.

Why Organize Physical Education?

Do we need to organize or plan anything as spontaneous and inevitable as the young child's vigorous movement? If we turn children loose at recess and let them play, won't they get what they need? It is true that very often the leaders will play hard and get exercise. But this may be at the expense of a large number who cannot keep up with them and who consequently stay on the outside watching the game. Both leaders and "fringers" lose something in this situation. Physical education is for all the children in the class, not merely the largest and the strongest. It includes the spastic, the polio victim, and those disadvantaged in other ways. Obviously, most children will need guidance if they are to learn to include all their classmates. They must come to see that this is "organized justice"[2] as well as decent consideration. In giving a fair chance to each, the privileged child learns as much as the handicapped child does in receiving. Such learnings come from good class procedure.

[2] A term adapted from Borgese's characterization of fascism as "organized injustice." See G. A. Borgese, *Goliath: The March of Fascism*. New York: The Viking Press, Inc., 1937.

New skills bring confidence and help emotional development.

In play, the child's emotions are involved. He needs help in developing control of them and in building up an increasingly mature pattern of good sportsmanship. For the child, this emotional control is the surest approach to the fundamentals of getting along with his peers, and sportsmanship increases his appreciation of ethical standards. By watching children at play, a trained observer can tell whether they have had the full benefits of well-organized and well-guided play experience. If the girl with leg braces is taking her turn on the climbing apparatus with encouragement; if the fat boy on first base gets coaching, not ridicule, from his teammates; and if the children are acting as accepted officials in their own games with a minimum of squabbling, then the observer knows that they have been well taught.

Children learn courage and balance from play on parallel ropes.

Organization is necessary to ensure breadth as well as quality in the child's experience in physical education. The child must learn many important motor skills in rhythm, in ball handling, in climbing, running, jumping, and in expressive movement. These skills must be organized in the curriculum and taught, just as skills in language arts, music, and arithmetic must be organized in the curriculum and taught.

There are, therefore, four basic reasons for organizing physical education. First, we enable all children to participate within the limits of their abilities. Second, by teaching the group that all must be helped to participate, we increase children's social and emotional maturity. Third, we teach the right ways of playing. When these ways have been learned, the play becomes once more spontaneous, but now it is useful, productive play for the whole class. Fourth, we organize to ensure the learning of a variety of important motor skills.

Good Use of Time

Good planning and teaching mean good use of time. The well-taught class moves easily to the play space and expands into activity without the restriction of fussy directions or overly careful formation. In some classes, for example, the children carry out and properly space the necessary equipment, then put it to use. Each child has something: a rope, a ball, a hoop, a pair of stilts, or the like. He uses it in his own way, with due consideration for others as he shares space with them. Or, if it is a day for games, the games are carefully selected so that everyone will be active most of the time. For example, the class plays Catch of Fish rather than Drop the Handkerchief.[3] The children play old games with great zest and improving strategy. They read about new games before coming to the playground in order to avoid long explanations. All games are organized, as far as possible, in the classroom, so that action can start as soon as the play space is reached. On many days, movement exploration, with all the children responding together, will prove a good investment of time. As the teacher makes suggestions or sets problems, the children try to find the answers in movements of different speed and strength.

[3] Catch of Fish is a game in which all players run most of the time. In Drop the Handkerchief, the circle stands still while one or two children run.

Planning in the classroom makes possible good use of time in the gymnasium.

Always, the teacher is alert to remove obstacles to action and to remedy time-wasting procedures that prevent learning because they prevent doing.

The Purpose and Principles of Physical Education

The *purpose* of physical education, implicit throughout the preceding discussion, should now be clear. The purpose of physical education is to secure the best possible development of all children and youth, especially along the closely related lines of physical growth, motor skill, emotional maturity, and social adjustment. Such fortunate development ensures total fitness, healthy growth, and the possession of rich recreational resources. It entails social adjustment in a free society.

Among the many *principles* that relate to physical education, a few of great importance will be stated here as guides to later study.

Movement

Since structure demands function, the child, built for movement, must move in order to develop normally. Movement becomes more effective as he grows older, and teaching increases this effectiveness. We have said that, in physical education, vigorous movement is planned as developmental experience. Basic to this development is the exploratory phase, in which the child focuses on what he wants to do and finds out what his body can do. He learns to control the quality of his movement, and comes to perceive space as its changing background. If problem solving is emphasized in teaching, the child thinks, invents activities, and remains freely expressive in his movement. This makes integration with sports, self-testing, and dance a natural process. Thus movement exploration becomes basic to all forms of physical education.

Development

The development of most children along interrelated lines of change follows a broad sequential pattern. However, each individual child proceeds at his own rate and at any age shows his own unique pattern within the larger one. His progress depends on the interaction of inner potential and external conditions. This means that the teacher should not think in terms of the average child or of standard performance. Instead, he should provide activities through which each child may try, in his own way, to realize his own powers to the full. Each child is recognized by the teacher when he improves, even though he may still be rather clumsy. So each one has some small triumph each day.

Indivisibility

The child should not be thought of as an aggregate of separate parts—body, mind, and spirit—but as a unified, organic whole. Moreover, development should be recognized as a total phenomenon. Physical growth and the development of motor skill, emotional maturity, and social adjustment may be observed separately, but they must be understood as interrelated changes in an indivisible organism. This means that the teacher plans for and watches all outcomes possible for each child. These plans, these outcomes, go well beyond exercise and fun.

Fitness

Total fitness is a condition of mental and moral health as well as physical vigor. It results, not from exercise alone, but from intelligent use of vigorous movement in teaching the child as a unified organism. Total fitness gives the power to endure hardship or to live in comfort without losing drive. It is basic to survival, both for the individual and for his society, but it will be maintained only if the individual accepts his responsibility to a society that he values.

Stress

Situations of stress are necessary to the child's best development, but the degree of stress should be adapted to the stage of development. In his natural play a child changes the situation when the stress becomes too great. When adults are in control, however, they often expose children to too much or too little stress, through lack of understanding of how much the child needs and of what he can endure.

Goals

The child's goals are set by his development and adaptive needs. He must try himself out; he is driven by his growing strength to see how strong he is today. The teacher can forget all about stars, ribbons, and other artificial awards in the physical education class. Teacher and children can enjoy together the gaiety and fun natural to an active experience in play. However, the teacher must be ready to underline and to clarify less obvious goals: "Charles, you're growing up; you used your own ball today. . . . Mary was very brave about her knee. . . . Bill's group got along as well as the big boys in the fifth grade!"

The art of expanding and improving the child's goals, or of substituting socially useful goals for those that are socially destructive, is one of the most rewarding and interesting responsibilities of all teaching.

Learning

The learner responds as a whole to the goals he adopts. If the child wants to throw a ball, he throws it. If it comes his way, he tries to catch it. Later, more complex "whole" patterns occur: bouncing and catching, tossing and catching, throwing against a house or a wall and catching. The teacher understands that repetition of these acts is satisfying, especially when the learner sees progress in skill. Therefore the teacher often suggests improvements in parts of the whole pattern, but practice to improve parts is always related again to the whole skill.

Self-direction

A free society depends on the capacity of its members for intelligent self-direction. At all ages and in all branches of education this capacity must be developed. In physical education regimented gymnastics have long since given way to solving problems in movement, devising strategy in games, inventing new activities with apparatus, and creating imaginative forms of dance. While the teacher is an indispensable guide to best learning, the children will get into action with a minimum of lost time if taught to take responsibility for self-direction.

Summary

Physical education is the use of vigorous movement as planned developmental experience. It is an integral and important part of education, the only part of the child's school day in which he is encouraged to move freely and taught to move effectively. Through vigorous movement, at least four aspects of the child's many-sided development may be guided: physical and organic growth, motor skill, emotional maturity, and social adjustment.

The purpose of physical education is to promote the best possible development in each of these four aspects, thus ensuring the child's total fitness as well as the acquisition of desirable resources in physical recreation at any stage of his development. This broad purpose will not be attained unless the subject is well organized and well taught.

Some of the principles basic to the conduct of physical education are briefly stated below:

Movement is essential to the child's normal development, since it is a function of his human structure. The teacher may improve the child's understanding and control of this function by setting various problems in movement for him to explore and solve.

Development proceeds according to general plan, but at the individual's own rate. Therefore the teacher considers each child's growth pattern, not attempting to hold or mold him to an age-grade norm.

Indivisibility is the chief characteristic of the child's organic unity. Therefore the teacher is concerned with his total behavior: how he thinks and feels as well as how he moves when he runs, jumps, climbs, dances, or plays games.

Total fitness is a state of physical vigor and high morale. Therefore the teacher must try to educate children, not merely exercise them.

Stress, in favorable degree, contributes to the child's development. Often the child is a better (intuitive) judge than the adult of the degree of stress he needs or can endure.

Goals depend on the child's developmental needs. The teacher expands and improves the child's goals, but does not try to impose others that are artificial or superficial.

Learning results when the child responds as a whole to the goals he adopts. The teacher may guide his practice of the whole skill or of various parts; the parts should be put together again into an improved whole pattern.

A free society must seek to develop intelligent self-direction through its educational program. Teachers of physical education will set problem-solving situations and encourage invention in movement exploration, games, self-testing, and creative dance. They will avoid regimented gymnastics and use only a minimum of completely teacher-directed activities.

Selected References

American Association for Health, Physical Education, and Recreation, *Leisure and the Schools*, 1961 Yearbook. Washington, D.C., 1961.

AAHPER, *Physical Education, an Interpretation.* Washington, D.C., 1956.

AAHPER, *School Packet: Why Physical Education?* Washington, D.C., 1954.

Duncan, Ray O., and Helen B. Watson, *Introduction to Physical Education.* New York: The Ronald Press Company, 1960, Chaps. 3, 12.

Oberteuffer, Delbert, *Physical Education*, rev. ed. New York: Harper & Row, Publishers, 1956, Chaps. 1, 2.

O'Keefe, Patric Ruth, and Anita Aldrich, *Education through Physical Activities*, 3d ed. St. Louis: The C. V. Mosby Company, 1959, Chap. 3.

Williams, Jesse Feiring, *Principles of Physical Education*, 7th ed. Philadelphia: W. B. Saunders Company, 1959, Chap. 1.

CHAPTER 2

The Child

Developmental facts and experiences

DURING THE GREATER PART OF THE HISTORY of the Western world men have regarded the mind and body as separate entities. This belief came from many sources, widely separated in time and space. For example, Simeon Stylites became famous by living on a pillar and trying to ignore his body, as did other hermits of the fifth century. Sanctity of the spirit was contrasted with grossness of the flesh in the religious teaching of Europe in the middle ages. The French philosopher Descartes wrote convincingly of dualism in the seventeenth century, and many other influences strengthened the idea, which now seems curious to us, that the body is a necessary but somewhat unworthy form of housing and transportation for the mind and spirit. This idea dominated education and the rearing of children until the last quarter of a century, by which time the findings of many sciences had made clear the essential wholeness of the human organism.

In Frederick Lewis Allen's phrase, it was "Only Yesterday" when most teachers wanted to work with the child's mind rather than his body. Only yesterday, our Puritan heritage demanded that the child's need to run, to shout, and to play be repressed as rigorously as sin.

The Child as a Unified Organism

Today's child lives more naturally than the child of yesterday, and his natural life is accepted and more clearly understood by the adults around him. Teachers today know that when a child comes to school, he leaves no part of himself at home. Neither does the teacher! There in the classroom each one of them moves, thinks, and feels, all at once and with one organism: his body. This body is a complex living structure, interesting and effective beyond any mechanical device yet invented by man. Moving, thinking, and feeling are so well synchronized in the human that neither child nor teacher is conscious of the integrating process in himself. Each one is aware, as the school day goes on, of what he wants to do. Each one tries, when the time seems ripe, to do it. Varying degrees of success attend his effort. The teacher, whose organism has matured through time, experience, and education, and whose level of effectiveness is, therefore, usually much higher than the child's, is sometimes at a loss to understand just what the child's level is. This is particularly true in certain aspects of the child's development, such as his physical growth and his developing motor skill, emotional maturity, and social adjustment.

In physical education classes the teacher has his best opportunity to observe the whole child in action, and to become familiar with his level of development. By the same token, these classes present perhaps the greatest challenge to fruitful teaching. As the child throws himself into play, he moves, thinks, and feels simultaneously and with all his energy. *How* he moves (skillfully or clumsily), *how* he thinks (quickly or slowly, with or without strategy), and *how* he feels (like cheating or playing fair) depends in great part on the teaching he is getting. But whether his learning is good or poor, it "sticks"; it becomes part of him because he has been wholly absorbed in the process; that is, in the game.

Interrelationship of Phases of Development

Because the teacher has learned that it is not realistic to take the child apart when studying him, he considers these various lines of development only as different dimensions of the child's total growth picture. There are, of course, many other dimensions not described in this text: intellectual horizons, imagination, concentration and perseverance, use of such cultural tools as language, and others. Although these also are related to a child's learning in physical education, they are perhaps not as closely related as are physical growth, motor skill, emotional maturity, and social adjustment. As Jersild has said:

> Motor development plays an important role as a vehicle for social development. Throughout childhood, and especially in the preschool and elementary school years, a child's social contacts with his peers are to a large extent made by way of common motor activities. Again, a child's motor development will have an important bearing upon the emotional features of his behavior. The child who is backward in his motor skills will, for example, have occasion to be angry or afraid in the face of obstacles or threats that an abler child will handle unemotionally. . . . What we do in education should be chosen with an eye to these interlocking relationships. What we provide for helping children to build competence in various motor activities, for example, is not simply an investment in healthy exercise or handy skills. It is also an investment in social and emotional adjustment. The child who is helped to become a good third baseman in a ball game may thereby reach first base in his efforts to become socially acceptable to other children.[1]

Breckenridge and Vincent are emphatic about the importance of instruction in motor skills:

> Instruction in motor skills can, through pointing out more efficient procedures, cut down waste movements and keep poor habits and false accessory movements at a minimum. Children must practice any new skill with satisfaction if learning is to proceed rapidly. The teacher can do much to keep motivation at a high level and to help the child retain self-confidence in his own ability. Unless there is a defect of muscles or nerves or bone structure, grace and free-flowing rhythmic movement should become the possession of every child. No child should be robbed of the joy which can be found in skillful bodily movement, of the social contacts it can provide during the preadolescent and adolescent periods, or of the contribution which adequate exercise and bodily expression can make to the general mental as well as physical health and vigor throughout life.[2]

[1] A. T. Jersild et al., Child Development and the Curriculum. New York: Bureau of Publications, Teachers College, Columbia University, 1946, pp. 23–24.
[2] Marian E. Breckenridge and E. Lee Vincent, Child Development, 4th ed. Philadelphia: W. B. Saunders Company, 1960, p. 319.

Individual Differences in Development

Although there is a sequence of development common to all children, the modern teacher knows that no two children grow in precisely the same way. Among other things, children differ in rate and uniformity of growth, in maximum potential, and in group status at any given time. How fast a child grows, how far he is going to get, how he differs from the "typical" or from his classmates in school—all these are determined by his particular growth pattern. Therefore the school and the home should not force him into any line or design of growth, nor hold him to specific age norms of achievement. They should, rather, provide the best possible conditions for growth so that the child may fulfill his potential and arrive at his own maturity levels in accordance with his own rate of growth.

Using Developmental Facts

In the brief summary of developmental facts that follows, no attempt will be made to describe characteristics by specific years. Beginning with important preschool years, there appears a common sequence of developmental steps or stages, each of which is essential to those that follow. During this sequence the child has experiences that either favor or retard his growth. Since each stage depends on those that precede, all of the child's experiences determine not only whether the boy of 11 will be as tall, as strong, as symmetrical as his age and inheritance permit, but also whether he will achieve his potential in skilled movement, in emotional control, and in getting along with other children.

Obviously, these developmental experiences are very important and should be carefully selected. Those selected for the physical education program affect so many dimensions of the child's total growth that they are crucially important. Only the best should be used. "It will probably do more good than harm" is not a suitable criterion for including a game, a dance, a song, a shop lesson, a reading project, or a type of athletic competition.

The rest of this chapter is devoted to a summary of developmental facts and their implications for the developmental experiences that should be included in a physical education program. The facts about physical growth are quoted from charts furnished the authors by Dr. Howard V. Meredith, research professor of the

Iowa Child Welfare Research Station. The facts about motor skill are drawn from various studies in the fields of child development and physical education. Facts about emotional maturity and social adjustment are derived from such authorities in child development as Breckenridge and Vincent, Gesell, Jersild, and Olson. Students interested in additional study may wish to explore the bibliography at the end of this chapter. The discussion is divided into three sections: *preschool*, from 3 to 5 years; *primary grades*, from 6 to 8 years; and *intermediate grades*, from 9 to 11 years.

Preschool: 3–5 Years

Physical Growth:
Developmental Facts

The average gain in weight during this period is 4½ pounds a year. The annual growth in height averages 2½ inches.

The legs grow faster than the arms; the arms grow faster than the trunk; and the trunk faster than the head.

This is not a period of tooth eruption. Ordinarily, the deciduous teeth have erupted before the age of 3 and the permanent teeth do not begin to erupt until after the age of 6.

The preschool period is a period of tooth and bone building. Bone-cell formation is active (the patellae and several of the wrist bones begin to ossify), and there are large additions to the enamel and dentine of many permanent teeth.

At the end of the period, at the age of 6, the typical child is 45 inches tall and weighs 45 pounds. Other averages are: arm length, 19½ inches; chest girth, 21 inches; upper arm girth, 7 inches; and leg girth, 9½ inches at the calf.

Motor Skills:
Developmental Facts

By the age of 3, walking and running are well established, but since balance is easier near the ground, the child often squats, creeps, or crawls when balance is threatened.

Climbing is natural and easy, since the child grips well with his hands.

Individual differences are apparent in the play interests and abilities of these 3-year-olds.

At 3½ or 4 years, the child can climb stairs using alternate upward steps.

During this period, the child learns to jump down, and later does a small broad jump (that is horizontally, along the ground).

Binocular vision is developing, but because fine focus is not possible, eye-hand coordination is rudimentary only.

Skill in ball handling is just beginning to develop.

The child can kick a ball from a standing position.

Physical Growth and Motor Skills: Developmental Experiences

Rapidly growing arms and legs demand use. The young child has an insistent need for activity. Opportunities must be provided to use the arms in climbing, hanging, pushing, and pulling; and to use the legs in kicking, running, jumping, climbing, and in various other forms of locomotion. Since the 3-year-old can grip well and suspend himself by his arms, he should have a chance to climb on metal frames with bars at different heights, on vertical ropes, and on parallel ropes and bars. Still simpler forms of apparatus may be improvised by using a slanted ladder, a bench, or a rounded pole. Tables and boxes may be arranged for climbing up and jumping down. Small, light mats should be used for landing from jumps, and for practicing such stunts as somersaults.

The child's lack of fine visual focus implies that balls should be large enough to be seen readily and caught with a rudimentary clasping motion. They should also be light enough to be thrown with a limited forearm motion. Medium-sized, brightly colored rubber utility balls are right for this age group.

All these skills and powers develop during the preschool years through daily informal play with balls and on apparatus. Enough equipment should be available so that no time is lost in waiting for turns; each child should have a ball, and only three or four children at a time should play on the same apparatus, depending on its size and type. This period of daily play should be supplemented by informal experiments with movement, rhythm, and inventive dramatic play, as described later.

As the child grows and develops, both teacher and parents should be alert to any signs of a physical handicap. Although most children develop normally, it is wise to catch defects of bones, joints, and muscles, as well as those of sight and hearing, early. The young child does not look like an adult, nor does he have adult postural contours and habits. He has a relatively large trunk and prominent abdomen, a flat upper back, a short and sometimes pronounced curve of the lower back. His feet are well padded but do not yet show much arch. His legs may be knock-kneed or, more rarely, bowed. Natural, active play, free movement and plenty of it, will assist the normal processes of change as he grows. Special exercises are necessary only in case of special defects. For example, any sign of asymmetry should be detected early. If one shoulder is higher than the other, if one leg is longer, if the ribs are unequally curved, then it is well to check with an orthopedic specialist and to follow his advice concerning special exercise or other treatment.

Emotional Maturity:
Developmental Facts

During the preschool period, the immediate, uncontrolled emotions of infancy become more subtle, more complex, and less direct. They are therefore more difficult for parents and teachers to understand.

Crying diminishes, and the child may be able to control it. It occurs less as a result of conflicts with playmates, falls, and bruises, more as an expression of anger at being thwarted or hurt by someone else.

Anger is provoked less by physical discomfort, more by difficulties with situations. The expression of anger is more often verbal; there is less physical aggression. Control of anger improves as various skills develop.

Fear is often learned from fearful adults; it takes the form of fear of animals, of being left alone, of the dark, of injury, or of other objects and situations. These fears are conditioned and may be overcome by reconditioning or by such favorable experiences as growth in power, development of new skills or general confidence, and play therapy.

Humor and gaiety are associated with play, physical activity, exciting physical sensations, slapstick, and other ego-satisfying situations.

Emotional Maturity:
Developmental Experiences

Normal progress toward emotional maturity depends on the child's basic feeling of security. This comes from love and acceptance, first in the home, later in school. Only love and acceptance will make the child sure of his place in the family group, work group, or play group. Constructive emotions are developed by contagion; the cheerful, happy, calm, parent or teacher provides an atmosphere favorable to the development of similar emotions in children. If the teacher enjoys play periods, accepts each child, and establishes a permissive and happy atmosphere, within a comfortable setting of orderly procedure, he is providing experiences favorable to emotional growth.

Children who are afraid of climbing should not be forced to climb. Rivalry in skill should be played down. "Set" stunts should not be required, but children should be encouraged to experiment, to invent, and to learn new skills, each one progressing at his own best rate. When the clumsy child makes progress, the teacher should comment favorably. As he improves in skill and confidence, this less able child will overcome fear, and will have fewer occasions for anger resulting from frustration. The child's natural impulse to seek comfort from the teacher if he has been hurt in play should be met warmly by the teacher. However, the teacher's natural impulse to lift the child up or down from apparatus should *not* be followed, since this slows the child's development of independence, skill, and judgment as to what he can do with safety. An occasional helping hand to the child who is timid or excessively overweight may give the confidence needed for learning. Verbal help as to how to get down from apparatus, or how to relax in jumping down from a small height leads to more efficient body movement.

Children are usually gay and happy while they are actively at play, but shouting and screaming probably create more tensions than they release. The resulting overstimulation is favorable neither to safety nor to improvement in skill.

Social Adjustment:
Developmental Facts

At the beginning of the preschool period, the child is socially dependent on adults.

Adult attitudes, as described in the previous section, build the framework of security and confidence upon which later adjustment depends. These attitudes are reflected in ease of discipline, happiness, affection, and welcome at home; in parents' helpfulness and loyalty; in parents' sharing of children's interests.

In a favorable environment, the child readily seeks comfort, help, and companionship from adults and shows his affection by climbing into an adult's lap or nestling in his arms.

In the course of developing independence, the child will show occasional resistance and self-assertion. At first this may be obstinate and unreasonable; later it will be more subtle. It may persist as negativism even in adult life.

The child will engage in "parallel play" with his parents, brothers and sisters, or neighbors. That is, he will play alongside the others, without sharing equipment or taking part in their activities. He can, however, maintain play in small groups for a short time.

The child's first response to other children during the preschool period has been observed to be friendly most of the time (about seven times out of eight).

The preschool child will guard his own possessions and his own rights while experimenting with those of others.

Aggressive behavior during the preschool period is to be expected frequently, but it is more than balanced by the number and duration of friendly acts. Some aggressive behavior is a normal part of early social development, necessary to self-confidence.

Social skills must be learned and practiced without too much adult interference.

Competition and rivalry with others, which appear prominently by the age of 4 or 5 years, are very much affected by the environment and by indirect control exerted by adults.

The child's dominance over others depends on his self-confidence in any situation; training can improve self-confidence. Children who have especially good bodily skills tend to be dominant.

Children who have little chance to practice and develop social skills in home and neighborhood play with other children may be handicapped in first efforts at social learning in school.

Social Adjustment:
Developmental Experiences

Social adjustment may be learned gradually through play. Simple beginnings are made in parallel play with balls, when children do not have to share a ball but merely share space as each plays with his own ball. Other forms of parallel play are found in exploring different kinds of movement: light running; heavy stamping; tiptoe and crouch walking; running in circles, zigzag lines, and straight lines; moving quickly and moving slowly. Through moving freely about, children can learn to share a large play space without colliding. This is one of the first adjustments they make easily. Fairly early in the preschool period, and with increasing skill, they may develop imitative and dramatic movements. These may be rhythmic and repetitious, but they are not necessarily so. Records, percussion instruments, television and radio programs may accompany this early "dance play."

Some 5-year-olds enjoy rhythmic play in small groups. The authors have seen leaders use tambourines with such groups, to set the rhythm of rapid running, alternating with stooping and jumping when the groups gathered together. More often, however, children of this age will improvise their own movements to their own rhythms.

Taking turns on apparatus involves more difficult skills of adjustment to others. At first, taking turns may be based on the child's sense of fairness, which develops early. Later, he may learn that consideration for others makes more fun for all. By the time he is 5, he may be ready for the impersonal discipline of a large group game, if the teacher is with the circle to remind all players that the rules apply to each one. Very few circle games, however, give much activity to all players. They should be used only occasionally, as a step in group adjustment.

By the time he is 5, the child may be able to work with four or six others in carrying mats, setting up simple movable equipment, and carrying supplies from storeroom to playroom. He enjoys these services because they make him feel competent and grown-up.

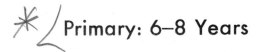 **Primary: 6–8 Years**

Physical Growth:
Developmental Facts

The average annual growth during this period is 5½ pounds in weight and 2 inches in height.

The chest grows faster than the abdomen, the legs faster than the trunk, and the face faster than the head.

The pulse and breathing rates decline, moving gradually toward their adult levels. By the age of 9 the rate per minute is rarely above 90 for a normal pulse, or 20 for normal respiration.

Typically, twelve permanent teeth erupt: four molars and eight incisors. There are wide individual differences: at age 9, for one child in five, the number of erupted permanent teeth is either less than ten or more than sixteen.

At the end of the period (at 9 years), height will vary from 48 to 58 inches, weight from 50 to 90 pounds, and chest girth from 20 to 29 inches.

Motor Skills:
Developmental Facts

The child's speed of reaction is about half that of the adult.

His locomotion has improved: steps lengthen in walking and running, balance is better, the use of arms as an aid in locomotion begins. Skipping, hopping, and galloping can readily be learned in the first grade.

At the age of 6, the child can catch medium-sized balls and use a full-arm swing as he throws from the shoulder. He can also change his stance, starting from a position with his feet apart and his body partially turned sideways. By the age of 9 he can handle small balls well and use a small baseball bat and tennis racket.

At the age of 6, he can bounce and catch a ball well and kick a ball on the run.

He can improve his skill in landing lightly as he jumps. He can jump over a small obstacle, progressing to fair form, and can make a good beginning at the high jump by 9 years.

Track skills are of interest both to boys and girls. Boys show superiority to girls in throwing.

Stunts are enjoyed; the child can control a front somersault at the age of 6, and can develop fair form in the handstand and the cartwheel during these years. More complex climbing and balance skills also develop.

The child is ready to learn swimming skills by the age of 6, if not earlier.

Physical Growth and Motor Skills:
Developmental Experiences

Since most youngsters become much larger and stronger during the primary grades, they can develop many new skills and are forever trying to see what they can do. They will run wherever there is space; climb, chin, and swing up wherever they can find a rope, a tree, or a crossbar; and throw or kick whatever is left loose to throw or kick. Apparently there is no stopping them, if anyone should want to, in this endless game of measuring up to their world. Motivation is no problem when there are so many new things to do, so many movements to try, so many stunts and tricks to invent. Perhaps it is more of a problem to find space, equipment, and class time and to provide guidance. But if the child is to have the best developmental experiences, these things must be made available.

Climbing apparatus is important for the arms, shoulders, and rapidly developing chest of the 6-year-old. Vertical ropes, horizontal or slanting ladders, low bars, the adjustable trapeze, or more elaborate metal frames will provide the needed opportunity to progress in strength as well as in the skills of pulling up the body weight, turning upside down, climbing up, balancing, climbing down or jumping down from apparatus. The conventional jungle gyms, teeters, or swings and slides seem to be less inviting and less challenging to invention than simpler, less expensive kinds of apparatus.[3] Jumping down continues to be an adventure, and to learn controlled relaxation in landing is to add a skill very useful to the child's safety in play. He may jump from benches, tables, boxes or platforms, provided they are stable and his landings are protected by soft surfaces and good techniques. As his legs lengthen and he learns to use his arms, he can jump further on the ground in a broad jump and jump over small hurdles and high-jump bars.

Since children differ so much in rate of growth and in growth potential, apparatus must be adaptable for use at different heights. It also follows that all children cannot be expected to do "standard" stunts or to reach the same level of ability. Each one should be relatively free to choose and to invent his own way of playing on apparatus.

Although most children seem to keep ceaselessly active, they will, if left to themselves, adequately balance activity and rest. The young child can, however, become absorbed and push himself to the point of exhaustion if he is caught in a competitive situation or in pseudoadult activities under pressure from adults. Such situations should be avoided, since his circulation and other fatigue-recovery mechanisms have not yet reached adult levels of efficiency.

By the age of 6, the child has become fairly sure of himself in walking and running, and enjoys such varied experiences as skipping, hopping, and galloping, either in rhythmic play or in movement classes without rhythmic accompaniment. By the third grade he has developed more agility and has begun to control his weight when he changes direction. All kinds of chasing and dodging games help in this, if the rules give all the children a chance for activity. Also useful is free movement in response to suggestions from the teacher. The teacher may ask the children to show how many different ways they can move to the wall and back. He may ask them to move freely around the room with light skipping, then with a very high skip. Gallop and slide-and-slide may also be used, with leads changing in a specified manner. In free movement, the teacher may help the child to distinguish and

[3] See Chapter 6 for a description of this kind of apparatus.

to show different qualities, such as quick and slow, light and strong, straight and curving, high up and low down. Movements of different parts of the body may be suggested: "Can you move your hands quickly and lightly? How high can you reach with your elbow? How far behind you? How high can your knees go?" Any number of problems may be invented by the teacher, and a great number of movement "answers" will be invented by the children if they are encouraged to be creative.

Some of this movement exploration will take place without sound accompaniment, and some will fit a definite rhythmic pattern set by drum, tom-tom, or tambourine. Some will take place in a small space, which the child thinks of as his own space, and some while moving about and sharing space. Some use may be made of appropriate singing games, but probably more use will be made of dance play to dramatize poems, stories, pictures, or songs that have been part of their other experiences during the day.

In his play with balls, the child should begin with medium-sized balls and progress to smaller ones. At the age of 9 he can control tennis balls quite well. He is responsive to instruction in form, and receptive to new stunts in ball handling: O'Leary, basketball dribble, tossing a ball against a wall, or shooting for baskets. In the latter activity the 8-year-old will be frustrated and may develop poor technique unless a low basket is set up and a relatively small, light ball is used. It is very important that every child have a ball to himself when he is experimenting with these skills. Of course, the class is organized in such a way that only one or two groups are playing with balls, so that from eight to sixteen balls per class are needed, not forty.

Stunts and self-testing activities will be used frequently throughout the primary grades. Many of them help to develop arm strength: for example, the wheelbarrow, the push-up from a half-kneeling position, the mule kick, and the tip-up. Somersaults will be done with more skill than at 4 years and should be practiced with emphasis on the tucked position of the head, on rolling up to a standing position, and on doing two in succession with little pause between. In these grades the extended cartwheel, done in even rhythm with balance held upright at the end, may be approached. Dual and combative stunts are favorite ways of testing and developing strength: double somersaults, Indian wrestle, and others.

First-grade children enjoy dramatizing in dance play what they are learning about Indians.

In general, only slight sex differences in skills and interests are apparent in the first three grades. Boys throw better; girls are better at cartwheels and other stunts; boys like contests and combative stunts better than girls do.

If facilities are available, by all means introduce some swimming into the program. Not only does it promote excellent all-around bodily development, but it introduces the element of controlled relaxation as no other form of physical education can. However, very thin children who chill easily should not be included in the group unless they feel ready for it. If they are included, they should have shorter swimming periods than the others.

Emotional Maturity:
Developmental Facts

The child's normal emotional development continues to depend on security and acceptance. Acceptance by his own age group is increasingly important as the child becomes less dependent on adults. He wants social approval and can usually control his own conduct to get it. Some children who are adept at getting the approval of adults, however, fail at the new task of getting approval from their own age group.

As the child's interests broaden and his activities become more varied, he has a greater range of emotional experiences.

The expression of his emotions is more controlled, therefore more removed from the source and harder to understand. Crying is repressed. The 6-year-old may be brave about physical injuries; hurt feelings, fatigue, or unjust punishment, on the other hand, may produce tears not only at 6, but also at 7 or 8.

Anger in social situations and in play groups is expressed at 6 and 7 by some fighting. Later, "big talk," gruffness, boasting, and "acting tough" take the place of physical aggressiveness. The child may even adopt costumes of tough adults—cowboys and gangsters—to give him a sense of power and competence in difficult situations.

Fear of physical danger is somewhat dispelled by developing skill and courage, but the child becomes susceptible to fears of the supernatural, of school failure, and of loss of popularity. Deeper fears induced by stimuli from radio and television appear at this age.

If the school program is not suited to his maturation level, the child will be bored by tasks too easy for him, or frustrated by tasks too difficult.

Laughter is aroused by incongruity or by the frailty and discomfiture of others. By the end of this period, children may enjoy elements of surprise as well as jokes on themselves.

Emotional Maturity:
Developmental Experiences

If the 6-year-old has not gone to nursery school or kindergarten, leaving home to begin the first grade often presents an emotional problem. This problem can be mitigated by acceptance from the teacher and the play group. Large group games, in which the teacher sets a warm social climate, are very helpful. The happy, secure, noncompetitive atmosphere already described is important in periods of play on apparatus, in stunts, and in free movement.

Expressive movement is an excellent way of giving vent to aggressive and hostile feeling without fighting. "Walk like a giant" may lead to heavy, angry stamping, with the child feeling as wicked as the worst of giants and perhaps emerging as a more relaxed and cheerful child. When the youngster is in the third grade he will read tales of heroes. If he acts them out in pantomime or dance plays, he will get the sense of power and adult competence he needs. He will also extend the range of his emotional experiences.

Including in the program a wide variety of activities of different degrees of difficulty, gives the slow child a chance for success and satisfaction while challenging the gifted child to go on with his inventions from "strength to strength." If the slow child has emotional difficulties, some special attention given to his motor skills and to his ability in games may make him feel more secure. It may help the child who fears loss of popularity or who has never attained it, who has never really been accepted by his group. At the same time, the teacher must respect and nurture the child's developing independence, which turns him gradually away from the teacher to his own age group. Marks of this developing independence are efforts to be brave about physical injuries and greater courage in trying new physical skills and stunts. These efforts should be encouraged by the teacher with recognition and commendation at strategic moments.

All adults must be careful to avoid the sarcasm and ridicule that causes self-consciousness, increases awkwardness, and interferes with the development of easy movement and motor skill.

Social Adjustment:
Developmental Facts

By the age of 6 the child should be able to learn that there are simple, impersonal rules that apply to everyone in his group. With the teacher's guidance, he should be able to give up his own wishes and follow these rules.

In his own self-directed play, the child develops increasing skill in playing with small groups. At the age of 6, these groups often dissolve in quarrels, with one or more, or even all, quitting the game. But by the age of 8, children have learned to muddle through disputes and maintain their groups for longer periods of play.

Natural play groups now become segregated, boys from girls. The boys' play is somewhat rougher, and other interests tend to differ as cultural roles become more clearly defined.

For both boys and girls, motor skills are important factors in group acceptance and group leadership.

The child learns to adjust to competitive situations both within a group and from group to group if these situations are not so intense as to upset his emotional balance.

Social Adjustment:
Developmental Experiences

As the child enters into the group games and play characteristic of this age, he makes different kinds of adjustment. Circle games, played in a fairly large group, may be the 6-year-old's first try at fitting into the discipline of group procedure under rules that are the same for everyone. Circle games may be used on the first days of school, but since, as has already been pointed out, most of them give little opportunity for activity, they should be used a few times only. The child will develop more naturally in small, self-directed groups, which should be started by the third or fourth week. Cooperative balance in these groups is precarious at the age of 6, and the teacher tends to step in and settle things. It is better to let the group shift, as it will, after a quarrel. Some will go out and some come in; gradually, the group will find its own way to maintain balance. By the age of about 8, the groups work along with only minor difficulties. Team feeling begins. Relay races in the third grade are genuine team efforts, with every youngster running when he is tagged. The 6-year-old, on the other hand, is likely to wait for his opposite in the next file, and to run an individual race with him. As soon as team feeling begins, rules come to be appreciated as giving each team an equal chance. Useful rules, well understood and well observed, give the child a sense of security.

In simple team games, such as Fish Net, children can improve team strategy, getting some elementary concept of organization for offense. In Cat and Rat, on the other hand, they will need coaching in defensive strategy as they assist the Rat.

Although boys and girls tend to form separate play groups on the playground and in their own yard play, class groups should be mixed. Complete segregation tends to foster sex antagonism; mixed play maintains some degree of mutual understanding.

Guidance in school play may modify other cultural pressures toward sex differences, aggression, and competition.

During this period the school and the home must face the problem of competition in games and try to understand its many significant aspects.[4] Of course, there is an element of competition in many other family and school situations. Children compete for the love and attention of parents and of teachers. Sensible adults play down this competition by giving affection freely and impartially, because they know it is necessary to the child's security. Building on this basic security, the child may develop the increasing emotional control he will need to stand up to the increasing strains he must face as an adolescent and an adult. The development of emotional control under stress is a slow process, achieved through successful adjustment at graduated levels of difficulty, until the child is able to take his place in our strenuously competitive society.

Some psychologists believe that games contribute to this development. Competition on the sand lot or school playground calls for control at the child's own level. It is not intense competition and most of the players can take it. Of late, however, there has been a tendency for adults to force youngsters into the "varsity" pattern. Eight-year-olds are dressed up in uniforms, play their games before a crowded stadium, and drive toward a national championship subjected to all the pressures that sometimes break a mature man. Parents and teachers who tolerate or promote this sort of competition frequently do not understand that it is an unnatural forcing process, not in keeping with the child's own rate of development. Perhaps they also derive a vicarious thrill from the child's prominence, and some entertainment from the incongruity of childish attempts to perform an adult role.

Parents who really understand competition and children will avoid many other forms besides intense athletic competition. They will not emphasize grades or compare accomplishments: "Why can't you do as well as Tom? I am sure you are as bright as he is." They will not ridicule poor performance or losers in any situation, nor will they humiliate children when they fail. They will, on the contrary, recognize every kind and degree of achievement and give every child some feeling of success. They themselves will have fun as they play with children, whether they

---

[4] Paul H. Mussen, John J. Conger and J. Kagan, *Child Development and Personality.* New York: Harper & Row, Publishers, 1963, pp. 486–593.

win or lose in games. They will show the child respect for the rules as "organized justice," necessary to give all players a fair chance. They will use a judicious mixture of praise and suggestions to call forth the child's best efforts.

A noncompetitive attitude is important in promoting safety in apparatus play. Remarks such as, "You can't do this stunt!" or, "Who can climb as high as Billy did?" may lead to efforts beyond the child's capacity, and to accidents. On apparatus, parallel play will continue, but small groups may stay together while moving from one piece of apparatus to another. The incidental learnings in adjustment here are very important. As children work in groups to take out and put back portable apparatus, or as they take their turns at play on apparatus, selfishness and shirking give way to roughly equal efforts in the face of group pressures.

During. this period, free movement about the room is really parallel play also, but it does require a considerate sharing of

Competition at the boys' own level produces good results in skill, fun, team play, and emotional control. Here the game is played under competent adult supervision but without the pressure of an adult audience's demands for a championship.

space. Expressive movement may become organized into panto-mime or dance plays through group planning and execution. This kind of creative group work reaches a peak later, but third-graders can make a very good beginning at it. They will also enjoy the group feeling that develops in simple folk dances and singing games.

Intermediate: 9–11 Years

Physical Growth:
Developmental Facts

The average annual growth during this period is 7 pounds in weight and 2 inches in height.

The rate of growth (gain for size) in height and weight gradually falls off during childhood. The minimum rate prior to adolescence is reached by the average girl between 9 and 10 years and by the average boy between 11 and 12.

Typically, four permanent bicuspids and two lower cuspids erupt between the ages of 9 and 11. The lower cuspids erupt approximately a year earlier in girls than in boys. At the age of 11 the number of permanent teeth varies from ten to twenty-eight.

At the age of 11 the average boy or girl weighs 75 pounds and is 56 inches tall. Other averages are: arm length, 24 inches; chest girth, 26 inches; upper-arm girth, 8 inches; leg girth, 11 inches at the calf.

Motor Skills:
Developmental Facts

During the intermediate years motor skills are still a factor in leadership, more definitely now with boys than with girls.

A marked maturation of motor skills occurs during this period. Locomotion is steadier, and is characterized by better form. There is more grace and expressiveness in walking, running, leaping, and skipping.

Track skills and interests increase.

Ball-handling skills increase; there is better balance and footwork in kicking. Bats, rackets, and clubs are readily used to propel balls.

Sex differences in general are more pronounced. Girls exhibit better form in tumbling, swimming, and dance; boys, in ball control and in all skills involving strength. Boys continue to enjoy combative skills and contests of strength; girls have much less aptitude for or interest in them. The average height for the standing vertical jump is the same for both boys and girls: 12 inches in the sixth grade; but the boys' top performance is 19 inches to the girls' 16. In the standing broad jump, boys' averages are somewhat better than girls': 4 feet 9 inches for fifth-grade boys to 4 feet 1 inch for fifth-grade girls; 4 feet 11 inches for sixth-grade boys to 4 feet 4 inches for sixth-grade girls. The boys' top performances are also superior to those of the girls: 6 feet 3 inches for fifth-grade boys to 5 feet 8 inches for fifth-grade girls; 6 feet 5 inches for sixth-grade boys to 5 feet 7 inches for sixth-grade girls.[5]

Physical Growth and Motor Skills:
Developmental Experiences

Sex differences in rate of growth will often create embarrassing situations in dance and movement classes if small boys are paired with large girls. It is probably better to let children choose their own partners throughout the intermediate grades.

Although the rate of growth decreases during the intermediate years, a very great improvement in skill and some increase in endurance take place. In no sense does the child slow down in active play; on the contrary, he needs to play harder, and for longer periods, than ever before. Although he develops greater endurance, he may need some protection from overfatigue, and he should not be placed in such an intensely competitive situation that the coach, the game, and the crowd will push him past healthy fatigue into exhaustion. Intramural games, with occasional invitations to play other schools, are, therefore, preferable at this age to interscholastics organized on the "varsity" pattern of leagues and tournaments.[6]

Increasing skill in handling balls, bats, stilts, jump ropes, and other forms of small apparatus gives the 10-year-old great

[5] Marjorie Latchaw, "Motor Achievement," *Research Quarterly*, 5:429, December, 1954.

[6] For an authoritative statement on this question, see Educational Policies Commission, *School Athletics*. Washington, D.C.: National Education Association, 1954. See also the statement of policy on competitive athletics for children by the American Academy of Pediatrics, Appendix A.

The intermediates are challenged by feats of increasing difficulty.

satisfaction. Equipment of the right size, and in sufficient quantity —a ball for every child in the squad that is playing with balls, for example—is an excellent investment. This investment produces especially good returns during the intermediate period, which is a period of rapidly developing skill, strength, and endurance. Play with small soccer and American footballs, small basketballs, softballs and hard baseballs, light bats, and tennis rackets and balls should be planned at least twice a week in season. The period from 9 to 11 is also a good time to begin elementary instruction in golf and tennis and to continue or start instruction in swimming and diving.

Large apparatus will challenge the 9- to 11-year-old to more difficult feats such as vaulting, chinning, hand traveling, or inverted balance, and handstands on apparatus. Most will enjoy advanced stunts, and almost all will have mastered cartwheels and headstands by the ninth year.

Free movement and movement problems provide opportunities for developing the really fine locomotor skills and the grace and expressiveness of which children are capable at this age. Just as increased ball-handling skills make team games more satisfying, so increased movement skills may lead into dance and dramatic play and make both of them absorbing creative experiences on a more mature level than before.

Emotional Maturity:
Developmental Facts

During the intermediate years the child's acceptance by his own group is essential to his feeling of security; at the same time, his independence of adults increases. However, he wants to be liked by adults. He forms loyalties outside the family, and may go through a hero-worshiping stage.

During this period the child is learning emotional control as well as concealment. Pressure from the child's peer group does not permit crying, and it is rare among most 10-year-olds.

Under favorable conditions, he is able to compensate for frustration in some efforts by successes in others, and to resolve conflicts by decision making, adjustment, and creative endeavor. He may, however, also resort to less fruitful compensatory methods, such as daydreaming, lethargy, excuses, gossiping, aggressive hostility, and psychosomatic illness; and he may have unresolved conflicts, leading, in turn, to neuroses.

The child is beginning to have insight into the emotional life of others; this insight serves as a basis for a more idealistic concept of sportsmanship.

Anger from frustration diminishes as the intermediate child grows in skills. However, the 10-year-old is not yet able to control outbursts of anger or the verbal assaults which he aims at the object of his rage. These weapons, often effective with his peers, only increase his difficulties with adults.

Some sex antagonism is likely to develop unless boys and girls have the experience of mixed play groups at school.

Inventiveness and creative ability, which are often lost in the routine of school tasks and skill standards, may be retained if adults are interested in encouraging them.

Persistence increases noticeably. During this period fear takes the form of worry about school success, specific mistakes, and more generalized feelings of guilt.

With adult guidance, the child can learn to accept surface differences in race, religion, and ability, and to look for basic human likenesses beneath the surface.

The development of humor parallels intellectual growth. The child enjoys puns and playing on words. By the age of 11 he begins to outgrow laughter at the expense of others.

Emotional Maturity:
Developmental Experiences

Although they may find it difficult, both parents and teachers should attempt to understand and to foster the child's growing independence, which is, after all, part of the business of growing up. They should also realize that the child must be accepted by his own age group, and should therefore endeavor to promote mutual acceptance among members of play groups.

In spite of his independence, the youngster still wants love and affection from parents and teachers—but this affection is not openly sought, nor should it be obtrusively expressed. When the 10-year-old scrapes his knee in a fall on the playground, he does not come running to the teacher as he did when he was 6, wanting to be held as well as cared for. He appreciates concern along with competent first-aid treatment, provided it is offered on a man-to-brave-man basis.

Some of the child's regard for adults is transferred to heroes somewhat removed from his daily orbit. An athletic champion, a movie star, a teacher, or a scoutmaster may become the model for the boy. Although the girl is equally susceptible to hero worship, her idol may be either a hero or a heroine, while the boy's —at this age—is always a hero. This susceptibility of the child to influence by example places a very real responsibility on the teacher to be admirable as well as admired.

Motor skill is a great asset to the child in winning group acceptance, more so among boys than among girls. At this age there seems to be a natural drifting into segregated play groups, which soon become fairly close-knit "gangs." The school, through coeducation, can counterbalance this tendency to some extent and prevent the lack of understanding between the sexes that results from complete isolation. Through the sixth grade, most physical education classes should be mixed. In both the fifth and the sixth grades, however, some provision should be made for boys to play the more rugged games, such as soccer and flag football, with teams of their own sex. Even in mixed classes, separate squads of boys and girls may be organized, depending on the skills involved.

The problem of heterosexual adjustment is less acute at this period than during adolescence, but square dancing and social dancing, when the children are ready for it, will be found helpful at both levels. Mixed classes, of course, are best for dancing, and also for movement exploration and dramatic play.

Dramatic play or pantomime is an excellent means of expressing the aggression which is part of normal development and which boys and girls must somehow channel into approved outlets. Youngsters between the ages of 9 and 11 have more strength and initiative than younger children, and so are beyond the bluster characteristic of the latter group. They enjoy planning an active portrayal of the lives of heroes they have read about. The role of villain may present an acceptable emotional outlet for the "problem boy," and dramatizing conflict gives everyone a good opportunity for the release of hostility. When the children themselves create dramatic sequences, they almost always seem to plan scenes of violence ending in sudden death. "Unchildlike," the beginning teacher thinks, and wonders whether he is harboring a class of monsters. As succeeding classes write and act out very similar dramas, the teacher learns to consider them natural and to be grateful for the safety valve they provide. Games and stunts having elements of combat serve much the same purpose.

In the 10-year-old's dramas, strength and virtue are always idealized, always victorious. Actually, the child is an idealist. He is beginning to understand how others feel. His concept of sportsmanship may now grow beyond that of living up to the rules so that everyone may have a fair chance to win; he may begin to see that everyone must have a fair chance, not only to win, but to enjoy playing. The child is developing the emotional control that goes along with this stage of sportsmanship. He does not have to boast when he wins, nor quarrel or make excuses when he loses. He is learning to compensate for frustration, and he sometimes succeeds in using his mistake as a basis for planning the next game.

However, none of this growth will occur by itself. It must be carefully fostered by the example and teaching of adults. The teacher's success in aiding emotional control depends on his understanding of the problems of individual children. His insight into the background of each child helps him to know the causes of immature behavior, to arrange experiences that may compensate for unusual fears and frustrations, and so promote greater balance.

Social Adjustment:
Developmental Facts

As social skills develop, play groups become more closely knit and take on a cohesive "gang" or "clique" character. Belonging to a gang is essential; the latter part of this period is often called the "gang age."

Groups have a great effect on the individual. "Groups can liberate what is socially meaningful in the person and give it direction and a chance for self-development much better than any individual can. . . . Not only momentary behaviors, but many deep springs of child personality are liberated in group situations. The child finds himself because others find him."[7]

Adults who employ democratic techniques in guiding children's groups are more successful than those who use autocratic or laissez-faire methods.

A "pal" of the child's own age and sex is a support to his growing independence and is necessary to his development.

Children become increasingly capable of complex organization, both in large and in small groups. They can make rules, officiate, and choose leaders on merit.

There is improvement in keeping aggression within socially accepted limits: fighting only according to the rules, getting ahead without cheating, winning with some degree of modesty.

It is important for the child to be part of a "good" gang, but good gang influence cannot be achieved by constantly shifting gangs. The child must do his part by adjusting and fitting in.

Some children are so successful in gang life that they never mature beyond it, never develop inner resources or other social techniques. "Enough but not too much" is a good guide for group participation.

Great individual differences are found in children's tendency toward socialization. Those who prefer more solitary occupations or association with smaller groups are not necessarily problem children, but those who are ostracized because of lack of skill in sports may become socially handicapped unless they find some other basis for acceptance.[8]

Leaders among children are moderately but not outstandingly superior in social status, intelligence, schoolwork, and motor skills. They tend to be more extroverted than children who do not become leaders.

Child leaders who use domination are not as successful as those who use understanding and social skill to bring about cooperation within their groups.[9]

---

[7] L. B. Murphy, *Social Behavior and Child Personality*. New York: Columbia University Press, 1937, p. 132.

[8] Moss Hart, *Act One*. New York: Random House, Inc., 1959, p. 30.

[9] Breckenridge and Vincent, *op. cit.*, p. 488.

Social Adjustment:
Developmental Experiences

Because this is the "gang age," team games become a vitally important experience in the intermediate grades. Close-knit team feeling is developed by progressive stages. The very simple relays and two-team games of the primary grades are succeeded by modified team games such as Long Base, hit pin baseball, and line soccer. These, in turn, lead to softball, flag football, and scramble basketball.

If teams are to become primary groups exerting real influence on their members, they should keep the same membership over a period of time. This period will lengthen as children get older, until the same teams are maintained throughout a season. Nine- or ten-year-olds are capable of electing competent leaders in their rooms as captains. Captains, in turn, should choose team members who will form a unified group. Obviously, this selection should be made from a class list rather than in the presence of the whole group during activity time. Not only does the latter method take too much time, but it drives home their inferior status to the children who are chosen last. After the choosing, if all the team names are read at once, all the players belong on the same basis; and it is the belonging that counts.

Most seasonal teams in the fifth and sixth grades will probably be all-boy or all-girl groups unless definite procedures for choosing mixed teams are agreed on. The teacher interested in sociometric techniques may find it useful to study the structure of these groups in order to be ready with counsel if it is requested or to arrange groups if this seems necessary.

Children in the intermediate grades can, with guidance, learn to officiate and to accept one another as officials. Their ability to get along together goes far beyond that of the 6- or 7-year-olds, who usually break up at the first disagreement.

If real leaders are elected as captains, the training received by these boys and girls of high potential can be of great value to our society in the future. Such leaders may be able to grow from domination to cooperation through the development of social skill and understanding. Many group discussions will take place and many group decisions will be made before, during, and after games. Line-ups, offensive and defensive strategy, and different plays will be decided. Evaluation by the whole team of its own success or failure will lead to planning for practice on needed skills or new plays. In looking for new resources, the group may develop the less obvious talents of its members and help the obscure child to find himself. But without wise adult guidance, team games can make the overly aggressive child still more aggressive and the withdrawn child still more withdrawn.

Both captain and team members will need help when they have a handicapped child on the team. How to give such a child his fair chance to play and at the same time give the team a chance to win presents a real problem in human relationships. The handicapped child must be protected in contact games. Perhaps he can be given a side-line job, watching plays and errors as he helps to keep score. Perhaps some other special provisions can be made. In one school, for example, a poliomyelitis victim wearing leg braces was given half the soccer goal to keep and ropes to hold to while he kicked. Often a child may bat while someone runs bases for him. A spastic on a softball team, for example, may choose a substitute batter and become his first-base coach. Of course, in play on apparatus and in swimming, the atypical child comes into his own. But in no case should such a youngster be left out entirely. Not only does he benefit from being included, but the normal children who plan ways of including him learn a great deal about social adjustment.

Other physical education experiences may also contribute to social development. In square dancing, the members of the square depend on one another, not only for fun, but to keep the pattern of the dance going smoothly. In movement exploration and modern dance, small groups often work together at a high level of planning and mutual understanding. These experiences may also call for boy-girl adjustment, although some of the movement and dance groups will choose problems best approached by girls or boys alone. Movement and dance call for qualities of expressiveness and imagination, which are sometimes overshadowed in games by strength and skill. Therefore, children who are not very successful at games may do much better in dance and movement. This possibility presents both an opportunity and a hazard. The teacher must not allow the natural athlete to feel out of place in dance groups, because he will then begin to think of dance or even movement exploration as a "sissy" activity. Problems calling for strong movement, and dances or dramatic play involving conflict, will serve to emphasize culturally accepted "masculine" qualities in addition to providing an outlet for aggressive feelings.

Summary

Human development follows a sequence common to all children. However, children differ in rate of growth, in maximum potential, and in degree of variation from the average at any given time. These differences should be considered both by the school and by the home if the unique developmental pattern of each child is to be understood. The school program in physical education should be so varied and individualized that each child will have experiences suited to his own developmental pattern, and to his level of maturation at any time.

Among the many different phases of development, the four that are of greatest interest to teachers of physical education are physical growth, motor skill, emotional maturity, and social adjustment. Since the child is a unified being, these different phases or lines of development are so closely interrelated that all must be considered in planning the program.

By definition, physical education is the use of vigorous movement as planned developmental experience. The program therefore consists of experiences carefully selected and arranged to provide the best possible conditions for growth. Such experiences can provide the best conditions only if they are based on the facts of physical growth, motor development, emotional maturity, and social adjustment as these have been ascertained by study of the child at various stages.

The preschool child's most rapid physical growth takes place in legs and arms. Between the ages of 3 and 5 the child has an insistent need for physical activity to foster this growth and to coordinate the use of his limbs. Climbing and jumping on play apparatus, and active play with medium-sized balls and other equipment, should form a large part of each preschool day. These activities should be supplemented by creative movement as well as by rhythmic and dramatic play. Parents and teachers should watch the child's body during these years to discover, in its early stages, any asymmetry that may appear.

If the young preschool child can go about his activities, both at home and at school, in an atmosphere of warm affection, cheerfulness, and serenity, he will have a good chance of developing security and stability. His first moves toward adjusting to other children in play situations should be guided, but without unnecessary interference. Preschool play will be parallel at first; later, there will be shared play in small groups; and at the end of the period there may be some circle games.

The child in the primary grades (6 to 8 years) feels the need to test his growing strength and skill. He will experiment with anything he can find to throw, to kick, to climb and balance on, or to jump on, from, or over. In other words, he wants to measure up to and to control his environment. Play on all kinds of large apparatus, and with such small equipment as balls, bats, jump ropes, and hoops, gives him this chance for control. Each new success contributes to his growing sense of independence as well as to his emotional stability through the overcoming of fear and frustration. Movement exploration in response to problems set by the teacher not only leads to additional control and skill, but may also provide a healthy outlet for the expression of aggression and other emotions. In playing with others, children of the first three grades should have guidance in developing social skills. Beginning with circle games to help to understand the operation of group rules, going on to small group games and then to the simpler team forms, the child accomplishes new adjustments at each stage. By the third grade he will be ready to take his place on a team and to join in the team's competitive effort. Team competition should, however, be kept on the child's own "sand-lot" level, not forced into an adult pattern of intensive contests and championships, if we want the child to develop at his own best rate.

The youngster in the intermediate grades (9 to 11 years) is at a "golden age" of motor skill. His growth rate slows down; he seems to know himself and what he can do; and he plays harder for longer periods than before. Balls of various types, rackets, bats, clubs, and track equipment will get incessant use. Equipment of the right size, and enough of it, is an excellent investment, yielding good returns in activity and skill. During this period boys and girls become increasingly independent of adults, and increasingly dependent on friends of their own age. They make such rapid strides in getting along together that by the fifth and sixth grades they form closely knit gangs or cliques. Belonging to one of these is a "must" at this age. Team games may give some children the feeling of belonging they crave. Such games should progress from the simple relays of the primary grades through modified team sports, such as Long Base and line soccer, to the more highly organized softball and flag football. Competition should still be kept at the youngsters' level: intramurals, which they themselves can run, are better than "varsity" leagues planned and organized by adults. However, adult example and guidance in games determine whether the intermediate's latent idealism, his more mature sportmanship, his concern for the handicapped, and his acceptance of persons of all colors, creeds, and conditions, will be developed or will remain potential only. To round out the intermediate's development, finally, it is necessary to provide the creative, emotional, and social experiences found in movement exploration and various types of dance.

At every level, and in every grade, careful selection of the best experiences is necessary for the child's optimum development. Wise planning of physical education experiences will do much to insure that the 11-year-old becomes as strong, as well built, as skillful, as stable, and as socially competent as his potential permits. How to organize these experiences in the school program is discussed in the following chapter.

Selected References

AAHPER, *Children in Focus*. Washington, D.C., 1954, Chaps. 4, 5.

Baldwin, A. L., *Behavior and Development in Childhood*. New York: Holt, Rinehart and Winston, Inc., 1955.

Baller, Warren, and Don Charles, *The Psychology of Human Growth and Development*. New York: Holt, Rinehart and Winston, Inc., 1961.

Boynton, Bernice, *A Study of the Rhythm of Physical Growth from Anthropometric Measurements on Girls Between Birth and Eighteen Years*. University of Iowa Studies in Child Welfare. Iowa City, Iowa: Department of Publications, State University of Iowa, 1936.

Breckenridge, Marian E., and E. Lee Vincent, *Child Development*, 4th ed. Philadelphia: W. B. Saunders Company, 1960.

Cowell, Charles, *Scientific Foundations of Physical Education*. New York: Harper & Row, Publishers, 1953, Chaps. 3, 4.

Doll, E. A., *The Osretsky Tests of Motor Proficiency*. Minneapolis: Educational Test Bureau, 1946.

English, Horace B., *Dynamics of Child Development*. New York: Holt, Rinehart and Winston, Inc., 1961, Chaps. 8, 12, 13.

Gesell, Arnold, and Frances Ilg, *The Child From Five to Ten*. New York: Harper & Row, Publishers, 1946.

Gutteridge, Mary V., *A Study of Motor Achievements of Young Children*. New York: Archives of Psychology No. 244, 1939.

Jersild, A. T., *et al.*, *Child Development and the Curriculum*. New York: Bureau of Publications, Teachers College, Columbia University, 1946.

Jones, H. E., *Motor Performance and Growth*. Berkeley, Calif.: University of California Press, 1948.

Kephart, Newell C., *The Slow Learner in the Classroom*. Columbus, Ohio: Charles E. Merrill Books, Inc., 1960, Chaps. 1, 3, 6.

McCandless, Boyd R., *Children and Adolescents Behavior and Development*. New York: Holt, Rinehart and Winston, Inc., 1961.

McGraw, Myrtle B., *Growth: A Study of Johnny and Jimmy*. Des Moines, Iowa: Appleton-Century-Crofts, 1935.

Meredith, Howard V., *A Study of Eighteen Anthropometric Measurements on Iowa City White Males Between Birth and Eighteen Years*. University of Iowa Studies in Child Welfare. Iowa City, Iowa: Department of Publications, State University of Iowa, 1935.

Meredith, Howard V., "Toward a Working Concept of Physical Growth," *American Journal of Orthodontics*, 3: 440–458, July 1945.

Meredith, Howard V., "A Descriptive Concept of Physical Development," *The Concept of Development*, ed. by Dale B. Harris. Minneapolis: University of Minnesota Press, 1957, pp. 109–122.

Meredith, Howard V., "Recent Studies On Growth of the Body and Face," *American Journal of Orthodontics*, 45: 110–124, February 1959.

Meredith, Howard V., "Methods of Studying Physical Growth," *Handbook of Research Methods in Child Development*, ed. by Paul E. Mussen. New York: John Wiley & Sons, Inc., 1960, pp. 201–251.

Millard, C. V., *Child Growth and Development*. Boston: D. C. Heath and Company, 1951.

Ministry of Education, *Moving and Growing*. London: Her Majesty's Stationery Office, 1952.

Mussen, Paul H., John J. Conger and J. Kagan, *Child Development and Personality*, 2d ed. New York: Harper & Row, Publishers, 1963.

Olson, Willard C., *Child Development*, 2d ed. Boston: D. C. Heath and Company, 1959.

Prescott, D. A., *The Child in the Educative Process*. New York: McGraw-Hill Book Company, Inc., 1957, Chaps. 10, 11.

Stratemeyer, Florence, *et al.*, *Developing a Curriculum for Modern Living*, 2d ed. New York: Bureau of Publications, Teachers College, Columbia University, 1957.

Updegraff, Ruth, *et al.*, *Practice in Preschool Education*. New York: McGraw-Hill Book Company, Inc., 1938.

CHAPTER 3

The Program

Organization of experiences

FROM THE PREVIOUS DISCUSSION it is obvious that the best developmental experiences should be carefully selected for the physical education program. Careful organization of these experiences to fit available time and space is also important. They need not, however, always take place according to a fixed schedule. Expressive movement, dramatic play, or dance based on stories can often be integrated with other classroom experiences, especially in the large, flexibly furnished classroom of the modern school. But there will be some time every day when each class needs space for running, throwing balls, working with apparatus, and moving about freely as individuals or as a group. This space, usually found in the gymnasium or on the playground, will have to be allocated to different classes at set times. Each class needs at least half an hour daily in such a space; a period of fifty minutes is better. Careful planning is necessary at each stage of program organization.

Planning the Use of Time and Space

To make a wise selection from the wealth of experiences available in physical education before organizing them into a working schedule, the teacher should look again at certain basic characteristics of development. We have defined physical education as the use of vigorous movement as planned developmental experience. What characteristics of development should be considered in planning? It seems obvious that the teacher should:

1. *Plan for continuity of experience.* Mursell has said: "Development never occurs as a series of self-contained stages, but is continuous growth."[1] Ball-handling skills, for example, have a long way to grow, from the 3-year-old's forearm thrust of a rubber ball to the mobilization of bodily strength achieved by the 11-year-old as he delivers a fast overarm throw. The preschool child's laborious scramble up an obstacle, his adventurous, somewhat uncertain jump down, do not change overnight to the intermediate's agile vault onto a larger box, and his high leap and easy landing in descent. These skills develop day by day, week by week, year by year, just as skills in language arts and arithmetic do. Short units of two weeks one year, three weeks the next, do not provide truly developmental experiences, nor does one period a week give much chance for development. Continuity is important. It is not inconsistent with variety.

2. *Plan for pupils' self-direction.* The child needs the chance to work, to experiment, to progress, to fail, to learn by himself.[2] He needs to invent new skills, new ways of using acquired skills, and ways of solving problems in movement as well as in arithmetic. Certain forms of physical education, such as self-testing, movement exploration, and creative dance, give more opportunity for self-direction than do others. Games and folk dances, on the other hand, which set a group pattern in which each member plays an assigned part, contribute more to other lines of development, such as social adjustment.

If, in self-testing the child is encouraged to invent new things and to improve skills he has already begun to acquire, he himself supplies variety to the program. In movement exploration the teacher sets progressively more complex problems, and the child

[1] James Mursell, *Developmental Teaching.* New York: McGraw-Hill Book Company, Inc., 1949, p. 68.
[2] *Ibid.*, p. 112.

directs his own responses into new and interesting patterns of movement. Again, variety within continuity is achieved by means of self-direction. This variety gives all children a chance to succeed and may prevent the feelings of inferiority that often inhibit the less skillful child. Childhood inhibition may persist as adult self-consciousness and awkwardness in movement.

Whatever the form of physical education, the modern teacher emphasizes orderly self-direction in order to get full use of class time for action.[3]

3. *Plan for individual differences in rate and pattern of development.* If children have freedom to select and direct their own activities, they seem to fit them into their own rate and pattern of development. Because they are very sensitive to pressure, it is best not to set grade standards of achievement by which children (and teachers) are evaluated. Slow children should not be pushed, nor should very capable children be held back. For this reason, it is more realistic to think of grade groupings (preschool, primary, and intermediate) rather than of separate grades in describing material. To label a dance suitable for the fifth grade does not recognize the fact that it may fit some fifth grades but be too advanced or too easy for others.

4. *Plan for many-sided development:* in physical growth, in motor skill, in emotional maturity, and in social adjustment. Different forms of physical education contribute to different phases of development in varying degrees. For example, self-testing promotes motor skill and emotional maturity, as do movement exploration and dance. Games make an important contribution to social adjustment. The skillful teacher who keeps all the children active, in any form of physical education whatsoever, is contributing to their physical growth and development. At the same time, in every lesson, his teaching methods take into consideration the total development of each class member.

Materials for Planning

Before discussing seasonal schedules for different age levels, it may be well to talk about materials for planning—that is, the different forms of physical education and the outcomes that the teacher may expect at different developmental stages.

[3] Elizabeth Halsey and Lorena Porter, "First Steps Toward Fitness," *Journal of Health, Physical Education, Recreation,* November 1958, pp. 40–41.

In this text various kinds of vigorous movement are grouped into four general forms of physical education: games, movement exploration, dance, and self-testing.

Games are played by children of all ages; they are described at length and in great number in most texts. The teacher is urged to select carefully from this wealth of material and to use each game he chooses not as a pastime, a fill-in, but as a truly developmental experience. Certain criteria may be helpful in making selections:

1. Does the game give the experience in social adjustment needed by the children at their present stage of development? Simple circle games, for example, are useful in the first few lessons of new first graders to give them the feeling of the group as a whole and the discipline of the rules of the game applying to all.

2. Does the game provide vigorous activity for all? One-goal games, such as Hill Dill, or two-goal games, such as Brownies and Fairies, will do this. Circle games in a large group, on the other hand, are almost useless for this purpose.

3. Does the game interest children? Do they choose it often?

4. Does it give opportunities to develop strategy, or to think while in action?

5. Does the game call for skills appropriate to the stage of motor development reached by the children? Does it develop useful skills?

6. Can it be directed by the children themselves?

7. Does the game provide for desirable ethical learnings? Duck on the Rock and Red Light put a premium on cheating, but they also allow for group control in enforcing the rules. Some relays have rules that cannot be enforced because they interfere too much with the runner's progress. If the runner gets by without obeying these rules, he is learning that it pays to cheat.

Most games need space, and should be played in the gymnasium, in the playroom, or on the playground. A few are suitable for the classroom.

Movement Exploration is an interesting development in physical education and as used in this text is basic, both in method and content, to all forms including games, dance, and self-testing. In brief, movement exploration is a planned series of problem-solving experiences through which the child learns to understand and control the many ways in which his body moves and to improve many different skills. The problems involve qualities of movement: fast or slow, strong or light, smoothly continuous or staccato. They also deal with such other factors as controlling momentum, focusing, adjusting energy and relaxation, using direction and space effectively, and communicating ideas and emotions.

Of course, children have always explored movement in their own way when free to do so. Here, however, these natural drives are channeled toward growth by means of carefully planned progression in problems set by the teacher and answered inventively by the children. Movement exploration is described in detail in Chapter 9.

The gymnasium, a large classroom with movable desks, a playroom, or the playground is suitable for movement exploration.

Dance is used in this text as an inclusive term. Rhythmic activities, folk dance, singing games, square dances, social dance, and creative dance are all brought together and considered as valuable forms of dance experience. The child shares, either as an individual or as a member of a group, in the dance experiences of his own and other cultures. It is natural for children to enjoy moving to music or to any rhythmic beat. If the dance experience is appropriate to the child's level of motor development, if it has

This metal frame encourages freedom of action in climbing, turning, and hanging while at the same time providing opportunities for group interaction.

meaning as dramatic expression or as part of an integrated activity, it can be a very happy experience. Competence in dance provides an important recreational resource for people of all ages. Dance activities are best carried on indoors—in the gymnasium, a large classroom with movable desks, or a playroom.

Self-testing is the term given to those forms of physical education in which the child tests his powers of control over his body and his environment. Large apparatus challenges him to climb, to jump off, to jump over, and to invent new ways of doing these things. Smaller pieces of equipment, such as balls, bats, and rackets, challenge him to manipulate them with skill. Stunts challenge him to control his body in space without reference to other objects. Self-testing activities may be carried on indoors or out, depending on the apparatus used.

Specific illustrations of these forms of physical education, and of the outcomes that may be obtained if they are well taught, are presented on the following pages for use in planning programs for each of the three school levels included in this text. The descriptions are followed by suggestions for time distribution and seasonal schedules.[4]

Materials for Planning: Preschool (3–5 Years)

Forms of Physical Education	*Outcomes*
GAMES	
Interest in small group games of free, imaginative nature develops at the end of this period.	Accepting rules as applying to self.
Large group games are introduced as needed to help in group adjustment. The teacher at first plays with the group, helping the children to understand the rules and to realize that they apply to each one.	Adjusting to behavior of others.
	Beginnings of strategy: thinking while playing.
	Fun.
	Listening; self-discipline.
Games of short duration and dramatic interest are chosen: Cat	

[4] More detailed descriptions of these forms of physical education will be found in Chapters 9, 10, 11, and 12.

A good toy: large enough to give some help in balance while it encourages action.

Kindergarten playtime (below).

and Rat, Duck, Duck, Goose, Drop the Handkerchief.

MOVEMENT EXPLORATION (See Chapter 9)

Teacher gives leads and suggestions but does not demonstrate; child invents own responses. "Look at the wall around our room. Can you touch it and come back without touching anything or anyone else? Can you do the same thing moving some other way? More quickly? How small can you be? How tall? How wide? How lightly can your feet move? How quickly can your hands move? Can they go high in the air? Low near the ground? Show us how strong your hands and arms are."

Finding out how the body can move.

Fun and satisfaction in movement.

Sharing space with others.

Inventing new ways of doing things.

Controlling quality of movement.

Expressing feeling by movement.

Activity, exercise, strength.

DANCE

The following dance activities are appropriate for the preschool program:

Informal movement to accompaniment of percussion instruments, nursery rhymes, jingles, poems, songs, and recorded music.

Games such as Stoop and Magic Carpet, in which players start and stop to accompaniment.

Singing games such as Looby Loo, Muffin Man, London Bridge, The Farmer in the Dell, Did You Ever See a Lassie?

Dance play: creative expression of everyday themes, stories, nursery rhymes, and so on.

Ability to attend and respond to rhythmic sounds.

Enjoyment of moving to music and other rhythms.

Individual expression.

Feeling for group patterns.

Keeping one's own place and making appropriate contribution to whole dance.

Skill and ease in locomotion.

Inventiveness.

SELF-TESTING

Large apparatus:

Climbing on tables, boxes, metal frames, ropes.

Jumping from heights of one to three feet and landing safely. Supporting body in hanging position.

Testing developing powers.

Satisfaction, fun.

Development of skill in getting over obstacles.

Development of skill in landing safely from jumps.

Balancing on low beam, walking. Trying new things.

Small equipment:

Throwing and catching large balls, beanbags.

Playing with jump rope.

Playing with large blocks.

Kicking balls.

Manipulating inner tubes, hoops, scooters, tricycles, roller skates.

Stunts:

Child identifies self with animals and inanimate objects—walks like a dog, cat, crab; hops like a bunny; bounces like a ball; jumps like a kangaroo or jack-in-the-box; rolls like a log.

Development of confidence, courage, independence.

Lessening of frustration.

Inventiveness, exploring, solving problems.

Recognizing own ability.

Working with others in taking out and putting up equipment.

Improvement of eye-hand coordination in manipulating many kinds of small objects.

Sharing space without conflict in parallel play.

Increasing responsibility in caring for equipment.

Activity, exercise, strength.

Time Distribution

Preschool children will spend much of their time in self-testing activities in their own play space, both indoors and outdoors. For some time every day, they will enjoy the simplest types of movement exploration. For 5-year-olds, the weekly plans will set aside time for elementary dance experiences and games.

The actual scheduling will be arranged flexibly, according to local situations and policies.

Time Distribution

Preschool (3–5 Years)

SELF-TESTING 60%

MOVEMENT 25% EXPLORATION

5% GAMES

10% DANCE

Materials for Planning: Primary Grades (6–8 Years)

Forms of Physical Education   *Outcomes*

GAMES

Interest in group games grows and experience in playing with others becomes important in social adjustment.

Large group games, such as Mickey Mouse, Garden Scamp, and Slap Jack, are enjoyed in the first days of the first grade. One-goal or two-goal games provide more activity: Hill Dill, Midnight, Brownies and Fairies, Chinese Wall.

Small group games, such as Stoop Tag, Link Tag, Galloping Lizzie, Jump Shoe, One Against Three, and Free and Caught, encourage activity and self-direction.

During this period the team idea emerges. Relays such as Tag the Goal Relay, Shuttle Relay, and Stride Ball Relay are enjoyed.

By the end of the period, interest shifts largely to simple team games: dodgeball varieties, kickball, soccer ball kick, Long Base.

Understanding rules as a way of giving each a fair chance.

Self-discipline under rules.

Admitting being caught.

Following directions.

Adjusting to behavior of others.

Recognition of sportsmanship as simple justice.

Fun.

Early concepts of leaders and members, in small groups and relay teams.

Skill in running, dodging, footwork, change of direction.

Ball-handling skills.

Beginning of team feeling.

Group planning and strategy.

Ability to choose captains and team members on merit.

Acceptance of children who differ in skill, and ability to play with them.

Activity, exercise, strength (of legs), if games give all a chance to be active most of the time.

MOVEMENT EXPLORATION (See Chapter 9)

Beginning with the very simple problems used for 5-year-olds, the teacher may suggest more complex ideas and progressively more difficult problems. He does not demonstrate, but encourages individual responses: "Show us your own space—how high is it, how wide, how far behind you, how far in front, how low? Can you move

Finding out how the body can move.

Fun and satisfaction in movement.

Understanding difference between one's own space and space shared with group.

Developing ideas of different directions and different levels in space: high, low, middle.

about the room very lightly and quickly? Can your hands be light and quick, just as your feet are? Now can you move slowly, with very strong, heavy feet? Strong hands, too? In your own space, how high can your knees go? How many ways will your elbow move? Can you make a circle with it? What else? Will it turn you around?"

Teacher and class together may develop expressive movement: "How do you move when you feel very happy? When your Dad asks if you want to go on a picnic? Can you carry the picnic basket? Is it heavy?" From here, the children will pick up the story, the teacher bringing out qualities of movement at different episodes.

Increased skill in locomotor and nonlocomotor movements.

Inventing new ways of moving.

Understanding how different parts of the body move.

Controlling speed and strength of movement in simple and more complex sequences, involving change of direction.

Expressing feeling in movement —freely, without self-consciousness.

Developing a "vocabulary" of movement through which feelings may be communicated.

Activity, exercise, strength.

DANCE

Rhythm skills:

Attending and responding to pulse, accent, tempo, and phrasing of accompaniment.

Rhythmic games.

Performing different locomotor movements to accompaniment— walk, run, hop, jump, skip, gallop, slide, leap. Later these may be combined into traditional dance steps such as the waltz run, step- hop, schottische.

Singing games: Round and Round the Village, Thread Follows the Needle.

Folk dances: Based on walk, run, skip, slide, or gallop—Dance of Greeting, Shoemaker's Dance, Carousel.

Play-party games: Fitting in with studies of pioneer life—Picking up Pawpaws, Skip to My Lou, Bow Belinda, Pop Goes the Weasel, Shoo, Fly.

Increased skill in locomotion.

Enjoyment of moving to rhythm and music: accuracy in response.

Adjustment to group; understanding total pattern and one's own part.

Feeling for ways and customs of other days and other people.

Inventiveness and imagination.

Integration of thought, feeling, action.

Simple form of creative planning and action as a group.

Better understanding of stories and centers of interest used in other parts of the school program.

Creative dance or dance play: Individually or as a group, plan and do a dance based on—things around us, pets, toys, weather, seasons, stories, centers of interest in social studies program. Familiar radio or television programs may also be used.

SELF-TESTING

Large apparatus: Climbing with increasing skill on ropes, poles, metal frames, climbing ladder.

Jumping from heights of two to four feet and landing safely.

Broad jump and low hurdle.

Jumping up, on, and over obstacles.

Turning upside down; skinning the cat; chinning; balancing on low and higher beam, on parallel bars, or on ropes.

Inventing new ways of doing all these things.

Small equipment: Ball-handling and kicking skills.

Using jump ropes, stilts, tether ball sets, hoops.

Using tennis and badminton rackets (at about 8 years) and paddles.

Stunts: Interest in identification continues—spinning like a top; kicking like a mule; imitating a measuring worm, coffee grinder, jumping jack, ball.

More difficult stunts challenge children at this age—tip-up, frog headstand, handstand, cartwheel, forward and backward roll, handstand with support.

Testing developing powers. Satisfaction, fun.

Greater skill in getting on or over obstacles, climbing, and chinning; jumping down, jumping over small obstacles, and broad jump (toward end of period).

Confidence, courage, independence.

Lessening of frustration.

Recognition of own capacities as well as limitations.

Inventiveness.

Flexibility, balance.

Cooperating with others in caring for and moving apparatus; taking turns; sharing space and small equipment.

Skill in throwing, catching, bouncing, and batting balls.

Skill in kicking, fielding, footwork.

Subjective control—that is, skillful use of the body in space without relation to other objects.

Activity, exercise, strength.

Learning safety in stunts—helping one another by "spotting."

Planning the Primary Schedule

Rapidly growing, ceaselessly active, constantly exploring, the primary child needs at least one daily instructional period in the play space. The schedules that follow are based on the usual thirty-minute period per day. Both dance and movement exploration are shown during the indoor season. Although the emphasis is still on self-testing, both movement exploration and games are assigned more time than in the preschool program.

The fall schedule could put periods of self-testing on successive days, then alternation with games the rest of the week. This arrangement simplifies organization—that is, setting up apparatus and taking care of balls, ropes, and other equipment. Children remember more easily if they repeat Monday's plan on Tuesday than if they have to wait until Wednesday.

Indoor and outdoor self-testing will differ, since both apparatus and surfacing differ. Stunts such as the headstand, somersault, and cartwheel can be practiced much more safely indoors. Rope jumping, ball handling, and playing with hoops and stilts are suitable for both indoor and outdoor periods. Use turf, if available; a sloping hillside is ideal.

The division of time between movement exploration and dance may be worked out experimentally by each teacher. During the last half of the winter term the two may be scheduled together, once a week, so that teachers who wish to use more rhythmic experience in movement problems or to carry directly from movement into creative dance may do so.

Time Distribution

Primary Grades (6–8 Years)

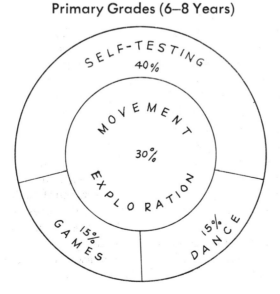

FALL SCHEDULE		September– October		OUTDOORS
Mon.	Tues.	Wed.	Thurs.	Fri.
	Movement		Exploration	
Games	Self-testing	Games	Self-testing	Games

WINTER SCHEDULE		November – March		INDOORS
Mon.	Tues.	Wed.	Thurs.	Fri.
	Movement		Exploration	
Games	Self-testing	Dance	Self-testing	Dance

SPRING SCHEDULE		April– May		OUTDOORS (INDOORS)
Mon.	Tues.	Wed.	Thurs.	Fri.
	Movement		Exploration	
Games	Self-testing	Games	Self-testing	Games

Materials for Planning:
Intermediate Grades (9–11 Years)

| Forms of Physical Education | Outcomes |

GAMES

Simple and modified team games, such as Dodgeball, Line Soccer, Alley Soccer, Base Football, Scramble Basketball, Flag Football, Hit Pin Baseball, Bombardment, Keep Away, Work Up, and Long Base provide experience in seasonal sports of immediate interest and help develop skills and strategy needed later in more advanced seasonal sports.

Tournaments within the class and within the school are important experiences.

Team personnel and captains should remain the same for as long a period as feasible.

Appreciation of rules as "organized justice"; recognition of sportsmanship as fair play and consideration, giving opponent same rights as own team.

Self-discipline in obeying rules and developing sportsmanlike conduct.

Strong "we" feeling in teams.

Belonging: being accepted by one's own group.

Acceptance of all players regardless of differences in skill, social status, race, religion, and emotional maturity.

Increase in variety of sports skills.

Simplified forms of individual sports may be introduced: paddle tennis, tether ball, table tennis, darts.

More difficult and expensive sports may also be introduced, depending on the resources of the school, camp, community, and family: swimming, tennis, golf, riding, and winter sports.

Understanding of offensive and defensive strategy.

Ability to plan team plays, as a group.

Ability to officiate and to accept classmates as officials.

Ability to plan and organize class procedure with help of teacher, or group procedure without adult help.

Willingness to accept and plan for participation of handicapped.

Fun, recreation.

Exercise, strength, endurance.

MOVEMENT EXPLORATION (See Chapter 9)

Continue previous experience, using more complex problems: "Show us a strong, quick movement, followed by a slow, light one. . . . Use all levels."

Introduce idea of direct, contrasted with indirect, movement.

Freedom from inhibition and embarrassment in movement.

Invention of new ways to express qualities of movement.

Understanding how different parts of the body may express different qualities of movement.

Four square is a good game for the fifth grade.

Follow diagrams from floor patterns; make original diagrams.

Dramatize themes of group interest: conflict, grief, and death as well as lighter themes will be chosen by the children. "We are the crowd coming out of the basketball game. Can you show by the way you move, which team won? Think of all the different characters in the crowd. Can your head and shoulders show us which one you are? . . . Will your group take any one of our instruments and do two light, slow movements, followed by a very strong quick movement?"

Use movement training in games: "How do you change focus in bombardment? In soccer? Flag football? . . . In playing on ropes is all your movement strong? What part is strong? What part is light? Is it fast or slow? How do you keep it slow when you are coming down the rope?"

Working with groups to create different movement patterns.

Using instruments to accompany group movement.

Understanding space in relation to quality (direct and indirect) and floor pattern.

Imagination and creative expression.

Emotional expression: release of hostility in an impersonal and approved manner.

Development of an increasingly interesting "vocabulary" of movement—that is, ways of moving that communicate an idea.

Fun, satisfaction, recreation.

Activity, exercise, strength, endurance.

Integration of thinking, feeling, and moving while absorbed in creative expression.

DANCE

Movement and rhythm skills: Exploring locomotor and body movements.

Performing complex dance steps such as schottische, polka, two-step, waltz.

Using musical symbols to describe rhythm of movement.

Folk dance: Simple dances, such as Gustaf's Skoal, Seven Jumps, Ach Ja.

More complicated dances, such as Little Man in a Fix, La Virgencita, Highland Schottische.

Square dance: Simple round dances, mixers.

Fun, enjoyment.

Increased skill in moving to rhythm within dance patterns.

Improved social adjustment.

Competence and confidence in meeting social situations.

Increased resources for home and school parties.

Increased appreciation of customs, history, and temperament of other peoples.

Understanding of part played by form and theme of a dance.

Creative imagination.

Use of "vocabulary" developed in movement exploration.

Creative dance: Choreographing original dances.

Social dance: May be taught in sixth grade, depending on need and interest of group.

Integration with various projects in social studies: United States backgrounds; family backgrounds; occupations; Western expansion; Latin America; Canada; Europe; Asia.

Ability to work intensively with a group in planning and performing original dances.

Integration of feeling, thinking, and moving, into effective expression.

SELF-TESTING

Large apparatus: Climbing more skillfully and to greater height on ropes.

Traveling hand over hand, or by swinging rotary motion, on horizontal bar or ladder.

Devising new vaults, wall-scaling techniques, and other means of getting over obstacles, depending on apparatus available.

Doing handstand, cartwheel, and handspring on apparatus; turning upside down from hanging position.

Inventing dual stunts on apparatus.

Small equipment: Ball handling.

Using lightweight basketballs, footballs, regulation softballs.

Propelling balls with bats, rackets, and clubs.

Performing with jump ropes individually, in couples, and in groups.

Track skills.

Stunts and tumbling: Continuous rolls, forward and backward.

Dive and roll.

Continuous cartwheels.

Handstand; walking on hands.

Pyramids.

Double and triple stunts.

Testing developing powers.

Satisfaction, fun, recreation.

Understanding need for practice.

Ability to sustain attention, continue practice, and devise new methods and techniques.

Increased ability to learn from observation, visual aids, and teaching suggestions.

Increased confidence, courage.

Inventiveness and ingenuity.

Cooperation with partner or group.

Acceptance of responsibility in moving, adjusting, and caring for apparatus.

Understanding and observance of safety regulations.

Increased skill in getting body over higher apparatus.

Flexibility, balance, agility.

Skill in using games and sports equipment.

Increasingly skillful use of the body in space, without relation to other objects (subjective control).

Activity, exercise, strength.

Adjustment to groups and squads, as leader or other squad member.

Is rope jumping a "sissy" sport? Not if prize fighters, athletes, and dancers all use it for conditioning and training in footwork. Boys and girls in some schools find it fun to invent couple and group variations.

Planning the Intermediate Schedule

The child in the intermediate grades is developing independence from adults by establishing his place in his own age group. For this reason, more emphasis is placed on games, and more attention should be given to the quality of group experience provided by games. During these years the emphasis on team spirit and functioning should gradually increase, until, by the age of 11, youngsters are competent in making fairly complex organizational arrangements.

Group experience is also provided through movement exploration and dance. In movement, groups may develop increasingly complex patterns to their own rhythmic accompaniment. This experience differs very little from the beginning choreography of modern dance, and movement may easily be integrated with modern dance in the sixth grade. However, if teachers have developed movement exploration into informal silent drama, they may wish to retain time for this valuable form of expression.

Social forms of dance (play-party games, folk and square dancing, and social dancing) are usually enjoyed very much at this age. However, social dancing should not be introduced until the class feels a definite need for it; this felt need provides the drive that will take children over the first awkward, self-conscious moments.

Self-testing continues to challenge the skill and strength which children in the intermediate grades are developing. Boys and girls will show different kinds of abilities now, and should probably be in separate squads.

The spring program may differ for 9-year-olds, who will want to see what they can do in track athletics, and 11-year-olds, whose main interest will be some form of softball. Skills in both track and softball are developing rapidly.

In fact, the great skill development of these years is likely to fascinate the physical education specialist. He may wish to take his small athletes as far as they can go. The classroom teacher should keep the balance now, mindful of the importance of the tasks of social adjustment and emotional maturity that face youngsters at this age. Only a varied physical education program will contribute to these lines of development.

Time Distribution

Intermediate Grades (9–11 Years)

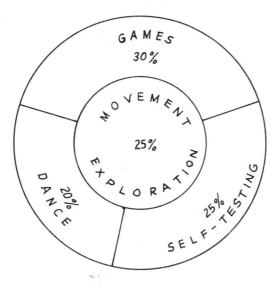

FALL SCHEDULE   September - October   OUTDOORS

Mon.	Tues.	Wed.	Thurs.	Fri.
Movement		*Exploration*		
Games	Self-testing	Games	Self-testing	Games

WINTER SCHEDULE   November— March   INDOORS

Mon.	Tues.	Wed.	Thurs.	Fri
Movement		*Exploration*		
Games	Self-testing	Dance	Self-testing	Dance

SPRING SCHEDULE   April - May   OUTDOORS (INDOORS)

Mon.	Tues.	Wed.	Thurs.	Fri.
Movement		*Exploration*		
Games	Self-testing	Games	Self-testing	Games

Planning with the Children

In most modern schools children will share in the teacher's planning at the preschool, primary, and intermediate levels. This does not mean that they will decide the basic framework of the program. Children in each grade may contribute at their own level, for example, by discussing what they need to practice. Such a discussion should take place in the classroom, before the activity period begins. Other preliminary planning should also be done before coming to the play space: who will take out the equipment, who will set up the portable apparatus, what each squad will do, what games will be played, and how they are played.

Children may help the classroom teacher plan language arts experiences related to games. Writing descriptions of favorite games and reading them to the rest of the class provides excellent practice in communicating meaningful material. This activity puts a premium on clarity and brevity, and often results in better game descriptions than any in the books.

Other forms of integration will develop naturally within the classroom and will involve the children in planning. For example, a story may have such great appeal that the children will wish to live the experience again in a song, in pantomime, in a dance, or in some other art form.

Planning for Every Child

Today, we believe that the handicapped or atypical child can best learn to live a normal life if he participates as fully as possible in the school life of normal children. The purpose of this procedure is to help him enlarge his sphere of activity and learn to live with his handicap without self-pity. It is also important for a group of normal children to be able to accept a handicapped child, and to give him every chance that a favorable social climate may give. For the atypical child, physical education is especially important. He needs all the fun he can have, all the strength and skill he can possibly develop. He needs recreation now and recreational resources for the future; he needs social adjustment for both present and future happiness.

Obviously, the handicapped child's participation should be cleared with the school or family physician for the protection of the teacher as well as the child. If the medical supervisor knows about the individualized forms of physical education in the program—movement exploration and self-testing activities—and if the teacher and the school nurse also make it clear that many games and dances are not too strenuous and demanding, the way will be cleared for specific medical advice. Overprotective parents should be urged to visit classes and see for themselves what the handicapped child is learning and doing. In extreme cases, where no activity is permitted beyond the minimum required for getting around, the child should still come with the class and help in small ways, such as counting equipment, officiating, keeping records, or using percussion instruments to accompany class work. He should never feel shut out from this very vital part of school life.

The exceptionally capable child, on the other hand, will also find much to challenge him in an individualized, nonstereotyped program. In self-testing, movement exploration, and creative dance, there is no limit to the progress he can make. In games, the natural leadership of the skilled player is recognized whenever captains and squad leaders are elected by the children. The

Noon-hour recreation: competition can be serious business.

teacher may help him to use his leadership constructively in coaching his team members. The extraclass program, discussed in the following section, will also give him satisfaction.

Extraclass Experiences in Physical Education

Noon-Hour Activities[5]

Children who must have their lunch at school are entitled to guidance during that hour as well as during any other part of the school day. Washing, toileting, a pleasant and nutritious meal,

[5] Mary L. Watrous, "Pupil Participation in Noon-hour Activities," *Guidance for Today's Children*, National Elementary Principal, 33d Yearbook. Washington, D.C.: National Education Association, 1954, p. 212.

rest and recreation are all very important. Informal play experiences should be provided as recreation. These may be quiet games, table games, or easy circle games for younger children. For the older ones there should be auditorium programs, play-party games, square dancing, play with small equipment, and stunts.

Older children often make good assistants in leading games for younger children. They may be trained for this leadership during the first month of the school year.

After-School Play

It is much better to have game tournaments after school than directly after lunch, if it can possibly be arranged. In one urban school, in the center of an apartment house district, after-school play clubs were formed for fifth and sixth graders. The clubs had tournaments out of doors in the fall and spring; indoors, in the gymnasium, during the winter. In a residential suburban town,

Noon-hour recreation: competition also can be fun.

close cooperation between the schools and the recreation commission permitted the utilization of elementary school buildings and playgrounds as a part of the town's recreational resources as soon as the school day was over. The commission's personnel conducted sports tournaments, craft projects in the workshop, and programs in music and drama in the auditorium, besides supervising the informal use of game rooms.

Recess

These brief interludes in the school day should probably be left for free activity. The teacher and the children need a break

A socialized recess period.

in the daily routine—a time to be active or quiet, as they choose. Teachers may learn a great deal about what the children are learning by watching their behavior on the playground when they are not under direct supervision. Do they carry on activities they have learned in class? Can they get games started by themselves? Are they careful of equipment? Do they play reasonably well together for their age and level of development? What happens to overly aggressive children? To withdrawn or overanxious ones? How much progress are they making in self-direction?

Informal Integration with Other Parts of the School Program

From time to time, both children and teachers will want to consult the physical education specialist about some project in health, social studies, or the arts. Here are sample questions that were asked of the specialist by children in a modern school, where the classroom teachers and the specialists consistently worked together:

> We have found our great-grandparents came from many of the dance countries—Scotland, France, Germany, Russia, and Sweden. Will you help us learn dances they might have known?—*Fourth grade*
> We are planning a party for our parents. Will you help us plan some mixers and square dances to teach them?—*Sixth grade*
> We have been having arguments in our soccer games. Can you come to our room next week and help us with the rules?—*Fifth grade*

Summary

To make each minute of the time given physical education yield the highest returns for the children, the teacher will want to do several things:

1. Know how children in general develop and what to expect of the children in his room. At the same time, find those who differ from the general pattern and give them individual thought.

2. Know what outcomes to expect from the different forms of physical education.

3. Plan the schedule within the limitations of time, space, and equipment available, using the different forms of physical education as developmental experiences to meet the special needs of his class.

4. When he has found the best program pattern for his group, maintain it long enough to ensure continuous growth. This may mean a season, a semester, or a year.

5. Challenge the children's inventiveness, keep a high proportion of pupil activity and self-direction in the lesson, and maintain good control.

6. Let the children help in planning and organizing the physical education class before coming to the gymnasium.

7. Include all the children: the handicapped, the overweight, the underweight, the highly skilled, the unskilled. Let each work at his own level. Help children to accept one another and to respect the special gifts each may have.

8. Plan noon-hour and after-school play as an educational experience. Watch play behavior at recess to see which learnings stay with the children.

9. Be available as a resource person when needed by other teachers.

Selected References

AAHPER, *Children and Fitness, A Program for Elementary Schools,* Report of the National Conference on Fitness of Children of Elementary School Age. Washington, D.C., 1960.

AAHPER, *Children in Focus: Their Health and Activity,* 1954 Yearbook. Washington, D.C., 1955, Chaps. 8, 16, 17.

Baker, Gertrude M., *The Modern Teacher of Physical Education.* Des Moines, Iowa: Appleton-Century-Crofts, 1940, Chaps. 2, 3, 4.

Cowell, Charles C., and Helen W. Hazelton, *Curriculum Designs in Physical Education.* Englewood Cliffs, N.J.: Prentice-Hall, Inc., 1955, Chap. 4.

McNeely, Simon, and Elsa Schneider, *Physical Education in the School Child's Day.* Washington, D.C.: U.S. Department of Health, Education and Welfare, 1950.

Mursell, James, *Developmental Teaching*. New York: McGraw-Hill Book Company, Inc., 1949.

Prescott, Daniel, *The Child in the Educative Process*. New York: McGraw-Hill Book Company, Inc., 1957.

Van Hagen, Winifred, Genevie Dexter, and Jesse Feiring Williams, *Physical Education in the Elementary Schools*. Sacramento: California State Department of Education, 1951, Chap. 4.

Watrous, Mary L., "Pupil Participation in Noon-hour Activities," *Guidance for Today's Children*, National Elementary Principal, 33d Yearbook. Washington, D.C.: National Education Association, 1954.

CHAPTER 4

The Lesson

Experience is a fine teacher. The vicarious experience of observing other classes is also helpful. Unfortunately, the best a book can do is to take the reader along for a look at some experienced teachers at work by describing their lessons as they appear to visitors. In this chapter, four such descriptions are followed by suggestions for evaluation, planning, and the selection of appropriate teaching methods.

Four Lessons

SECOND GRADE—MOVEMENT EXPLORATION—NOVEMBER

As thirty 7-year-olds come into the gymnasium, faces light up and bodies quicken into action. The children fan out over the room, doing all kinds of stunts. Half a dozen are trying cartwheels, with varying degrees of success. Some are doing bunny hops (crouching, springing forward, landing first on hands, then on feet). Some are running on all fours (dog run), some are putting hands down and kicking both feet up behind them (mule kick). Others are just skipping with arms and knees lifting high and lightly at each step. For all this activity in a comparatively small room, there seems to be little confusion.

The teacher, Miss Arnes, comes in with the last ones. She is a quiet-mannered young woman with a pleasant face and an alert look which seems to take in every child at a glance. After the children have had about five minutes of continuous action, the teacher strikes a tom-tom rather softly. Every child slows down, then stops and listens.

"Please find your own space and show us how large it is." Each child moves to some prearranged part of the room and begins to stretch and reach in every direction without moving his feet, which are spread a little for balance. "How much room do you have on the floor? Can you show us with your hands? How far can you reach behind you? On each side? Good. How small can you be?" (Children double up, most of them lying on side clasping knees.) "Good. You look like small balls. Do you think you can roll once around, like a ball, without going out of your own space?" (This is accomplished after two or three tries.) "How tall can you be? Yes, that's fine. Most of you look taller than you did last week." (Children stand on tiptoe, stretching arms over head, and give an added stretch to show that they are really growing.) "Can you move your hands and feet lightly and quickly inside your own space? . . . Still quickly, but with strong movements, let your feet take you around the room, anywhere, as long as you do not touch any one else." (Children respond with a great variety of movements. When their feet are to be strong and quick, some stamp, some jump forward or sideways, with emphasis. Rhythms as well as steps differ. Hands and arms show forceful movements, and faces express effort.) "Find your own 'space. That was very good. When you are doing strong things with your arms and feet, how do you feel?" "Strong," says Therese; "Mad," says Jack. "Yes, and let your faces show how you feel if you want to. Like to try that again?" (This time some very ferocious expressions develop.) "Come back to your own space, sit down, and I'll tell you about a hard one. . . . Do you think you could do strong, quick movements, first high up, then low down? Then could you change, starting low, going to middle, and last of all high up?" (Children seem to understand the idea of moving at different levels, although they do better at middle and high levels than at low ones.) "Find your own space and sit down. . . . How could we do that better?" ("We weren't fast enough!" . . . "Didn't get down!" . . . "Let's try it slow!") Teacher: "Good idea. Suppose we try a slow, light movement, very low."

In the midst of this: "I'm after Indians," says Betty. "So am I!" . . . "I'm an Indian!" Realistic conflict is in the making, but the teacher forestalls it by giving the children a chance to plan a drama. After one boy's suggestion that all the girls be Indians is indignantly rejected by Betty, because she thought of the game first, they decide that everyone who is wearing red can be a "Redskin," and a simple drama of fight and flight is developed. Both are enacted symbolically, the "fight" being the shooting of flintlocks by the settlers, of bows and arrows by the Indians. The lesson then ends with each child resting in his own space, lying on the floor, for a brief moment or two before returning to the classroom. In all, almost thirty minutes have been spent in the gymnasium.

THIRD GRADE—SELF-TESTING—SEPTEMBER

This group is all business as it comes out to the hard-surfaced playground. Eight children are carrying the two upper segments of a vaulting box which they put together in one corner of the playground. Four have a mat which they place at the end of the box. Two have a bag of balls, two others a box in which jump ropes are neatly coiled. Four carry a thick pole about 6 inches in diameter. Four more carry two supporting stands for the pole and all eight work at setting it up. Six carry six small boxes which are set up to make three hurdles in a row by putting a wand across two boxes for each hurdle. There is also a horizontal ladder, apparently a permanent fixture, in another corner of the playground. All the apparatus is distributed advantageously about the playground, and the children form in squads, one at each piece of apparatus or set of equipment. Miss Brown, who is the teacher of this class, has come out with the children and has given help as needed with the setting up and distributing of apparatus and equipment. With no additional signals, children begin to use the equipment.

At the box, which is about 3 feet high, most of the children do a crouch jump up, putting both hands on the box and jumping up with both feet. Then they do a crouch jump along the top. After this they stand up and jump off the end where the mat is. One boy substitutes a forward roll along the top, another pulls himself along the top with his hands, like a seal, and does a somersault off the end, first letting himself down onto the mat with his hands.

In the group with balls, each child has an inflated rubber ball about 7 inches in diameter. With these, all kinds of ball-handling skills are being tried: throwing against the wall and catching; bouncing high and catching the ball as it comes down; dribbling; and juggling of a simple kind. Two boys are playing together. First they do a bounce pass to each other, then, at the teacher's suggestion, they bring in another boy, and keep two balls going around their small circle.

There are enough jump ropes for every child in the squad to have one, and most of the children are doing various individual jumping routines. Others are practicing in pairs.

At the hurdles, each child takes his turn at clearing the three in series, replacing any wand he may have knocked off.

The horizontal ladder is used for chinning, for jumping up, for hanging, for jumping down, and for forward travel, hand over hand on the rungs. One boy with rather large hands and long legs has experimented until he can travel forward while holding on to the sides of the ladder. When Miss Brown gives him a hint about using a sideways swing of his body, the youngster is able to take longer "steps" with his hands and gets along with much less effort.

On the horizontal pole, some children jump up to a "front rest" (supporting the weight, nearly vertical, on hands and thighs), then do a somersault over the bar and drop down. Others do a cat walk along the top on hands and feet, while still others do a kind of sloth walk, holding from underneath with hands and knees.

The teacher seems to be everywhere, encouraging all the children, especially those who do new things and the less able who are making the slightest improvement. She notices that there appears to be a general weakness in landings, so she stops the class and asks the children to "find a space" in which they can practice jumping and landing.

During their work on this problem in movement she helps the children get the feeling as well as an understanding of expending and receiving force, which are so important in jumping high and landing easily. To emphasize the use of arms as an additional factor in expending force when jumping "as high as possible," she suggests that the children make a shape in the air as they jump. After a few minutes of such practice, she asks each half of the class to demonstrate for the other half in turn. As the children look for the highest jump, the most interesting shape, and the softest landing, she asks them to tell *why* each one was effective. After a short evaluation of the work of each group, she tells them to return to their squads and then to shift to the next set of equipment.

In thirty minutes each squad has practiced at two stations. Since this third grade has self-testing three times each week in the fall, the children understand that they will all have a turn at each station during the week. At the end of the period, apparatus is carried in by the same children who took it out.

FIFTH GRADE—GAMES—OCTOBER

About forty 10-year-olds come running out to the playground and form files behind their team captains, making six teams in all. Six children bring out three large sacks of balls. Each child wears a colored band across his chest, over one shoulder, and under the opposite arm. The children sort into teams by color: gold, green, red, blue, purple, and brown. One girl, who seems to be room leader, briefly announces: "Remember, we decided to play double-team dodgeball, with Golds and Greens in the center first, then Reds and Blues, then Purples and Browns. Each side has five minutes in. Get ready!"

The teams hurry out to their section of the field, which is divided into three equal parts by two cross lines. Captains of the four end-section teams go to the sacks and each brings back a ball for his team. A boy on crutches at the center of the sideline has a whistle and a watch. "Captains ready?" Each captain puts up his hand after looking to see that his team *is* ready. The boy blows his whistle, and the game is on.

For five minutes, the end teams try to hit some Green or Gold player in the center. With four balls going, there seems to be a great deal of action. When a center player is hit, he goes outside the field of play; apparently he may field any ball that goes outside. He then plays a kind of "keep-away" with the end teams, who try to get their balls back.

The whistle blows, and time is called. "Center teams get five points!" (There are five players left in.) The teams rotate, and the game is on for two more five-minute periods. Score: Greens and Golds, 5; Reds and Blues, 2; Purples and Browns, 3.

The teacher, a man who seems to be in his middle thirties, now takes over. Mr. Clark: "How did it go today?" A chorus of voices answers: "Better!" . . . "Terrible!" . . . "We missed the ball, and the kids on the outside kept it. Can we go out and take it away from them, Mr. Clark?" Mr. Clark: "What are the keep-away rules?" Someone calls out: "Same as basketball; can't fight over it, but can tie it up." Mr. Clark: "That's right; end teams can go outside, but center team players, once out, cannot come into the field. Is there anything you need to practice?" Again a chorus of voices: "Just throwing straight!" . . . "No, you don't throw straight at a guy, you throw where he's running to!" . . . Mr. Clark: "In other words, you shift your focus as your opponent runs and where do you focus?" . . . "Depends on how fast he is." . . . "Where you think he is going to be when the ball gets there." . . . Mr. Clark: "Good, we shall practice that." . . . "Another thing, Mr. Clark, we have to practice catching." . . . Mr. Clark: "Remember how your hands move when you catch?" . . . "First easy, then strong." . . . "How do you keep your eye on the ball when there are four balls?" . . . Mr. Clark: "Good question. I would say watch as many as you can, change focus fast, change your own direction, and keep moving. Think for a moment which of these things you want to work on in a short session right now. Take your own space." The children scatter over the room, each one starting to work as he feels the need. Some go through catching motions, reaching, relaxing, and firming hand control; some practice jumping and reaching for tie ball; some pair off, going to the end of the playground and taking turns trying to hit the other while he is running. Mr. Clark straightens out the traffic rules for this group, and then says, "Let's begin with these same problems next time, working where you are now. Captains bring the balls and color bands, and we'll go in."

SIXTH GRADE—DANCE—FEBRUARY

"The sixth graders have a dance on Fridays during the winter months," Miss Thomas explains. She adds that mixed parties are beginning to interest this group, and that knowing what to do and how is of immediate concern. On this particular Friday, the group is undoubtedly eager for class; wet combs have brought a certain degree of order to the boys' hair, they are wearing their brightest shirts; the girls swish their full skirts with an air of subdued excitement.

Since evaluation and planning followed last Friday's class, Miss Thomas gives a quick review in the classroom as the children change into gym shoes. Charles and Eddie, "leaders" for the day, leave ahead of the others to set up the victrola and arrange the records in order. As the class enters the gymnasium, a snappy march is heard. The girls and boys begin walking counterclockwise around the gymnasium, and all have found a partner before getting around once. Eddie lifts the needle, and the partners race to form a large circle for the first singing game, Bingo—a mixer dance with a continuous change of partners which tends to minimize the importance of the first choice. The dance also provides a good review of the "grand right and left"; several children need help with the weaving, but on the third try all goes well.

Miss Thomas then raises her hand to signal "listening" and tells the class that the polka they are to learn that day forms the basis of many lively dances. A few children who have learned the polka the year before in Miss Smith's room agree to demonstrate. In open dance position, three couples demonstrate the "face-to-face" and "back-to-back" polka. Miss Thomas tells the group that they can learn the same dance step easily by trying a few "problems." She suggests that they warm up by doing a few slides counterclockwise in time with the music. She then instructs them to continue sliding in the same direction, but to change the lead foot with each change of phrase; that is, to slide eight steps with the left foot leading, then eight steps with the right. The class finds these directions easy, but strenuous to follow. After a few moments, the youngsters sit down on the floor to recover their breath while Miss Thomas describes the next problem as "a matter of arithmetic, namely, division." They are to repeat the slides as before, first doing eight slides with each foot leading, then four, and finally two, continuing with the twos until the music stops. Again, the group solves this problem easily.

After another try, Miss Thomas commends the class for learning the pattern so well, but asks for suggestions on ways of improving the quality of movement, explaining that the polka is characterized by lightness and lilt.

John thinks that they were covering too much space, and Joan suggests that they try it with partners, as the three couples had demonstrated it. They then practice again, this time with partners. The music is stopped frequently, and each time the girls are asked to move forward to the next boy in the circle. After several changes Miss Thomas tells the group that they were doing the polka so well that the next time she would teach them the Finger Polka, a dance which is a favorite in many groups and is found in one form or another in almost every country.

There is just time, at the end of the class, to review the two dances that have been selected in preplanning. The children quickly form sets for Captain Jinks. Before the last dance, Barnacle Bill, the girls of each set are asked to move on to another partner. Then the dancing period is over and the children walk informally to their rooms, stopping with relish at the drinking fountain on the way.

Analysis and Evaluation

Whether or not the reader approves of all the procedures just described, he will probably find basic similarities of organization and certain favorable outcomes common to all the lessons described. Most physical education lessons are organized around such procedures as these:

Preplanning. Preplanning is the only part of the lesson that always comes at the same time, of necessity. The other parts may be shifted about, emphasized, or omitted, depending upon the main objective of the lesson. Preplanning is done in the classroom, preferably, so that each child will know what to do when he gets to the play space.

Pupil-directed activity. A well-trained class comes into the play space and into purposeful activity at the same time. Whether this is the informal stunt-like play described in the second grade movement lesson, the individual "work session" mentioned in the fifth grade game lesson, or the immediate arranging and use of apparatus as was described for the third grade, pupil-directed activity should be developed by good teaching. It saves a great deal of time and is very satisfying to the children, since it gives them the feeling of competence.

Teacher-planned problems in movement. Themes for the problems come from the fundamentals of movement (pp. 174–176). They furnish the "main content" of lessons in movement exploration, and in other forms of physical education reinforce learnings in specific skills and understandings as needed. "See how light your body can be when you jump down from the apparatus?" "How can you use your body more effectively when you change direction quickly?" Through these problems the learnings in movement fundamentals are used well in other activities.

Main content of lesson. This refers to the game or dance to be played or performed, or the apparatus or equipment to be used and enjoyed with improving skill.

Evaluation. Children discuss their progress and what they need to practice. Evaluation can be made when a break is needed or at the end of the lesson. It should be brief and to the point in order not to take too much time from activity.

Equally important as analyzing is evaluating teaching methods in terms of outcomes—what the children do, and what they are getting from the lesson. The visitor can make only a tentative judgment on the basis of single impressions, but the teacher can evaluate the children's development during a season, a semester, a year, or several years. Thus he will know whether he has been providing effective developmental experiences in daily physical education lessons.

As an aid to evaluation, many teachers like to use definite criteria, such as the following:

1. Does the child show drive toward a goal which fits in with class goals?

2. Is the child made happy and secure by orderly class procedures in a warm, permissive social climate?

3. Do the children get enough vigorous activity to improve in strength and endurance?

4. Are they given a chance to test developing skills and the power to control various objects in their environment?

5. Do they show increased skill in both objective control (manipulation of small objects or use of large apparatus) and subjective control (use of the body in space, without relation to objects)?

6. Are their confidence and independence increasing with increased skill?

7. Can they use movement to express ideas and emotions without self-consciousness?

8. Do they have approved outlets for feelings of hostility and aggression?

9. Are they inventive—do they think creatively while exploring movement, dancing, playing games, or playing with equipment?

10. Are they having fun? Showing satisfaction and enjoyment? Developing recreational resources?

11. Are there opportunities for developing that degree of social adjustment appropriate to the maturation level of the class?

12. Are the groups within the class learning to accept others of different backgrounds and abilities so that all may have a feeling of belonging, or being wanted?

13. Do the children have the chance to evaluate and plan for class activities in accordance with their maturity?

14. Do they understand the purpose of game rules and safety rules, accept them, and live up to them?

15. Are they as competent in self-direction and self-discipline as their age permits?

16. Do they take good care of apparatus and equipment?

17. Is there evidence of integration of the child's experiences? Is he absorbed in what he is doing? Is his physical education class related to the rest of his school experience?

18. Does each child have a chance to work at his own level of ability and receive recognition for any improvement he makes?

"Can they use movement to express ideas and emotions without self-consciousness?"

Not all of these criteria will apply to any one lesson, since different forms of physical education have different outcomes. For example, criteria 7 and 8 are specifically applicable to the lesson in movement exploration. Criteria 4 and 9 are met by the third-grade lesson in self-testing activities; 12 and 14 by the dodgeball lesson; and 5 and 17 by the dance lesson. Most of the other criteria are met by all the lessons, as they should be by almost every good lesson in any form of physical education. Of course, many other criteria might well be used, depending on the emphasis and objectives of the individual teacher; each one will want to set up his own list for evaluating his own work.

Meeting the Criteria of a Good Lesson

Listing the criteria of a good lesson will not ensure good teaching. In addition, the method by which the teacher carries out his plan is important. Formerly, method could be reduced to 1–2–3 pedagogy. Now, it is considered best to let the teacher work out his own method on the basis of his understanding of how children develop and how they learn. Suggestions based on methods by which experienced teachers have met the criteria listed earlier in this chapter may, however, be of help.

Criteria 1 and 4 (drive toward goal and testing developing powers):

If the teacher has secured enough apparatus and equipment to go around, the normal child's drive will be to test his powers. The class will have to discuss and adopt rules for safety, non-interference, and consideration of others. The wording of these may be worked out in language arts, and graphic arts posters illustrating them may be made. But the day-by-day observance of the rules comes from quiet reminders and insistence, day by day, from the teacher.

Criterion 2 (orderly, warm, permissive classroom atmosphere):

The balance between an orderly and a permissive atmosphere is not achieved in a day. It requires, to begin with, warmth on the part of a teacher, expressing a genuine liking for children and an imaginative understanding of their thoughts and feelings. The teacher must learn to:

1. Teach the basic courtesy of listening.

2. Tie orderly procedure to what the children want to do: "We can have more time to play if we work together quietly to get the gymnasium ready."

3. Be consistently firm as well as pleasantly controlled.

4. Use a quieting signal for attention: a chord on the piano, the raised hand, the low voice, are all better than the shrill whistle. Children are sometimes overstimulated and "jittery" in games. The teacher's composure and quiet insistence on courtesy will help to calm them.

5. Speak clearly but quietly as soon as the class is attentive. Be brief but definite in words and calm in tone. Do not let discussion wander; compliment those who contribute; and then get action going immediately. "You have listened well, and have done some good thinking. We all agreed to try what Bob and Mary Lou suggested. See whether you can remember, when you play, to do these things."

6. Help the children understand that too much noise and excitement keep a player from doing his best. In a physical education class no one wants or expects to hear a pin drop, but no one should tolerate bedlam.

7. Prepare for the troublemakers. Try to understand their real drives. Do they want attention? If so, think up some device for letting them help before trouble starts. Know who needs to be separated from whom to preserve the peace.

8. Sense when hostilities are brewing. The best of classes may not get through a rainy day in the fall, or a warm and muggy spring afternoon, at its customary even pace. These are probably the times for a good rowdy game of Bombardment, where everyone is knocking down Indian clubs and the noise is wonderful. In movement exploration, strong, quick movements, loud percussion instruments, and dramas of conflict will help to ease the tension.

Criterion 3 (vigorous activity):

1. Select "every-child-active" rather than "most-children-waiting" games.

2. Plan preliminary organization of teams, practice, games, and so forth, in classroom.

3. At beginning of year, teach self-direction and sharing of space, so that whole class may try out stunts, informally, when children first come into the gymnasium. Accustom children to an

individual work session at the beginning of the period, where each one goes to his own space and starts to work immediately on some movement pattern or problem that interests him.

4. In self-testing activities, have children understand ahead of time where apparatus and equipment belong, who is to take portable equipment out, and where each squad is to go for its play. Let them start without waiting to be told what to do.

5. In dance or games, have children change formations informally and quickly. "For this relay, we need squad files behind the white line." . . . "Two large circles, boys on outside going clockwise, girls on inside, going the other way."

6. If new games are to be played, directions may be read as part of reading practice before the class comes to the play space.

7. Have evaluating discussions when children need a rest; keep them short and to the point; follow them with more activity, using suggestions made during the evaluation period.

8. Avoid elaborate directions, long-winded explanations, and wordy demonstrations.

9. Use large group games only as necessary at the appropriate stage in children's social development. Small group play provides more activity.

10. Insist on enough balls, jump ropes, and other equipment so that each child has something to play with.

11. Gradually lengthen active play periods and give fewer rest periods, in order to build endurance.

Criteria 5 and 6 (skill, confidence, and independence):

1. Let children try skills at first without a demonstration, watching to prevent growth of faulty habits.

2. Later demonstrate, or have skilled class member demonstrate, when there is need for help with such basic skills as throwing, catching, jumping, relaxed landing.

3. After demonstration of the skill, let class try the whole before practicing any part. Later, practice of parts may be needed, but this should be followed immediately by trying the whole skill again.

4. Confidence and independence develop if the child has a chance to work out his own problems and receives recognition for initiative as well as success.

5. To improve subjective control, emphasize exploration of movement in response to requests for different movement qualities. Do not demonstrate response, since this will lead to imitation.

Children with talent may develop a great deal of skill.

Criterion 7 (expression of feeling without self-consciousness):

Keep child's attention on the idea, or the problem, by simple directions and short statements. Do not comment on his movement as such.

Criterion 8 (outlets for aggression):

Use noisy games, combative stunts, dramas of conflict and symbolic destruction. Again, keep the child's attention on the idea, to avoid increasing interpersonal tensions.

Criterion 9 (inventiveness, creative thinking):

Recognize new ways of doing things on apparatus, interesting original patterns in dance or in movement, good strategy in games. Stop stereotyped playing, and ask children how they might outwit their opponents. Encourage team huddles, even after relay races.

Criterion 10 (enjoyment):

Have a good time yourself, whether you play with the class or not. Plan carefully enough so that you do not have to worry about what comes next in the lesson. Avoid striving for perfection in nonessentials. Help the class to understand that screaming prevents fun for all.

Criteria 11, 12, 13 (group adjustment):

1. Taking into consideration the age of your class, do not expect too much or be satisfied with too little in the area of group adjustment.

2. Give groups—teams, squads, or dance groups—time to make their plans. Let them work out their difficulties without intervention unless they reach an impasse.

3. At the intermediate level, train leaders to give everyone a chance and to help the less skilled and the handicapped to be accepted.

4. At the intermediate level, develop a strong group feeling. Keep the personnel of teams the same for as long a period as seems feasible. Let teams have their own colors and team names.

5. Study the natural groupings within the class by means of sociometric techniques (see page 165). Give isolates a chance to be in a group with at least one child of their choice.

Criterion 14 (accepting rules):

One or two infractions of the rules may be handled by pupil officials and a quiet word from the teacher. Several infractions should be made the occasion for class discussion of the purpose of the rules, why each player has to know and keep them, and why it creates difficulties for the team if any member breaks the rules. Safety rules should be handled in the same way.

Criterion 15 (self-direction and self-discipline):

Trust the children to get activities under way. Compliment them when they do this well. If they think of new ways to play old games, let the class try them. With intermediates, relate the self-control needed in class to what they are learning in social studies about the self-discipline necessary in a free society.

Criterion 16 (responsibility for apparatus and equipment):

Integrate a study of the cost of equipment and apparatus with number skills. "Do you like having enough balls so that each of you can have one to play with? Some schools do not have enough money to buy one ball for each child in the class. If a ball is lost, how much money would be needed to replace it? How long would it take to earn it?"

Criterion 17 (integration):

The child readily becomes absorbed in movement exploration or in creative dance if he is allowed to work out ideas, problems, and feelings in his own way, or in his group's way. Do not interrupt this process until it is time for a rest, or until several children in the class are no longer concentrating. Integration of physical education with other subjects should not be forced, but should grow naturally out of situations that arise in class. Some of these are described in detail in Chapter 7.

Criterion 18 (individualized teaching):

Many of the activities in the lessons described in this chapter call for individual response. If the teacher does not urge children beyond their limits when they are below average or hold them back when they are above average, they will select the things they can do successfully. On apparatus, for example, no child should be urged against his own will to try any prescribed stunt. Competing with more able children should be discouraged, and set standards of performance for age or grade should not be used for producing motivation.

Planning

On the basis of evaluation, the teacher will plan for his next lesson. Teachers in training are often skeptical about detailed lesson planning. They like to ask experienced teachers whether they still make out plans for their work, and are shocked when the best of the older teachers say, "Plan? Of course. How else could I know what we're doing?" The authors agree completely with the latter point of view. While granting that details of planning are more important to the beginner than to the experienced teacher, they maintain that continuous, systematic evaluation of past lessons, and subsequent planning of future lessons, is the direct road to improving the experiences offered the children. And that, after all, is the most important consideration.

It is the business of the professional course in teaching physical education to help teachers in training learn how to plan and evaluate effectively. They may then become self-directing and continue to grow in competence, even if they have little or no supervisory help in their jobs. In making his lesson plan, the teacher thinks ahead about what he hopes the children will achieve (specific objectives), what experiences will be provided in the lesson (class procedures), and what questions class and teacher will ask each other at the end of the lesson (evaluation). The plan for the third-grade self-testing lesson described earlier in this chapter, for example, might read as shown on the following pages.

DAILY LESSON PLAN

Name_____   Unit_____Self-Testing_____
Date_____No.___30___   Equipment for 6 Stations
Class Time____30 minutes_____   6 boxes, 3 wands   6 jump ropes
Grade___Third_____   Swedish box   6 balls
                                            horizontal ladder   30 color bands
                                            horizontal pole,
                                            supports

Objectives

1. To improve control of balance and force through use of equipment
2. To increase strength and flexibility through vigorous participation
3. To provide for creativity through stress on individual achievement
4. To improve understanding and powers of observation through guided evaluation
5. To help children grow in self-direction and ability to work together

Activity and Time Allotment	Procedures	Coaching Suggestions and Anticipated Problems
Planning in Classroom — 5 min.	Organization: (1) As group leaders pass out color bands, explain arrangement and use of equipment at the six stations by means of a chart. (2) Name starting station for each color squad; ask each squad to take out and return equipment for first station. (3) Explain procedure for lesson: each squad will have time to work at two stations, reviewing and/or working out and perfecting individual patterns	Note to student or beginning teacher: this part of the lesson plan is an indispensable step in the eventual success or failure of the lesson.
Practice in Squads — 6 min.	Individual Help: Move from squad to squad giving individual coaching and group help as needed.	As an exercise in "anticipating problems", consider situations that might.

Activity and Time Allotment	Procedures	Coaching Suggestions and Anticipated Problems
Movement Exploration — 8 min.	Teacher-Directed Problems: Have children find a space; show "how high they can jump; how softly they can land." After ample practice, ask for suggestions of techniques that result in effective use of force in take-off and landing. Apply to use of force in throwing and catching. Repeat problem in jumping, asking children to "show the kinds of shapes they can make with their bodies while in the air." Have half of the class observe the other half in turn, looking for interesting shapes, as well as for techniques of jumping that need further work. After evaluation of the work of each group, dismiss children for work at second station. Encourage them to work for better control of force as they practice and to experiment with "making shapes" as they jump from the box.	develop during each step of this hypothetical lesson.
Practice in Squads — 8 min.	Individual Help	
Dismissal — 3 min.	Returning Equipment: Signal for "listening" by raising hand; remind children of procedure to be followed for returning equipment. Explain that children in each squad will be given opportunity to show movement patterns they worked out to class during the next self-testing lesson.	

How closely does the teacher follow his plan? If it is an appropriate plan and there is nothing unusual about the children's response, he may carry it out just as written. Often, however, changes will come as a result of the spontaneous reaction of children, who are always ready to provide the unexpected. For example, the plan for the second-grade lesson in movement exploration might have had several items that were discarded when Indians entered the picture. Or, the teacher might have planned a dramatic finish, leaving the theme to the children's invention. Perhaps, on the other hand, she foresaw that "slow, light movement at a low level" was bound to suggest hunting, and that Indians were bound to be hunted by settlers.

Summary

This has been a practical chapter. Descriptions of four different physical education lessons with four different grades were followed by a list of criteria for evaluating the lessons. Planning and evaluation have been presented as complementary steps in progressing toward better lessons. The methods by which experienced teachers have tried to meet the criteria have been described in some detail.

The central theme of understanding the development and drives of children runs throughout this chapter. Beyond this understanding, the teacher must have confidence in the human capacity for growth if he is to give each child a chance to work along the lines of growth best for him. If he can communicate his confidence to the children in such a way as to build mutual respect and rapport, he is well on the way to professional competence. He may then go beyond competence toward the artistry which is teaching at its best.

Selected References

AAHPER, *Developing Democratic Human Relations Through Health Education, Physical Education, and Recreation,* 1st Yearbook. Washington, D.C., 1951, Chap. 7.

Baker, Gertrude M., *The Modern Teacher of Physical Education.* Des Moines, Iowa: Appleton-Century-Crofts, 1940, Chap. 5.

Halsey, Elizabeth, and Lorena Porter, "First Steps Toward Fitness," *Journal of Health, Physical Education, and Recreation,* November 1958, pp. 40–41.

Prater, Betty, "Improving the Product," *Journal of Health, Physical Education, and Recreation,* April 1961, pp. 24–25.

Treves, Joan, "More Time to Teach," *Journal of Health, Physical Education, and Recreation,* April 1961, pp. 26–27.

CHAPTER 5

The Teacher

THERE ARE MANY EXCELLENT REASONS why well-qualified young men and women select teaching for a career. As a profession, it provides a good life for the teacher, rewarded by community respect and liking in addition to his self-respect and his salary. Moreover, each day of successful teaching contributes to good school living for the children who are taught. Children live almost half of their waking hours in school, and it is the classroom teacher who makes their school lives rich or poor, happy or miserable, developmental or limiting. It is the classroom teacher, with the help of the specialist (and often without such help) who may provide truly developmental experiences in physical education. It is the reward of both teacher and specialist to see their children develop in vigor, freedom of movement, emotional stability, and social responsiveness. It is also rewarding for the teachers to share the fun, the absorption, and the gaiety of the children as they play. As soon as it is time for the physical education lesson, the children express happy anticipation. One fifth-grade boy announced to the physical education specialist that he liked her. "Do you know why I like you?" he went on, "It's because you do lively things with us."

The classroom teacher and the specialist work together as a teaching team, each one contributing what he can best give to the physical education program.

The Contribution of the Classroom Teacher

The social climate of any classroom depends on the personality and ability of the teacher. Warmth, acceptance, security, and challenge will be felt by each child if the teacher accepts each one as a person, whether gifted, average, or handicapped; if the teacher is even-tempered as well as friendly; and if he is ingenious in planning learning experiences. In such a climate children develop favorable attitudes toward the specialist and toward the experiences he has planned.

The classroom teacher knows the child as a total personality and knows his school day as a total experience. He should be familiar with the child's home, neighborhood, and community background, since this kind of information is invaluable for understanding his behavior and for estimating what to expect in the way of accomplishment. The classroom teacher also knows the child as a member of a group. If he supplements daily observation with sociometric studies, he will be able to assist wisely in group organization and group play. As a result of daily contact, the classroom teacher is in a favorable position to know when the child needs a certain kind of emotional experience and what type of group pressure or support will help him most.

Because the classroom teacher works in all subject areas, he can readily coordinate learnings in other areas with the content of the physical education program. It is the classroom teacher who knows whether children's work in social studies would benefit from learning the folk dances of Scandinavia or Latin America. He knows, when small children begin to develop number concepts, what type of scorekeeping experiences in games will provide needed practice. He can tell from his work in language arts when children are ready to read game descriptions, to write them, and to stand up and tell them to the class. He knows, therefore, when to ask the physical education specialist for help so that the child's various learnings may be well integrated.

Can you treat them all alike? A look at their faces on the first day of school gives the answer.

In schools that have changed from traditional to more flexible types of organization, classroom teachers are encouraged to specialize along the lines of their interests and ability, and then act as resource teachers in their special fields. In-service training or summer courses in physical education are available to teachers wishing more work in this field.

It is the classroom teacher, furthermore, who helps to carry on throughout the day the learnings begun in physical education. Standing and sitting well, moving quickly and lightly, carrying objects efficiently, relaxing completely—these skills are useful to children throughout the day and, as a matter of fact, throughout life. The classroom teacher who knows how important they are will give them the proper emphasis, not only in the physical education class, but during the remainder of the school day as well.

The Contribution of the Physical Education Specialist

Whether he serves the children through direct teaching, as a consultant to classroom teachers, or as a coordinator of physical education activities in several schools, the physical education specialist constantly draws on his own professional training, experience, and continuing study.

He is, first of all, in possession of scientific knowledge concerning the child's physical growth and developmental needs. Are the activity lessons vigorous enough to increase endurance? Are they too demanding, so that they result in exhaustion rather than healthy fatigue? At what age are children's skeletal structures vulnerable to strain, and what activities might cause strain? When is growth energy particularly needed? What safety precautions are used by the alert supervisor? What methods of evaluation will give most accurate and useful information about the children's fitness? The answers to these and dozens of similar questions may help to protect as well as stimulate children's physical growth.

Second, the physical education specialist also has a great deal of information about motor skills, information useful to the classroom teacher, to parents, to school administrators, to camp directors and recreation directors—to anyone, in fact, who works and plays with children. When should children begin to have swimming lessons? What kind of balls are needed for first graders? Will fifth-grade children develop bad habits if they try to shoot baskets at official heights with regulation balls? Can you *teach* running, or do you simply let children run? What is good form in throwing for 6-year-olds? What is good movement? To some of these questions, no answers have yet been scientifically determined, but the specialist knows what clinical evidence is available and what the authorities say. The answers are important to the child's optimum development in motor skills.

Third, the specialist is familiar with a wealth of material in different forms of physical education. His knowledge will give variety and interest to the program. He can analyze the outcomes of different games, and select those that will give the necessary practice in the motor skill most in need of development at any given time. He knows how to modify activities to provide more or less exercise, as needed. He also knows, if his training has been broad enough, what dances may readily be integrated with the study of various geographical regions or historical periods. He is informed about the emotional outcomes of competition and of dramatic play. He has analyzed the social experience provided by different games, dance groupings, squad and team activities.

Fourth, the specialist knows short cuts to class organization that will give the greatest amount of activity participation in class time.[1]

In short, his knowledge and experience are very helpful to the classroom teacher, in enriching the program, suggesting more effective methods of class organization, in integrating physical education with other areas of the curriculum, in meeting problems of interpersonal relations, and in meeting problems of individual development.

The Contribution of the Children

Whenever school people talk about "experience as a teacher," they are saying that children teach the teacher. In his very first days of laboratory teaching, the teacher-in-training discovers that the children are teachers. Sometimes they are rugged, sometimes amusing, almost always surprising; and on good days they are very fine teachers indeed. The child is the only one who can help the teacher bridge the gap between "what the book says" and "what we can do in our school."

In an atmosphere of rapport, children, as consumers, will evaluate very frankly what they have accomplished in a lesson. Their appraisal provides valuable information that supplements, underlines, or corrects the teacher's estimate. Some children, in self-directed activity, will prove to the teacher that his preconceived ideas of their ability were mistaken. In play on large apparatus, they will select and try stunts that seem feasible to them, even though these may be well beyond or far short of what the teacher had thought they could do. The same thing is true in

[1] Elizabeth Halsey and Lorena Porter, "First Steps Toward Fitness," *Journal of Health, Physical Education, and Recreation,* November 1958, pp. 40–41; Betty Prater, "Improving the Product," and Joan Treves, "More Time to Teach," both in *JHPER,* April 1961, pp. 24–28.

movement exploration, dramatic play, and creative dance. One ninth-grade teacher had many misgivings when the least skilled group in her grade decided to dance "The Rime of the Ancient Mariner." The dance they produced was significant, however; and when offered in a program it held the respectful interest of a sophisticated audience.

The Contribution of the Principal

Administrative policies may promote or obstruct the physical education program, and the school principal plays a very important part in its success. His understanding support will ensure enough time to develop total fitness; and enough space so that special events will not crowd physical education classes out of the gymnasium; enough equipment so that the children's time is not wasted waiting for the ball to come their way, for example, or waiting for their turn on the ropes. The understanding principal, knowing children as children, will be able to resist pressures toward intense competition of the varsity type, and will promote competition suitable for elementary school age levels. He will think of physical education as education in addition to exercise, and he will create an atmosphere in which teamwork to solve problems of health and physical education is facilitated.

Such teamwork of all school personnel, from principal to child, will also enlist the cooperation of parents. This is necessary for protecting the health of the child who returns to activity after illness, in providing enrichment for the highly skilled and encouragement for the unskilled, in meeting behavior problems, and in dealing with other exigencies.

Health Information Essential in Teaching Physical Education

All teachers need information about the physical and mental health of the children they teach and about procedures that will improve their health. Ideally the classroom teacher works with specialists in these fields: the school physician or nurse, the guidance counselor, and the physical education and health education teachers. The importance of teamwork among them, reinforced by cooperation from the school principal, parents, and family physician has been emphasized in the previous section. Such a team approach will build positive health values for all children as well as encourage exceptional children. However, it may be that the classroom teacher does not have the opportunity to consult health specialists. In such a situation it is very necessary that he have access to specific information. Some of this information closely related to teaching physical education is given in the rest of the chapter.

Health Appraisal

Periodic health examinations should be given to all children at least three or four times during school life. It should be an educational experience in which good health findings are pointed out, and defects detected, recorded, and followed up at a later date. If possible this should be done by the family physician, with records made available to the school and recommendations given directly to the parents who are present at the examination. In situations where poverty or indifference prevent this procedure, or where services of a school physician are available, other provisions are usually made.[2]

The classroom teacher is often responsible for giving screening tests of vision and hearing annually, for recording results on the child's cumulative health record, for referring defects to the proper specialists, and for watching to see that corrective measures are employed.

Continuous observation of the child's health is a natural function of the alert, well-educated teacher. It is much more useful than the "daily inspection" formerly advised but too often found to become a mechanical routine. Space prevents listing here the symptoms of children's diseases[3], but it is important for the teacher to note symptoms that may appear during vigorous exercise and that warn of malfunction. If any of the following

[2] Alma Nemir, *The School Health Program*. Philadelphia: W. B. Saunders Company, 1959, pp. 297–301.

[3] Clair V. Langton, Ross L. Allen, and Philip Wexler, *School Health Organization and Services*. New York: The Ronald Press Company, 1961, pp. 199–207.

occur, the information should be passed on to parents and the family physician:

1. Extremes of underactivity or overactivity in free play.

2. Breathlessness, pallor, or bluish tinge of skin or lips during average amount of activity.

3. Undue fatigue after activity, and very slow recovery.

4. Obvious palpitation of the heart during exercise and undue coughing.

5. Pain, swelling, limitation of movement.

6. Obvious asymmetries of structure or movement, uncoordinated movement.

7. Weakness, poor posture.

8. Undue anxiety or fear in everyday situations.

Exercise and Rest

As pointed out in Chapter 1, exercise is necessary to normal health and development. The amount of vigorous activity needed by normal children is estimated to be from two to four hours daily, depending on their level of development.[4] Most authorities agree on the following facts:

1. The child will not overtax his heart in everyday play situations, provided he has a normal heart.[5]

2. To develop endurance (a vital factor in fitness) activity should increase gradually in intensity and duration over a long period of time.[6]

3. Children and youth may go beyond the stage of healthful activity to harmful exhaustion if they are overstimulated as they may be by highly organized competition.[7]

4. During periods of rapid growth, the child or youth is especially vulnerable to energy depletion and to injury of the long bones. Games such as tackle football should, therefore, be avoided during these periods.[8]

[4] *Journal of Health, Physical Education, and Recreation,* 25:25, January 1954.

[5] A. H. Steinhaus, "The Role of Exercise in Physical Fitness," *Journal of Health, Physical Education, and Recreation,* 14:299–300, June 1943.

[6] *Ibid.*

[7] American Association for Health, Physical Education, and Recreation, and American Medical Association, Joint Committee on Athletic Competition for Children of Elementary and Junior High School Age, *Desirable Athletic Competition for Children.* Washington, D.C.: AAHPER, 1942.

[8] W. M. Krogman, "Child Growth and Football," *Journal of Health, Physical Education, and Recreation,* 26:12, September 1955.

5. After illness or an operation, the physician's recommendation should be received before the child resumes normal physical activity.

6. Handicapped children should not be excluded from physical education, but should take part in modified activity approved by the physician in charge.

Small children take shorter intervals of activity and rest than older ones. In preschool, kindergarten, and first grade, provision is made for complete rest on floor pads for all children at appropriate intervals. Endurance gradually increases and by the time a child has reached fifth grade, he should be able to go through the school day without rest. As stated earlier, a brief period of evaluation or discussion during or at the end of the physical education lesson will give the rest needed after very vigorous movement. Of course, handicapped and convalescent children are much more vulnerable to fatigue and so should be watched.

Posture and Feet

Good posture is important to the child's health. It permits effective use of his body, gives respiratory and digestive organs favorable working space, helps to prevent later back strain, and contributes to an appearance of alertness, confidence, and grace in movement. Most children who have plenty of vigorous movement will develop the muscular strength necessary to hold the body erect. However, some will deviate, and so will need special help.

The classroom teacher should keep in mind the fact that the young child's contours are not those of an adult. His upper back will usually be flat, but his shoulder blades may be prominent. His abdomen protrudes, and his lower back will show a short but often marked hollow. Gradually abdominal strength and control improve, the lower back lengthens and moderates its hollow, and if enough of the right type of arm and shoulder exercise is provided the scapulae (shoulder blades) are held closer to the back.

This normal development is, of course, facilitated by vigorous exercise of arm, shoulder girdle, back and abdominal musculature. Such exercise is not found in most game or dance experience (fine for leg muscles) but is best provided by movement exploration and self-testing, especially climbing, swinging by the arms, and upside down stunts on apparatus.

The teacher should watch for asymmetry that shows in a front or back view. One high shoulder, sideways curve of spine or tilt of hips, habitual sitting or standing with weight on one side, all need attention from a specialist. Corrective exercises should be done only by the physical education specialist on recommendation of the physician in charge. The classroom teacher can improve environmental factors such as poorly adjusted seats, poor lighting, and overlong sessions of sitting. He can watch for individual handicaps of vision, hearing, fatigue, malnutrition, ill-fitting shoes and clothing, and emotional instability—all of which may affect posture. The teacher will do well to introduce a "movement break" even if there is no time to go to the gymnasium. He can motivate good posture and remind children to "sit tall" or to "stand tall and easy," avoiding the old admonition "shoulders back" which usually produced strain and hollow back.

Strong, well-shaped feet are essential for effective movement and for weight bearing. While the preschool child usually has well-padded feet, the two arches (long and transverse) so essential to foot function need the protection of shoes that fit well and give support. The classroom teacher should watch for symptoms of malfunctioning feet, such as toeing out and rolling over on the inside border of the feet in walking. For observation as well as for best development of foot strength, children should take off both shoes *and* stockings before indoor physical education classes, and keep them off during the lesson, provided floors are smooth but not slippery.

Fitness and Health

Nationwide attention has been focused on fitness by the expressed concern of two United States presidents, the Operation Fitness[9] conducted by the AAHPER, and state programs with the same aim. It is important that local schools carry out these plans. Fitness may be described as health plus, that is, the extent to which a child or adult is free from illness and free to work or play with maximum vigor and endurance. This is more than a physical condition; since the human organism is indivisible, morale plays its part. To reach their highest effectiveness, physical strength and vigor must be reinforced with emotional drive and stability.

[9] See Appendix.

The classroom teacher can contribute to this national program in the following ways:

1. Cooperate with local administrators and specialists if they are putting Operation Fitness into your school system.

2. If no local program is as yet underway, it is better to start in your own room than to wait. First, test for fitness as described in Chapter 8, then teach to overcome the weaknesses revealed by the test, and at the end of the year retest and report your results to the principal.

3. Weaknesses may be overcome by stepping up the daily amount of vigorous movement and improving motivation. Muscular strength is improved by use of muscles. Endurance develops as the total amount of muscular work done is increased each day. For best results in either strength or endurance, psychological factors must be considered. If strength and endurance are important goals to the child, he will work hard toward them. If an activity itself is fun, very interesting, and demanding, he may keep right on until the teacher stops him or real fatigue sets in.

Children are easily motivated for movement exploration and self-testing. Moreover, each of these activities may be planned to strengthen the muscle systems generally below par in our children. These are the muscles of arms, shoulder girdle, back, lateral trunk, and abdomen. Games and dance also are easily motivated, but they develop chiefly leg strength and general endurance. Calisthenics may be useful for specific muscle weaknesses, but on the whole they are uninteresting to children, who easily become bored and go through them listlessly. Nor do they have the important elements of self-direction, problem solving, improvement of useful skills, group cooperation and adjustment, invention, and creativity that are attainable outcomes from movement exploration, games, self-testing, and dance.

Most parents will cooperate if they are informed of their children's lack of fitness and if they know what to do about it.

Safety and First Aid

Safety education is a positive program of teaching children to live safely with situations that may at times be dangerous in their world. This can be done by providing experience in meeting hazards under careful teaching and supervision. At the same time prevention of accidents through care in the construction, selection, and maintenance of school facilities and equipment is essential.

When a child plays on apparatus he may be meeting hazards. The school's part in preventing accidents is to see that the apparatus is safe in type, solid in construction, kept in good condition and repair, and placed on a surface suitable for landing from it.[10] The class should be organized in such a way that there are only a few children at each piece of apparatus. The teacher's part is to give instruction in how to land and how to grip firmly. He will be wise to let a child try those things he feels he can do, and not urge him to go beyond what he senses is within range of his ability. The teacher gives the child verbal help if he needs it, but not manual help. He will see also that the child is not pressured by competition with more able children or by a set of required "class achievements." In the opinion of most experts tackle football and regulation basketball are not in accord with elementary children's abilities and do not belong in the elementary school program.

The elementary school children themselves can take responsibility for making their playground a safer place to play.[11] A playground committee or council made up of representatives from different rooms helps to set up safety rules, to practice and help others with safety skills, to spot hazards in games, and to meet everyday safety problems with problem-solving techniques.

Certain safety skills are taught in self-testing: balance and footwork in changing direction; landing from different heights on different surfaces; relaxation and control of momentum in falling; keeping a strong grip; "spotting" or assisting the learner in stunts; consideration of others in sharing apparatus, and sharing the play space without touching or bumping. Some accidents are caused by defects of vision, hearing, and other bodily functions. Some may have psychological origins. If a child is repeatedly injured, his parents and the physician in charge should be consulted.

The National Safety Council compiles statistics on accidents from reports sent in by thousands of school systems. Less than half of school accidents occur in organized activities on play-

[10] See Chapter 6.
[11] Phyllis A. Glaser, "A School Playground Council in Action," *Journal of Health, Physical Education, and Recreation,* 32:27, September 1961.

grounds or playfields, in playrooms or gymnasiums. The incidence rates differ for different ages.[12]

First aid is a useful skill for all teachers. There should be at least one person certified in this field in each elementary school.

Mental Health and Emotional Stability

Since the child is an indivisible organism, many facets of his personality develop simultaneously, and it is no news to the teacher that mental health is an inseparable part of the total health picture. Certain outcomes favorable to mental health may be expected from well-taught physical education classes: increased confidence with developing skill, happiness and enjoyment, relief from tensions that build up in a sedentary school day, acceptance of one's limitations in capacity and making the most of them, and integration of one's physical and emotional powers of control. In any classroom, however, there are some children who have problems in mental health that show up as deviations from accepted behavior. Some of these are briefly discussed in the following pages.

1. What can be done for the child who simply does not participate? In such a situation, the teacher must look below surface behavior, knowing that this may be a troubled child who needs understanding and warm acceptance even more than the happier children who are enjoying their play. The first thing to do is to try to find out why the child acts as he does. The following are some possible reasons:

a. He may be overanxious, afraid of being unable to do what the other children can do and therefore of being ridiculed by them and blamed by the teacher. If this is the difficulty, do not force his participation. Since his natural drive to try his powers has been crippled, let his curiosity take him into the easiest thing he sees to do. Praise him quietly for participating, and for any success he may have. Do not ask him to demonstrate. Do not let him be "It" in games, especially in those games where the child who is "It" has little power and needs skill or drive to catch the others.

b. He may be a model in all other schoolwork, precise and orderly, and unwilling to risk his reputation for neatness and cleanliness in what seems to him rough-and-tumble

[12] National Safety Council, *Accident Facts.* Chicago, 1961, pp. 89–93.

play. Again, do not force participation. Praise him when he finally does join in. Let him see that you approve of his activities, and do not mention any of his varieties of "goodness." If he has aptitude for skills of any kind, see that he has a chance to improve and to demonstrate them. Perhaps you can visit his home, and obtain encouragement of the new experience he is enjoying at school.

c. There may be physical handicaps—obesity, undernourishment, defects of vision or of hearing—which make him feel safer on the side lines. Correction of handicaps and learning to live with them is needed here. Let the other children urge the handicapped child to play, and make sure that they are considerate of him.

d. He may hit upon nonparticipation as a device for getting attention from the teacher. Give him the attention he needs, and let him feel that you understand and accept him. Tell him that you would like to see him playing with the other children because you know he would have fun. Do not ignore him, but gently urge him to participate.

2. What should be done with the overly aggressive, overactive child who participates in everything anyone else is doing and who is a roving troublemaker unless controlled? Again, this behavior cannot be dealt with on a temporary or superficial basis. The teacher must know why the child acts as he does. Meanwhile, he should accept him as a child-in-need and let him feel the support of basic understanding and affection, which the child probably needs very much.

When class work suffers because of the aggressive child's behavior, it is necessary to be firm in stopping him; but it is unwise to be harsh or obviously angry. Meanwhile, every possible acceptable channel for the expression of his hostility should be tried. If the class is playing a game in which the aggressive child is breaking rules, switch to movement exploration and give several problems in strong movement before you give any in light movement. Encourage movement dramas growing out of the hero-villain theme. The aggressive child will usually be chosen to play the villain, or you can see that he is. This gives him an opportunity to act out his hostility, and is excellent therapy.[13] Do not

[13] Karl Menninger, *Love Against Hate*. New York: Harcourt, Brace & World, Inc., 1942, pp. 172–182.

expect immediate rapport or rapid improvement, and be patient in meeting relapses after some improvement has occurred.

The extremely aggressive child may need expert help. If the community has such resources, the child should be referred, through the school principal and the school physician, to a clinical psychologist, who will send him on to a psychiatrist if necessary, or to a treatment home if one is available.[14]

3. What can be done if the class as a whole gets restless or downright unruly? This rarely happens if children are given enough activity which they have helped to plan carefully before coming to the gymnasium. If children come into a beautiful, big space that invites running and must then sit down and contemplate it while the teacher explains a game, the class is lost before it begins. Or if they must practice making a circle until they can do it without pushing or pulling, the process may last the whole period because pushing and pulling are the only attractive activities offered.

If the teacher can foresee restlessness about to overcome an ordinarily well-behaved class, the sooner he can get them out of the classroom and into vigorous activity, the better. In such a situation, movement exploration beginning with familiar problems and self-testing activities are preferable to games and dances, unless these are vigorous and well known to the class. Recently, a very skillful and experienced classroom teacher, working with the school curriculum committee, came out strongly in favor of a daily period of physical education. "I don't know much about physical education, and have never liked it for myself," she said. "I only know that Tuesdays and Thursdays, when we don't have it, are hard days for my class and for me. We just don't get as much done."

If disorder is not the exception but a daily occurrence in your room, it might be well to explore these possible causes:

a. Is the climate of your room hostile because you have tightened up and are using an overdose of punishment?

b. Are you using emotional blackmail with your class? Some teachers win most of the children in the class through affection, which they then use consciously as a means of control. This method will sooner or later divide the group

[14] See Fritz Redl and David Wineman, *The Aggressive Child.* New York: The Free Press of Glencoe, 1957. Also, Bruno Bettelheim, *Love Is Not Enough.* New York: The Free Press of Glencoe, 1950.

into "ins" and "outs." Throughout this text, the teacher has been urged to extend acceptance, warmth, and understanding to all children. When he implies that those who do forbidden things or who do not do assigned tasks will lose his affection, the general rapport with and confidence of the class is lost.

c. Are you emphasizing competition and rivalry as motivation? Competition is a necessary part of games, and it is bound to occur in other school experiences, but it may be emphasized or played down according to the teacher's philosophy. Overemphasis sooner or later establishes an atmosphere of hostility. Moreover, it tends to make the withdrawn child still more withdrawn and the aggressive child still more aggressive. As Hein has pointed out, "Learnings in sports competition must be as carefully graduated as are learnings in other fields."[15]

4. What can be done if groups and teams do not work well together? Make certain, first, that the form of group organization is suited to the children's level of maturation (see Chapters 2 and 3). If you are making decisions for the group in an autocratic manner, or if the group varies too much in ability or socioeconomic status, the "we" feeling will probably never develop. On the other hand, if you are giving children too much responsibility, they may become insecure and exclusive in their reactions to the rest of the class.

5. What should be done if the children are unsportsmanlike in their behavior? First, examine your own concept of the kind of behavior you should try to develop at their age level. Perhaps you are asking for the civilized, complicated behavior that taxes adult self-control. Start where the children are; go on gradually, expecting to do much reteaching; and be ready to repeat explanations with patience.

In fact, this is the procedure that must be followed in all teaching: talking, explaining, planning, discussing, acting, and evaluating.[16] In the teaching of self-discipline and good sportsmanship, children should contribute to all of these procedures, but they should not be expected to deal with the lawbreaker.

[15] Fred V. Hein, "What Stand on Competition?,"*Children in Focus.* Washington, D.C.: American Association for Health, Physical Education, and Recreation, 1954, p. 159.

[16] James L. Hymes, *Behavior and Misbehavior.* Englewood Cliffs, N.J.: Prentice-Hall, Inc., 1955, p. 20.

Since the problem of consistent infraction of the rules may well involve the emotional conflicts of troubled children, it is beyond the ability of the other children to solve. Such a problem is basically the responsibility of the teacher.

At this point, the young teacher-in-training may feel appalled by the amount he is supposed to know. Every profession has the same effect on the beginner. Teaching, as a profession, is especially demanding, because it deals with the most complex, important, and interesting things in the world: human beings. It catches them when they are young and have much to learn. And the beginning teacher has much to learn, too. Actually, the modern college student's preparation for teaching is very much like on-the-job training in industry. To study–discuss–plan–teach–make mistakes–analyze mistakes–plan again–teach again (but better not make the same mistakes again!)—surely this process is the familiar learning by doing, and it works. It works faster and more efficiently with the help of an experienced supervising teacher, who can give insight into the practical workings of basic principles and help the student evaluate his own teaching.

In addition to broad knowledge, however, the young teacher should take with him a capacity for liking children, for laughing with them, for accepting them at any stage of development, and for understanding their problems and their "growing pains." It is especially important that he concentrate on what is happening to the children. The sooner he can forget himself and see what is happening to the children in his class, the sooner he begins to teach instead of going through the motions. When he begins to teach, the children begin to learn—and that is when the fun begins for everyone.

Summary

Teachers who bring children the fun and activity of physical education lessons will be rewarded by seeing the children grow and by sharing in their enjoyment.

Both the classroom teacher and the specialist contribute to the success of the physical education program. The classroom teacher sets the social climate and contributes his knowledge of each child as a total personality, of his background in school, home, and community, and of his group relationships. He knows when physical education may be integrated to advantage with other subject areas. It is only when the classroom teacher continues through the day the teaching of posture and movement begun in physical education classes that these learnings take hold.

In addition to his specialized knowledge of games, movement exploration, self-testing activities, and dance, the specialist uses his background in health, safety, movement analysis, and child development to serve the children and to help the classroom teacher.

The child also contributes to the program. His response shows both teachers whether their estimates of his development were correct, and his evaluation of class progress is important to future planning.

The elementary school principal is a key figure in the success of the physical education program. If he understands the child's need for all-around development through vigorous movement he will give adequate time, space, equipment, and general support to physical education.

The day-by-day teamwork of classroom teacher, specialist, and children should be reinforced by the help of administrators, other teachers, and parents whenever the need occurs.

If the classroom teacher has no specialist to help him, he will have to fill the gap through his own study. He may wish to become a resource teacher in physical education if his school permits flexible interchange of classes. This will require in-service training and summer study. All teachers will find in this chapter specific information in certain areas related to physical education: health, safety, fitness, posture, mental health, and behavior problems.

Teaching is a demanding profession because what happens to human beings is of crucial importance. As soon as the beginning teacher forgets himself and sees what is happening to the children in his class, his real teaching begins.

Selected References

AAHPER, *Children in Focus: Their Health and Activity*, 1954 Yearbook. Washington, D.C., 1955, Chaps. 9, 10, 11, 12, 13, 14, 19.

Baker, Harry J., *Exceptional Children*, 3d ed. New York: The Macmillan Company, 1959, Chaps. 3, 4, 5, 6.

Davies, Evelyn, *The Elementary School Child and His Posture Patterns.* Des Moines, Iowa: Appleton-Century-Crofts, 1958.

Glaser, Phyllis A., "A School Playground Council in Action," *Journal of Health, Physical Education, and Recreation,* 32:27, September 1961.

Joint Committee on Health Problems in Education of the NEA and AMA, *Health Appraisal of School Children,* 3d ed. Washington, D.C., 1961.

Joint Committee on Health Problems in Education of the NEA and AMA, *Health Education,* 5th ed. Washington, D.C., 1961.

Langton, Clair V., Ross L. Allen, and Philip Wexler, *School Health Organization and Services.* New York: The Ronald Press Company, 1961.

Menninger, Karl, *Love Against Hate.* New York: Harcourt, Brace & World, Inc., 1942.

National Safety Council, *Accident Facts,* Annual Report. Chicago, 1961.

Nemir, Alma, *The School Health Program.* Philadelphia: W. B. Saunders Company, 1959.

Oberteuffer, Delbert, *School Health Education,* 3d ed. New York: Harper & Row, Publishers, 1960.

Redl, Fritz, and David Wineman, *The Aggressive Child.* New York: The Free Press of Glencoe, 1957.

CHAPTER 6

The Play Space

THE PROGRAM IN PHYSICAL EDUCATION is carried on within limits of space and equipment. What is accomplished by the teacher during each lesson depends, to some degree at least, on these factors. It therefore seems advisable to include in this text descriptions of space and equipment adequate for the developmental program in physical education. Although beginning teachers are seldom asked to plan playgrounds or to buy equipment, they often serve on committees that present the needs of the elementary school to administrative officers. In addition, they are responsible for securing the interest of parents in providing a favorable environment for children's play, both at school and at home.

Outdoor Play Space

For many years we have known that children should play out of doors as often as the weather permits. More zest for play, the speed-up of metabolism, and the greater irradiation of body proc-

117

esses by direct sunlight are some of the important health reasons for preferring outdoor activity to indoor.

The outdoor play space should be planned functionally; that is, according to the needs of the different age groups using it. Children of all ages need a level space, appropriately surfaced, equipped with permanent as well as portable apparatus, enclosed by protective fencing, and large enough to accommodate peak loads in activities desirable for the age level of the group. Hilly sites should be terraced, and low sites provided with artificial drainage. In addition to these general requirements, there are specific requirements for each age group.

Preschool Play Space: 3–5 Years

Size: 10,000 square feet minimum.

Surfacing: Mostly turf; some hard surfacing for locomotor toys such as tricycles, toy automobiles, and roller skates. Soft surface, such as sawdust, sawdust mixed with sand, or tanbark, to a depth of 12 inches under apparatus.

Trees and shrubbery are essential for shade, landscaping, and climbing. Play porches and patios are desirable.

Equipment:

Sandbox, covered.

Construction area, including building boxes, cinder blocks, wood and lumber scraps.

Project area, for art and other project activities.

Area for pets.

Wading pool, with fountain, sprinkler, or hose for water play.

Permanent apparatus, including horizontal and slanting ladders, vertical and parallel ropes, horizontal bars, supported poles, monkey rings, rope ladders, and "creative" equipment.

Portable apparatus, including low tables, small hurdles, boxes, and benches.

Play equipment, including balls of various sizes, jump ropes, tire casings, old inner tubes, hoops, sand tools, and locomotor toys.

Primary Play Space: 6–8 Years

Size: 2–4 acres.

Surfacing: Some turf, mostly hard surfacing for games and play with small equipment; soft surface under apparatus.

Houses in the playground village are child-size, but strong enough for climbing.

Trees and shrubbery around edges, to avoid interference with games and ball throwing yet provide shade for such special activities as crafts and construction.

Equipment:

Construction area, as for preschool group, with addition of larger scraps and some tools.

Project area, for use as an extraclass laboratory.

Area for pets and experimental animals.

Permanent apparatus, including horizontal and slanting ladders, horizontal bars, supported poles, monkey rings, rope ladders, vertical and parallel ropes, tubular and metal stands for climbing, "creative" equipment.

Portable apparatus, including tables, hurdles, planks with hooks, saw horses for support, low balance beams.

Play equipment, including balls of various sizes, bats and paddles, jump ropes, tire casings, wheeled toys, stilts, construction equipment, bands of different colors to distinguish squads and teams.

Intermediate Play Space: 9–11 Years

Size: 3–5 acres.

Surfacing: Hard-surfaced area laid out in courts for team games, individual games such as paddle tennis and tether ball, and play with balls and other small equipment. Turf for field games such as softball and soccer and for some track and field events. Soft surface under apparatus and in jumping pits.

Equipment:

Construction and project areas in shade.

Camping area, equipped with outdoor oven, barbecue pit, council fireplace, and ring.

Permanent apparatus, as for primary group, but with addition of broad- and high-jump pits and take-off boards, poles for tether ball.

Portable apparatus, as for primary group, but with addition of standards for high jump, volleyball, volleyball nets.

Play equipment, including junior-sized softballs, soccer balls, volleyballs, basketballs, and footballs; regulation tennis and handballs, bats, paddles, and rackets; jump ropes, roller skates, stilts, pogo sticks, small vaulting poles, deck tennis rings, shuffleboard pushers and disks, aerial darts, paddles and birds; bands of different colors to distinguish squads and teams.

Indoor Play Space

In a small elementary school, the gymnasium or playroom serves all grades in the school, often for more than one purpose. At noon it may be a lunchroom, at times a music practice room, at other times an auditorium, and in the evening it may serve as a community recreation room. The use of such a multipurpose room must be scheduled with care and with due regard for priority of need. The room must be constructed and equipped with various purposes in mind. Obviously, there must be adjoining storage space large enough for a variety of equipment. A platform is essential for auditorium use, and an adjacent kitchen is needed if the room is to be used as a lunchroom. In a large school it is more economical, in terms of both scheduling and maintenance, to plan separate facilities for most of these purposes. All special-purpose rooms should be available for community recreation after school is over for the day.

Size and Surfacing

An elementary gymnasium or playroom should be at least 60 by 40 feet; 70 by 50 feet is recommended. Flooring should be resilient, durable, perfectly smooth and level, not slippery, and easy to care for. Resilience is very important in structural and functional foot hygiene. The developing double arch of the small child's foot, and the developing strength of foot muscles all through the early years, require resilience in flooring as well as training in use. Hardwood is the most satisfactory resilient surface now available. However, a hardwood floor requires care in maintenance and is more difficult to keep clean than a floor of rubber or asphalt tile. For this reason, the use of the gymnasium as a lunchroom is not advisable, regardless of the size of the school.

Equipment for the Indoor Play Space

Gymnasium equipment must be portable or removable so that space may be cleared for various forms of physical education. Some types of apparatus, such as ropes, climbing ladders, basketball goals and bleachers, may be suspended or recessed when not in use. Other types may be kept in a storage room, being brought out and put away by class members. The storage room should have a door into the hall as well as into the gymnasium, so that boxes of balls, jump ropes, and other items may be taken to and from the playground without entering the gymnasium. For reasons of safety, various items of mechanical equipment should be recessed. It must be remembered, however, that large expanses of wall space are needed for ball play. Recessing of equipment should be planned accordingly. The following items of equipment are needed in the gymnasium:

For climbing, hanging, and various suspension skills: Vertical ropes in sets of four or six; parallel ropes; portable climbing frames; large, strong boxes, arranged in steps; supported bars; horizontal and vertical or slanting ladders; horizontal and parallel bars.

For jumping: Mats, platforms, small boxes with light poles placed across for hurdles, strong tables, benches, Swedish vaulting boxes and horses.

For balance: Low beam, high beam, or English "form."

For play and games: Balls of all types and various junior sizes; jump ropes; bats, paddles, and rackets; stilts and small vaulting poles; deck tennis, shuffleboard, and badminton equipment (fleece or yarn balls instead of birds); hoops; colored shoulder bands for teams and squads.

For dance and movement exploration: Percussion instruments, record player, records, piano.

Supervision of Play Space

Whenever either playground or gymnasium is the site of class or extraclass activities, responsible leadership should be provided. This means planned instruction during class time and planned supervision during extraclass use at the noon hour or after school.

Supervision is planned according to the general policy of the school. It should, however, always be constructive guidance rather than mere police duty. As such, it includes the following responsibilities:

1. Preliminary and frequent subsequent checks to see that the play area is free of trash, obstacles, and removable hazards, such as loose gravel on hard surfaces.

2. Firmness in enforcing general rules and in developing children's self-discipline. A children's playground council helps here.

3. Observing, and helping children to understand and observe, the general plan for extraclass use of facilities—for example, the schedule of intramurals and the time set aside for general, unscheduled play.

4. Assigning the use of space, equipment, and apparatus to prevent congestion; checking the return of small equipment and portable apparatus.

5. Assisting intermediates in carrying out their own plans of organization.

6. Constant watchfulness of all groups to see that they are considerate of others and that safety practices are being followed.

7. Teamwork with other school personnel in reporting problems and planning for better use of playgrounds.

Care of Facilities and Equipment

The following steps should be taken to provide reasonable care and maintenance of physical education facilities and equipment:

1. Seasonal cleaning and painting. The use of bright paints can add to attractiveness of apparatus.

2. Protective treatment of wood, ropes, and nets to prevent weathering.

3. Ensuring stability of upright apparatus by setting it in concrete[1] and keeping guy wires and cables taut.

4. Removing damaged apparatus and equipment and securing prompt repair and return.

5. Raking and cleaning sandboxes; keeping jumping pits and soft ground under and around apparatus dug up and raked to prevent packing and free of trash or other obstacles; renewing filling as needed.

6. Keeping small equipment in boxes; jump ropes coiled and tied; balls dusted and stacked; bats, rackets, and paddles dusted, inspected, and stacked; colored bands tied by colors.

7. Carrying mats, never dragging them. Protecting old mats with washable covers; cleaning new plastic mats as necessary.

8. Cleaning grounds or floor daily; sweeping paved surfaces free of gravel; keeping fences repaired.

9. Keeping markings clear.

Safety Measures

As has been pointed out in the previous chapter, the school safety program provides education as well as protection.

Safety education means teaching the child to live safely in a world of hazards, but it does not mean that additional hazards have to be provided by the school. Safe apparatus, good care and repair of apparatus, and careful supervision of activities on the play area are all vital factors in the promotion of safety. Some additional factors may be listed here:

[1] Never, however, permit concrete platforms under apparatus.

1. Instruction in the safe use of apparatus and in safety skills.

2. Teaching children consideration for others and responsibility for the safety of others.

3. Teaching children responsibility for their own safety.

4. Careful recording and review of accidents, followed by correction or elimination of causes.

Community Use of Play Areas

Most schools practice close cooperation with the community and make their facilities available for community use after school hours. Such a policy makes the following outdoor facilities desirable:

1. Facilities for picnics and outdoor cooking. A camping area, already listed as desirable for children in the intermediate grades, will serve this purpose.

2. A hard-surfaced area, at least 60 by 90 feet, for square dancing, with a loud-speaker system for music and caller.

3. A lighted area for night softball, croquet, horseshoes, archery, shuffleboard, deck tennis, and volleyball.

Community use of indoor facilities requires the following:

1. A separate entrance to the facilities to be used, and provision for shutting off the rest of the building.

2. Equipping of the gymnasium for square and folk dancing, volleyball, deck tennis, paddle tennis, shuffleboard, badminton, and table tennis.

3. A club room with kitchen facilities for evening PTA and club meetings.

Recent Developments in Playground Equipment

Some forms of playground equipment that have been used for a long time are becoming obsolete and are gradually being discarded. Often called "sit-and-ride" items, they do not represent as good an investment of school money as the simpler types currently recommended. A word about the disadvantages of each of these forms of equipment may be in order here.

Swings: Enjoyed by preschool children but not developmental; space-consuming; dangerous when too close together.

Teeters: Dangerous; not developmental.

Slides: Very expensive; enjoyed by preschool children but not really developmental.

Giant stride: Dangerous.

Merry-go-round: Expensive; not developmental.[2]

Creative Equipment

Traditional equipment is being in part supplanted, in part supplemented, by so-called creative equipment or by improvised, homemade apparatus. Creative equipment, which is more or less abstract in design, may be used in a variety of ways. Playground executives who have installed such equipment like it, as the following letters indicate:

> The newer equipment unquestionably holds the children's interest and certainly gives them opportunity for the invention of "games" both of an individual and a group nature. This, in turn, increases the amount of physical exercise they do, since they play for a longer period of time.[3]
>
> The use of new creative type of equipment gives the child the opportunity to use his imaginative talents in climbing over odd shapes of steel or reinforced concrete.
>
> We have found that where new type of equipment is being used, although we have not eliminated swings and slides, the attendance has increased three or four times.[4]

The amount of exercise possible on this type of apparatus again depends on what the child wants to do. If the child visualizes the apparatus as something requiring a great amount of move-

---

[2] By "not developmental" the authors mean that the equipment does not provide much actual exercise, is not really conducive to improvement in strength or skill, and affords little opportunity for inventing new things to do. In fact, the natural desire of the child to see what else he can do leads him to dangerous variations of the accepted use of these "one-way" devices. For example, children soon get bored with going down a slide in a safe sitting position, and may try standing up, facing backwards, or other hazardous innovations.

[3] Personal communication from Robert W. Crawford, Recreation Commissioner, Philadelphia, January 19, 1956.

[4] *Ibid*, November 1, 1961.

ment, then he'll perform a great amount of movement. It is our opinion that the needs of the child will tend to dictate what the apparatus means to him; therefore, if he needs a lot of exercise, the apparatus will provide that for him.

Because of the absence of moving parts, the creative apparatus, as presently available, is completely safe—or as safe as playground apparatus can ever be. We feel that if you remove all elements of danger from apparatus, then there will be no challenge in it for the children.

Unfortunately, it is true that the creative playground equipment available currently is relatively expensive in initial outlay. It is our opinion that the maintenance cost and the like will be considerably lower than is found with traditional apparatus.[5]

Accurate records have been kept of those areas where conventional type playgrounds were replaced by new, modern, and functional facilities. These records show that the newer facilities are attracting an 800 per cent increase in participation.[6]

Among the pioneers of modern playground design is Joseph Brown, professor of sculpture at Princeton University. The various forms of play apparatus he has invented, although structurally safe, permit a variety of activities. Some of these forms are mobile enough to provide a framework that shifts as other children on the apparatus move. This unpredictability, he believes, tends to stimulate creativity.[7]

Improvised Equipment

Many schools wishing to equip a playground on a limited budget have saved a great deal of money by using equipment that is at hand or that has been made in the school shop. Obsolete tables or desks may be reconditioned and used for vaulting or jumping obstacles. Community resources may yield both materials and labor—"do-it-yourself" enthusiasts in the PTA have equipped playgrounds in more than one community. A few examples of improvised equipment are given here.

1. Local tree surgeons or city foresters may be able to contribute short, thick tree trunks. Left horizontal, these may serve

[5] Personal communication from John A. Turner, Superintendent of Recreation, City of St. Louis, January 10, 1956.

[6] Robert W. Crawford, "A New Look for Philadelphia," *Recreation*, 49:322, September 1956.

[7] Joseph Brown, "One Body—One Mind—One Person," *Recreation*, 47:576, December 1954.

Can you go all the way by yourself? The best part of it is that there's no train coming.

This improvised animal is excellent for climbing.

as climbing or vaulting obstacles; set vertically in a cement base, they may be used as climbing and jumping obstacles by older children. Longer sections may be made into slanting poles by rigging them to a supporting wall or fence; or a balancing tree may be set up, about 2 or 3 feet from the ground, on wooden supports.

2. Ladders may be donated, reconditioned, and used on stout supports horizontally or vertically.

3. Hardwood planks, set between two chairs, may be used for vaulting, balance stunts, and jumping down.

4. Strong packing boxes, finished and painted, make good apparatus for climbing and jumping down. When used as supports for light sticks, they serve for jumping or hurdling.

5. Obsolete equipment may serve many purposes. Old streetcar tracks are good for balancing; children find a variety of uses for old culverts; even old fire trucks, with the motors removed, have been used on some playgrounds.

For several years the Glencoe, Illinois, primary schools have had a fire engine, a steam roller, and a concrete culvert on the grounds. The area is in constant use by second and third graders during free activity periods. The apparatus is usually teeming with youngsters, although some of the third graders prefer games. The kindergarten and first-grade children go over to this part of the grounds as a special treat; they swarm and climb over the apparatus with obvious enjoyment. All teachers feel that the children enjoy these pieces of apparatus now as much as they ever did.[8]

Schools With Modern Playgrounds

The Association for Childhood Education, International, has appointed a committee to study problems related to playgrounds for children. This committee has secured reports about recent projects in planning and developing the outdoor play areas of their schools from several association members. The reports are used as a resource file on the subject. The authors have had access to this file and have received permission to publish some of the

[8] Based on a personal communication from Norman Erickson, Principal, Central School, Glencoe, Illinois.

reports from those who wrote them. They are included in this chapter as specific illustrations of local problems, solved by the ingenuity of local school personnel in cooperation with members of parent groups.

CAROLE HIGHLANDS SCHOOL, TAKOMA PARK, MARYLAND[9]

The Carole Highlands Elementary School was opened in 1953. It consisted of twelve classrooms, a multipurpose room, kitchen, library, teachers' room, and infirmary. In 1955 four new rooms and additional blacktop were added, and the play area enlarged.

The school is located in a suburban community of approximately one thousand five hundred homes, two miles north of Washington, D.C., in Prince George's County, Maryland. The school property consists of eight acres of beautifully wooded land. About two acres comprise the building site and playground. This area fortunately is level land with fairly good drainage. A large lawn, which was well seeded by the builders, borders the northeast side of the building. Two other level areas with beautiful trees comprise the southern entrance to the school. On the west side of the building there are garden spaces approximately 6 by 12 feet for the primary grades to use. A blacktop semihard surfaced area was placed in the rear of the school, and laid off in circles and rectangles for games. This is bordered by another large space for softball, playground equipment, and so forth. Softball diamonds were laid out and the Board of Education was asked to erect a backstop.

Our social studies program of 1953 centered almost entirely on the new school. The primary classes chose for their project the garden plots by their outside doors. The children brought cuttings of various plants, such as geraniums, coleus, and begonia. The cuttings were started indoors and rooted before being planted in the gardens. The third-grade class collected wild flowers and transplanted them in their garden plot. Others studied the trees and labeled them. Birdhouses and feeding stations were put up in trees around the building. The fourth, fifth, and sixth grades made rock gardens and collected shrubs, plants, bulbs, and cuttings to beautify the grounds. One fifth-grade class, with the help of parents, built a fireplace. The State Forester's Office assisted the upper grades in planning a nature trail. The foresters furnished enough seedlings so that each child in the school had one to plant. The dry summer of 1954 caused the loss of many of these.

[9] Report by Frances Lindahl, Principal.

This climbing apparatus provides good arm, leg, and trunk exercise for several children.

Each year the teachers and children plan ways to continue the work that was started the first year. Rose bushes, various shrubs, tulips, narcissus, daffodils, iris, and chrysanthemums have been added. It is a continuous process and has many possibilities.

County and neighborhood organizations have also added to our facilities. The County's active summer recreation program used the school for its activities and has erected sandboxes that benefit our younger children. A civic association of the community has donated picnic tables and money for improving the facilities.

The Board of Education furnished swings, chinning bars, and seesaws the first year, and this year added a new set of swings. Our PTA donated money to buy an additional set of swings. Basketball poles and baskets were erected on the blacktop area. Standards for volleyball and other games were furnished by the Board of Education. It also furnished funds each year for equipment suitable for all grade levels. The PTA, in cooperation with the Board of Education, is now working on a project which consists of cinder blocks and tile pipes. An outdoor stage, a fort, and a ramp with a fireman's pole will be completed this year. A group of parents will clear a large space under the trees near the primary rooms in which to place simple and inexpensive devices for small group play, such as discarded rails from railroad tracks for balancing, wooden horses made from logs, and low chinning bars. Another small group area will have a broad jumping pit, horseshoe pegs, and pitchers' boxes.

Each year we plan to add other features. We feel that this type of playground equipment is very valuable because of its creative play possibilities.

BROOKS SCHOOL, GREENSBORO, NORTH CAROLINA[10]

Brooks School is one of the seventeen elementary schools of Greensboro, a city of 80,000 population. The school was opened in a new school district in September, 1951, and since that time has grown from an enrollment of 360 with 12 teachers to an enrollment of 706 with 21 teachers. A new wing was added in 1953.

The year before the building was completed we were housed in a nearby church. As we watched the building progress and acquainted ourselves with the twenty-five acres comprising the grounds, we realized the necessity of planning for a suitable playground for this very modern school. It has not been possible, financially, for Greensboro to equip its playground, so the members of the new PTA took this job as their first project.

The first committee appointed was composed entirely of men who worked with me in making plans for "homemade" equipment. Meetings were called in the spring and volunteers offered to make what they could during the summer.

In August, just before the school opened in September, the real fun started. The fathers, as many as twenty at a time, gathered in the late afternoons and went to work. This is a community of well-to-do people and the men welcomed the opportunity to get out of their offices and do some real hard work with their hands. Many mothers "hung around" and helped to do some of the easier work, and one evening they brought supper for the group, which made it possible for the work to continue late into the evening.

Some of the equipment installed was the result of original ideas, some pieces were copied from magazines, and some copied from standard playground equipment. At the end of the first year's work the value of all this was estimated at $1,500, but the actual cost to us was $40.

Since the first year we have added much more, have repaired and replaced some, and have laid a 55- by 70-foot concrete-paved area marked off for circle and line games. This area did cost, but an interested father gave us a big reduction since the PTA was to raise the money needed.

I would like to list what we have, and would like to add that the children, grades one through six, love all of this. Here they are (all homemade): a railroad track for balancing; box hockey

10 Report by Carrie Phillips, Principal.

(3); tether ball poles (5); tire swings (8); climbing pole (1); monkey logs for climbing, and so forth (3 sets); acting and horizontal bars (8); cable swings (6); ring toss boards (2); basketball goals (6); backstops for baseball fields (2); horse made from pipe (1); tunnel made with large terra-cotta pipes (1); sandboxes made with logs (4); seesaws (5); handball boards (2); posts for net games (3 sets); innumerable large stumps and logs for numerous activities.

The physical education program is so organized that each grade has a directed play period every morning for group games and for learning to use the equipment. In the afternoon they have independent play periods with a teacher in charge of as many as four grades at a time. They use the equipment then, learning to play together, taking turns and so on. It is also used in the mornings before school opens with student patrols in charge, but there is no "room recess."

Beginning this year, a father who is in the science department of Woman's College of the University of North Carolina, which is located in Greensboro, has agreed to serve as chairman of a committee of parents, teachers, and students to lay out a nature trail through the woods on our playground. Along this trail another committee will build a picnic area, with a grill, tables, and benches. The PTA will finance this project. However, much of the material will be donated, and all the labor will be done by our own folks.

I can't omit our interest in birds and flowers. The children have put up thirty-two birdhouses and bird feeding stations. The contents of a "bread box" for leftover bread in the cafeteria furnish part of the bird food we need. We have two large bird baths, also.

During the first year each student in school planted one or more jonquil bulbs. Since then they have planted many more and a Garden Club, composed of "Brooks Parents," has added hundreds of iris and tulip bulbs. All of these, with the regular forest of dogwood trees in the front yard, make Brooks a "thing of beauty and a joy forever" for parents, students, and teachers.

J. ENOS RAY SCHOOL
PRINCE GEORGE'S COUNTY, MARYLAND[11]

For those interested in developing small areas I would like to offer a description of what one kindergarten teacher and the parents have done with less than a quarter of an acre of ground.

[11] Report by Frances Lindahl, Principal, Carole Highlands School, Prince George's County, Maryland.

. . . Money was raised by the parents to erect the building in 1948 and each year additions are made to the facilities.

For imaginative play, a ramp leading to a platform built over a large drainage pipe may be converted into a boat, a cave, or a watchtower. A fireman's pole provides a quick and easy method of descent. To add to its attractiveness, brightly colored paints were used.

Cinder blocks giving the appearance of a miniature fort give the children many opportunities for storybook play. One day it is the Alamo; another time it is a house, with plywood boards forming the roof and separating the rooms. These same boards may be used as a slide when more active play is desired. Sometimes it is a grandstand for the basketball games. Space has been saved by utilizing the side of the building as a support for the basketball net.

An 8-foot wire fence along the side of a deep ravine makes possible the use of a small area beside the building. A number of 3-foot steel poles with a concrete base have been placed in the ground. Beside each pole is a cinder block for a seat. Table tops or steering wheels fitted with couplings can be screwed to the tops of these poles. The children will be able to use the table tops for clay modeling, or any activity involving tables, and the wheels for imaginary automobiles, boats, and so forth. Along the fence, wire baskets will be fastened for holding clay or other materials.

An old school bus was purchased, and is being converted into "The Magic Bus." The bus will have a face, lights for eyes, grill for nose, bumper for mouth. Inside the bus, shelves and racks will be installed for books, crayons, drawing paper, and so on. Also included will be buzzers, bells, lights, and other small-muscle manipulators. Low-voltage electricity will be used. Boards are being made that can be placed across seats facing each other for children to work on. Numerous imaginative play possibilities can readily be seen.

NORTHGATE SCHOOL, SEATTLE, WASHINGTON[12]

We have a problem in Seattle of cloudy weather and mild rain, especially during the late fall, winter, and early spring months. Any gravel, grass, or sand and loam playground becomes almost impossible to use consistently even when properly drained. Consequently, practically all of our smaller playgrounds and parts of our larger playgrounds are blacktop (semihard surfaced). We find we can use them almost immediately after a rain. They

[12] Report by William L. McRea, Principal.

drain and dry off reasonably fast. No harm is done to rubber balls, which we use in playing on wet surfaces.

We have regular playground markings that we paint on the surface of the blacktop. Examples of our markings are: softball diamonds for the upper grades, and for the lower grades if space permits; goal lines for touch football; goal lines for soccer; volleyball courts; basketball key for outdoor basketball hoops; circles of various sizes; markings for hopscotch, snails, squares, standing hop, step, and jump, and for volley-tether ball.

We have fixed equipment for some of the limited-area play space on which hopscotch, squares, jump rope, and the like may be included and located away from the running and ball games. We have exercise bars 30 inches and 34 inches high for children to turn on. These have proved one of the most popular pieces of equipment. We have climbing poles 10 feet high for climbing. Some schools have climbing trees installed through the courtesy of the PTA. These are placed away from the running areas.

Schools that have planned their playground space for grade level and for efficient use of all play space find their playground problems are less; that it provides more useful, safe recreational opportunities. It is an aid to the teachers on ground duty and helps the children in their own freedom in selecting games.

The teacher can plan for goal games, circle games, relays, limited-area games, seasonal sports, and miscellaneous games in her physical education program. The carry-over for noon-hour and recess games as well as for after school play is very good.

Our playgrounds can now be used most of the year regardless of weather. We find less serious accidents on the blacktop than with the old gravel and sand or loam type of play spaces. We find that using limited fixed equipment with proper safety instruction is most valuable in preventing accidents. Our safety instruction stresses safety on the playground, school grounds, and in the classroom, and is a part of the regular instruction program.

Summary

Standards for the equipment and supervision of outdoor and indoor play areas used by different age groups have been outlined in this chapter and illustrated by detailed descriptions of four school playground developments. Current practice reveals the following:

1. Many forms of traditional playground apparatus are being supplanted by either creative or improvised equipment.

2. Creative equipment (so named because its abstract form may suggest different uses to different children) usually calls forth inventive, nonstereotyped reactions.

3. Improvised equipment is being made by PTA members and by students and teachers in the school shop. Obsolete pieces of school furniture, old buses and fire engines, tree trunks, and culverts reappear on the playground, to be utilized by imaginative children.

4. Bituminous surfacing for multipurpose areas is cleaner, less dangerous, and more useful in rainy seasons than clay, sand and loam, gravel, or crushed rock, and is being increasingly used to replace these other materials.

5. Community participation in planning, building, financing, and enjoying school recreation facilities is increasing.

6. Apparatus is returning to the gymnasium. Children need it for all-round physical development, for testing their developing skills and powers, and for sheer fun, inventiveness, and confidence.

7. If children have enough apparatus as well as play materials, and if they have free access to both, they will be busy at things we would like to have them do and there will be less vandalism and destructive activity in school neighborhoods.

8. Apparatus and equipment constantly and vigorously used need careful maintenance and periodic replacement.

9. Supervision of play areas at play time should be constructive guidance rather than mere police duty.

Selected References

Butler, George D., *Recreation Areas*, 2d ed. New York: The Ronald Press Company, 1958.

Gabrielson, M. Alexander, and Caswell Miles, *Sports and Recreation Facilities for School and Community*. Englewood Cliffs, N.J.: Prentice-Hall, Inc., 1958.

Heffernan, Helen, and Charles Bursch, *Curriculum and the Elementary School Plant*. Washington, D.C.: Association for Supervision and Curriculum Development, 1958.

CHAPTER 7

Integration

INTEGRATION IS A MUCH-ABUSED CATCHWORD, with many different meanings. But it is, after all, a useful word if it is not too heavily loaded, and if its meaning is clearly understood. In this book it means "bringing together into a unified whole." The integrated person succeeds in bringing together all his powers for effective action toward his goal. In an integrated school environment, different learnings from many sources are brought together and so related as to focus on a problem. The ideal child in the ideal school, then, would have his own abilities and the resources of his environment freely available, without conflict or inconsistency, when he wants to work out a problem. It is unnecessary to add that this condition remains largely in the realm of the ideal. Why doesn't it exist? What stands in the way of its realization? Perhaps we should look more closely at this matter of integration and how it develops.

The child's level of development determines the *scope* of integration, but it does not necessarily affect the *degree* of integration. A baby may be better integrated at 6 months than he will be at 6 years, or at 16. The beautifully integrated organism with which he begins life[1] may or may not maintain its integrity

[1] C. S. Sherrington, *Integrative Action of the Nervous System*. New Haven, Conn.: Yale University Press, 1911.

137

as cultural pressures toward disintegration come into play.[2] Family, church, school, recreation, work—these different aspects of modern life split up the individual's day. Moreover, they divide his experiences and often his beliefs and even his loyalties. Specialization within each of these areas makes for further division. The school has in the past fostered this specialization, with its divisive effect on the child's personality, through subject-matter isolation. What the child learned was not organized into any pattern that made sense or that gave satisfaction because of its wholeness. Nor did these separate subjects, often unrelated to the child's interests, challenge the integrated use of his powers.

The modern school has tried to remedy this splintering of the child's experience in many ways. Relatedness has been emphasized by various curricular devices: correlation, fusion, core programs, and unit planning, to mention a few. In this chapter, relatedness between physical education and other subject areas will be discussed. These related experiences may be developed in any form of curricular organization.

Language Arts

Children write clearly when asked to describe their favorite games so that other children may play them. In Cleveland Heights an experiment was conducted with the third and fourth grades throughout the school system.[3] Half of the grades wrote descriptions of selected games they had played. The other half read the descriptions and, under pupil leadership, played the games. The second group also critized the game descriptions, revising those that were incomplete or not clear. A surprising number needed no revision.

> The experiment proved not only that children had ability in composition but also a command over a far greater vocabulary than was previously supposed by the writer. The project of having the children play and then write the games served as a vital and stimulating motivation for reading and composition

[2] J. S. Plant, *Personality and the Cultural Pattern*. Cambridge, Mass.: Published for the Commonwealth Fund by Harvard University Press, 1937, p. 127.

[3] Louise Kent Hale, "Construction of Reading Material in Games." Unpublished M.A. Thesis, for State University of Iowa, 1940.

because the material for the experiment was so closely related to the child's interests and experiences. The fact that the interest of the children and teachers was sustained throughout and beyond the completion of the work proved that the project was a pertinent one. That the children wrote with clarity and accuracy, and improved in ability to organize their thoughts on paper, is evidence of the educational soundness of the procedure employed.

Teachers gained by the experiment. The appreciation of children's choices, the change of emphasis in leadership, and the integration of physical education with the reading and composition were evidences of their growth. There was an increase of interest in all games and in the identification of many new ones. The establishment and application of the criteria for judging games was an innovation, and it placed an entirely different light upon the selection of games.[4]

The Cleveland Heights study also led children to produce "game books," and to direct their own game programs. A monograph containing the forty best game descriptions was prepared and widely used in the schools for reading preliminary to playing the games.

Later, the writing-reading-playing program was introduced in the second grade with equal success. Still later, recreational material was gathered from stories the intermediates wrote about "What I Do with the Family to Have Fun." Illustrated booklets on family recreation were prepared in each school for members of the PTA. Not the least valuable outcome of this project was the insight into children's backgrounds which teachers obtained through reading their stories about family play. A project of this kind might easily be related to the study of family life in social studies classes.

Malloy, in describing a coordinated reading program, discusses the contribution of one physical education teacher as he has observed it. The teacher writes sports words on the scoreboard in the gymnasium, then presents verbal context clues to the class and has someone read the appropriate word from the list. After describing the reading work in other special fields, Malloy concludes that the classroom teacher plays the major role in the teaching of reading by providing instruction and practice in the basic skills. He continues:

[4] *Ibid.*, p. 34.

Then the alertness of teachers in the special fields develops sequential learnings in the whole reading program. This means more than the mere perusal of a course of study. Both classroom and special subject teachers exchange information and plan together.

Here, then, is one answer that shows real promise for enriching the reading experience. Children apply their classroom learnings and build on their skills in other interest areas. Special teachers develop an abiding interest in the learnings of children in the classroom, and classroom teachers find new avenues of expression for use in their classes.[5]

Sometimes stories which are told, written, or read by the children grip their imagination to such an extent that, in their wish to identify themselves with the characters, they will be stimulated to dramatize it, pantomime it, or dance it. One of the authors saw remarkably good work in movement and silent drama, or miming, while visiting the schools of West Riding, England. Whenever stories from language arts or incidents described in social studies classes appeal to the children, mimes are worked out to dramatize them. Miming in English schools is impressive because the children's movement is sincere, not self-conscious, controlled and often beautiful. These qualities develop after movement has become a part of the curriculum; before this, the mimes may be hampered by conscious efforts at coordination. The change has been described by Stone:

In the first mime, the kings in their walk to Bethlehem were thinking only of how best to control their bodies to the slow beat demanded of their steps by the music played. In the second Nativity, through confidence gained and control of the body, they were able to walk to Bethlehem as they felt the kings would walk to Bethlehem. After they had been through this dance or movement experience they used their bodies in mimes to the full extension. There was no longer need to tell a child to make a gesture. The body easily responded to the emotional stimulus roused by the part the children were portraying. . . . There was a oneness between the emotional self and the physical body.[6]

[5] Robert Malloy, "They, Too, Teach Reading," *Reading for Today's Children*, National Elementary Principal, 33d Yearbook. Washington, D.C.: National Education Association, 1955, p. 128.

[6] Peter Stone, *Story of a School*. London: Her Majesty's Stationery Office, 1949, p. 16.

Music

Music, rhythm, and dance are so often integrated that a special section on music and physical education is almost superflous. A few suggestions may, however, prove helpful.

Singing games should be selected jointly by music and physical education specialists. For best results, have one half of the class sing while the other moves; then change. Through coordinated scheduling, percussion instruments and rhythm bands may be used both in music classes and as accompaniment to creative rhythms in physical education classes.

Small children enjoy acting out short songs about animals. Older girls like to make up songs and chants to rope jumping and to ball-bouncing routines such as O'Leary. The rhythms of poems, chants, songs, and musical recordings fascinate children

A square dance party is a fine opportunity for integration: Music directs the cowboy band; Social Studies help with gay costumes and the theme of the party; Physical Education teaches the dances and the calls.

Music teachers can help any rhythm program with a rhythm band.

and lead them to dance movement. Murray[7] and Pierce[8] have given many suggestions in this area which teachers will find useful.

Early American folk songs, as well as those from other countries, can be related to folk dances of the same national origin. Musical programs for the public are always enhanced by dances, related in either time or place to the music performed.

Social Studies

Studies of other countries are incomplete unless pupils have a chance to dance characteristic national or regional dances. Ashton,[9] in her definitive study, has pointed out that children feel

[7] Ruth Murray, *Dance in Elementary Education*. New York: Harper & Row, Publishers, 1953, pp. 77–95.

[8] Anne E. Pierce, *Teaching Music in the Elementary School*. New York: Holt, Rinehart and Winston, Inc., 1959, Chaps. 6, 9.

[9] Dudley Ashton, "An Ethnological Approach to Regional Dance." Unpublished Ph.D. Dissertation, for State University of Iowa, 1951, p. 422.

their way into a more complete understanding of the temperament and customs of other cultures if they dance as peoples of those cultures have danced. This applies, of course, to studies in history as well as in geography. To feel the stately deportment and balance of the minuet is worth pages from a textbook in reconstructing court formality or the formal nature of Colonial society when it was still tied to British and European ways. Contrasting with this formal pattern are the vigorous, slapdash play-party games of the frontier settlements, which illuminate many characteristics of frontier life.

The contrast between Greek and Roman civilizations may be highlighted by a study of Greek and Roman athletic festivals. Undertaken jointly by social studies and physical education teachers, such a study might well terminate in an athletic pageant to which the parents were invited.

When children know that their grandparents danced Czechoslovakian dances as children in the homeland, when they can borrow grandmother's beautifully embroidered native costume as a model for pageant costumes, their appreciation of our heterogeneous cultural background is strengthened. Acceptance of cul-

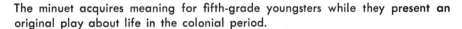

The minuet acquires meaning for fifth-grade youngsters while they present an original play about life in the colonial period.

Sixth-grade boys enjoy performing "The Old Men's Dance" as part of a unit on Mexico.

tural differences may be furthered by the development in the children's own inheritance.

All social studies programs include a study of the community. Such a study should include the community's recreational facilities, and preferably a visit to the community recreation center, during which the director can acquaint children with its function and program. Social studies programs also include a study of family life, in which recreation plays an important part. Questions such as, "What games can you play with the family?" "What can you do in your own backyard playground?" may be answered most effectively through the combined efforts of the social studies teacher and the physical education teacher.

One of the most important purposes of the social studies program is the fostering of socialized behavior, which is essential to a free society. Physical education shares this purpose. In the conduct of games, group dances, team sports, and after-school play groups, democratic procedures are carefully planned and carried out. In order to teach a conscious appreciation of these procedures, however, it may be valuable to time both discussion and action in physical education classes to coincide with similar discussions in social studies classes.

Crafts and Shop Work

When students in the intermediate grades have enough skill to make games equipment, they will be interested in such projects both for their own and for school use. Shuffleboard disks and pushers, paddles for aerial darts and paddle tennis, stands for tether ball, boxes to hold small equipment, bows and arrows of a simple kind, stilts—all these make good construction projects.

In crafts, children can make yarn balls, rope rings for deck tennis, beanbags and target boards, and table games such as checkers. They can also make percussion instruments such as rhythm sticks, drums, wood blocks, tambourines, cymbals, triangles, and castanets.[10]

To make sure that these projects are introduced at a time when they will benefit children most in their construction work, the physical education teacher must plan ahead with the teachers of crafts and shop. The request for games equipment should not be made a few days before the equipment is actually needed.

[10] Pierce, *op. cit.*. p. 81.

These boys are absorbed; their varied learnings are focused together in one project and are therefore integrated. Does physical education have a place in this project?

Arithmetic

Games provide many situations calling for numerical skills. Problems may range in difficulty from the simplest scorekeeping to equalizing relay teams, measuring courts for different games, and, finally, computing batting averages and the percentage of baskets made out of total shots taken. These problems should be used at appropriate times both by specialists and by classroom teachers, not only to develop numerical skills but also to increase readiness for learning them. Often the more difficult problems will increase the youngster's understanding and appreciation of the usefulness of arithmetic in the things he likes to do.

Health

One of our large cereal producers has cleverly related food habits to athletics by marketing a product as the "Breakfast of Champions." Girls as well as boys, at least in the primary grades, want to be champions in athletics. When they get older, girls want to excel in dancing, acting, skating, swimming, riding, and skiing, while boys still see themselves spotlighted in the stadium or ball park. These drives certainly furnish the basis for teaching simple rules of proper eating, sleeping, exercising, and bathing. In some schools children have written letters (language arts again!) to performers they admire, asking what training rules they would advise. Often the letters are answered, and some of the answers have been very helpful.

The school health appraisal, or any partial checkup, should be a teaching situation. If the physical education specialist examines backs, feet, and posture, he will detect the children who need help, and will know the type of help they need. At the same time he will tell the children enough about themselves to promote good response to special help. Motivation will then be on a positive rather than a negative basis.

Health posters and health calendars can be joint products of health, physical education, and graphic arts classes. One fourth-grade class chose "Play and Health" as a topic for special study at a time when parents were talking about a possible playground bond issue. As a result of various committee reports, the children obtained facts on play and growth, play and sleeping, play and eating, play and posture, play and safety. Posters illustrating these facts made a very favorable impression on parents who attended the school's open house.

In another school, health calendars became a graphic arts project, which was carried on throughout the year. On the calendars were marked "weeks" when various phases of healthful living were to be stressed.

Visual Arts

In addition to the posters and calendars already described, many possibilities exist for relating physical education and art. The attractiveness of the game and family recreation books produced in the Cleveland Heights schools were enhanced by illustrations and brightly colored cover designs. Murals of children at

The Art Department helps prepare for a picnic in the park.

play in different countries have been used to decorate the walls of playrooms. Children working in clay will often choose a subject from their favorite game, sport, stunt, or dance.

The integral relationship between movement and art has been well expressed by Stone:

> And soon it became obvious that the creative urge expressed in all the arts comes from the same source. Although the way it is expressed in each art is somewhat different, all the arts have a common beginning.
>
> That common beginning is movement—movement, something primitive and fundamental, so it seems to me: not movement for expressing emotion or ideas, which becomes Dance: not movement which makes us feel we want to say something, which is Drama: not movement for developing bodily strength or skills, which is Physical Training: but movement for movement's sake, the starting point of all the arts.[11]

Science

Natural avenues of integration between science and physical education are provided by the child's desires for physical strength, for growth, and for skill. His questions about these points may lead the class to ask the science teacher or some other resource person for help in answering such questions as these:

1. Why am I so much smaller than Bill, although I am 12 and he is 10?

2. Are all tall basketball players good because they are tall?

3. Are short runners faster than tall ones?

4. They say kids get earaches from swimming in the Y pool, but I can swim in the lake hours every day and never feel it. Can you get earaches from washing inside your ear?

5. When we fed our rats milk they grew bigger than the others. Could I get bigger by drinking more milk? Why did the man in the movie feed his fighting dog meat, but drink milk himself?

6. Why do I get a pain in my side when I run fast?

The answers to these questions can lead to general discussions of such topics as heredity and environment, individual differences, food as a source of energy, and regulations for public health and

[11] Stone, *op. cit.,* p. 15.

safety. Most of these topics are also related to health education, and plans should be made for integrating the work in these three fields.

School Camping and Outdoor Education

Almost half of our states have programs in school camping, and almost half of our teacher education programs in physical education include courses in camp leadership. This does not mean, of course, that physical education specialists necessarily direct school camps, or that the camping program consists mainly of physical education activities. On the contrary, most school camps would agree with the policy of the San Diego City-County Camp Commission: "An organized program of competitive sports has no place in the Cuyamaca program. The children are so occupied in exploring and living in their new environment that they have little desire for this type of play."[12]

However, since the school camp endeavors to provide an integrated experience in outdoor living, usually extending over a period of at least a week, vigorous physical activity as planned developmental experience is definitely a part of the camping program. Hiking over trails and over rough terrain is necessary for exploration by land, and boating, for those who swim well, provides an alternative method of exploration in lake and stream country. Scouting for wildlife demands skill in moving noiselessly over a great variety of obstacles, in changing pace and direction, and in getting up- and downhill easily. Campcraft and woodcraft—even fire building and outdoor cooking—depend on skill in manipulating small objects and equipment. Folk and square dancing are popular forms of evening recreation.

Smith's account of some of the projects that may be planned in the school camp gives some idea of the physical endurance to be developed:

> Some examples of program activities are exploration hikes; lumbering activities; glacial trips; hikes to quaking bogs; ex-

[12] Winifred Van Hagen, Genevie Dexter, and J. F. Williams, *Physical Education in the Elementary School*. Sacramento: California State Department of Education, 1951, p. 289.

ploring gravel pits; gathering and preparing wild fruits for camp use; visiting farm wood lots, orchards, and sawmills; maple sugaring; discovering marrow and muck quarries; cook-outs; study of lakes; reforestation projects; game census; building trails and shelters; construction and use of weather stations; fire fighting; and exploring abandoned, modern, and experimental farms.[13]

In most schools it is the children in the intermediate grades who go to camp for a week, spring or fall, at some established camp site, accompanied by classroom teachers who guide their vivid learning experiences. Additional counselors are recruited from school personnel so that there is one counselor for every eight to ten children. Parents and other members of the community sometimes serve as volunteer leaders if they are qualified.

In one school-camping project directed by the supervisor of physical education, parents as well as children participated in making the decision to camp. Then the parents were kept informed of the step-by-step progress of preplanning by letters, bulletins, a two-day school demonstration of camping procedures, and a precamp visit to the camp site. Teachers were interested in the possibilities of integrating learnings from a variety of fields; both parents and teachers made favorable evaluations of the children's experience at camp.[14]

Although elementary school teachers who have good rapport with children and are flexible in their own recreational interests may get along well at camp without special training, they will find such preparation very useful. In-service training is provided by some school systems. A recent study of the content and organization of a week's course in camp for classroom teachers lists the following objectives, based on criteria approved by experts:

1. To acquire certain basic outdoor skills and to accumulate a repertoire of camp activities.
2. To learn the roles of campers and counselor through routine camp duties, such as cabin living, meal routine, and camp government.
3. To explore the out-of-doors as an outdoor laboratory for natural science, conservation, and other selected subjects.

[13] Julian Smith, "Community School Camping," *Children in Focus.* Washington, D.C.: American Association for Health, Physical Education, and Recreation, 1954, p. 199.

[14] Jean Young, "The Outdoor Classroom of the Will Rogers School." Mimeographed report, Pontiac, Mich., 1960.

4. To discover new methods of teaching *and* learning in an informal situation through experimentation with camper learning projects.
5. To analyze the problems of a child's adjustment to the camp situation.
6. To become acquainted with the literature on the school camp movement and especially source materials for program activities.
7. To investigate the unique learning possibilities inherent in the camp setting: What can best be taught in camp?
8. To learn techniques of promoting camper health, safety, and comfort.
9. To develop an understanding of the organization of a school camp.
10. To practice techniques of planning for and evaluation of a camp curriculum.[15]

Teachers preparing for elementary school work may find camp leadership courses interesting and useful electives in their undergraduate programs. Such courses may also be offered in summer schools or special workshops. Sometimes a brief introductory course will be enough to give the teacher the security needed for a happy camp experience.

The examples given in this chapter of integration in the environment could be multiplied, and probably will be multiplied, by the classroom teacher as he gains insight into the process. Let us now look briefly at integration as it applies to the child.

We have said that the integrated person brings all his powers to bear on a goal he has selected or approved. It is this kind of behavior which the various forms of physical education seek to develop. Moreover, it is only through physical education that the school promotes the integration of basic structural elements—bones and large muscles—into the individual's whole functioning. Whenever the child sees clearly what he wants to do and how to try to do it, whenever the green light is on, permitting or promoting the effort, he goes ahead. All his powers, for example, are used in competitive games. For the most part his play is not "child's play" to the child. It is neither casual nor effortless. All his powers are called on as he tests them out in play on apparatus, or as he explores various possibilities in movement. If he is ab-

---

[15] Jean Harristhal, "Training for School Camp Leaders." Unpublished M.A. Thesis, for State University of Iowa, 1953, p. 21.

sorbed in what he is doing, and if he is making headway, he is showing integrated behavior.

Integration within a group, so that the group moves effectively toward its objective, is another desirable outcome of physical education when it is well guided. An integrated group is able to work together without much friction. Personal wishes are subordinated to the common goal, and as the goal is approached and then achieved, group feeling is strong and morale is high. With the help of the perceptive teacher, this integration may be achieved in games, movement exploration, and dance.

Thus, inner consistency, belonging to an effective group, and understanding relationships in the environment are all aspects of total integration. At any developmental level, total integration is basic to mental health. Conversely, as Stevenson has pointed out, "mental illness is itself a breakdown in the mental integrity of a person."[16] Both integration of the physical education teacher into the school faculty and of the physical education program into the school program are necessary to an atmosphere that promotes mental health throughout the school. To quote again from Stevenson:

> It is evident from the above that a concern for mental health is not an adjunct or an addition to a program for health, physical education, and recreation. It is of the essence. Without concern for building the child into a whole-hearted being, there is no education. In the sound program a concern for mental health comes without strain, hardly making itself evident, because like the mentally healthy child it has become an inextricable part of the whole.[17]

Summary

Integration has been defined as "bringing together into a unified whole"; the integrated child brings his powers together in effective action; the integrated school brings together various

[16] George S. Stevenson, "Promoting Mental Health," *Children in Focus.* Washington, D.C.: American Association for Health, Physical Education, and Recreation, 1954, p. 182.
[17] *Ibid.*

parts of the curriculum in a related pattern that has meaning for the child.

Physical education may be related to almost all other subjects. Examples are given of integration with language arts, music, social studies, crafts and shop work, arithmetic, health, art, science, and school camping.

Integration of basic skeletal and muscular structure into total functioning is promoted by physical education. This integration may be seen in many vigorous activities in which the child becomes absorbed. The degree of absorption seems to be related to the degree of integration.

Groups as well as individuals are more effective when integrated. Group integration depends on how well the teacher understands the group process, and how well he is able to guide group activities.

All aspects of integration are important in promoting good mental health in the school.

Selected References

Humphrey, James H., *Elementary School Physical Education*, Part II. New York: Harper & Row, Publishers, 1958.

Kraus, Richard, *Play Activities*. New York: McGraw-Hill Book Company, 1957.

Murray, Ruth, *Dance in Elementary Education*, 2d ed. New York: Harper & Row, Publishers, 1962.

Pierce, Anne E., *Teaching Music in the Elementary School*. New York: Holt, Rinehart and Winston, Inc., 1959.

Radler, D. H., and Newell C. Kephart, *Success Through Play*. New York: Harper & Row, Publishers, 1960, Chaps. 3, 4.

Sheehy, Emma D., *Children Discover Music and Dance*. New York: Holt, Rinehart and Winston, Inc., 1959, Chaps. 7, 8.

Smith, Julian, "Outdoor Education," *Recreation*, October 1961.

Stone, Peter, *Story of a School*. London: Her Majesty's Stationery Office, 1949.

CHAPTER 8

Evaluation

EVALUATION SEEMS NECESSARY FOR LEARNING. Thorndike once had a group of subjects, each of whom tried to toss marbles into a small box behind him. When the subjects could not tell by sight or sound whether or not the marbles dropped into the box, their performance did not improve. But when the box was placed on a hard surface, so that the unsuccessful tosses made a different noise, the subjects learned as usual.

"How am I doing?" is a natural question. Children are not ashamed to ask it in so many words. College students are asking it when they want more than a pass or fail grade. "How am I doing?" is a vague question, however, because it asks for evaluation of progress without saying what *kind* of progress—that is, without telling the goal involved. Let us suppose, for example, that a college student is taking the marble-tossing test, that she has developed skill and is getting a high score. Her boy friend comes in for his trial. Fully aware of his need to be "tops," the girl deliberately reduces her score. "I didn't do so well," she says to the boy as they walk away from the laboratory; but she is really "doing pretty well" toward her own special goal.

If we want to agree on what we are talking about, we would have to say that evaluating is estimating progress toward a *known*

155

goal. The estimate may be precise and objective, like a score in marble tossing, or it may be vague and subjective, like the girl's sensing of the boy's pleasure in having the better score. Ultimately, evaluation is only a step in the process of learning to live more intelligently and to work more effectively. Unless this process is continuous, effectiveness is lost. In other words, evaluation without follow-up is an expensive way to waste time.

Good teaching implies that the whole class plans together, works together, and then evaluates progress before going on to new plans. This process, which has been discussed as part of the physical education lesson in Chapter 4, may be described as informal evaluation of short-term progress. The method involves (1) critical discussion of what class members have observed in class activity; (2) agreement on what has been accomplished; (3) appraisal of what remains to be done; (4) planning how to get it done; and (5) carrying out the plans.

Evaluation of long-term change, which occurs less frequently, is used to estimate progress toward more remote developmental goals. It proceeds more formally, by means of more precise and objective techniques. Techniques vary, of course, depending on the goal. A review of some important techniques and their uses follows.

Evaluation of Physical Growth

Measures of height and weight give precise and accurate information about the individual child's present status in relation to the average for his age. However, status at any one time is not so important as the pattern of growth shown by repeated measurements. A record of yearly measurements should be part of the child's cumulative file from preschool through high school. Interpretation of the information will be aided by the use of some of the modern methods of recording and analyzing data, such as the Wetzel Grid or the Iowa Growth Charts.[1] By revealing the child's deviation from his own pattern of growth, these charts direct attention to such possible causes as changes in nutrition, general health, or other growth factors.

[1] Free copies of these charts are available from the Bureau of Health Education, American Medical Association.

The school lunch offers an excellent opportunity for health teaching, through both visual displays and guidance in selecting good food in the lunch room.

Evaluation of Health Status

Medical examinations have been discussed briefly in Chapter 5. In addition to the periodic examinations given to all children, those pupils showing serious deviation from normal health conditions and those engaging in strenuous athletic competition need more frequent examinations to be given at the discretion of the physician.[2]

The scope of the medical examination and the extent to which it is used determine its value. The school health records should be

[2] Delbert Oberteuffer, *School Health Education*. New York: Harper & Row, Publishers, 1949, p. 215.

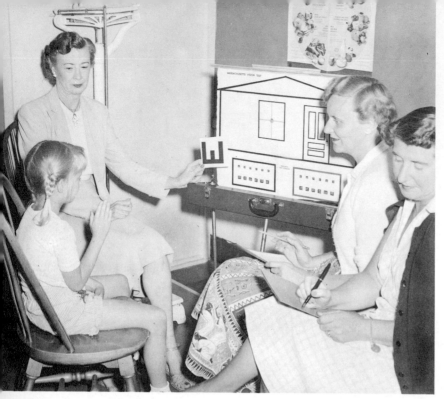

The annual screening test for vision, a joint project of parents and the school nurse.

The audiometer test, when available, is given by the school nurse.

planned jointly by those using them, or their representatives.[3] It is advisable to have the record include personal history of diseases and immunization data from examinations of physicians and dentists, teachers' observations, data from screening tests, and recommendations for program, including the type of exercise and the remedial measures considered desirable. Obviously the record is cumulative, pertinent facts and observations being added as they become available. The record should be in two parts, one for the files of the examining physician, the other for the school files.

This record should serve as a basis for nurse-teacher conferences concerning the needs of each child. In some schools health guidance and teaching is focused on individual needs by setting up an individual plan or work sheet.[4] Nurse and teacher agree on the child's health goals for the year. The teacher makes progress reports on these, and a final summary goes into the cumulative record.

Because the classroom teacher knows his students well and is alert to their needs, his observations of their day-by-day health condition is significant. He notes obvious changes such as coughing, sneezing, running nose, inflamed or watery eyes, profuse sweating, pallor, flushed face, rash, discharge from ears, swelling or lumps, other skin blemishes, fatigue, and complaints about not feeling well. If any of these conditions are observed, the child should be sent to the office of the nurse or principal, who decides whether he should remain in school or whether his parents should take him home. A child should not be sent home alone.

The teacher is not a physician, of course, and does not diagnose or give treatment. His function is to detect the first signs of any illness or abnormal condition so that these may receive expert attention; to understand the youngsters in his class and adapt the school program to their special needs as they appear; and to integrate screening techniques with health guidance and teaching.[5] He must be very careful to keep health information about individuals out of school gossip. Health records are to be used professionally and confidentially.

[3] Joint Committee on Health Problems in Education of the NEA and the AMA, *Health Appraisal of School Children*, 3d ed. Washington, D.C.: NEA, 1961, p. 7.

[4] Maude A. Brown, "A Coordinated Health Program," *American Journal of Public Health*, 34:1142, November 1944.

[5] Helen M. Starr, "What Emphases in Health?" *Children in Focus*. Washington, D.C.: American Association for Health, Physical Education, and Recreation, 1954, p. 118.

Evaluation of Physical Performance

Tests of physical fitness are widely used in our schools. They vary from school to school and state to state, although those constructed and standardized by the American Association for Health, Physical Education, and Recreation seem to be the ones most generally used. Most tests measure such components as strength of abdominal, back, and arm muscles, agility in running and jumping, skill in throwing, and endurance in performing various tasks. The child's total score in comparison with national, state, or local norms is considered an indication of his present status in physical competence, one of the bases for total fitness. Most of these tests are designed and used with children and youth from the fifth grade through the twelfth.[6]

Because of individual differences in capacity and rate of development, the results of fitness tests are most significant when used to evaluate a child's progress rather than to compare his status with that of other children or with national norms.[7]

When the local school system decides to adopt a city-wide fitness program, a committee composed of those who are to use the test results, or their representatives, should be formed. The following steps are suggested for the guidance of such a committee:

1. Secure copies of the bulletin of the President's Council on Youth Fitness, *Youth Physical Fitness*.[8] If it seems advisable to compare with other testing programs, state or local, secure those tests, directions for their administering and norms.

2. Compare the items in each manual of tests, and decide which set best measures the fitness objectives of the local physical education program, which is most feasible to administer, and which will best motivate the children.

3. Select one program and try a pilot project with one or two schools. Evaluate procedures.

4. After making needed changes in administrative procedures give the tests at the beginning and toward the end of the school year on a city-wide basis.

[6] However, the Denver city schools have been using tests in all grades for a number of years.

[7] Report of Conference on Fitness, *op. cit.*, p. 38.

[8] President's Council on Youth Fitness, *Youth Physical Fitness*. Washington, D.C.: Government Printing Office, 1961.

5. Analyze results and use them advisedly to provide motivation, to screen children needing special help, and to measure their progress, improve instruction, and interpret the program.

Many tests of motor skill have been developed and standardized in a half century of experimentation. Some are designed to predict how quickly children will learn new skills, and are called tests of motor educability. Others, called motor capacity tests, are designed to give information about inherent skill. Some investigators have used the term "general motor ability" to mean achievement in basic motor skills or achievement plus educability.[9] Like fitness testing, most of these attempts to measure motor skill have been carried on at high school and college levels. Some studies have been made of preschool children, and only a few exist of children in the elementary age group. The table on the next page has been prepared as a summary of the better-known elementary school tests appearing in the literature.

Use of Norms or Standards

Height-weight measurements, fitness and motor skill tests yield results that may be statistically treated to give national, regional, or local norms. If, however, the goal is the most satisfactory progress of the individual toward achievement of his own potential, norms are to be used with caution. Fortunately, officials in modern school systems no longer judge a teacher or a school by pupil scores relative to norms or standards:

> Evaluation, concerned as it is with individual and group behavior changes in a unique situation, is concerned only indirectly with standards or norms gathered in a given school or from among several schools. Standardized tests may be used in appraisal, but what they reveal cannot be accepted as being to a school's credit or discredit except insofar as the findings are qualified in view of the sought values and outcomes established by a study of the status and needs of the particular group of children involved.[10]

[9] M. Gladys Scott and Esther French, *Evaluation in Physical Education*. St. Louis: The C. V. Mosby Company, 1950, p. 192.

[10] Harold G. Shane and E. T. McSwain, *Evaluation and the Elementary School Curriculum*. New York: Holt, Rinehart and Winston, Inc., 1951, p. 57.

SELECTED TESTS OF MOTOR SKILL FOR ELEMENTARY GRADES (Grades One through Six)

Test	Stated Purpose	Items	Use of Results	Reference
Brace Test	To measure inherent motor skill, 8 to 18	Stunts	Homogeneous grouping Evaluating progress	D. K. Brace, *Measuring Motor Ability* (New York: A. S. Barnes & Company, Inc., 1927).
Iowa Brace Test	To measure motor educability, ages 6 to 22	Stunts	Homogeneous grouping Evaluating progress	C. H. McCloy and Norma Young, *Tests and Measurements in Health and Physical Education*, 3d ed. (Des Moines, Iowa: Appleton-Century-Crofts, 1954.)
Cozens Achievement Scales	To score achievement according to performance and age, height, weight, ages 6 to 16	Track and field events	Evaluating status Evaluating program Classifying for competition	N. P. Neilson and F. W. Cozens, *Achievement Scales in Physical Education for Boys and Girls in Elementary and Junior High School* (Sacramento: California State Department of Education, 1934.)
Carpenter Mat Tests	To measure motor educability of children in the first three grades	Hops and jumps	Homogeneous grouping Evaluating progress	Aileen Carpenter, "Tests of Motor Educability in the First Three Grades," *Child Development*, December 1940.
McCloy General Motor Capacity Test	To measure general motor capacity or innate potentiality, ages 9 to 22	Classification index; jumps, stunts	Predicting possible achievement Guidance	McCloy, *op. cit.*, pp. 114–126.
Carpenter General Motor Capacity Tests	To measure general motor capacity in the first three grades	Classification index; jumps, stunts	Predicting possible achievement Guidance	Aileen Carpenter, "Measuring General Motor Capacity and General Motor Achievement in the First Three Grades," *Research Quarterly*, 13:444, December 1942.
McCloy General Motor Achievement Test	To measure general motor achievement, ages 9 to 22	Strength tests; track and field events	Evaluating status Deriving achievement quotient	McCloy, *op. cit.* pp. 208–214.
Carpenter General Motor Achievement Test	To measure general motor achievement in the first three grades	Broad jump, shot put, weight lifting	Evaluating status Deriving achievement quotient	Aileen Carpenter, "Measuring General Motor Capacity and General Motor Achievement in the First Three Grades," *Research Quarterly*, 13:444, December 1942.
Latchaw Motor Achievement Test	To measure motor achievement in the intermediate grades (fifth and sixth)	Throwing, running, jumping, kicking, striking	Evaluating status Evaluating progress Guidance	Marjorie Latchaw, "Motor Achievement," *Research Quarterly*, 25: 429, December 1954.

A city school in a privileged district may, for example, find its pupils underprivileged in opportunities for vigorous play after school hours. Apartment houses, elevators, chauffeured limousines, television, and radio, may take most of the active play out of the child's day. If there is an occasional trip to the park with a maid and the dog, both child and dog may be kept more or less on leash. A teacher in such a school who notes that the children in his room seem somewhat stiff, awkward, and easily fatigued during the physical education period will want to compare them objectively and accurately with others in order to take a better look at their needs. Standardized tests of strength and skill will help him in this analysis. If he finds that the children are significantly below average, he will plan with the rest of the school staff gradually to increase the length of the play periods and the intensity of the exercise. But he will offer the children encouragement rather than put on pressure, and he will be more concerned with the progress of individuals than with his room average. He will also try to look at the total health picture of the children. The same tests given at the end of the term or the year will show both the teacher and the children just what has been accomplished.

Care must be taken to keep standardized tests from standardizing the curriculum. In some schools so much emphasis is put on the results of skill tests that the teacher is greatly tempted to drill on test items. If he yields to this temptation, the child will lose his spontaneous pleasure in seeing what new skills he can invent. The broad physical education program, including all kinds of self-testing stunts, games, dance, and movement exploration, will be whittled down to the closely directed practice of a limited number of skills. The resulting loss to child, teacher, and school is very great indeed.

Another danger in using standardized tests lies in the fact that competition for high scores can ruin the atmosphere of a classroom by making the teacher nervous and increasing the children's anxiety. Then tension and the edge of overstimulation may replace the freely creative, happy, absorbed activity that helps children to do their best. Only when the school is free from the fear of scores can teachers and children learn to respect individual differences and to value each child's best effort, regardless of whether it is relatively good or relatively poor.

Evaluation of Emotional Maturity and Social Adjustment

No precise measures of progress toward emotional maturity and social adjustment have been widely accepted, but many devices are being used to extend and clarify teachers' subjective estimates. Materials and techniques used for this purpose include planned observations; adjustment indices; interviews; activity and anecdotal records; sociometric tests; recordings; films; children's letters, diaries, experience check lists, and autobiographies; creative writing; projective techniques; parent-teacher conferences; interest inventories; and problem check lists. Some of these materials and techniques may be used by the classroom teacher or the physical education specialist; others, such as adjustment indices, personality rating scales, and projective tests, are best interpreted by clinical psychologists or psychiatrists.

Information relating to emotional maturity and social adjustment is usually kept in the child's cumulative file, together with profile sheets from standardized tests, health and physical examination records, yearly case-study summaries, and whatever other permanent records the school may use. This cumulative record file permits each teacher to gain perspective by studying the child's pattern of development in preceding years as well as his progress during the current year. The information stimulates the teacher's interest in individuals, permits a teamwork approach to problems, and is basic to successful guidance.[11]

Physical education classes yield valuable anecdotal material for the cumulative file because of the continuous and obvious interaction of children. In recording individual behavior, however, the teacher must select significant instances and describe them objectively. The following hypothetical entries might be made on the same day in the life of the same 10-year-old boy, for example, but they differ greatly in guidance value:

> Tommie was aggressive again, running around to every squad and making trouble. When I talked to him he did not cooperate as

[11] National Elementary Principal, 33d Yearbook, *Guidance for Today's Children*. Washington, D.C.: National Education Association, 1954, p. 172.

most of the children do. When I told him he would have to go to the principal's office if he could not behave in the gymnasium, he did stay in his own squad, but he kept on making trouble there. I despair of getting him to stop quarreling with the others.

Tommie did not take his turn in his own squad, but went to each of the other squads and tried to go in ahead of the squad members who were waiting. When I asked him why we planned to have each squad stay at its own apparatus until all changed, he answered readily that it gave everyone the same chance. When asked, "Can you go back to your own squad, go to the end, and take the same chance as the others?" he said he could, and did. Perhaps he needs more attention than I have given him.

Various kinds of sociometric devices may be used in the physical education program to obtain information about social adjustment. The method of having captains choose teams[12] is a rough sociometric device, but it may be too rough in some cases. It is not always successful in giving isolates the best group environment, nor does it always help the teacher to understand the complexity of group structure within the class. To accomplish these objectives, the teacher may find it desirable to construct a *sociogram;* that is, a diagram of the pattern of acceptance and rejection within a group.

In investigating this pattern, the teacher must use care to prevent damage to personality. One way of discovering the relationships that exist within a group might be to distribute cards to all the children, with these directions: "Next week we shall have new squads. It will help me in forming the squads if each of you gives me some names. At the top of the card, write the names of three people you would like on your squad—first, second, and third choices. Then draw a line and write the name of anyone you would rather not have on your squad." The responses might be charted either as a simple diagram of person-to-person relationships[13] or as a more complex diagram showing subgroups within the class.[14]

---

[12] Such choices should never be made in the actual classroom situation. See Chapter 2.

[13] Hilda Taba and Deborah Elkins, *With Focus on Human Relations.* Washington, D.C.: American Council on Education, 1950, pp. 191, 192.

[14] E. F. Pflieger and G. L. Weston, *Emotional Adjustment: A Key to Good Citizenship.* Detroit: Wayne State University Press, 1953, pp. 19–23, 60–67.

Evaluation of the Physical Education Program

The physical education program is a good one if the children are making satisfactory progress in physical growth, motor development, emotional maturity, and social adjustment. As has already been pointed out, no statistical information, such as a comparison of school or class averages with national or local norms, gives a clear picture of individual progress. For this reason, yearly case-study summaries should supplement reports on standardized tests. These, together with an appraisal of the program in operation, should help teachers, supervisors, and other administrators to evaluate the contribution of physical education to the goals of the school.

The following criteria of a good physical education program[15] are suggested as an aid to evaluation:

Time

1. Is enough time allotted to the physical education program to ensure adequate development? (A minimum of thirty minutes daily is needed.)

2. Is this time well invested? Is every child active?

Space and Equipment

3. Is there enough space to permit free movement?

4. Is there enough equipment so that each child has some piece of small equipment for his own use, or is each child in a group of three or four sharing a piece of large apparatus?

5. Is all available space and equipment used? Do children show responsibility in using space and caring for equipment?

Program

6. Are activities varied?

7. Are activities suited to the children's maturation level?

8. Is physical education integrated with the rest of the school program?

Health

9. Do children appear fit? Do they show good physiological response to strenuous activity? Is health screening evident?

[15] Detailed criteria of good teaching will be found in Chapter 4. See also N. P. Neilson and Winifred Van Hagen, *Physical Education for Elementary Schools*, rev. ed. New York: A. S. Barnes & Company, Inc., 1954, pp. 114–119.

10. Are handicapped and atypical children helped by a program especially adapted to their needs? Are they accepted, as far as possible, as participants in the rest of the program?

Safety

11. Is safety teaching evident? Are children learning the skills of safety? Do they accept responsibility for their own safety and for that of their classmates?

Skill

12. Are children moving well? Freely?

13. Do their skills seem to be well developed for their level of maturation? Meet criteria of movement fundamentals?

Emotional Maturity

14. Do children move confidently? Without fear?

15. Do they invent new things to do? Show independence and initiative?

16. Are they developing persistence?

17. Can they judge their own abilities?

18. Is the class situation stimulating enough to demand self-control? Is it excessively stimulating, leading to tension, frustration, and regression to immature behavior?

Social Adjustment

19. Is there a warm social climate in the class? Do all the children feel accepted? Are the handicapped participating with the help of other children?

20. Is aggression controlled? Is consideration for others shown in sharing space, equipment, and apparatus?

21. Do teams, squads, and other groups get along together as well as can be expected at that particular age level?

22. Do children show self-direction and self-discipline? Does the teacher guide rather than dominate?

Evaluation in a Democratic Society

Evaluation in American schools has certain characteristics that can be found only in a democratic society. Freedom of inquiry is one; we are free to find out how everyone is doing, from the youngest child to the highest authority in the system. Freedom of speech is another; in teachers' meetings and committees, we are free to discuss results that are poor as well as results that are good. Freedom to plan and to experiment is a third; we all assume responsibility for acting on the results of evaluation. Everyone contributes, the majority decides, and all carry out the decision.

It is true that we encounter limitations of money, of time, of facilities. Now and then we encounter human obstacles as well. But in our society we do not have to consult the party line before we know what to think. We do not have our evaluating and our planning done for us; we are not told what and how to teach, nor how to use children to promote the interests of the party. All of us—children, teachers, administrators, and community members —are learning together to use our developing powers *with* one another rather than *over* subordinates. Through free and careful evaluation, we may learn more quickly and more effectively.

Summary

Evaluation is an estimate of progress toward a known goal. It is a necessary step in the continuous process of learning: defining the goal, planning and working toward the goal, evaluating progress made, revising plans and methods according to what has been learned from evaluation, trying the new approach, and re-evaluating.

Evaluation may be accomplished through precise, objective measurement or through subjective estimate. It may be used informally, to review daily progress in class, or more formally, to assess long-term progress.

Precise measurement of certain outcomes in physical education is possible: increase in height and weight, and improvement in physical fitness and motor skill tests can be determined objectively. Age norms for physical growth and physical performance tests are available but these are less important than the individual pattern of growth shown by each child's cumulative record.

Less precise than measures of physical growth and motor development are the many devices for estimating progress toward emotional maturity and social adjustment, such as sociograms, anecdotal records, and projective tests. These are useful in supplementing teachers' opinions; the results they yield should also be kept in cumulative individual record files.

The classroom teacher should evaluate each day the immediate health status of the children in order to discover those who show early symptoms of disease or other malfunctioning.

Certain precautions should be taken in setting up and administering a testing program. Test results should be used to guide individual pupils, not to evaluate the success of teachers or schools. When tests are used for the latter purpose, the tendency is to teach with the tests in mind, thereby limiting the children's experience, or to encourage competition for high scores, thereby increasing the tension under which teachers and children work.

To evaluate the total program of physical education, certain operational criteria have been suggested. These, together with yearly case-study summaries, will keep teachers and administrators informed about the kind of program they have and how it is working out.

Evaluation in American schools is characterized by such democratic procedures as free inquiry, free speech, and free enterprise. It is a broad responsibility, distributed among children, teachers, administrators, and community, according to the ability of each group to contribute. Evaluation is conducive to learning to work together, to using our powers *with* one another rather than *over* subordinates.

Selected References

AAHPER, *Children and Fitness, A Program for Elementary Schools,* Report of the National Conference on Fitness of Children of Elementary School Age. Washington, D.C., 1960.

Andrews, Gladys, Jeanette Saurborn, and Elsa Schneider, *Physical Education for Today's Boys and Girls.* Boston: Allyn and Bacon, Inc., 1960, Chap. 4.

Lane, Howard, and Mary Beauchamp, *Understanding Human Development.* Englewood Cliffs, N.J.: Prentice-Hall, Inc., 1959, Chap. 15.

President's Council on Youth Fitness, *Youth Physical Fitness,* Report. Washington, D.C.: Government Printing Office, 1961.

Scott, M. Gladys, and Esther French, *Measurement and Evaluation in Physical Education.* Dubuque, Iowa: William C. Brown Company, Publishers, 1959, Chaps. 8, 9.

Willgoose, Carl, *Evaluation in Health Education and Physical Education.* New York: McGraw-Hill Book Company, Inc., 1961, Chaps. 1, 8, 10.

CHAPTER 9

Movement Exploration

Introduction

HUMAN MOVEMENT HAS BEEN STUDIED from many angles. Industrial engineers have worked to eliminate unnecessary movement by time-motion analyses. Specialists in salesmanship have tried to teach the carriage that gives the best image of confidence and enthusiasm. Psychologists have studied movement as a projection of human personality. Orthopedists have recorded deviations from the normal in posture and gait as possible symptoms of pathological conditions in bone, joint, or muscle. Producers of drama on the stage or screen know that movement as well as spoken words tell the audience of tragedy, conflict, or joy; hesitation or decision; and give depth to the portrayal of character.

In physical education, skills of movement have been taught with success. In fact, physical education has been the only part of the school program that specifically has had this responsibility. Teachers and coaches taught the skills of each sport separately: blocking and tackling in football; batting and bunting in baseball; trapping and passing in soccer, and special patterns in swimming, diving, and figure skating. We have studied the human mechanism in courses such as anatomy, kinesiology, physiology and correctives, believing (quite rightly) that we should know the scientific basis of its structure and function. However, putting together the information about bones, joints, and muscles, leverage and other mechanical principles, into a useful, teachable understanding of movement at various age levels has yet to be accomplished, although promising beginnings have been made. There has also been a search for core learnings in performance that might be applied to many different specific skills and so short-cut the development of all of them. Among the many interesting approaches toward synthesis of our knowledge and experience is the elementary school program that we have called movement exploration.

Movement Exploration: Definition and Origin

Of course, children have always explored movement in their own way whenever they were free to do so. Here, however, we use the term to mean part of the physical education program. In brief, movement exploration may be defined as planned problem-solving experiences, progressing in difficulty, through which the child learns to understand and control the many ways in which his body may move and thus to improve many skills. Years of practical experiment and study have evolved a framework of what might be called fundamentals of movement. Within this framework the problems are organized into a sequence of pro-gressive learnings.

Much of the pioneer experimenting in movement was done by Rudolph Laban.[1] English experts in physical education began working with Laban's basic theories of weight, time, and space, adapting them to children's understanding and activities. They found children readily responsive and capable of original and creative work in developing their own action patterns built on

[1] Rudolph Laban, artist, choreographer, author, and teacher of contemporary dance widely known for many years in Central Europe escaped from Nazi Germany to England where he established and directed a center for the Art of Movement until his death in 1958.

"... older children have gone on to expressive movement in silent drama, or pantomime."

various qualities of movement. As it progressed, the work became very generally accepted as a means of developing skill and agility in other activities.

In some English schools older children have gone on to expressive movement in silent drama, or pantomime. Using stories from the language arts or social studies the children plan and perform group drama, which becomes for them an absorbing art form. Their skilled movement and freedom from self-consciousness often give these "mimes" moments of compelling expressiveness and beauty.

In this country, also, movement exploration has a long history. As far back as the summer of 1926, Margaret H'Doubler conducted a workshop in Fundamentals of Movement relating to dance, sports, and other activities. Ruth Glassow[2] published a text on fundamentals as applied to college classes, and many others have added to literature and practice at the college level. Much work has been done at the elementary school level, and movement exploration is widely accepted as an important part of the curriculum.

Not only does it develop useful skill, but it is vigorous, it is fun, it calls for invention, imagination, and problem solving—all

[2] Ruth Glassow, *Fundamentals in Physical Education.* Philadelphia: Lea & Febiger, 1932.

shown as each child finds his own solution in movement to problems set by the teacher, the class, or himself. A very important part of movement exploration is the teacher's part in guiding children so that they will use the skills and understandings they are acquiring in this form of physical education to improve their performance in other forms such as games, sports, self-testing, and dance. Thus movement exploration becomes a useful method of learning as well as valuable content in the program.

Content

The content of movement exploration is found in problems based on the fundamentals of movement that are common to all forms of physical education. Those identified in this text are described below.[3] The components listed under each of the fundamentals serve as the themes for lessons organized by the teacher around one or more problems. Progression through a series of lessons or from one grade to another is achieved by leading children from the exploration of simple patterns to those involving variations and combinations so that complex patterns and greater skills are evolved. In all lessons knowledge and understanding of principles of movement are fostered through guided observations and evaluation; also the children's capacity for working with partners or in small groups is improved.

Fundamentals of Movement

1. *Focus on purpose: Why do we move?* Best learning occurs when the child is working toward a purpose (goal) he has adopted. The effectiveness of his movement depends, in part, on how well he focuses on that purpose. The teacher helps each child to accept increasingly complex goals:

[3] Adapted from Rudolph Laban's principles of movement as presented at the workshop on movement exploration held at the State University of Iowa, Summer 1961. Director: Lorena Porter. Contributions from others recognized in Preface.

To learn new ways of moving, new skills.

To find out, explore use of equipment and apparatus.

To solve problems, invent movement patterns.

To express feelings, tell a story in movement.

To use movement better in a game or dance.

To grow stronger, more fit.

2. *Perception of space: Where do we move?* Very early the child may learn the difference between his own space in the play-room and the common space, where everyone moves freely with-out interfering with anyone else. He then goes on to other learn-ings:

> Direction: floor patterns in circles, in straight lines, forward, backward, sideways, diagonally; space patterns.
>
> Level: moving high, low, or in between.
>
> Range: making large or small movements, variations.
>
> Game patterns: anticipating movement of opponents and of teammates; throwing ahead of a moving target and inter-cepting a moving object; picking openings on offense and covering openings on defense.

3. *Control of quality of movement: How do we move?* If the child learns to feel and control different elements of move-ment singly in the beginning and in combinations of increasing complexity later, he will eventually learn and control a variety of skills, and use movement to express ideas. The elements taught are:

> Speed: fast or slow, with variations.
>
> Force: strong or light.
>
> Configuration: straight or twisting, curved, devious; out from the center of the body, or in toward the center.
>
> Continuity: smoothly sustained or with sudden breaks and holds.

4. *Use of body: With what do we move?* The body's capa-bilities for movement, joint action, interdependence of parts, elementary application of mechanical principles—this knowledge is of great interest to the child, and may well be taught at differ-ent grade levels; in the intermediate grades it may be integrated with appropriate learnings in science.

> Parts of the body and how they move: joint action of flexion, extension, and rotation in neck, spine, shoulder girdle, arms, elbows, wrists, hands, trunk, hips, legs, ankles, feet; interdependence of moving parts.

Locomotor movement: walk, run, hop, jump, gallop, skip, slide, leap; combinations and variations.

Nonlocomotor movement: bend, stretch, twist, push, pull, swing, fall; combinations and variations.

Balance: on what parts of the body can balance be maintained; moving from one balanced position to another; moving through space with body weight carried on different parts of body; keeping balance when changing direction at full speed; when playing a ball that is hard to reach.

Posture: balance of effort and relaxation in walking, sitting, standing.

5. *Relationship: With whom do we move?* Basic consideration for others is taught in every lesson.

In exploring space: using common space without interfering with others; moving with a partner or group to make a floor pattern; moving with others at different levels.

In controlling quality of movement: moving with partner in matching or contrasting actions; moving with a group in telling a story or expressing an idea.

In self-testing: working together in taking out, putting away and using equipment; doing double or group stunts.

In games: being a useful part of a group, a side, a team; helping to evaluate class progress.

In dance: working well with a partner or a group.

Movement fundamentals and their component parts will be made more specific and more inclusive later in the chapter, when problems are described in detail.

Method

As the child applies these fundamentals of movement in other forms of physical education he is using movement exploration as a method of improving a variety of skills. Whether he is successful in this application depends on how his learning is being guided and on what methods of teaching are followed in his class.

First of all, movement exploration should use the problem-solving method. It should follow such basic procedures as: (1) setting the problem; (2) experimentation by the children; (3)

observation and evaluation; (4) additional practice using points gained from evaluation. Answers to the problems, of course, are in movements rather than words. The movements will differ as individual children find the answer valid for each. The teacher does not demonstrate, encourage imitation, nor require any one best answer. Thus the children are not afraid to be different, and the teacher feels free to let them progress in their own way, each at his own rate. The result is a class atmosphere in which imagination has free play; invention becomes active and varied.[4] Improvement occurs through observation and evaluation, practiced when rest periods are needed. Evaluation is positive and encouraging rather than negative. If one group is watching another in action, the observers are asked what they liked about what they saw. With guided experience in observation they will watch for quality of movement, body leads, level and direction, or whatever fundamentals are involved in the problem. Of course improvement is helped by the teacher's suggestions: "Can you make a straighter line with your legs and feet?" "Can your arms help your feet to make your skipping light?" Sometimes these suggestions are made to individuals, sometimes to the whole class. Evaluations and suggestions must be brief and to the point, leaving most of the time for vigorous movement.

Obviously, self-direction is an important characteristic of method in movement exploration, as in other forms of physical education. Even first graders, given to understand that they may practice stunts they like (always using the common space well) as soon as they come into the gymnasium, will start right out with bunny hops, high skipping, cartwheels, and other lively action. Fortunately they *want* to be active, and when they understand that responsible self-direction is the quickest way to get into the things they want to do, they will be motivated to take this responsibility. In many second and third grades, children will sometimes start their individual "work sessions" with only a reminder that they may work at their own problems. These problems are the child's own selection to meet his particular needs for improvement in the skills to be used in the rest of the lesson, be it games, self-testing, movement exploration, or dance. Habits and skills of self-direction should persist as he grows older, and help the individual to watch, analyze, and plan his own learning, both in school and in out-of-school recreation.

[4] Robert Scofield, "A Creative Climate," *Educational Leadership*, October 1960, p. 5.

Illustrative Problems—Primary Grades

The following problems are arranged in order of difficulty. Each is identified with the movement fundamental it is designed to teach, although it may contribute to others. The description of the problem is not, of course, a lesson plan. It is merely a help to the teacher as she works out her own plan; while the teachers' approach to the problem, and what may be expected as the children's response are given in some detail, these may best be used as guides rather than blueprints. In each lesson, for example, the teacher will work out her own way of setting the focus on purpose, and of developing good person-to-person relationships. A few specific suggestions may be helpful:

Do not demonstrate. Let each child find his own way of moving to answer the questions. Usually, children will move freely and spontaneously when asked whether they can do this or that. But if the class is fond of discussion and accustomed to it, be sure that the children understand that these questions call for movements, not words. If they need encouragement, you might say, "Let's see whether you can . . ." Occasionally, individual children may be asked to show the class what they are doing, but the others should not be urged to imitate.

Do not be afraid to repeat problems. Children love to do again the things they know well. They demand their favorite stories over and over again; they play the same games with zest; they will stretch up and about as they touch the boundaries of "their space" lesson after lesson without being bored. Of course, they will invent variations on the familiar themes and show increased skill in executing them.

Make sure that the children are barefoot and in clothes that allow free movement.

Use rhythm instruments very sparingly at first. If an attempt at uniform rhythm is made too early, much of the variety, spontaneity, and inventiveness of the children's responses will be lost.

Encourage original responses. Encourage the clumsy and the timid. Often the withdrawn or anxious child, who may not be good at games, will find himself in this part of the program. He needs approval of his first efforts if he is to get off to a good start.

Use imagery occasionally, but not often enough to make children dependent on it. If the child can abstract the quality of lightness and perceive it in many movements, he will not have to wait to be a snowflake or a fairy. He will be able to make general use of the quality as he moves.

Talk sense to children. They like it better in the long run than the nonsense of an overdramatic, ingratiating, or patronizing approach.

The list given below may help in organizing lessons in such a way that all fundamentals are taught.

Movement Fundamental	*Problem Numbers*
Perception of space	1, 4, 5, 9, 12, 15, 17, 18, 24, 27, 30,
Control of quality movement	2, 8, 11, 13, 16, 20, 21, 25, 29
Use of body	3, 6, 7, 11, 14, 19, 22, 23, 28, 33, 34, 35
Focus on purpose; expressive movement	29, 31

DESCRIPTION OF PROBLEMS[5]

1. Perception of space: child's own space and common space

Teacher's approach: This is a fine big room for play, look around . . . all this space we can play in together. Can you go and touch the nearest wall and come back to where you are without touching anything else? . . . Stand so that you have plenty of space for yourself—this is your own space. Can you touch the top of it? . . . Stretch way up! . . . The front of it? . . . Can you touch the back of it without moving your feet? . . . Does it go way out to the side? . . . Let's see how far it goes away from your feet—on the floor, at your waist, above your head. . . .

Children's response: Usually they will stretch in every direction with real satisfaction. After this, they will know where their space is, and will return to it and stay in it if that is indicated.

2. Control of quality: fast movement

Teacher's approach: Pick out a spot a long way from your own space . . . point to it . . . run to it as fast as you can and stop on it . . . now come back to your own space as fast as you can. . . . What took you to the spot and back so fast? (Feet) Yes, let's see whether your feet can move fast right in your own space. . . . If you are not standing on your feet, can they move even faster? Try it. . . . Can your arms move fast, too? . . . Can both your arms and your feet move fast? . . . Stand up and see whether you can go out to that same spot and back, moving both arms and feet very fast. . . .

[5] A series of three dots is used to indicate movement by the class.

Children's response: When they are "not standing" on their feet, some will sit down immediately, some will lie down. It does not matter which they do; in fact, it is good if they do different things. The important thing is to get them either lying or sitting. Make sure they *move* in answer to your questions.

3. Use of body: changing its dimensions

Teacher's approach: See how far out you can stretch—both arms, both feet. . . . Now squeeze in until you are very small . . . stretch out again until you are very wide. . . . Can you be very tall and thin? . . .

Children's response: When stretching out, they will put arms and legs far apart. When trying to squeeze in, they will curl up, either lying on the side, on the back, or crouching face down.

4. Perception of space: circular movement

Teacher's approach: Let's see again how small you can be. . . . Good. You look like balls—can you roll like a ball? . . . Can you roll around in your own space? . . . Stand up and show me with your arms where you went when you rolled like a ball. . . . What do you call that thing you just made? (Circle)

Children's response: They will curl up and, at your suggestion, clasp their knees. This helps them tip over and roll up again. They will enjoy repeating this maneuver several times. "Where you went" should suggest a circle; make sure that they trace a circle in the air.

5. Perception of space: circular pattern on floor

Teacher's approach: Can you make your feet take you around the floor in a big circle? . . . See whether some of you can go in the same circle. . . . Can we make another circle? . . . As you go around in the circle, try to see what different things your feet will do. . . . Now go the other way in your circle and try some things, all of us doing the same things with our feet. . . .

Children's response: Probably they will all readily make a circle, both in the air (Problem 4) and on the floor. If eight to ten children join together, the circle will be about the right size. This may be a good time to identify skipping and galloping. When they are all trying the same step, the tom-tom may help to get a uniform response.

6. Use of body: feet

Teacher's approach: In your own space can your feet move very fast, right where you are? . . . Sit down and see how many ways your feet can move (be sure shoes and socks are off). . . . Yes, they can bend and stretch, and roll around—all in the ankle. Try little jumps in your own space, and think what your feet do (bend when you come down, and stretch when you go up). . . . Good, let's try it again and think what else bends and stretches (Knees). . . . Now see if your feet can take you in a circle, and if they can do all the things they did last time. (Use same approach to explain use of hands.)

Children's response: Some will see that their feet can circle at the ankle, and some will want to explore their toes. This is fine if it does not take too much time. See if they can keep their feet or hands moving while they talk about them.

7. Use of body: how hands can lead the body's movement

Teacher's approach: Stand in your own space and show me again how far you can stretch out. . . . What do your hands do? . . . Yes, they go far apart—they go first. How tall can you be? . . . What did your hands do? . . . Yes, they went up high, they were the *leaders*. See whether your hands can lead you to the wall and back. . . . Try just one hand leading you . . . now the other one. . . . Let your right hand take you in a small circle . . . then the left hand. . . . Good—most of you changed and went around the circle the other way when you changed hands. See whether each hand can take you in a larger circle. . . .

Children's response: This is a problem to which they might tend to respond verbally. Keep them moving. When one hand is leading, see whether they can get the idea of stretching it out so far that it actually turns the shoulders and trunk as it pulls the body along. Then they will see more easily that each hand leads in a different direction.

8. Control of quality: speed and strength

Teacher's approach: Let's see what else your hands can do. Can they move quickly? . . . Slowly? . . . How strong are they? . . . See

These second-grade children are exploring different points of balance.

whether they can be strong and quick. . . . Can they make your whole body strong and quick? . . . Can they be light and quick? . . . Make your whole body light and quick? . . .

Children's response: When their hands are "strong," they will clench their fists and contract arm muscles. If they have difficulty with the "whole body" movement, tell them to move away from their own space, in and out among the others in the large space, so that they will feel freer to move. Use plenty of encouragement here in their first attempt to show differences in speed and strength of movement.

9. Perception of space: different shapes for children's own space

Teacher's approach: Show me your own space again. . . . It looks to me like a big bubble. Does it shine when you see it in the sun? Does it have different colors? Try painting in all the different colors—behind you, in front of you, all around you. . . . Make a new little bubble and show me how small it is. . . . Let's see it get larger . . . higher . . . wider. . . . Paint in lots of color, and make the biggest bubble you ever saw. . . . Does anyone live in something different? Show us and let us tell you what it is. . . . Shall we all help them paint their spaces? . . .

Children's response: They will have much to tell you about blowing bubbles, and perhaps the idea of bubbles can be elicited from them. Or they may suggest boxes, little huts, corrals—almost anything. It does not matter, as long as they can paint it and stretch thoroughly while doing it.

10. Use of body: feet—where they can move; how they can move

Teacher's approach: Remember when your feet took you in a circle? See whether they can take you in a small circle right in your own space. . . . What can they do besides walk and run? (Jump, skip, gallop, hop) Find out how many things they can do while they are taking you to the wall and back. . . . Good—now see whether your feet can go higher than your head. . . . Can they go high in front of your head? . . . Behind your head? . . .

Children's response: It is time now for the children to name the things their feet do—to learn the words *jump, skip, gallop, hop,* and the names of other steps they may try. When they are asked to put their feet high, they will try such different things as a mule kick, handstand, headstand, shoulder stand, and cartwheel. Do not expect them all to try the same thing or to do what they try equally well. If they do not know what to do when asked whether they can put their feet high in front of their head, tell them it will be easy if they start by lying down on their backs.

11. Control of quality: speed and strength

Teacher's approach: Grip hard with your feet and legs while they take you in and out, past other children, to each corner of the room and

Running with a partner is fun! Six-year-olds try giant steps.

back again to your own space. . . . Keep gripping, and try to make your feet and legs slow as well as strong. . . . Can your hands be strong and slow, also? . . . How do you feel when your hands and feet are strong and slow? Show me by your faces how you feel as you do strong, slow movements again. . . . Good.

Now try changing to light and slow—very light with your feet— hands, too—but still slow. . . . How do you feel when you do this? Now let your hands move very quickly and lightly . . . let them go right down to the floor . . . pat the floor quickly and lightly . . . what does it sound like? Yes, like rain. Now let your hands go high, still very quick and light hands. . . . Can they take you up in the air higher still? Very quick little jumps; both hands and feet are light and quick. . . . Now bring your hands down to middle height, neither high nor low, but still quick and light. . . .

Try jumping with your hands on your hips. . . . Now let them help your feet get up with high light jumps. . . . All the children who are wearing something blue sit down by Hugh and watch the others jump high and light. . . . What did you see that you liked (verbal response here). . . . Good, the hands swing up and then down; yes, Bobby re- membered to stretch his ankles and knees as he went up, and bend them when he came down. Now blues jump and the others come over here and watch. . . . Good. Did you see some strong arms and light feet?

Children's response: When they are strong and slow, they feel like a giant, or very big, or very fierce. Encourage a variety of expressions, both verbal and facial, but do not call attention to the facial expression of an individual, however remarkable it may be. It is important to avoid self-consciousness, and if the children seem self-conscious, do not men- tion the feeling part of the problem until they appear to be uninhibited again.

They should now get the feeling of a strong upswing of the arms to help in jumping.

12. Perception of space: straight lines

Teacher's approach: Let's see how long and thin you can be. . . . Yes, lying down and stretching is one good way to be long. What do you all look like? (Sticks, bats, arrows) Can you show me how an arrow goes through the air? . . . Did you go fast or slow? Straight or in a circle? Let's try it all going the same way. . . . Now again, going the other way. . . . How do you look like a sharp arrow when you stop? (Stop standing up)

Children's response: They will all want to slide on the floor at the end of the arrow's flight. If the floor is not suitable for this, tell them at the beginning that a good, sharp, swift arrow will stick in the ground instead of falling down at the end of its flight.

13. Control of quality: continuous and broken movement

Teacher's approach: An arrow always stops after a while. What else moves and then stops? (Automobiles, fish, birds) Can you think of something that moves fast and then can stop still, suddenly? (Bicycle, cow pony, fish) I wonder whether you can run very fast, and then, when you hear the tom-tom, stop suddenly. . . . (Repeat this until they get the idea of starting fast, going in one direction, stopping suddenly, and then going in another direction.) Now see whether you can stop yourself without any help from the tom-tom. . . . Remember to stop with your feet apart and your weight right over them so that you keep your balance.

Children's response: At first they will lose their balance, fall down, and clown a bit on the sudden stops. Help them to see that it is very important, in playing such games as basketball, ice hockey, and football, to be able to start and stop fast without losing balance.

14. Use of the body: elbows—where they can move; how they can lead the body in movement

Teacher's approach: Crouch down in your own space. . . . Show me what your left elbow can do. . . . How can it move? (Up, down, forward, back, around in a circle) Let your body move with your elbow. . . . How far around to the back will your left elbow take you? . . . How far the other way around will your right elbow take you? . . . Now move your elbow up. . . . As it keeps moving up, let's see what happens to the rest of you. . . . Yes, some of you have strong elbows that move so far they take you right up on your feet. Can your elbow pull you to the wall, leading your feet? . . . See whether your other elbow can turn you around and lead you back. . . . Can you do the whole thing without stopping? . . .

Children's response: As they move the elbow forward, back, and around, let a trunk-twisting movement develop. Try to sustain the twisting as they move from low to middle level. Probably some will go into the twist; if that happens let them do it for awhile and then ask them to try the twist without using the elbows to see what happens (much harder). If they do not start the twist you had better refrain from mentioning it.

15. Perception of space: level

Teacher's approach: What crawls along the ground? (Snakes, spiders, ants) Let's see how close to the ground you can move. . . . What is very high when it moves? (Boy on stilts, giant, long-legged clown) Show us how tall you can be. . . . Can you walk that way? . . . How do you go way up when you run? . . . When you skip? . . . Try walking, changing levels when I give you the word. Start high . . . low . . . middle . . . low . . . middle . . . high. . . . Now face your partner and join both hands. Stay in the same place and change levels, one going up while the other goes down. . . . Where do you meet?

Children's response: Some children pick up the idea of different levels very readily and use them naturally in inventing movements. Others stay conventionally at the middle level in everything. From time to time, and in different problems, remind them to use different levels. Better use group observation here to encourage change of level; the low level is especially difficult for children.

16. Control of quality: speed and strength

Teacher's approach: Crouch down close to the ground, keeping on your feet. . . . Shoot your arms out fast, wide apart. . . . Try it again. . . . Now shoot both arms and legs out, quick as you can, and far apart. . . . Good. That was a *quick* and *strong* movement. See whether you can do something else that is quick and strong . . . keep on. . . . Now try quick, light movements. . . . Try something harder: do your quick, strong movement once; stop still; then do your quick, light movement several times. . . . Good. Now the other way: a quick, light movement once, then a quick, strong movement several times. . . .

Children's response: In the first movement, all the children will go from low to high. Later, if any use different levels as they work on the qualities, compliment them and let them demonstrate so that the others can see that this adds interest to the movements.

17. Perception of space: direction and range

Teacher's approach: This morning I saw something while I was coming to school. Perhaps you saw it too: It moved very fast, way up in the sky, and it left a trail so you could tell just where it had been. (Jet plane) Who wants to show us on the chalkboard just where the jet went? . . . Good. Will you all show me with your arms, in the air? . . . Now can you show me this same path of the jet across the gym? . . . Should this be a fast, light movement, or a fast, strong movement? (Boys will say strong, being more sensitive to engine beat.) Do jet planes always make the same picture? (Take them as far as they want to go on skywriting, expressing it by moving through floor patterns of planes they have seen. If they demonstrate other types of planes, see whether they modify the quality of their movement, making it slightly slower and possibly lighter.)

Children's response: If they do not readily pick up the idea of making a floor pattern from an air pattern, spend more time on the latter. Have them make large movements and small movements, and then see whether they can put the same picture on the floor in a small movement with their finger. Then ask them to make the movement so big that they will have to have their feet take them all around the gym.

18. Perception of space: moving at different levels

Teacher's approach: How many of you have ever traveled in an airplane? Did you feel very high? Remember the day we moved from high to low to middle? If you wanted to travel, but did not want to go as high as a plane, how could you go at about middle level? (Auto, train) Try a trip across the gym and back, using both plane and car. . . . Suppose you had to travel by water, could you go at a high level? (Ocean liner, hydroplane) At a low level? (Canoe, rowboat, speedboat, submarine) Let's see: Can you take a trip, quite a long trip, all around the gymnasium space, and change from one thing to another? . . . (Fit

"*. . . a slow, light movement.*"

this movement into any work they may have had on transportation.) This time, see whether both movement and level of travel can tell me what kind of transportation you are using. . . .

Children's response: If they have worked in groups before, this is a good time to have them do so, letting one group show the others a trip it is taking. They can work up a rather elaborate script, including various things that happened on the trip. A master of ceremonies reads the script, a chorus may show the mode of travel, and the rest may pantomime special events.

19. Use of body: knees

Teacher's approach: Show me your knees. . . . How high can they go? . . . How low? . . . How far apart? . . . How close together? . . . Can they go higher than your hips? . . . See whether you can do this: run very fast and then let both knees go very high at once. . . . What did you do? (Jumped) Now move more slowly, letting first one knee, then the other, go high. . . . What was that? (Gallop or skip) What do your knees do when you try to see how tall and thin you can be? (Stretch) When you move at a very low level? (Bend) When you are in between? (Bend a little)

Children's response: At the first attempt to get the knees high, some children will do what they did in getting the feet high, that is, cartwheels and handstands. Concentrating on getting the *knees* high, higher than the feet, will produce jumps and skips.

20. Control of quality: change from slow and strong to slow and light

Teacher's approach: Let's try a slow, strong movement. Everything is slow and strong: hands, elbows, knees, and feet. . . . How do you feel? Let it show in your face. . . . Now do a slow, light movement. . . . Try the slow, strong movement first, then the slow light movement, without stopping between. . . . Would you like to try this with a partner? You do your movement while your partner does his; both of you are slow and strong, but you are doing different things. . . . Now both of you are slow and light. . . . Try changing from one to the other without stopping, just keep going. . . .

Children's response: If they seem in the least self-conscious about "How do you feel," do not stress this idea until they come back to it themselves. However, letting them express anger and aggressiveness during strong movements is a very good way of getting these feelings out of their system in an approved manner.

21. Control of quality: changes from quick and strong to quick and light

Teacher's approach: (As in Problem 20. When they are working with partners, let the children try alternating their movements as follows.) Do you think you might try responding to each other with your movement? Jack can do his strong, quick movement while Joe watches —will you two show us? . . . Now Joe does his while Jack watches. . . . Good. All try this. . . . Now try it with your light, quick movements, first one of the partners, then the other. . . . Watch your partner.

Children's response: They have fun with this, and usually become completely absorbed in what each pair is doing. This is a good problem for group observation.

22. Use of body: leads by elbows and other parts of body

Teacher's approach: Remember when your elbows took you to the wall and back? Try letting your left elbow take you in a very small circle in your own space. . . . Can your right elbow take you in a circle? . . . Which way did the right one take you? (Opposite, to the right) Do you suppose your nose could lead you to a corner of the room and back? . . . Can your nose take you all over the gym? . . . Now try having your hips lead you, first backward, then forward. . . . Which is easier? (Back) Stand in your own space, and see whether your hips can move over to the left without moving your feet—way over, farther than your head . . . now to the right, way over to the right. . . . Can you make a circle with your hips while your feet stay still . . . and your head stays in its place? . . . Try the other way around. . . . How can you get your hips higher than your head? . . . Good.

Children's response: There is a good deal of humor in this problem, which they will probably enjoy. First the nose lead will make them look like old men, then the hip lead will make them feel funny. However, both will give them better control and flexibility.

23. Use of body: feet

Teacher's approach: Sit down in your own space and put your feet straight out in front of you. . . . Feet are important; they take you where you want to go; they can move you lightly, strongly, fast, or slow. How far forward can you stretch your toes? . . . How far back can you bend them? . . . Can you bend them so far back that the heels are ahead of them? . . . Keep trying, moving the toes both forward and back. . . . Now lie on your back and put your feet in the air. . . . How high can you get your toes? . . . Your heels? . . . Try to get your heels higher than your toes . . . yes, you'll have to bend your toes back. Still lying on your back, move your feet lightly and quickly. . . . Can you make a small circle in the air with your left toes? . . . Try a larger circle. . . . Do the same with your right toes . . . both sets of toes . . . heels. . . . Stand up and see whether you can walk to the wall and back on your heels. . . . Do the same on your toes. . . . Now run. . . . Which are you on when you run, toes or heels? Remember the other steps we have tried? Do as many as you can think of. (Skip, gallop, hop, jump, leap) Which did you use, toes or heels? (Both) See whether you can go sideways, with

one foot following the other and doing just what the first foot does. . . .
(This may go into slide-and-slide, and then progress into the polka if the
children are ready as follows.) Good. Now try going the other way,
with the other foot going first . . . slide, and slide, and slide. . . . Try it
first one way, then the other. . . . Do four slides one way, then four the
other. . . . Can you do two slides one way, then two the other way? . . .
Good. It will be easier if you start with a little hop, and then hop when
you change. Try it: hop, slide and slide, hop, slide and slide, and so
on. . . .

Children's response: Like all problems in movement exploration,
this should be done without shoes or stockings. Children will be interested in feeling their feet and toes with their hands to see how strong
and yet flexible they are. Since foot strength is so important to a child,
besides laying the foundation for foot strength in adult life, this problem may be repeated often. If the progression here is too fast, take it in
two lessons. Bring out the fact that moving on the toes is necessary to
light steps, but that the heels always help the toes. Unless both move
easily and work hard, no child can run as fast as he wants to or play for
long without getting tired.

24. Control of quality: configuration at different levels

Teacher's approach: What do you know that turns around and
around, very fast, and then falls over? (Top) Show me how a top spins.
. . . Does your top wind up with a string? Mike, do you want to wind us
all up? . . . Watch when he pulls the string! . . . Can someone wind us
up so we'll go the other way? Fine, Betty—remember to go the other
way when she pulls the string. . . . Does your Dad have a tool that turns
something? (Screwdriver) What is the difference between the way a
screwdriver moves and the way a top moves? (Slower, stronger, from
high to low, does not fall over) See whether your elbow can screw you
down to the floor. . . . Now let the other elbow unscrew you, so that
you come up the other way. . . .

Children's response: You will have to think of something else if you
do not want the tops falling all over the floor. They will want to do this
several times, and of course they should because it is such fun. When
the screwdriver is used, be sure the movement is a strong twist.

25. Control of quality: change of quality pattern at different levels

Teacher's approach: See whether you can do a quick, light movement, very high. . . . Now a quick, strong movement that goes from middle to low. . . . Do both movements, one after the other, several times,
stopping when you are low and then going on up to the high level. . . .
Do you want to try this with a partner? First you do your movement,
then he does his, the way we did the other day. Remember? . . .

Children's response: If they are ready, the next step is to do these
patterns in a group. You may ask three or four children to demonstrate,

and then ask those who would like to work with each of them on his movement to join him. Later the groups may get percussion instruments and beat out the rhythm while they do the movement pattern. Group observation will help.

26. Expressive movement: difference between winning and losing

Teacher's approach: Does your Dad take you to the basketball games? How do the people look and walk when they are going out of the field house? . . . If they have lost the game, do they look and walk differently from the way they do when they win? Show me how you moved when you came home last time, and let me guess whether you lost or won. . . .

Children's response: Some other situation may be a better one to dramatize in your group, of course. The important thing is to show two contrasting feelings through movement.

27. Perception of space: air and floor patterns of numbers

Teacher's approach: Can you write a number in the air with your arm? . . . Could you put the same number on the floor by running? . . . Good—I can read most of your numbers. Take a partner, run your number on the floor, and let your partner guess it. . . . Take turns.

Children's response: If they are doing work in numbers that can be integrated with this problem, try doing so.

28. Use of body: chest and back

Teacher's approach: Remember how your elbows led you around the other day? Try having your elbow lead you to the wall and back. . . . Let's try a chest lead. Which way would you go? . . . Yes, forward. Now can your back lead you back to place? . . . Some of you let your hips lead you back, as we did the other day. Try it again, chest leading to the wall, back leading back. . . . Stand on your hands and knees, and see how high your back can go . . . humps right up, doesn't it? How low can you make it go? . . . Yes, it is a big hollow now. . . . Try it again; hump it up first . . . now hollow. . . . Try a hard one: Sit back on your heels, and see whether you can hump your back. . . . What happens to your chest? Yes, it goes down. See whether you can hollow your back. . . . What happens to your chest? Does it come up? Can you take out the hollow, straighten your back, and still keep your chest high? . . . (If they manage this well, or when they have, try the last part from a standing position, being careful to get rid of the hollow, but not to "freeze" in this position. To avoid this, have them walk lightly around, keeping tall.

Children's response: This coordination, the localization of control over the long back muscles, is difficult, and the problem may have to be divided or repeated several times. If you think a little imagery will help, the humping may be likened to an angry cat.

29. Control of quality: configuration

Teacher's approach: Can you do a strong, quick movement using arms and legs in straight lines out and in? . . . Try your arms straight up and down, while your legs do what they did before. . . . (Here have group evaluation.) Can you make your legs go straight up and down? . . . Now see if you can change everything: do any kind of a slow movement in your own space, making curved lines first with arms, then with legs, then with body. . . . See how many of these movements you can do at once. . . .

Children's response: In the first part they will not have much trouble, especially if they think of lying down when they make their legs go straight up and down. They will not have much trouble with doing curving movements separately, but combining them may be too difficult. Use observation and evaluation here. Be sure these movements are kept slow, or they will be doing the twist.

30. Perception of space: from pictures to floor patterns

Teacher's approach: Would you like to try drawing some pictures on the board that we could follow by moving around the gym? . . . These are very nice; look at them all. Are there any you want to try? Sue's? Fine. Will four or five of you go with her and help her work it out? . . . (In this way, get them all working in small groups, on designs of their own choosing.) Some of you can do one part of the picture, while some are doing another—you do not all have to do each part. . . . Bob, would your group show us how you were working out your design? . . . What did you like about it? (If they used variety in quality of movement and in levels, be sure to bring this out in the evaluation by the group.) Try your own picture again, and see whether you can make it more interesting. (Let them work out their own difficulties, with the feeling, however, that you are there to help them.)

Children's response: You may have to rearrange groups to make sure that some creative talent is present in each group. Encourage planning by doing, not merely by talking. If they wish to use percussion instruments as accompaniment, let each group have its own instrument and use it as needed for its own design.

31. Expressive movement

Teacher's approach: Remember a picnic you went on with your family? Perhaps you found some very interesting things while you were exploring in the woods—or perhaps you saw some things you were afraid of. Let's tell that story by the way you move, and save the words until later. . . .

Children's response: They love this chance at dramatization, and, with encouragement, will progress from mere charades to a more general expression of themes: conflict, triumph, defeat, heroic adventure.

Let groups work together on other themes from many sources. The children may wish to dramatize the life of heroes they have read about in social studies. Poems, songs, drawings, or favorite stories may be the source for movement dramas. In working out movement patterns for these dramas, help the children to keep the movement general and abstract, using the qualities, levels, and varieties of movement they have been working on in their problems. But do not tell them what to do, nor what patterns to follow. The things they do should come out of their own feeling of how a person in a given situation would act and move. Vocalization should be rare, since these are dramas in movement.

32. Use of body: bending and stretching in different joints

Teacher's approach: Sit down in your own space and count the number of joints in your body that you can touch. . . . How many? Good. Why do we have to have so many? (So we can do a lot of movements.) . . . See if you can bend all the joints in your hips, legs, and feet, both legs working together. . . . Now see how far you can stretch them. . . . Try the same thing with your shoulders, arms, hands, fingers. . . . Can you bend and stretch your spine? . . . Stand up and see what else your spine can do . . . (Twist and bend sideways) Try running lightly and not too fast anywhere in the room. . . . Think as you run whether your arms and legs are bending or stretching. . . . Now skip (use a tom-tom) . . . gallop . . . run to your own space. . . . What did your spine do when you were running? (Bent forward a little) Can you touch the floor without bending your knees . . . bob up a little and down again, several times, and see if you can get closer to the floor . . . Good. Where do you bend when you do this? (Hips and spine) . . . Can you keep your spine straight and bend just at the hips. . . . (Group observation.)

Children's response: There are a great many possible variations of this lesson, such as walking without bending the knees, bending the body sideways as well as forward and back, and twisting. This offers fine integration with a health education lesson on body structure. Be sure the children appreciate the greater mobility of the shoulder girdle, arms, and hands for the variety of things they have to do; the greater strength and reduced mobility of spine, hips, knees, ankles and feet for security in bearing the body weight. They will do a great variety of movements in this problem if they start from different positions.

33. Use of body: good posture

Teacher's approach: Review Problem 28 with practice of walking tall and easy. Then go on to remind them of joint movement. As you walk does your spine bend any? . . . (Yes, enough so you are not stiff) Stop in your own space and relax slowly, all over. . . . Pretty soon you will be on the floor . . . Lie in any easy position. Now when you get up and stand tall, what has to work? (Muscles) . . . Why do your muscles have to work? (Against your weight, against gravity) Yes, so good posture, standing tall, is a sign of strength, balance, and flexibility. Now try walking in good posture and see what else you have to have. . . . (Skill) (Use group observation here.)

Children's response: This will not be difficult for them to understand especially if it is integrated with science. The boys will talk about zero G, and they may ask questions about why the cosmonauts get dizzy when they are in the state of weightlessness. They will also be interested in thinking of erect posture as a phase of evolutionary development, so that man has to work at it all the time. (See the next problem.)

34. Use of body: erect posture

Teacher's approach: Today we shall explore the way different kinds of animals move. Do you know any living thing that moves around but has no arms or legs? (Fish, snakes) See if you can move around without using arms and legs. . . . Now suppose you had four legs like your cat or your dog. . . . What is the next animal going up the scale in the animal kingdom? (Ape family) How do they get about? . . . Do they use both arms and legs? (Can go either way.) Can they use their arms better than humans do? Why? (Arms are longer; hands are bigger, more like feet) Does that help them? How? (Climbing trees and swinging from tree to tree) Now try moving around the room like the human beings you are, both fast and slow . . . with a partner see how many kinds of steps you can use. . . . Now one partner in each pair sit down, and the other show each stage in evolution, beginning without any arms or legs. . . . Which boys and girls finally looked most like human beings? Why? (They are tall, hold heads high, stand easy but erect.) Now the others stand while their partners watch. . . . Did you all see some that looked very human? Yes, I thought they were very good. Let's all sit down, and sit like apes . . . now like humans . . . What's the difference? (Apes have hunched shoulders and forward heads.) How does it help man to sit, stand, and walk erect? (Hands and arms are free to do things; he looks more confident, more graceful; he is built for erect posture.) Yes, he is built to stand straight, but he has to work at it all the time with skill and strength against the pull of gravity.

Children's response: They will enjoy this, and if you are not careful they will want to remain at lower levels in the animal kingdom! That is why it is better to talk about apes than monkeys and to avoid imitating horses, which many children will do endlessly; also plan ahead what you are going to do about animal noises. While this posture lesson may get temporary good results, children have to be reminded to keep good posture habits often. You should make these reminders constructive.

Which runners are well focused? Which are using energy at the finish? This photograph also shows temperamental differences in response to competition.

Which girl shows the best movement? Why?

This boy is controlling momentum well. Could he use the same technique on a turf field?

The rules of hopscotch require that the player have a foot in each square. How does this contribute to good movement?

Problems for Intermediate Grades

Teaching Suggestions

Movement exploration is an essential part of the intermediate physical education program not only because of its intrinsic worth, but also because it facilitates learning in sports skills, dance, and drama. In the intermediate grades many of the learnings in movement exploration may be applied to sports skills, which are high in the interest of children at this time. For example, if youngsters are executing a "punch," they should discover that it is a stronger movement when they take a step with it, thus using the entire body. Similarly, a step is necessary for a strong throw in any ball game. Through movement exploration, the concept of putting the whole body in motion is associated with the execution of a strong movement in any part of the body. Continuity and strength are experienced together.

Those problems in movement exploration which are based on the expression of an idea or an emotion easily lead into dance and drama. The class may start with a familiar story, telling it through their own inventions in movement, with individuals and groups portraying events and feelings. As the movement develops, words may be introduced spontaneously if there seems to be a need for them to supplement the movement. Drama developed in this way eliminates memorized lines as well as memorized movements and gestures. The children are freed of the artificial or superficial manner often assumed in a play when they are not able to *feel* the character they are attempting to portray.

Children in grades four, five, and six who have not had movement exploration before should go quickly through the problems for the primary grades so that they will understand the elementary ideas of quality, space, and control of different parts of the body. They may, of course, omit such simple problems as Problem 2, and combine others, such as Problems 3, 4, and 5. Some group activity should be introduced as soon as the teacher is sure that they are working well and without self-consciousness. Groups may be formed casually in the gym as the group projects start, or possibly in the classroom before going to the gym. It is not necessary to choose leaders and then have the leaders choose squads; nor is it necessary to keep the same groups from day to day. If class members are not familiar with the informal method of grouping themselves, it may be desirable at first for the teacher to determine the groupings. During the first few lessons, the teacher may mention some accomplishments of those children who are selected infrequently, thus making them more acceptable to the rest of the class. It is not advisable to permit children to group themselves if they openly reject any of their classmates. If at any time the boys show a tendency to exclude girls from their groups, this tendency may be accepted as natural in the intermediate grades. Although all of their work should not be done in sex-separated groups, boys by themselves will often produce original ideas, with much strength and variety in their movements.

The difficulty of problems for the intermediate grades increases rapidly, necessitating repetition with minor variations by the teacher. As has been said before, children enjoy repeating problems; and their feeling of satisfaction grows as skill increases.

Accompaniment may be used to add interest to the patterns developed by the children, as suggested in problems toward the end of the intermediate series. Whether the accompaniment is provided by rhythm instruments or improvised on the piano, it should be used with care. If the teacher or the children come to depend on accompaniment to set the rhythm or the mood of what they are to do, their own creative products will be limited and certain restrictions will have been imposed on the free working of their imagination.

Group response, as a unified effort, develops gradually. When children in the intermediate grades first begin working in groups, the result will probably be independent movement presented simultaneously. Slowly, they may develop the idea of integrating their movements through one or more of the following:

1. Relating the movement of each individual to that of the others in the group.

2. Working for variety in level, direction, and range.

3. Consciously using focus.

4. Developing floor patterns for group movement.

5. Using the total available space.

The following list may help in organizing lessons in such a way that different fundamentals will be taught. It must be remembered that the description of the problem is not a lesson plan.

Movement Fundamental	Problem Numbers
Perception of space	35, 39, 43
Control of quality of movement	37, 38, 41, 44, 45, 46, 47, 48, 49, 50, 55, 60
Use of body	32, 36, 42, 51, 52, 58, 59
Posture	33, 34
Focus on purpose: expressive movement	40, 53, 54, 56, 57, 61

DESCRIPTION OF PROBLEMS[6]

35. Perception of space: different floor patterns, changing quality of movement and body leads

Teacher's approach: Can you make straight lines while you are running quickly and lightly? . . . Change your direction as you need to, but still keep the line of your running straight. . . . Take a partner and, running together, make a letter Z. . . . Try another letter which has all straight lines. . . . Now a letter with both straight and curved lines. . . . Can you do a light, quick walk and make a star? . . . Now try the same thing with a different lead; that is, let your arm or your head or your elbow lead you. . . . Try this: Use a slow, light movement with a chest lead, and make a lot of script *L*'s—nice, round lines. . . . Now can you underline what you have written by letting your hips lead you backward in a strong, quick run? . . . Remember that we give the name *direct* to a straight movement and *indirect* to a curved movement. Right in your own space, show me direct and indirect movements of your arms . . . elbows . . . body. . . .

Children's response: The last part of the problem, in their own space, should lead to axial movements (twisting and turning of the body). If it does not, remind them.

36. Use of body: maintaining balance when changing direction

Teacher's approach: Can you walk to the black line, then suddenly run to the white line at the end of the gym as fast as you can, and stop before you go over the white line? Try it. . . . Now turn around, run back fast to the black line, change to a walk, and walk slowly back to this starting line. . . . Sue, Stevie, Harry, and Dick did that very well; let's watch them. . . . What was good about their changes? (They did not run too far; they stopped with their feet apart and their weight right over their feet; they were at a lower level when they stopped.)

This next one is harder. I'll tell you what to do, and then we'll have a race. Start at the black line, and when I say "Go" run as fast as you

[6] A series of three dots is used to indicate movement by the class.

can to touch the white line with your feet, then turn and run back to finish at the black line, without stopping. Ready—Go! . . . Good, Stevie. I was watching to see how he would turn, and he did these things: Short, quick, strong steps as he got near the white line; leaned back as he touched the line; turned quickly and started the other way with short, quick, strong steps. All try again. . . . Much better. Now in your groups try running very fast in a zigzag pattern—straight lines, no curves. . . . Did you try leaning as you changed? Short, quick steps as you changed? Try again. . . .

Children's response: They really improve markedly if this problem is repeated, and it is an excellent one for providing activity as well as skill practice. They will soon learn to think ahead so as to shorten their step and lean in the direction they are going. Sooner or later, someone is going to point out that this is what makes for good running in soccer or flag football, if they are that far along. When repeating this problem, try sometimes having them "zig" fast and "zag" slowly.

37. Control of quality: working out patterns with a partner

Teacher's approach: Take a partner and work out some movement patterns. Yours and your partner's need not be the same, but they should have the same qualities. First do a quick, light, direct movement, then a quick, strong, direct movement, and keep repeating them in that order. . . . Now try doing your movement patterns alternately; first Charles does his while George watches, and then they change. . . .

Children's response: If they are rusty on movement qualities, you might review Problems 20, 21, and 25 in the primary series. Repeat this work until they are sure of how to make quality patterns. Also try changing speed in the second pattern.

38. Control of quality: working out patterns in groups

Teacher's approach: In your groups, make up your own patterns of slow, indirect, light movement, followed by slow, indirect, strong movement. . . . Try changing levels between the two patterns. . . . Now use different speeds in the two patterns. . . . Make sure you are using different levels. . . . Do the two patterns give you different feelings? (Strong makes you feel more serious, and so forth) Good; if you feel any difference, show it as you do the patterns. . . .

Children's response: Do not insist on expression of feeling if there is any self-consciousness, and do not point out pupils who are very expressive. The latter practice may induce insincerity along with self-consciousness.

39. Perception of space: change of focus in baseball

Teacher's approach: When you are at bat in a softball game, what do you look at? Show me. . . . What does the coach say? (Keep your eye on the ball.) Now suppose you have hit the ball and are running to first base, what do you look at? (First baseman)

Let's try this: Each group dramatize a softball situation. See whether you can figure out where your eyes look as you play, and what you pay attention to. . . . Good; really looks like a game. What do you look at as the game changes? (Depends on what you are doing—when hitting or catching the ball, look at the ball; when running to a base, look at the baseman.) Where does the rest of the team look? (If on the bench, they look at runners; if in the field, they watch action to put the runner out: keep paying attention to what you are trying to do.) Can we say that to be a good player you must *focus* on the *purpose* of what you are doing? Take a partner who runs about as fast as you do, and line up at the other end of the gym, in pairs. We are going to race to this black line, one pair at a time, as Bob gives the signal—but one runner is going to watch his opponent, and the other is going to watch the goal. Ready, Bob? . . . Try it again, changing the focus. . . .

Children's response: They are old enough to generalize, and the boys are especially interested in what will make them skillful at sports. When they get the idea of the race, let several pairs run at once. If they have not matched themselves evenly, shift them. Usually a runner will be slowed up by watching another runner. Bring out the fact that, in running fast, all action must be in the direction of the run, since force is best applied in the desired direction of movement. Swinging arms across the body instead of straight forward and back, toeing out or in instead of straight ahead—these will prevent greatest speed.

40. Focus on purpose: expressive movement

Teacher's approach: Each group join hands with the leader at one end. Move along together at a light walk. Watch to see what the leader is looking at. Look at it yourself. . . . Janie's group moved right toward the thing they were looking at. Try changing your focus. . . . Watch Ted's group a moment; do they tell you a story? (Coming in to see something, or hear something, then finding something different)

Remember the story, "————" which you read last week? Would each group like to try dramatizing it? Think of how the focus changes as you go through what happens. . . . (Watch one or two dramatizations, then generalize.) How does focus help a drama? (Makes it more real, more exciting, tells you what is coming) Can we say that to act out a good dramatization, the group must focus on what it wants to say? How is this like focus in a game? (Focus on what you want to do, in both.)

Children's response: They enjoy dramatization, and can improvise one quickly if they are familiar with the story. Some groups, however, may need at least two lessons. They may be surprised to find that there are the same factors of good movement in sports and in this class.

41. Control of quality: two quality patterns with different leads and floor patterns

Teacher's approach: In your groups, make up your own pattern of a quick, indirect, light movement, followed by a quick, direct, light movement. While you are working, try to use different floor patterns. . . . Good. Now try to remember all the different parts of your body that can lead in movements, and use as many as you can. . . . Why was that better? (More interesting, showed what we could do) Wes, show us what you can do. . . . Now shall we try changing the focus when we change from one quality pattern to the other? . . .

Children's response: Whether this takes one or two lessons depends on the aptitude of your class. Move along as fast as they want to go.

42. Use of body: flexibility and range of movement

Teacher's approach: How many of you can put your feet together, straighten your knees, bend forward, and touch the floor without bending your knees? . . . Try it again. . . . Bob up and down, and see if you come nearer. . . . Did you ever see football players do this for a warm-up? What else do they do? (Airplane exercise) Arms horizontal, feet apart, bend and twist to touch left foot with right hand, then come up straight and go down the opposite way. . . . Why do they do these exercises? Yes, they must be flexible so that they can kick well; so that they won't get hurt. Who else practices flexibility stunts? (Tumblers, swimmers, circus people, dancers) Here is one the dancers do—let's try it. (Sit on the floor with feet wide apart, bend forward to touch your left foot with the right hand, then up straight, then the opposite.) . . . Why do dancers need to be flexible? (To do more things, have better movement) Yes, to get the best movement in sports, in tumbling, in dance, or in anything else, you need flexibility, or good range of movement in your joints. Remember you bend in the spine and hip joint, and twist in the spine and trunk. In dance you can use big, wide movements to say certain things. Suppose half of you come toward the rest with arms wide and long, light, leaping steps, then stop near them. . . . The rest of you back away with small steps, pull your arms in toward the body, and go down to a lower level. What is the difference between the things the two groups said with their movements? (Friendly—afraid; come along—no; victory—defeat; free—slave)

Children's response: As in Problem 39, they will be interested in factors that make for skill in sports. If the effect of range of movement on the expression of emotion needs more work, use additional group patterns. Have children work out similar floor patterns, differing only in range—for example, let them spread out over the gym in large squares or circles, then make very small circles or squares, using very short steps.

43. Perception of space: changing range of movements

Teacher's approach: Remember the quality patterns you worked out the other day? (Quick, indirect, light, followed by quick, direct, light) You did very well in getting different floor patterns, leads, and focus. Now see whether you can change the range of movement, also. Have some large movements, some very small movements; some wide, some narrow. . . .

Children's response: They should be able to do this readily unless they have forgotten the patterns. If they have, encourage them to work out new ones, and emphasize the difference in range of movement.

44. Control of quality: change of quality pattern by changing one quality

Teacher's approach: Let's see a direct, quick, strong movement of the arms . . . of the legs . . . of the whole body, moving away from your space. . . . (Write on the board "direct, quick, strong.") What would your pattern be if you were to change just one quality? Who can write it? . . . Who can write a different one? . . . (After each pupil's contribution except the last, write the original pattern.) Finally, the following sequence appears on the board:

> Direct, quick, strong
> Indirect, quick, strong
> Direct, quick, strong
> Direct, slow, strong
> Direct, quick, strong
> Direct, quick, light

I wonder whether you could do these one after another without getting mixed up. . . . Was that hard? Carol had a good idea; she used the same pattern for "direct, quick, strong" each time.

How would you like to try this in your group? Any suggestions? (Work out with them the idea of different movements for the variations and the same movement for the original pattern each time it is repeated.) Now see whether you can move through the six parts without stopping between. . . . Frances' group had an interesting way of emphasizing the original pattern each time it was repeated. Will you show us what you did? . . . What did they use? (Focus—focused on center of group)

Children's response: This is a difficult problem, which cannot be mastered in one lesson but will require several repetitions. Continuous movement from one pattern to another should not be introduced during the first lesson, as it is here, but should be delayed until the class is ready for it. Soon the pupils will point out that this is like a poem or a song with a chorus—the uniform group movement to the direct, quick, strong pattern. This idea, together with centering the focus on the chorus each time, may help them.

45. **Control of quality: identifying different quality patterns used in daily life (punch and slash)**

Teacher's approach: Let's start with direct, quick, strong movements. . . . Do a different movement with the same qualities. . . . Now another. . . . Can you think of a name that would fit all these different movements? What would you call all direct, quick, strong movements? (*Thrust, punch,* and so on) Do we use thrusting movements in athletics and at work? (Hammering a nail, volleyball serve, broad jump, punch in boxing, kneading bread, shot put) Do some of these movements and see whether they are really direct, quick, strong in quality. . . .

Remember how we changed to indirect, quick, strong movements? Do some of these and see whether you can find a name for them. . . . (*Slash, snap,* and so on) How do we use a slashing movement? (Cracking a whip, shaking a rug, high jump) Can you imitate some of these and feel the quality pattern of the slash? . . .

Children's response: Some pupils will be helped by this verbalizing, and some will not. It should not be forced unless it seems to stimulate thinking and understanding as well as interest. Keep the class active as much of the time as possible, even if some verbalizing is indicated.

46. **Control of quality: identifying two more quality patterns (pressing and tapping)**

Teacher's approach: Remember the two patterns we used as verses the other day? One was direct, slow, strong. Try a number of movements with that pattern until you have a name for it. . . . (*Pushing, pressing*) How do we use it? (Ironing, pushing a car, tug of war, action of a bulldozer or steam roller) The other pattern was direct, quick, light. Try it out and find a name for it. . . . (*Tapping, dabbing*) How do we use it? (Typing, bouncing a ball) Now, with a partner, try alternating these two movements. First both of you do pressing, then tapping; after that one of you does the pressing, and the other responds with a tapping movement. . . .

Children's response: They may have different names for these movements, and if they keep the characteristic qualities of the patterns, that is all right. Explain that having names for patterns is a short cut in talking about them, but that it will not work unless everyone uses the same names. Therefore, they should agree on the names they want to use.

47. **Control of quality: emotional components of different quality patterns; making a movement "poem"**

Teacher's approach: Remember the movement poem your groups did the other day, with a chorus and three verses? If we used our new names for these patterns, the "poem" might go like this: *punch, press, punch, slash, punch, tap.* Let's have the groups go through these patterns again, always keeping the same pattern for the chorus. . . . Now, as you do these different patterns, see whether you can feel a different mood in each one. . . . Try to agree on the feeling in your own group. . . . Will each group show the rest of us its movement poem? We shall watch to see whether our idea of the feeling of the pattern agrees with yours. . . . What are these feelings? (*Punch*—courage, hope, and so on; *press*—determination, domination, persistence; *slash*—cruelty, victory; *tap*—trying out, curiosity, teasing) Try your "poem" again in your groups, and let your feelings come out. . . .

Children's response: They may have many other feelings besides these, or they may not mention any of these. If their feelings seem authentic, and if there is some agreement, accept their ideas. After all, they are the ones who have invented the patterns and (presumably) have the feelings as they execute them. If they still balk at emotional expression, do not force it. But if they go along with it, they are ready for the next two problems.

48. Control of quality: identifying new quality patterns (float, glide, flick, wring)

Teacher's approach: We might start with a quality pattern that is the exact opposite of a punch. What qualities would it have? (Indirect, slow, light) That is right. See whether you can put that into movement, doing something with interesting variety. . . . How would you name it? (*Float*) How do we use movements like that? (Slow waltz, lob in tennis, "sculling" in swimming, silent paddle in canoeing, folding eggs into a cake batter) Now let's change one quality—which one? All right, change indirect to direct, and see whether you can do a direct, slow, light movement. . . . How do you want to name it? (*Glide*) How do we use it? (Smooth walk, parts of dance steps and swimming strokes, painting a fence) Try the two together: *float, glide, float.* . . . Sandra had an interesting pattern because she used different body leads and different levels, and changed the focus in the glide movement. Now let's change another quality in the float—the second one. Try an indirect, fast, light movement. . . . What do you think we should call it? (*Flick, toss*) How do we use it? (Tossing a ball sideways, dusting a chair) What is the last change we can make in the pattern of the float? Indirect, slow, strong is correct. Can you name it? (*Corkscrew, wring*) How do we use it? (Wringing out clothes or using corkscrews, parallel parking without power steering)

Children's response: Whether or not they pick this up readily will determine whether they need two or more lessons on this problem. If they are really ready for it and are working well, all four quality patterns may be named in one lesson, although they will receive additional practice in another lesson.

49. Control of quality of movement: making a new "poem" with new quality patterns

Teacher's approach: Would you like to make a new "poem" from the four new quality patterns, with a float for the chorus? Let's agree on the order: *float, glide, float, toss, float, wring.* Try it in your groups, using the same movement for the float each time. Remember to get as much variety in floor pattern, level, and range as you can, and change the focus when that will help. . . .

Children's response: They will need time to work out interesting patterns, perhaps two more lessons. However, it might be well to have each group present its "poem" at the end of the first class in order to get suggestions from the group and to have an immediate goal for the lesson.

50. Control of quality: emotional components of new poems

Teacher's approach: I would like to see once more the interesting "poems" you worked out last time. As you do them, see whether you can sense the feeling of each, and how it changes from verse to chorus, from chorus to the next verse. What is the feeling of the float? (Dreamy, letting go, relaxed) The glide? (Slow but sure, mysterious, dangerous) The toss? (Could not care less, sophisticated) The wring? (Working hard, putting on the pressure) Suppose you go through your patterns again, showing your feelings. . . . See whether thinking of focus and range of movement will help you. . . .

Children's response: By this time they should be well aware of the feeling aspect of movement, and should be enjoying the chance to communicate their feelings. Of course, not all will be equally good at this, but even the ones who are less expressive should be absorbed in trying.

51. Use of body: locomotor movement and balance

Teacher's approach: Today we might try combinations of the way we move through space. Move anywhere in the common space using as many different kinds of steps as you remember. . . . Let's have Betty write down the names of the steps you tell her. Now in your groups work out some combinations of these different steps. . . . Shall we watch Sally's group repeat their pattern? . . . What did they do? (Four walks, two hops, and a jump) Will Bill's group show us what they were doing? (Four gallops, two leaps, and a jump) Half of you try Sally's pattern and half try Bill's; think while you are doing these how your spine and head are helping. . . . (Erect on walks and hops, leans forward a little on gallops and jumps) How do your head and spine help when you run? All try. . . . (Lean forward) Why do they lean when you are going fast? (Balance) Yes, one important thing in balance is to keep your weight right over your feet. Can you show how you learned to change direction by running to the black line, and then in the opposite direction to the white line? . . . Now something harder. Can you run straight forward, touch the black line with one foot, then run directly to the right without losing your balance? . . .

Children's response: Of course they will use different patterns from the ones indicated here, but be sure they try most of the different steps in combination. In the balance part of the problem use group observation to bring out the fact the good runner shortens his step and leans slightly in the new direction as he approaches the turning point. They will tell you that this is what a good ball player does in any game where he changes direction, and what a figure skater does, also.

52. Use of body: nonlocomotor movement and maintaining balance on different parts of the body

Teacher's approach: Today let's try to see what your body can do right in your own space without moving into the common space. . . . Now tell Helen what you did so she can write the movements on the chalkboard. Try combining three of these movements and make a nice pattern by repeating it. . . . Get in your groups anywhere in the common space and decide on a pattern you would all like to do. . . . Good. (Try group observation and evaluation here, watching to see what the head and spine do to help in each movement.) Now in your own space we shall try some balance stunts. See if you can balance first on four, then three, then two, then one part of your body. . . . Now try the two and one, but use different points of balance. . . . Can you do a strong, quick movement in the common space and suddenly come to your balance position? . . . Good. Try the same movement but come to a different balance position. . . . Now come back to your own space and try three of those nonlocomotor movements you did at first, finishing with a balance on three points. . . . Keep on with this pattern to see if you can make it better. . . .

Children's response: They will think up many movements, and the list should include bend, stretch, twist, push, pull, swing, fall, with variations. When they do guided observation bring out not only what the spine does, but change of level and body leads. (Hand, elbow, shoulder, knee, and so forth)

53. Expressive movement: exchanging ideas with a partner

Teacher's approach: Remember when you did movement poems with a good deal of feeling. Today we might try to have partners reply to each other. Let's see what happens when one of you decides to do strong movements, and the other replies with light movements. . . . This time, as you reply, keep everything the same as in your partner's quality pattern except strength. If Tom starts out with a wringing movement, how would Sally answer? Yes, with a floating movement. All of you try it. . . . Now start with a slash. . . . This time choose the quality you will change, but change just one. . . .

Children's response: As they get more and more dramatic, you might try having a commentator work with each pair, and put into words the meaning of their movements.

54. Expressive movement: telling what you have seen at the circus

Teacher's approach: Everyone is going to the circus—the crowd goes in first. Think of all the characters you might see in that crowd; can you tell us by the way you move which character you are? . . . . Now the performers are ready to go in. Do you think your shoulders can tell us which performer you are? . . . Bill, will you show us your performer? . . . What was he? . . . (Lion tamer) How did you know? (Shoulders were strong; showed he had confidence; focused his eyes and his shoulders on the lions)

Children's response: If they are getting too concrete in their imitations, select the more abstract ones to demonstrate.

55. Control of quality: review of basic quality patterns

Teacher's approach: Let's repeat the names of all the different quality patterns we have learned. . . . Good. Do any one of them in at least two ways. . . . Watch Ted, Jane, Mary Lou, and Steve. As soon as you know which pattern any one of them is doing, come and tell me. . . . Now go through the same quality pattern, but change the floor pattern and the range. . . . All of you do one of the other patterns twice, and be sure to change focus between the two. . . . Now use different levels. . . . Is there any one of the patterns you do not know, or cannot do? (If any are mentioned, have the whole class do them together.)

Children's response: They will need several lessons to be able to use different combinations of movement qualities in a variety of ways. Let them use their own terms for the basic quality patterns if they have agreed on them. Use group observation and evaluation.

56. Expressive movement: telling what you have seen

Teacher's approach: If you went into a railway station in a large city you might see many kinds of persons and groups. Here are some: tired travelers, the team that won, the team that lost, strangers in the city, nervous parents. (Put these titles on the board.) Suppose you join your groups, and quickly decide which one you want to tell about. As soon as you know, put your initials on the board beside the title you have selected. Before we start planning, let's decide on some of the things we want to remember as we do this. (Show general feeling rather than merely imitating actions; use all we know about variety of movement, focus, range, direction, and so on.)

Children's response: Usually they are very good at this problem. For another lesson, you might let them suggest their own subjects. To overcome the tendency toward excessive detail and concreteness in action, select some patterns for demonstration to the class and allow time for discussion and evaluation.

57. Expressive movement: exchanging ideas with a partner

Teacher's approach: Take a partner, and exchange ideas through different quality patterns. First one partner does a pattern; then the other replies. We did this the other day by changing one quality in the pattern the first partner used. Today you are free to change as many qualities as you wish, or none at all. If your partner uses the floating type of pattern to say that it is a warm, sunny day and he feels lazy, you may answer the same way if you wish, or you may tell him to snap out of it. . . . You are doing very well with this, and I believe almost anyone could understand your ideas. Would you like to try having a commentator interpret what you are saying? (Use a volunteer for the commentator and have him go with one couple. Let the others watch and listen to anything that is especially good.)

Children's response: If the procedure of using a commentator seems fruitful, let them work in threes next time and take turns, two doing the movement and one commenting.

58. Use of body: locomotor movement with rhythmic accompaniment

Teacher's approach: Take a partner and try as many different kinds of steps as you can think of, such as running, skipping, and ———? (Leaping, hopping, galloping, sliding) . . . Now each couple join another so that you are in fours. All four join hands and do the same thing. . . . Say what you are doing as you do it. . . . I noticed that you kept time with the words; that is, the words came out right with the beat of your feet. Try this pattern: skip, and skip, and run-run-run. Keep on with it. . . . Think of some other step patterns yourselves, and use variety in direction in order to make different floor patterns. . . . Which fours would like to try one of these instruments to help with the rhythm? . . . Very good: I noticed that Edward was able to beat the tom-tom and do the step pattern at the same time. That is hard, but some of the rest of you might like to try it. . . .

Children's response: Although this is the first specific problem in rhythmic accompaniment in this series, the children will have had other rhythmic experiences in dance and in music. Therefore let them go as fast as they want to. The problem is introduced here as a beginning in integrating movement exploration with modern dance.

59. Use of body: locomotor and nonlocomotor movement with rhythmic accompaniment

Teacher's approach: Let's try this in your groups: First, get any rhythm instrument your group would like to use from the collection up here on the platform. Then let's all skip and beat out the accompaniment. . . . Now try gallop . . . slide-and-slide . . . run four, walk two . . . three runs and a hop . . . three skips and a jump. . . . Now try making up some different rhythmic patterns in your group, and accompany them. Change the range of your movements as you do the rhythmic pattern. . . . Now change the focus. . . . Shall we try something harder? Try a nonlocomotor movement right where you are. . . . (Remember push, pull, swing, and so forth) See if there is a rhythm pattern your group can make up with these movements. . . .

Children's response: Differences in ability will show up very soon. The problem of individualizing instruction while the children are working in groups is a real one. What each individual needs depends not only on his coordination but also on his temperament. Some will be helped by a more highly skilled friend while working in an average group; others may be lost in an average group and gain confidence only if placed in a group of generally lower ability. Usually such a group needs special help from the teacher or from a mature pupil who combines skill with patience. It may take several lessons in locomotor movement before you can get to the nonlocomotor part. This will depend on how fast your children pick up skill in the rhythmic accompaniment.

60. Control of quality: rhythmic accompaniment to different quality patterns

Teacher's approach: Today we shall try something you may find quite difficult. We shall beat time on our instruments to accompany a quality pattern. This is more complicated than merely keeping time to steps. Would you like to start with one of you doing a strong, quick, indirect movement, followed by a strong, slow, direct movement? Whom are you going to ask to do the movement? Fine; Sam, will you repeat your patterns several times so that we can all beat the rhythm on the floor as you move? . . . Now will each group get the rhythm instrument it wants, and go right into some quality pattern it knows well. As soon as you can, accompany the movement with your instrument. . . .

Children's response: The accompaniment may not be very skillful unless you have been able to integrate this lesson with some instrumental work in music. But it will serve the purpose of helping children to feel the rhythmic pattern of an axial movement as well as a locomotor movement, and it will improve with practice.

61. Expressive movement: each group communicates a different idea

Teacher's approach: (Before class begins, put these phrases or other, similar ones on the board.)

Will you help me?

I'm stronger than you are.

Let's be friends.
Catch the thieves!
Don't be afraid!
Let's find out.

Will each group choose one of these phrases to work on, and put your initials next to it? This is something you are going to express to each other, and later to the rest of the class, through your movement. You may carry the theme beyond this phrase, of course. Remember, as you work on it, to use all the things you know: feeling, levels, focus, floor patterns, range, and variety of body movement. Let's have something interesting; do not be satisfied with just everyday imitation.

Children's response: If they become absorbed in this, give them another lesson or two to work on it. Then let them go on, choosing the themes they want. They may wish to develop some of the things they have been reading about into a silent drama. When they ask to use percussion instruments or seem responsive to a suggestion to do so, let them try.

Illustrative Problems

Fundamentals of Movement Applied to Other Forms of Physical Education

Eight short problems are described below to illustrate the way in which movement exploration may be used in self-testing and in games. Both the teacher and the children will devise other problems to help with the things they need to practice, and the children will learn to use these problems in their individual "work sessions" at the beginning of class.

Self-testing

62. Use of body: relaxed landings (see also Problems 6, 9, 10, 22)

Teacher's approach: Shall we see how light our jumps can be? In your own space do small jumps up and down; keep them so light we cannot hear you. . . . Now three small jumps and one high one, and keep on repeating that. . . . All sit down. How did you keep the high jump light? (Bent knees more, made it easy coming down) Good, shall we watch some of you? (Select four or five who do it well.) . . . Did you notice how Freddie kept the big jump light? (Went right down and touched his hands to the floor) Try it again, three times, and then roll over. . . . Good. How does this help you when you are using the big apparatus? (Learn to jump down easily) Yes, suppose that the next time you come in and see the apparatus out each of you goes to your own space and starts right out with this pattern, working to make the jumps lighter each time.

Children's response: Usually, they need to practice this, and like to as well. This is a good problem for a "work session," and they can develop endurance by repeating the pattern more often.

63. Use of body: curling and extension

Teacher's approach: Start in any position you like and try to curl up, bending in all your joints. . . . Now stretch out, slowly. . . . Good. Try it again from a different position; keep both bending and stretching slow. . . . Now see if you can curl up slowly, and then stretch out as fast as you can. . . . Now try in three parts: first curl up slowly, then shoot out as wide and fast as you can, then relax easily and quickly right down to the floor. . . . Good. Keep repeating and try to make the three parts slow and light, quick and strong, then quick and light. . . .

Children's response: They will want to collapse with a bang, but group observation and evaluation will help them to make it a lighter movement, and they can easily see that in falling this way they will not get hurt.

64. Use of body: twisting, turning, falling, rolling (see also Problem 13)

Teacher's approach: In your own space look in as many directions as you can without moving your feet. . . . What part of you does move? And how? (Trunk, spine, hips, knees, shoulders—all twist) Now let your feet move, turning you around in your space until you are back again where you started. . . . Try this a little faster. . . . Now go around the other way. . . . Can you do a hard pattern? First turn around two or three times, quite fast, then a relaxed fall, then roll over once and up on your feet again to repeat the whole thing. . . . Good.

Children's response: During their group observation point out the qualities of lightness, continuity, and indirect configuration of the movement. They will see that this helps them in many stunts as well as in landing from apparatus.

65. Use of body: rules of balance, points of balance

Teacher's approach: Lean forward as far as you can without falling. . . . When you feel yourself falling, what do you do? Yes, your feet move forward to get under your weight. Try the same thing sideways. . . . Do your feet move sideways? Yes. And so we have the first rule of balance: keep your feet directly under your weight. Here is another rule we can work out: take a partner, grasp right hands and brace right feet against each other. Now try to keep your own feet still while you push and pull your partner so he has to move one (or both) of his feet. . . . Try different positions of your feet, always keeping your right foot braced against his right foot. . . . What is the best way? Yes, a stride position. Can you make a rule? (A wide base makes better balance than a narrow base.) Another rule? (The lower your weight, the better your balance.) Try balancing on just one part of your body. . . . Now on two parts. . . . Change these any way you wish. . . . Is it easier if you have two points of balance on the same side of your body, or on different sides? Why?

Children's response: If they do the two parts readily, go on to three or four parts, and a smooth continuous movement changing to different points of balance in turn. In group evaluation, help them to know how important balance is in all their games and stunts. They can also try fast movements stopping suddenly on one or more points of balance.

Games[7]

66. Control of quality: slow and light

Teacher's approach: In the game Brownies and Fairies, is there any part that you would like to practice? (Walking on tiptoe) Yes, that is a very important part of the game. Is it fast or slow? (Slow) Is it strong or light? (Very light) I shall stand over here with my back to you, and you see how close you can come before I hear you. When I hear you I shall beat the tom-tom and turn around, and you run as fast as you can to the black line. . . .

Children's response: It will be hard for them to do a slow movement like the tiptoe approach at the beginning of the lesson unless they have come into the room doing very lively stunts. After the stunts they will be ready for the practice of a slow, light movement. Later they can learn to try this practice with a partner, who claps his hands instead of using the tom-tom, and who pursues the tiptoeing player.

67. Relationships: running and twirling with three others in a small circle so as to progress toward a goal

Teacher's approach: When we play Indian Twirl it is quite hard for the circles to keep together when they go around and move forward at the same time. Would you like to try this first walking and then running? Fine. Get your groups and pick a goal right ahead of your group. Suppose one group tries this, and when they get to their goal, the second group starts out. As soon as you can go all the way walking without

[7] Before the following problems in movement exploration are carried out, it is suggested that the children review the games Brownies and Fairies, Indian Twirl, Hit, Bounce, and Catch, and Bounce Ball Relay which are described in Chapter 11.

losing your circle or touching any other group, you may try it running. . . .

Children's response: This is a very good test of the children's ability
to work together in a small group and also to keep from interfering with
others. Be sure there is plenty of room. If the space is small, have only
two circles practicing at once, the others observing.

68. Relationship: recovering balls without touching any other player (soccer or utility ball)

Teacher's approach: Today we shall play a game that will help you
to keep from interfering with others in the common space. Will all the
children except Caroline's group get a ball from the bag and go back
to your own space. You may play with your ball anywhere in the common space, using your feet, not your hands to control it. Caroline's
group are It. Each one of them is going to try to capture a ball, using
his feet to control it, and not touching any other player. If you lose your
ball, you are It, and whoever has captured your ball may play with it.
If you touch someone else, you are "dead" and have to come over to this
wall to practice noninterference.

Children's response: The "dead" group will practice in a line, passing each other by weaving in and out, keeping their arms folded. When
any one of them does this well, you may bring him back to life by a
favorable comment, and send him back to the It group. They get
plenty of activity in this game as well as practice in noninterference
and use of feet to control the ball. Later they may wish to try this practice with a pat-bounce or basketball dribble instead of using their feet.
In group evaluation point out the fact that this problem helps them
when they play soccer or basketball, not only in control of the ball, but
in avoiding fouls.

69. Control of quality: application to throwing and catching

Teacher's approach: When we play Hit, Bounce, and Catch, what
do you have trouble with? (Throwing hard enough; catching the ball
on the first bounce; getting too excited) Today we can practice without
counting, so you will not get so excited, and can take time to do everything right. Let's do this in partners—one watch and coach the other
until the signal for you to change.

Children's response: In group observation and evaluation, help
them to see that in the first part of the throw they move the arm well
back, twisting the trunk but looking straight ahead. This part of the
throw is indirect, light, and slow. Then the actual throw is indirect,
quick, and strong, and the follow-through is directly toward the wall.
Point out that to catch well, they should focus their eyes on the ball and
move toward it with their feet well under their weight. Then they

should reach forward with a light movement of the hands and draw them back with the ball in a quick strong movement, fingers firm on the ball. As they practice and improve in skill, point out that the best movements are continuous, without jerks or holds, from catch to throw to catch, and so on. If there is only one softball for every four or more players, have half of the class do a problem preparing for Bounce Ball Relay. In this they may play with one or two others at the most, depending on the number of tennis balls, and go through the same skills called for in the game, but starting at a walk and working up to full speed. Be sure that the group observes the change of direction of the bounce in the three parts of the game, the change of speed of the runner to keep close to the ball as it bounces and the change of force needed to make the third long bounce to the player next in line. Both of these problems are for advanced intermediates, and they can see the improvement in their skills when they actually play the game.

Outcomes of Movement Exploration

The following criteria may help the teacher evaluate the progress of his class. As they progress he will develop other criteria that seem important to him.

Mastery of Fundamentals of Movement

Focus on purpose; does each child: Understand the purpose of the lesson and work toward it? Eagerly explore new apparatus and what he can do on it? Invent movement patterns that show appropriate response to problems? Work with absorption to improve performance of his patterns? Enjoy telling a story or expressing feeling by movement?

Perception of space; does each child: Understand and respect the difference between his own space and the common space? Move in varied and meaningful floor patterns? Move at different levels? Show contrasting large movements in the common space and small range movements in his own space? Perceive the best space in his opponents' field to bat the ball or to run when carrying the ball?

Control of quality of movement; does each child: Show that he *feels* the difference between strong and light movement? Control speed and change it when advisable? Understand the difference between various configurations; between straight and curving movements? Develop continuity of movement in a familiar pattern? Know when and how to break continuity in a "hold"? See the application of quality patterns to everyday movements? Demonstrate the effect of changing one or two components in a pattern? Show natural emotional response when doing patterns of different quality?

Use of body; does each child: Show interest in the possibility of movement in various joints? Use different parts of the body as "leads" in movement patterns? Show ease, continuity, lightness, control of speed, and direct forward movement in such steps as walking, running, and skipping? Understand and use his body correctly in other locomotor and nonlocomotor movements? Maintain balance using different parts of the body as points of support? Move fast and change direction without losing balance? Show ability to sit, stand, and walk with erect posture, and care about working toward a "sit tall, stand tall" position? Understand the need for flexibility, strength, and forward direction in foot action? Improve in use of feet? Improve skill in relaxed light landing from jumps?

Relationships; does each child: Enjoy working with a partner? With a group? Show willingness to do his share? Control the tendency to interfere with others? Take responsibility? Listen to others in group discussion and try their ideas as well as his own? Improve in fitting his independent movement patterns to those of his partner or the group? Choose good leaders, take their suggestions, and see that they consider others? Respect the umpire even if it is someone of his own age?

Response to Method

Problem solving; does each child: Understand and accept the class problem? Work at it eagerly with freedom in experimenting and invention? Practice his own movement "solution" to improve it? Join in class observation and evaluation, relating what he sees to the purpose of the problem? Gain pointers from class evaluation using suggestions and new insights to improve his own work? Learn to treat his own difficulties as problems and work out practice patterns that will help him? Use these practice patterns whenever he has a chance for a work session? Apply this problem approach to other forms of physical education?

Invention and creativity; does each child: Feel that it is better to find his own answer than to imitate someone else? Know that no one will make fun of him if he is different from the others? Feel free from anxiety even if he works more slowly than the others? Improve in using his imagination? Move without self-consciousness, absorbed in the problem he is trying to answer? Enjoy problems calling for expressive movement?

Self-direction; does each child: Start responsible activity as soon as he comes into the play space? Know that he can explore use of small or large apparatus as soon as he has helped to set it up? Remember safety rules? Remember that everyone has the same right to a good time in the gym that he has? Realize that the more capable they all are at managing class organization, the more time they will have for the active things they want to do? Remember his own problems, and start his own work session on some one of the problems?

Use of Criteria

As the teacher uses these criteria to check on progress, he will find the "no" answers pointing to areas that need emphasis. First, of course, he tries to analyze the reasons why his class has not made more progress in these areas. Perhaps they need more practice in certain areas, and he will find the classified lists of problems for primary or intermediate grades useful. Perhaps he needs to modify his method: he may want to give more help on certain details, or he may want to give more guided responsibility. If he is a teacher-in-training, he has the advantage of advice from a supervisor who is working closely with his group of beginning teachers. If he is a teacher-in-service he has his own experience and knowledge of the children as resources. He may also have the advantage of a supervisor specially trained in physical education who may be ready with suggestions. Of course, the school library of references and films will help.

In the last analysis, the teacher himself will use the problem-solving technique. He will identify his problems, use all available resources to devise new approaches, experiment with the approach that seems most fruitful, and use criteria to evaluate progress with this new method. He knows that problem solving works with the children; on a different level it may work with the teacher!

Selected References

Anderson, Harold H., (ed.), *Creativity and Its Cultivation*. New York: Harper & Row, Publishers, 1959, Chaps. 6, 7.

Andrews, Gladys, Jeanette Saurborn, and Elsa Schneider, *Physical Education for Today's Boys and Girls*. Boston: Allyn and Bacon, Inc., 1960, Chap. 4.

Broer, Marion R., *Efficiency of Human Movement*. Philadelphia: W. B. Saunders Company, 1960, Chaps. 1, 2, 10, 11, 12, 27, 28.

Department of Education, Ministry of Education, *Physical Education Junior Division, Grades 4, 5, 6*. Toronto, Canada, 1955.

Detroit Public Schools, *Exploration of Basic Movements in Physical Education*. Detroit: Publications Department of Detroit Public Schools, 1960.

Glassow, Ruth, *Fundamentals in Physical Education*. Philadelphia: Lea & Febiger, 1932.

Halsey, Elizabeth, "England's Children Invent Activities," *Journal of Health, Physical Education, and Recreation*, 26:32, December, 1955.

Halsman, P., *Philippe Halsman's Jump Book*. New York: Simon and Schuster, Inc., 1959.

H'Doubler, Margaret, *The Dance and Its Place in Education*. New York: Harcourt, Brace & World, Inc., 1925, Chap. 4.

Kelley, Ellen Davis, *Teaching Posture and Body Mechanics*. New York: A. S. Barnes & Company, Inc., 1949, Chaps. 5, 9.

Laban, Rudolf, *Modern Educational Dance*. London: Macdonald & Evans, Ltd., 1948.

Ministry of Education, *Moving and Growing*. London: Her Majesty's Stationery Office, 1952.

Ministry of Education, *Planning the Program*. London: Her Majesty's Stationery Office, 1953.

Morison, Ruth, *Educational Gymnastics*. Liverpool: I. M. Marsh College of Physical Education, 1956.

Radler, D. H., with Newell C. Kephart, *Success Through Play*, Part I. New York: Harper & Row, Publishers, 1960.

Wessel, Janet, *Movement Fundamentals*. Englewood Cliffs, N.J.: Prentice-Hall, Inc., 1957.

CHAPTER 10

Self-Testing

No OTHER PHASE of the physical education program contributes more to the development of specific traits of physical fitness than do self-testing activities. Current testing programs at national, state and local levels demonstrate the fact that large numbers of American children are inadequately developed in selected measures of physical fitness such as strength, endurance, flexibility and physical skills. Weakness in strength of arms and shoulder girdle is especially apparent—a situation attributed to the fact that children today have less opportunity to climb trees, vault fences, and participate in other childhood activities natural to previous generations. Many self-testing activities demand vigorous use of trunk and upper extremities. All yield a high amount of purposeful activity within the class period because of the focus on individual rather than group activities. Several experimental studies show that significant improvement in muscular fitness is made by children in relatively short periods of time through regular participation in selected self-testing activities.[1]

[1] Lucille Ingrid Magnusson, *The Effect of a Specific Activity on Children with Low Muscular Fitness*, Ph.D. Dissertation, T1957 M199. Iowa City, Iowa: Department of Publications, State University of Iowa, 1957. See also Margaret Ruth Morris, *Measured Effects on Children in Primary Grades from Use of Selected Playground Equipment*, Ph.D. Dissertation, T1955 M877. Iowa City, Iowa: Department of Publications, State University of Iowa, 1955.

The term "self-testing" is used in physical education to designate those forms of physical education in which the child tests his powers of control over the environment. Developmental activities in stunts, tumbling, use of small equipment and apparatus, and track and field are described in this chapter. All of these activities except track and field are ones in which the child competes only with himself. Each child is encouraged by the structure of the lesson or situation to select a goal appropriate to his level of readiness and work toward the attainment of it with encouragement and guidance from the teacher. Track and field activities are included because, although competition takes place between individuals instead of with one's self, the skills involved are developed through self-testing.

In a sense motor development *per se* might be described as a continuing process of self-testing for the child. No sooner does he learn to walk or run, hop or jump, swing or slide, than he experiments with countless variations in time, space and force. Running on tiptoes, spinning about, walking railings, sliding downstairs, standing in swings or on teeters—children are constantly daring. They experiment with new types of learning that require courage and control. Unfortunately, much of this experimentation takes place in situations or on obstacles not considered appropriate, and so the child's drive to learn is often squelched by parental and teacher "don'ts".

The homemade, portable apparatus shown below is of simple construction.

The task of the elementary school is to structure the self-testing program so that increasingly complex challenges are provided for the children each year, in situations as free as possible from competition and undue hazards. Interest in the possible uses of the body remains a dominant one during these years. Invaluable learnings include not only the refinement of previously learned skills, but the acquisition of many new ones which the environmental opportunities suggest. Unfortunately, customary provisions for this phase of the program are stereotyped in a majority of schools. Equipment is limited and little in the way of more challenging apparatus is provided for children beyond kindergarten or primary grades. Concerted action of parents, administrators, and teachers is needed to improve the growing-learning environment of children through self-testing.

Suggestions for Teaching

Setting the Stage

The self-testing program should provide children with opportunities and freedom to experiment and explore situations rich in resources—ideas, equipment, apparatus. It should provide chil-

It can be arranged in various ways for increasingly difficult challenges.

dren the opportunity to solve problems—to try out two or more ways of doing something. Apparatus should be provided for indoor use, as well as on the playground, in order to provide for continuous practice throughout the school year. It should be of such a variety that children are encouraged to engage daily in the natural activities of childhood—climbing, hanging, balancing, vaulting, jumping in its many forms, as well as running, throwing and manipulating objects.

Small equipment such as beanbags, balls, hoops, and jump ropes should be provided in sufficient quantities for all children in a class to practice simultaneously. Other equipment such as deck tennis rings, wands, Indian clubs, tether balls and a variety of striking equipment—paddles, racquets and bats—should be provided at the ratio of one to every six children for the largest class. Central storage of equipment in places accessible to all classes can be worked out so that sufficient equipment for any one class is feasible in the budget of most schools. In schools where such provisions are not available, children are frequently able and always eager to supplement the school supplies by bringing balls and hoops from home. The ingenious teacher will think of countless types of improvised equipment. For example, handles of discarded brooms serve well as wands, milk cartons for Indian clubs, and automobile tires for obstacles and challenges.

Organizing the Lesson

The self-testing lesson falls quite naturally in two parts. One consists of teacher-directed problems on fundamentals of movement basic to successful achievement in a specific activity of the lesson, whether it be apparatus work, use of a piece of equipment, or group work in pyramid building. The other part consists of practicing that activity—the "stage is set," the situation structured, so that children engage in self-directed activity with the teacher as helper.

In the part of the lesson devoted to teacher-directed problems, floor work is planned in movement exploration that helps children achieve immediate as well as long range goals. For example, experimentation with relaxed landings from jumps off the floor should be practiced before experimentation with jumps over or off apparatus is encouraged. Experimentation with various parts of the body supporting the body weight should be practiced on the floor before setting up situations that involve balance on beams or

Cat Walk

Crab Walk

Lame Dog Walk

Kick Like a Mule

Hop Like a Bunny

Seal Crawl

Measuring-Worm Walk

Variations in patterns that children may discover in response to the challenge: "Show how you can move through space using *hands and feet* to support the body."

boxes. Practicing test-type stunts such as the mule kick or tip-up provides fun and immediate satisfaction for beginners in stunts and tumbling. Repeated practice develops the arm strength and coordination essential to successful achievement in more advanced stunts such as cartwheels, head and hand stands, and rope climbing. (Illustrative problems of the first type are found in the chapter entitled "Movement Exploration." Developmental stunts of the latter type are described in the succeeding sections of this chapter.)

The quality of self-directed practice in the second portion of the lesson is tantamount to the quality of preplanning by the teacher and class, but children must be helped to select goals appropriate to the fundamentals emphasized in the lesson. Then each child is encouraged to experiment with the equipment (or whatever else is involved in the lesson) and to work out for himself and practice patterns of movement.

Practice; observation and evaluation; further practice—these are the important sequential steps for improvement in quality and control of individual patterns. In addition, children must be taught to set up and return apparatus or equipment, and must review procedures for helping one another. Until habits of sustained practice are developed, it is advisable to organize the class into small groups which select a starting station and change to another on signal. During this part of the lesson, the teacher circulates among the groups giving help and encouragement as needed. See the diagrams on pages 225–226 for illustrative floor plans for this phase of the lesson.

Safety Measures

Teaching children control of movement in the use of their bodies or in the use of equipment and apparatus is an invaluable means of helping them learn to meet the hazards of daily living. The best safety measure in helping them develop such control is to allow each child to find his own solution to problems set by the teacher or the situation. Children should learn to respect individual differences and to compete with themselves rather than with others in the group.

Spotting, that is, guarding and assisting a performer, is advisable when children experiment with vaulting activities and with balance stunts performed on apparatus. Children should be

Examples of Floor Plans for Self-Testing Stations

Tossing balls through elevated hoop.

Ditch jumping: over long ropes extended on floor.

Jumping to touch heads to color bands. (Bands are tied to long rope, elevated to long poles to give necessary height.)

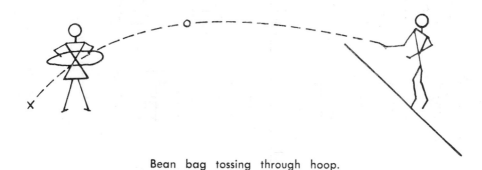

Bean bag tossing through hoop.

Examples of Floor Plans for Self-Testing Stations

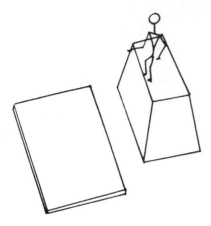

Box—jumping on and off.

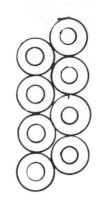

Obstacle (tire) run.

High jump.

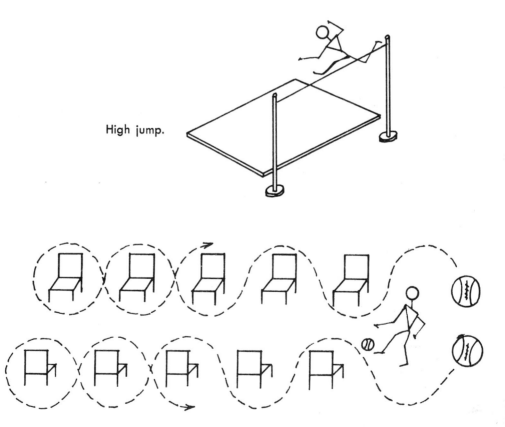

Obstacle run: controlling ball with feet.

taught to indicate their intentions in such instances, so that the teacher or a child can be ready to lend assistance.

Apparatus must be carefully spaced so that courteous and safe traffic is maintained. "Relationship," a fundamental of movement discussed in the previous chapter, permeates all lessons at all levels. Improvised apparatus should be used only under the teacher's supervision. Permanently installed apparatus should meet high standards of construction and installation. It should be inspected regularly for signs of stress and weakness. Soft turf, sand, or mats should be used under apparatus, for jumping activities, and for many stunts. Functional dress and gym shoes should be required. Children should be encouraged to perform in bare feet when the play area is suitable.

In selecting and teaching stunts, the teacher should keep in mind children's anatomical limitations. The following are a few points to remember:

1. Avoid stunts that put a strain on ligaments surrounding the knee and hip joints (for example, the dwarf walk, knee dip, and split).

2. Avoid stunts that involve hyperextension of the back (for example, the bridge and back bend).

3. Avoid heavy lifting by the child. He should not be permitted to carry a weight approximating his own. The epiphyses have not ossified in childhood, and may be distorted or malformed as a result of lifting excessive weights.

Description of Stunts

The stunts described in this section are organized according to type and arranged in order of difficulty. Each stunt provides a challenge for the child until he masters it regardless of the age at which he is first introduced to it. He enjoys practicing a specific stunt until he learns it, if it is within his level of ability; then he enjoys performing it for the sake of "the doing." Thus, specific aspects of muscular fitness are improved. However, individual differences in abilities preclude the fact that all children in a class can or will learn any particular stunt. Each child should be encouraged to learn some of each type of stunt and to improve his own record rather than to compete with class members of more or less ability.

Test-Type Stunts

The specific factor or factors of muscular fitness emphasized in each stunt is indicated, though all involve a degree of strength, agility, coordination and flexibility.

FIVE PIGS (Flexibility)

Stand with feet together.

Bob up and down trying to touch each toe in turn without bending knees.

Say the nursery rhyme "This little pig went to market," and so on bobbing on each of the accented words and stretching hands overhead at the end of each line.

DRUM (Strength of trunk and thighs)

Lie on back with legs straight and toes pointed, arms at side.

Drum on floor with heels (only a few quick repeats in the beginning); work up to making drum beat patterns.

HUMAN BALL (General flexibility)

Sit down crossing legs, knees bent, hands inside knees and around outside ankles, clasped in front of ankles.

Roll down on right shoulder, on back, on left shoulder, and up. Repeat to make a complete circle.

Complete circles several times one way; then reverse the direction.

COFFEE GRINDER (Strength of arms)

Start in a sitting position.

Place one hand on the floor and the other on the hip.

Walk feet away from the body until the body is in an inclined plane (straight line, no sagging or humping of hips).

Walk in a complete circle about the supporting hand, keeping the body in a straight line.

Try the stunt with the other hand.

JUMPING JACK (Coordination)

Assume a squat position.

Spring to an extended position with weight on the heels.

HEEL CLICK (Coordination, flexibility)

Stand in stride position.

Jump, flexing knees, and touch heels of both feet with finger tips before descending.

TOE TOUCH (Coordination, flexibility)

Stand in stride position.

Jump and touch toes, extending legs forward. Do not bend knees; try to keep legs perfectly straight.

JUMP AND TURN (Coordination, strength)

Stand with feet together and on a line. Use a crack in the floor or an imaginary line.

Wind body like a top.

Jump and turn all the way around, landing with feet in starting position and without losing balance.

TURK SIT AND STAND (Leg strength, coordination)

Sit in cross-legged position with feet close to the body and as nearly flat on the floor as possible.

Stand without changing the position of the feet and without touching the floor with any part of the body except the feet.

Try going up and down several times without stopping, like an elevator.

THREAD THE NEEDLE (General flexibility)

Keep hands in clasped position in front of body.

Step over the hands, one foot at a time, without releasing handclasp; then walk backward through hands to starting position.

EGG SIT (Flexibility, balance)

Sit in knee-flexed position, with hands grasping ankles.

Extend legs, maintaining grasp, and rock back into balanced position.

Can you hold this position three seconds? Five seconds?

SINGLE SQUAT (Leg strength, balance)

Balance on one foot, with opposite leg extended forward.

Perform knee bend with supporting leg and return to standing position without losing balance or touching hands to floor.

UP-SWING (Coordination)

Assume kneeling position, with weight on balls of feet.

Swing arms back and then quickly forward in order to gain momentum and swing up to standing position.

UP-SPRING (Coordination)

Assume kneeling position, with feet extended (as opposed to the position of the feet in the stunt above).

Swing arms back and then quickly forward while springing (jumping) to standing position.

BEAR DANCE (Leg strength, balance)

Assume a squat position.

Jump and extend one foot diagonally forward, then the other.

See whether you can repeat in quick succession. Five times? Ten?

JUMP FOOT (Coordination)

Stand with side toward a wall.

Move outside foot in front of inside foot and place it firmly against the wall, about a foot from the floor.

Spring from inside foot over raised leg without removing foot from wall.

STRENGTH OF ABDOMINALS

Lie flat on your back, with knees flexed.

With partner holding legs down, see how many times you can curl forward to a sitting position.

Note: Teach children to exhale on each forward curl.

ENDURANCE

See how many times you can curl up in one minute.

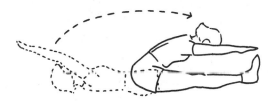

STRENGTH OF ARMS

How many push-ups can you do? (Knee-hand push-ups, as in the illustration, are recommended for elementary school children.)

FLEXIBILITY

Stand up straight.

How far can you reach toward the floor without bending your knees? Can you reach the floor? Can you reach between your feet and beyond your heels?

Combative Stunts

ROOSTER FIGHT

Face your opponent with arms folded across chest, weight on one foot, and other foot raised.

On signal, try to push him off balance either with arms, which must be kept folded across chest, or with shoulders.

HAND WRESTLE

Face your opponent with right hands joined, weight on one foot, and other foot raised.

On signal, attempt to cause opponent to touch the free foot to the floor.

PULL ACROSS

Opponents face each other on opposite sides of a dividing line.

On signal, grasp right hands and attempt to pull the other across the line.

INDIAN LEG WRESTLE

Opponents lie side by side, facing in opposite directions, with inside legs hooked together.

On signal, raise inside leg three times, returning to the hooked-knee position between extensions.

When knees are hooked for the third time, attempt to force your opponent's shoulders from contact with the floor; that is, to roll in any direction.

Basic Tumbling Stunts

The tumbling stunts below are described in developmental stages, or steps, with each step constituting a complete stunt less difficult than the one that follows. Step 1 of each series is appropriate for most primary-grade children, yet remains an important step for any beginning tumbling group, whether its members are 6 or 16 years of age. Learning is usually more rapid during the primary years, however, since flexibility is not limited by growth spurts.

FORWARD ROLL

Step 1:
Place hands flat on mat, shoulder width apart, with fingers pointed in.

Tuck head as far between knees as possible.

Push with the feet and roll in a ball, with the hands supporting your weight.

Land on upper back.

Roll to sitting or standing position.

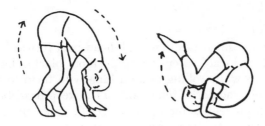

Step 2:

Roll to sitting position as described in Step 1.

Clasp hands over knees and come to a standing position.

(This step gives polish to the forward roll.)

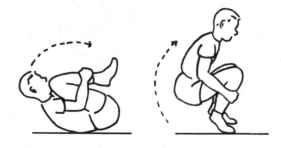

Step 3:

Perform Step 2 using a two- or three-step approach; that is, take several steps, jump lightly on both feet, and spring into forward roll.

Step 4:

Perform the forward roll over a rolled-up mat; through a hoop.

(Diving over or through an object should be attempted only after the children have mastered the first three steps. Inventing ways of diving should be initiated by the children rather than directed by the teacher.)

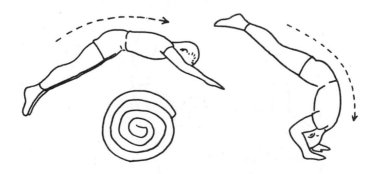

BACKWARD ROLL

Step 1:

Begin in squat position, with head bent forward.

Roll backward in curled-up position, placing hands flat on either side of ears while rolling and pushing with them to complete the roll.

(Pupils should be reminded (a) to keep head bent forward while rolling to prevent bumping and (b) to make the roll continuous in order to secure the necessary momentum.)

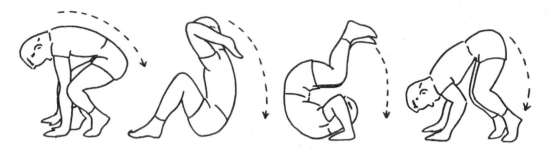

Step 2: From standing position to standing position.

Begin in semistanding position, with knees slightly flexed.

Roll as above.

(The additional momentum gained from starting in this position, together with a strong push of the hands, enables the performer to land on his feet rather than his knees. He is in position to perform a second roll or a series of rolls.)

Step 3: Backward roll with extension.

Perform Step 2 with a strong push of the hands and an extension of the feet while weight is on hands in order to assume a brief handstand position before snapping feet down for landing.

HANDSTAND

Step 1: Mule kick.

Place weight on hands and kick the feet into the air.

See how many times you can kick before losing balance and returning weight to the feet.

Step 2: Handstand using wall for support.

(Free practice is preferable to detailed instructions, other than those regarding safety. When children show ability in maintaining balance on hands in Step 1, they are ready to try Step 2. They should be instructed to face the same wall of the playroom in order to eliminate the risk of kicking one another.)

To begin the stunt, place hands on floor about a foot from the wall.

Swing leg up straight and throw head back to aid in balance.

(A child who has mastered this stunt should demonstrate.)

HEADSTAND

Step 1: Tip-up.

Stand with feet about shoulder width apart.

Bend, and place one hand flat on floor in front of each foot, with fingers pointing straight ahead.

Place knees on top of bent elbows, pressing forward slowly until weight is supported on hands.

Place head well back to aid in balance.

Step 2: Tripod.

Begin as in the tip-up, but lower head to floor, placing it about a foot in front of hands. The tripod arrangement of head and hands gives a firm foundation for this upside-down position.

(A chalk diagram or folded paper model helps children to visualize triangular support essential to successful performance of stunt.)

Step 3: Headstand with aid of partner.

Face your partner, standing at arm's length from him.

Performer: Make the tripod, then slowly raise feet, with helper aiding in balance as feet are extended. Point toes and arch back slightly to aid in balance.

Helper: Aid in descent by placing one hand on performer's thigh and seeing that he flexes knees and descends slowly.

Step 4: Headstand.

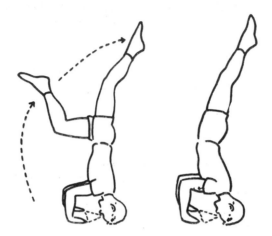

CARTWHEELS

Children should be reminded to check their own space carefully when practicing this stunt in order to avoid kicking someone. Such practice is an excellent activity when children first enter the playroom or arrive on the playground, since it does not necessitate the use of mats. An open turf area on the playground makes a good practice spot. Children should be instructed always to face in the same direction during practice, so that they can be responsible for clearing those in front of them. Free practice is preferable at the beginning, with the suggestion that they try a low cartwheel after having had considerable practice in the mule kick. The following analysis may be useful for coaching cues.

Step 1: Low cartwheel (without hip extension).

(The analysis is for a cartwheel to the *left* but it may be started to right if child prefers.)

Begin in stride position, placing left hand on floor.

Move right hand over the left one and place it on floor, also, about a foot beyond the left.

While weight is supported on hands, lift right and then left foot and cross over hands.

As body turns release left and right hands in turn, with a pushing action, which helps you turn and regain balance on your feet.

Step 2:
Practice series of low cartwheels.

Step 3:
Practice cartwheel with hip extension, keeping elbows and legs straight.

TUMBLING

Tumbling consists of a series of stunts—either of the same stunt or of a combination of different ones—performed in smooth, continuous sequence. As children become proficient in the basic tumbling stunts, they enjoy practicing them in sequence and creating new and interesting combinations. Two variations of the cartwheel, described next, permit smoother transition into the forward or backward roll and will challenge children who are able to perform continuous cartwheels.

ROUND-OFF

When feet are in stride position overhead, as in the regular cartwheel, bring feet together in mid-air, then land on both feet simultaneously.

You will land facing the direction from which you came, so continue with a backward roll.

TINSICA

When feet are in stride position overhead, as in the regular cartwheel, give an added push with the last hand down, causing the body to turn or flip into a forward position in landing.

Then follow with a forward roll.

The following combinations of stunts can be performed by most intermediate-grade children, provided they have had ample opportunity to practice basic stunts during the primary years: Continuous Cartwheels, Continuous Forward Rolls, Continuous Backward Rolls, Walking On Hands, Round-Off and Backward Roll, Tinsica and Forward Roll.

Couple Stunts and Pyramids

Stunts and pyramids involving precision in control of movement, cooperation, and teamwork become increasingly useful and appealing during intermediate grades. A few of the couple stunts appearing first on the list are appropriate for primary children, also. These stunts offer excellent opportunities for children to develop appreciation and respect for the wide differences in growth and abilities that result during intermediate years. Respect is earned when the rapidly growing child proves his strength as a base of support, or when the "featherweight" demonstrates balance and control of movement as top man on the pyramid.

Children should be helped to understand and apply principles of good movement. In addition to observing the safety factors discussed earlier in this chapter, it is imperative to (1) require spotters, or safety men, for all stunts involving lifting, balance, or support; (2) discuss mechanical principles involved in such activities; and (3) discuss correct and careful placement of the feet on the "base" in supporting stunts. For example, feet should be placed on strong parts of the body (the thighs or the shoulders) rather than on a weak parts, such as the hollow of the back.

WRINGER

Join hands with your partner and raise them high.

Turn under *joined hands* and stand back to back and then continue turning in the same direction to face each other.

Try to complete the turns several times in quick succession without loosening handclasp.

WHEELBARROW

Stand facing in the same direction as your partner, with one immediately behind the other.

Partner in front places hands on floor, and the other grasps one of his thighs with each hand.

Walk forward. (Partner in front, who is walking on hands, should set pace. If he is pushed too fast, he may get hurt.)

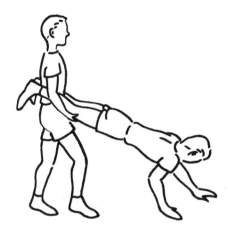

ROCKING CHAIR

Sit facing your partner with knees flexed and feet flat on the floor.

Sit on your partner's feet and place your hands on his shoulders.

As the "chair" rocks, the partner facing forward supports his own weight by partially standing on his own feet. This gives an illusion of being lifted in the air.

(Children enjoy performing this stunt to the accompaniment of a lullaby.)

BACK-TO-BACK-RISE (Chinese get-up)

Sit back to back with your partner, keeping arms locked, knees flexed, and feet flat on the floor.

Go up and down together (like an elevator) by leaning against each other and pushing with the feet. (For success in this stunt, children must keep backs erect and adjust to partner's weight throughout.)

Can you repeat stunt five times without losing your balance? Ten?

ANGEL BALANCE

Base: lie on mat with legs raised and knees slightly bent, and place feet diagonally alongside of top's pelvic bones.

Base: grasp top's hands and straighten legs, raising top into balanced horizontal position.

SITTING BALANCE

Base: lie on mat with legs raised and knees slightly bent.

Top: sit well back on feet of base and extend arms back, grasping hands of base to aid in balance.

As base straightens legs, top extends arms to side.

(Spotter should be alert to aid top in maintaining balance throughout the performance of this stunt.)

Angel Balance

Sitting Balance

HORIZONTAL STAND

Base: lie on mat with knees bent and feet flat on mat.

Top: place hands on base's knees and support weight while base grasps your ankles, with thumbs below and on inside of legs, and raises you to horizontal position.

KNEE-SHOULDER STAND

Base: lie on mat with knees bent and feet flat on mat.

Top: perform a handstand on knees of base with shoulder support by base.

Horizontal Stand   **Knee-Shoulder Stand**

ONE-KNEE BALANCE

Top: perform knee balance on back of base.

TRIANGLE

Top: stand in front of base, but facing in same direction as base.

Top: bend over, place hands on floor, and lift one foot off floor.

Base: with knees slightly bent, grasp top's feet, which are extended in turn, and place one on either shoulder.

Base: straighten knees slowly while top maintains straight-arm position and arches back slightly.

Top: maintain straight-arm position and arch back slightly.

ONE-LEG BALANCE

Base: assume erect, balanced position on one knee.

Top: place right foot diagonally across base's thigh, holding on to his shoulder for balance. Then step up to an erect position extending free leg backward.

Base: aid top in balance by holding him at the knee.

THIGH MOUNT

Base: stoop down so that top can sit on your shoulders.

Then assume a half-standing position and duck head, helping top come to a standing position on your thighs.

Base: support top by grasping him above knees and leaning backward to maintain your balance.

(This stunt requires considerable help from spotter until base and top learn to coordinate balance and timing.)

Thigh Mount

One-Knee Balance

HEADSTAND ARCHWAYS

Sides: face base and form a tripod. On signal, extend legs to headstand position (in turn).

Base: grasp ankles of each to aid in their support.

HANDSTAND ARCHWAYS

Sides: face base, standing at arm's length from him.

Base: grasp ankles of sides as they perform a handstand.

SKIN THE SNAKE

(Suggested for six to eight children.)

Line up in single file and stand in stride position.

Thigh mount and headstands.

Headstand archways.

Skin the snake.

Bend forward and extend right hand between knees to person behind; extend left hand forward and grasp right hand of person in front.

Last person in line sit, then lie down flat on floor with feet together while line moves backward over you.

As each person reaches end of line he lies down also.

Last person to reach end of line reverse procedure. Walk forward, straddling line, and pull next person to his feet.

Continue until all are in original position.

(It is imperative that children keep feet close together while lying on floor in order to avoid tripping members of team who pass over them.)

MERRY-GO-ROUND

(Suggested for six to ten children, half of them "lightweight" compared to the others.)

Lightweights and heavyweights stand alternately.

Form a circle and take a double wrist-lock grasp.

Lightweights sit on floor with legs extended and feet together.

At the signal, supporting children take one step backward, while those who are seated raise their hips to bring the body into a straight, inclined position.

Supporting children take small, sliding steps in one direction, while lightweights take small pivot steps on heels to put "merry-go-round" in motion.

A few examples of simple pyramids are given later in the chapter. Children will enjoy working out these as well as creating their own designs.

Merry-go-round.

Opening of the rose.

The bridge.

Tumble down.

Use of Small Equipment

Examples of developmental experiences with various kinds of small equipment are given below. "Problems" range from the simple to the more difficult and may serve as suggestions to the teacher of either the primary or intermediate grades. Also, progression within each example is possible and desirable through (1) changes in timing, force, or use of space, and (2) expansion from individual experimentation and patterns to work with partners or small groups in cooperative patterns. Intermediate grade children enjoy working out sequences of patterns into routines set to accompaniment. Balls, beanbags, hoops, Indian clubs, wands, and rings all lend themselves well to creative work.

BALLS

Guided play

(Balls of different sizes and kinds should be available for experimentation and practice.)

Teacher-directed problems

How many times can you bounce and catch the ball?

Can you throw the ball into the sky? How many times can you throw it high and catch it?

How high can you bounce the ball? How many times can you clap your hands before catching it?

How long can you bounce it? How many times can you pat-bounce (dribble) the ball without stopping?

With what other parts of the body can you bounce the ball?

Can you move through space controlling the ball with your feet?

With the ball placed between your feet, toss the ball from your feet and catch it with your hands.

As you bounce the ball can you make the ball travel around your body without changing the position of your feet?

Can you make the ball travel between your legs? Make a figure-eight?

With your weight supported on one foot only, can you bounce the ball continuously while turning to face different parts of the room?

Pat-bounce the ball and swing each leg over in turn.

Bounce the ball in or over markings or obstacles on the floor, such as circles, hoops, ropes, Indian clubs.

Pat-bounce the ball in all directions and around obstacles.

Throw and catch the ball while running in all directions.

Practice in ball handling through teacher-directed problems.

Guide (dribble) the ball around obstacles with feet.

Pat-bounce the ball with right and left hand in turn.

Jump over the ball as it bounces.

Juggle the ball; roll it up and down arms; bounce it **on arm or** head; balance it on one finger, and so forth.

Similar to above, working with partner or in threes.

Games with two, three, or four children

See:

Dodgeball in Three's.

Tether Ball.

Four Square.

Relays.

"Make up" games; groups of three, four, five children.

Contests

Target games (concentric circles on wall, frames).

Bowling.

Distance throwing.

BEANBAGS

Walk and run with beanbag balanced on head.

Jump with beanbag between feet, ankles, knees.

Pass or throw beanbag with feet—from one side to the other when in "tall" sitting position; overhead when lying on back.

Hop with beanbag balanced on free foot.

Jump or hop over beanbags scattered over floor.

Pick up scattered beanbags while hopping and balancing on one foot.

Throw beanbag upward with feet and catch with hands.

(See examples in use of balls.)

SHORT ROPES

Experiment with various foot patterns while turning ropes forward or backward in own space. (Jump; hop; skip; gallop; polka.)

Use any of the above foot patterns while moving through space; experiment with various directions and levels.

In couples with one person turning, work out patterns involving changes in timing or directions; with one person using a ball.

Use variations in types of swings: cross hands, forward, back.

Use variations in types of swings (rope held in both hands together): overhead, either side or under feet while maintaining jumping rhythm with feet.

Create patterns using combinations of foot and rope movements; put together patterns into a sequence and set to an accompaniment.

Work out patterns in pairs; small or large group.

LONG ROPES

Many forms of running jumps can be performed over a long elastic rope. The teacher and a child hold the ends of the rope at an appropriate level for jumping. The rope may be folded in the middle so that each holds two ends. It can then be stretched apart, parallel to the ground, for broad jumping, or held with one strand above the other for window jumping. Many other variations suggested and enjoyed by children are possible. Since five or six children can jump at one time, long ropes provide a great deal of activity in a brief period of time.[2]

For the ordinary long rope #10 window sash is the most satisfactory weight. Enough long rope should be provided for instructional periods so that children can work in small groups with not more than two or three waiting turns. Use variations in foot patterns and in timing or in types of swings.

[2] The rope used in the photographs on page 250 is called a "Magician's Rope," and was obtained from Frau Liselott Diem, Sporthockschule Kolm, Kolm-Mungersdorf-Stadion, Germany, for approximately $3.00 in U.S. currency.

Opposite page:
The elastic rope, imported from Germany, may be used in many ways.

Window jumping through the elastic rope (center).

Jumping over the elastic rope (bottom).

Skipping with crossed-arm swing requires coordination and timing. Can a boy use these skills in sports?

Two ropes with two turners, ropes turned in opposite directions (Double Dutch).

Two ropes with two turners plus short rope turned by jumpers.

Two ropes with two turners, ball bouncing by jumper.

Two ropes with four turners, ropes crossing in center (Egg Beater).

As above, jumper turns short rope.

Children enjoy working out these variations in foot and turning patterns, chanting rhymes either of local origin or of universal popularity. The following are some of the rhymes that can be used.

> Old Man Daisy.
> He went crazy,
> Up the ladder
> Down the ladder
> Went Old Man Daisy.

I asked my Mother for fifteen cents
To see the elephant jump the fence.
He jumped so high he reached the sky;
And never came back 'till the Fourth of July.

Teddy Bear, Teddy Bear, turn around,
Teddy Bear, Teddy Bear, touch the ground,
Teddy Bear, Teddy Bear, say your prayers,
Teddy Bear, Teddy Bear, climb the stairs,
Teddy Bear, Teddy Bear, show your shoe,
Teddy Bear, Teddy Bear, now skid-doo.

(The action is suited to the words.)

1—2 buckle my shoe
3—4 shut the door
5—6 pick up sticks
7—8 lay them straight
9—10 big fat hen
11—12 ring the bell
13—14 maids a-courting
15—16 girls a-fixing
17—18 boys a-waiting
19—20 that's a-plenty

Chickity, Chickity, Chop,
How many times before I stop?

Mabel, Mabel, set the table.
Don't forget the salt, pepper, vinegar, mustard.

Charlie Chaplin sat on a pin
How many inches did it go in?
1, 2, 3, 4, 5, 6, and so on.

Cinderella, dressed in white,
Went upstairs to clean the flues,
How many flues did she clean?
1, 2, 3, 4, 5, 6, and so on.

"Fire, Fire," says Mrs. McGuire.
"Where, where," says Mrs. O'Dare.
"At the fair," says Mrs. Blair,
"And it burns hotter and hotter."

(Regular jumping occurs until the last word, "hotter.")

Down in the valley
Where the green grass grows,
Sat little Mary as sweet as a rose.
Along came Johnny
And kissed her on the nose.
How many kisses did she get?
1, 2, 3, 4, 5, 6, and so on until a miss is made.

Down in the meadow
Where the green grass grows
There sat Mary (name of jumper)
As sweet as a rose.
She sang and she sang
And she sang so sweet
Along came Joe (boy friend)
And kissed her on the cheek.
How many kisses did she get? (Count)

WANDS

Jump over wand held at knee height by partner; cat-spring over;
hop over.

Balance end of wand on tips of fingers while walking and changing
direction.

Place one end of wand on floor and hold vertically with one hand
on top; run around three times.

In pairs, stand several feet apart, each partner holding wand vertically in front with one end resting on floor. On signal, race across and
catch partner's wand before it falls.

Place one end of wand on floor and hold vertically with one hand
on top; release wand while lifting one leg over it and catch it before it
falls.

Hold wand in front of body, parallel with floor. Step over wand
one foot at a time; stand straight; then step back over it in same fashion.

Begin as above; swing wand forward and back, jumping over it.

In a set of three: two children support a wand at each end waist
high or lower; the third child uses wand as support to turn on (a low
horizontal bar) or hurdle over.

HOOPS

Bowl (roll) the hoop while running freely.

Spin the hoop and run around it. How many times can you run
around it before it falls?

Use hoop as you do a jump rope. Skip in place, turning hoop forward; backward.

Twirling the hoop requires
flexibility and skill.

A sixth-grade girl twirls two
hoops.

Twirl hoop about wrist, arm, ankle, waist.

Swing hoop in different planes—in front of body, from side-to-side or forward and back. Change supporting hand at end of each completed swing without breaking rhythm.

Develop swing patterns and arrange a sequence; set to an accompaniment.

(As before, work out couple, small, or large group arrangements.)

COLOR BANDS[3]

Place color band on floor. See whether you can balance on one foot and pick up band with toes of free foot.

Sit on floor and place color band to one side. See whether you can reach across with opposite foot, pick up band, and put it down on other side.

Sit on floor and place band behind you, about 2 feet away. Roll backward, reaching feet overhead, and try to pick up band with feet; then roll to sitting position again.

Use of Apparatus

Suggestions for various types of play equipment and apparatus are given in Chapter 6, and later in this chapter. These include both permanently installed playground equipment suitable for children's recreational use and apparatus for instructional purposes only. Obviously, if either is used for class instruction, the teacher's supervision and guidance are required.

Several teaching stations are desirable for the organized lesson so that children may practice various developmental activities in a class period—jumping of various types, vaulting, climbing, balancing—with children moving from one station to another during the period.[4] Such variety should be introduced

[3] Color bands for identifying teams are easily made from carpet binding, which is available in assorted colors. Sew together both ends of two 30-inch strips. These can be worn diagonally across the trunk by looping them over one shoulder and under the opposite arm. They can also be looped together and used for marking lines or boundaries on the playing field. They are especially useful for manipulatory exercises of the feet, examples of which appear in the text.

[4] The films, *Physical Education for Primary Grades* and *Movement Education in Elementary Grade Physical Education,* demonstrate class organization and the exploratory approach in use of apparatus. Both are available from the Bureau of Audio-Visual Extension, State University of Iowa, Iowa City.

What is the shape of the body in the air? Which leads to easier control in landing?

over a period of time. When apparatus work is introduced to a class, all children should be given the opportunity to try out and get the feel of each piece before being given specific challenges or problems to solve. As the teacher needs to guide children in such exploration, other stations might better include self-testing activities or games in which some of the children can work independently.

After preliminary exploration of a specific piece of apparatus, problems based on fundamentals of movement should be set in such a manner that all children can succeed. (Examples of such problems are on the following pages.) Since most apparatus involves forms of jumping, landing, collapsing, rolling, curling, extension and balance or support on various body parts, these particular uses of the body should be incorporated in each lesson in both the preliminary work on the floor and in challenges set on the apparatus.

Developmental Experiences

LOW INCLINED PLANKS AND LADDERS, BALANCE BEAMS

Cross over (one side to the other), supporting weight on hands.
Travel from one end to the other:

1. Keeping close to the apparatus.
2. Using extension at some time.
3. Balancing on different parts of the body.
4. Showing change in timing; force; use of space.

Work with partner, each starting at opposite ends:
1. Use matching or contrasting patterns of movement.
2. Pass partner, using the same level of space; different level.

Use small equipment, beanbags, balls, hoops, and wands as you travel.

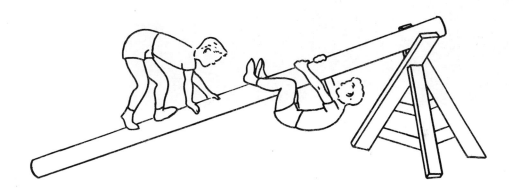

SWEDISH BOX (Stage, heavy table or other improvisation)

Note: Guided observation and evaluation are important at this stage of experimentation. Look for symmetrical and asymmetrical use of body. Which use of the body results in better impetus in take off? In balance and control in landing?

Climb up and off.
Climb up and balance and climb off.
Jump on and off; curl and roll.
Jump on; curl and extend the body in jumping off.
Jump on; try different points of balance; jump off.
Jump on and off, making a shape in the air before landing.
Jump on; jump off on swinging rope.
Practice and improve above patterns; create others involving changes in fundamentals.

Leap from platform, touching toes.

Dismounting from a three point balance on a Swedish box.

Making a symmetrical shape in the air.

Making an interesting shape in the air.   Symmetrical vault by a fourth-grade boy.

JUMPING STANDARDS (Small portable standards; wand or pole over two boxes)

Find different ways of crossing over or under.
Show how high you can jump while crossing over.

JUMPING PIT (Sawdust lined pit for outside use; lined mat for inside)

Jump for distance.
Jump for height: Try to touch a pole, hoop, or other object suspended from the ceiling or supported by a child elevated on table.

VAULTING BOX OR BUCK (Chair, low boxes or other improvisations, firmly anchored)

Do preliminary problems as above; proceed to others:
Cross over, supporting weight on hands.
Curl and/or extend the body, supporting weight on hands.
Cross over, using symmetrical and/or asymmetrical patterns.

GRIP

Children should be taught to grasp with the thumb in opposition to the fingers when climbing, hanging, or swinging on any piece of apparatus. This makes for a stronger grip and minimizes a tendency to slip when hands become moist from exercise.

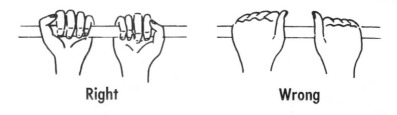

Right　　　　　　　　**Wrong**

CLIMBING ROPES AND POLES

Wrap feet around (the rope or pole) in such a way that they support the weight during successive pulls of the arms.

Place one foot on top of the other, with the rope between them.

Carry the feet well forward, so that the rope may be gripped between the calf muscles of the upper leg and the shin of the lower leg. This permits a firm locking grip of the knees, which hold the rope between them while arms and hip muscles are moving the body upward.

Gripping the rope or pole with the thighs will also help to support the weight.

When you descend, let the feet serve as brakes while you move the hands one below the other. (The danger of getting a rope burn by sliding down should be pointed out.)

Challenges such as the ones below enable all children to achieve success in using ropes or poles. Help them develop the arm strength needed for climbing and *descending* ropes safely.

Show different ways of moving the feet while supporting your weight with your hands.

Show different ways of moving your body while supporting your weight with your hands.

Curl and extend your body as many times as possible while supporting your weight with your hands.

Climbing a rope.

Bicycling.

Reverse hang.

Success in a new adventure.

SWINGING (Rings, trapeze, rope)

Children should be taught how to dismount safely from any piece of swinging apparatus. At the back of the swing, momentum is temporarily halted, and a perpendicular drop to the floor can be made *only* at that point. The following stunts may be tried:

Swing low and dismount.
Swing by knees from rings.
Swing on rope from Swedish box; dismount on mat placed at proper distance.
Swing on rope from Swedish box over jump standard; dismount on mat.
Swing on rope from floor to Swedish box; balance and dismount on mat.

CLIMBING FRAMES (Horizontal bar, parallel bars, beams, ladder, doorway bar)

Children should have the opportunity to progress from low to high frames and to experiment with ways of using them. They will invent traditional stunts such as the ones listed here as well as experiment with many variations and combinations. They should be encouraged to practice patterns working toward good control and flow of movement.

LOW FRAMES

Front rest and forward roll

Grasp bar and extend arms, resting body against bar.

Lower head, relax arms, and roll forward. Landing should be soft and controlled.

Hang by knees

Lift legs up and over bar and flex knees to a locked position.

Lower body slowly to upside down position.

Skin the cat

Grasp bar and slowly roll over backward by kicking feet overhead; bend knees and keep head down to assist in the execution of this stunt.

As feet touch the mat, give a slight push and roll back to original position.

Bird's nest

Grasp bar and raise toes, anchoring them on bar between hands.

Arch back, reversing angle of the hips, and lift the head to form the "nest."

HIGH FRAMES

Passive hanging

Hold body weight as long as possible.
Drop and land softly.

Active hanging

As above, but contract muscles into active position, holding head high and pointing toes.

Flexed-arm hanging

Grasp bar; raise body into flexed-arm position.
Hold as long as possible.
Drop and land softly.

Traveling (horizontal ladder)

Travel forward, one rung at a time; travel backwards.
Travel forward, skipping one or two rungs.
Travel along side of ladder.

One-knee mount

Jump up and grasp bar, swinging one leg up and over it; flex knee to a locked position.

Climbing tower designed and constructed for a small playroom.

Horizontal bars of graduated heights permit different stunts.

Swing free leg downward to start swinging action of body.

When body is above level of bar, grasp bar for support and swing free leg over bar to finish in sitting position.

Chinning

Grasp bar with palm of hand toward body.

Flex arms until chin is level with top of the bar.

Extend arms and repeat as many times as possible.

Variations of stunts done on low frames

Track and Field

Many activities included in the self-testing program are among those generally known as track and field events. There is a decided difference in emphasis, however, between the two forms of physical education. In self-testing activities the child is encouraged to compete with himself; track and field events are designed to test the child in competition with others. The goals are to win events or to set records—natural ones for children in the upper elementary grades.

Events

Official track events include dashes and relays, usually run on a circular track. Official field events include the standing and running broad jumps, the hop-step and jump, the high jump, the pole vault, the discus and javelin throws, and the shot put. Modifications of these and sundry novelty events are usually included in the elementary school program, since the purpose is to provide desirable competition for all children.

The reader is referred to the chart below, entitled "Track and Field Events for Intermediate-Grade Children," for recommendations of specific events appropriate to a specific grade and sex. These recommendations are based on evidence from numerous research studies which indicate that prepubertal boys and girls do not differ significantly in factors basic to success in physical performance except strength. Since the broad jump, distance throw, distance kick, discus, and shot put are all activities in which strength plays a primary role, it is advisable to separate boys and girls for these events. In activities primarily involving speed and coordination, girls and boys do equally well.

TRACK AND FIELD EVENTS FOR INTERMEDIATE-GRADE CHILDREN

Event	Grade	Boys and Girls Together	Boys	Girls
Track				
40-yard Dash	4, 5	X	X	X
50-yard Dash	6	X	X	X
40-yard Shuttle Relay	4, 5	X	X	X
50-yard Shuttle Relay	6	X	X	X
Relay (circular track)	6	X	X	X
Novelty Relays (obstacle, three-legged, sack, potato, hopping, and so on)	4, 5, 6	X	X	X
Field				
High Jump	4, 5, 6	X	X	X
Running Broad Jump	4, 5, 6		X	X
Standing Broad Jump	4, 5, 6		X	X
Standing Hop-Step-Jump	5, 6	X	X	X
Ball Throw for Distance (softball, basketball)	4, 5, 6		X	X
Soccer Kick for Distance	4, 5, 6		X	X
Ball Throw for Accuracy	4, 5, 6	X	X	X
Shot Put (8–10 pounds)	6		X	
Novelty Events (rope skipping, hoop twirling, juggling, tug-of-war)	4, 5, 6	X	X	X

Skills

Equipment

Turf, track, or smooth surface with an area 20 or more feet beyond the finish line; stop watch.

The starting position

The crouch start is used advantageously by fifth- or sixth-grade children. Younger children seem to do just as well with a standing start.

Directions for the crouch start

On the signal "Ready," kneel with hands placed behind the starting line and perpendicularly below the shoulders.

On the signal "Get set," lift knee and shift weight to forward position, distributing it between feet and hands.

On the signal "Go!" propel yourself forward with a forceful push of the feet and hands.

Action

Gradually assume a semierect running position as your body is propelled forward with the push.

Reach maximum speed as soon as possible, and maintain it until after crossing the finish line.

Record

Taken to the nearest tenth of a second.

Equipment

High jump standards, cross bar, jumping pit or layers of mats if done indoors.

Directions for starting position

Stand at the right or left side of the pole, whichever seems natural.

Action

Approach the pole with a slow, springy, comparatively short run at an angle of 30–45 degrees to the cross bar.

Take off on the foot away from the bar—the foot nearest the bar goes over first and the take-off foot trails in a scissorlike action.

Extend both legs (straight) during the jump and lift the arms in a propulsive manner to get additional lift.

Land on both feet.

Score

Two trials are allowed at each of successively higher levels. The jumper is eliminated on the third miss. The highest successful jump is recorded.

BROAD JUMP

Equipment

Jumping pit or long mat for indoor use; measuring tape; take-off board.

Directions for starting position

Assume a semicrouched position with toes behind the take-off board.

Action

Have body weight forward as your feet push off.

Curl body momentarily.

Thrust arms forward forcibly and extend legs to gain distance.

Land on both feet with weight carrying forward.

Score

The measurement is made to that part of the body closest to the take-off line. The jumper should walk forward out of the pit or off the mat. The best of three trials is recorded.

RUNNING BROAD JUMP

Equipment

Jumping pit and take-off board; long gymnasium mat if done indoors.

Directions for starting position

Stand far enough away from the take-off board to gain top running speed by the time you reach it.

Action

Run at top speed to gain maximum momentum.

Take off from board on one foot without breaking stride. Body weight should be directly over the jumping foot.

As you spring, throw arms forcibly forward above the head, and extend the legs forward in walking action.

Land on both feet at the same time with body in a forward direction.

Score

The measurement is taken at the mark made closest to the take-off board. The best of three trials is recorded.

STANDING HOP-STEP AND JUMP

Equipment

Jumping pit or long gymnasium mat if done indoors. Starting line sufficiently behind the pit or the mat to allow ample distance for the hop-step.

Directions for starting position

Stand on one foot, toe back of starting line, other foot up and not touching the ground.

Action

Hop forward on standing foot—one long hop; step forward on other foot—one long step.

Jump forward, extending legs, and land on both feet.

(The hop and step follow each other in quick succession to give momentum to the jump. In landing, the weight of the body should be forward to increase the distance and avoid falling back.)

Score

Measure distance from starting line to the heel or part of the body that finishes nearest the starting line.

Procedures for administering other events are self-explanatory. Selection of events should be made on the basis of the needs and interests of the children in a particular school, and the available space and equipment. See page 270 for an illustrative layout of area.

Track and Field Meets

In many elementary schools, modified track and field meets are the central attraction at end-of-school festivities, such as the annual school picnic or a basket supper held for entire families.

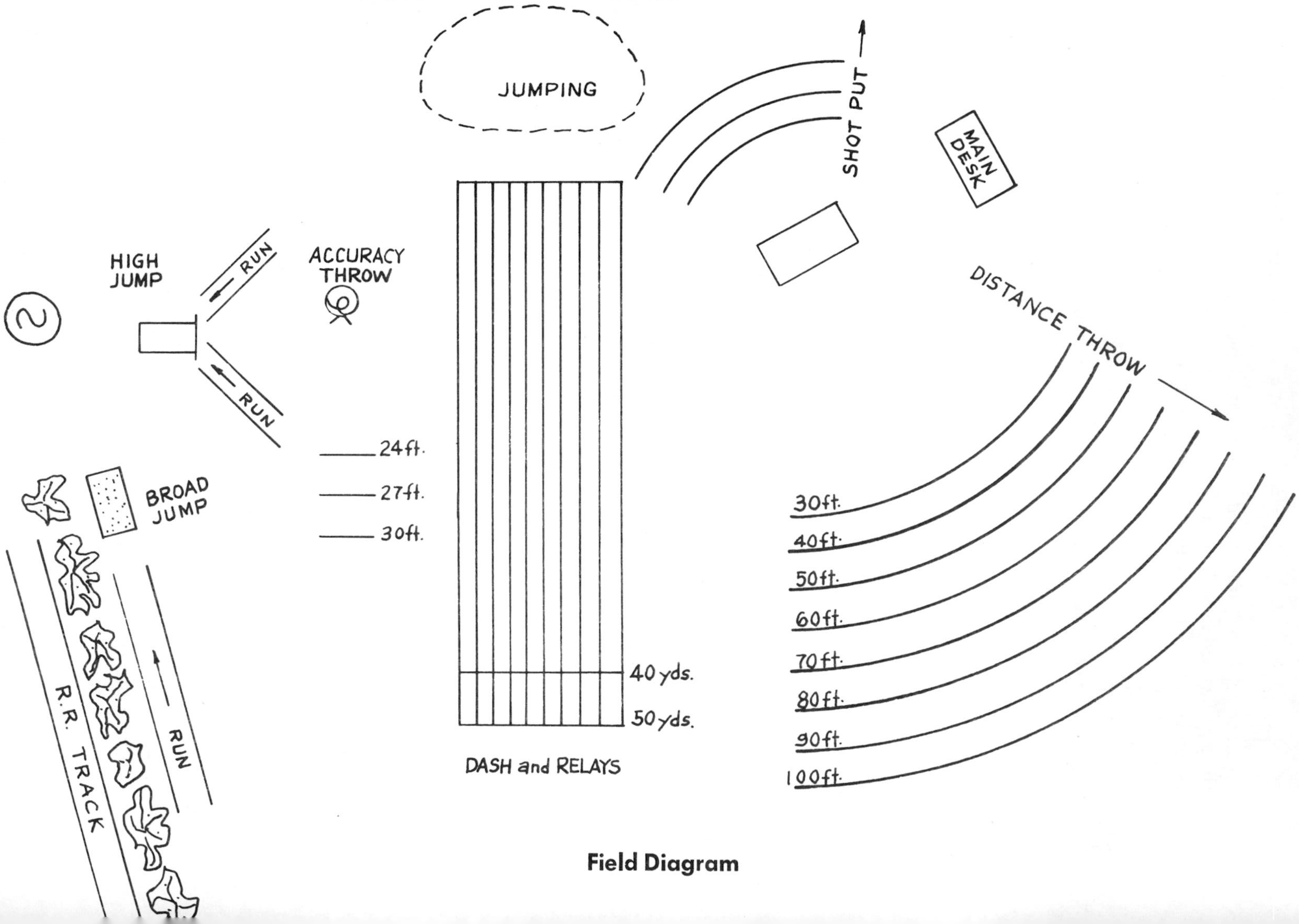

Field Diagram

MAIN DESK

DISTANCE THROW

SHOT PUT

30ft. 40ft. 50ft. 60ft. 70ft. 80ft. 90ft. 100ft.

JUMPING

40 yds.
50 yds.

DASH and RELAYS

ACCURACY THROW

24 ft.
27 ft.
30 ft.

HIGH JUMP

RUN   RUN

BROAD JUMP

RUN

R.R. TRACK

②

In some communities, track and field meets are organized for the intermediate-grade children of all the schools. Frequently, a track and field meet is arranged as a culminating activity in physical education and is held either during regular class time or after school.

Whatever the situation, desirable competition for intermediate-grade children in track and field events requires classification of children and selection of activities suited to their development. It is generally accepted that such competitive events are not suited to the needs and interests of primary-grade children. If they are in attendance at the festivities mentioned above, treasure hunts, games, and other suitable activities should be planned for them.

Classification of Children

The Neilson-Cozens Classification Index[5] provides a sound basis for classifying children 10 years of age and older for competition in a track and field meet. However for preadolescent children either an age or grade basis provides a satisfactory basis. When possible, a system of establishing levels of ability is preferable to either of the above. In preliminary practice, children establish records in the various events. The meet is then organized similarly to a golf tournament in which handicaps are established. For example, entrants for the high jump event, regardless of age or sex, would be classified on the basis of previous best records and on class performance, as follows:

Class A	3 feet 6 inches to 4 feet and over
Class B	3 feet to 3 feet 6 inches
Class C	2 feet 6 inches to 3 feet
Class D	2 feet to 2 feet 6 inches

Classifications for other events would be established similarly— on the basis of the range of scores established in a group. Since it is the usual practice to limit the number of events children can enter in a meet to two or three, they would make their selection

[5] American Association for Health, Physical Education, and Recreation, *Youth Fitness Test Manual.* Washington, D.C., 1958. See also Winifred Van Hagen, Genevie Dexter, and Jesse Feiring Williams, *Physical Education for Elementary Schools.* Sacramento: California State Department of Education, 1951.

on the basis of demonstrated ability for specific classes of each event.

Organization of Meet

A steering committee composed of children and teachers should be responsible for organizing and conducting a track and field meet. Teams containing an equal number of children from each age, height, or weight group or ability level provide a satisfactory basis for competition. The use of teams shifts the emphasis from individual to group scores and accentuates the "we" spirit of the day. By limiting the number of entries and scheduling a sufficient number of events, all children can be given a chance to participate. If there are children who do not wish to compete, they may serve as official starters, timers, and scorers. Such a track meet, run for and by the children, can provide them with a variety of valuable developmental experiences.

Selected References

Braithwaite, Molly, *Medau Rhythmic Movement*. London: The Associated Press Ltd., 1955.

Bresnahan, George T., W. W. Tuttle, and Francis N. Cretzmeyer, *Track and Field Athletics*. St. Louis: The C. V. Mosby Company, 1960.

Carlquist, Maja, and Tora Amylong, *Balance and Rhythm in Exercise*. New York: The Viking Press, Inc., 1951.

Diem, Liselott, *Who Can*. Frankfort A. M./Germany: Wilhelm Limpert Publisher, 1955. (Copyright U.S.A. by George Williams College, Chicago, 1957.)

Horne, Virginia Lee, *Stunts and Tumbling for Girls*. New York: A. S. Barnes & Company, Inc., 1943.

Ministry of Education, *Physical Education in the Primary School*. London: Her Majesty's Stationery Office, 1952.

Morison, Ruth, *Educational Gymnastics*. Liverpool, England: I. M. Marsh College of Physical Education, 1956.

Munden, I., *Suggestions for Use of Small Apparatus*, rev. ed. London: Physical Education Association of Great Britain and Northern Ireland, 1949.

Rodgers, Martin, *A Handbook of Stunts*. New York: The Macmillan Company, 1928.

U.S. Navy, *Gymnastics and Tumbling*. Annapolis, Maryland: U.S. Naval Institute, 1944.

Van Hagen, Winifred, Genevie Dexter, and Jesse Feiring Williams, *Physical Education in Elementary Schools*. Sacramento: California State Department of Education, 1951.

CHAPTER 11

Games

CHAPTERS 3 AND 4 HAVE DISCUSSED THE PLANNING of the physical education program and have pointed out how important it is to select the best learning experiences from the variety available. In this chapter, approximately one hundred games, carefully selected from several hundred, are described. All are written in a direct and simple style. The descriptions are meant to be read by children; indeed, some have actually been written by children.[1] This is done so that the children may integrate reading for meaning in language arts and preparation for play in physical education.

Experiment and experience have taught the authors that this integration of reading and playing also contributes to the child's ability in self-direction. After reading the descriptions as written, the class usually is able to play the game with little or no additional direction, apparently obtaining a clear picture of how to play. However, if the teacher is used to detailed statements of the rules (as in the official rule books of football, baseball, and other

[1] Game descriptions marked with an asterisk (*) were written by children in the Cleveland Heights schools under the direction of Louise Kent Hale.

adult sports) these descriptions will seem to him oversimplified, and may leave some of his questions unanswered. He will find additional information in *Notes for the Teacher* at the end of the game description, and if more rules are needed, the teacher and class may work them out as they play. It is well to remember that a few basic rules, strictly observed, work better than a large number, which the child has difficulty in remembering and therefore tends to disregard.

This method of reading descriptions and then playing the game does not mean that the teacher relinquishes control of the situation to the children. On the contrary, his function is extremely important: to guide that complex of educative processes that goes into a game situation, to see to it that the game is well played, and to ensure the fullest possible use of the educative resources that are thereby presented.

The game descriptions are divided into two groups: the first is intended for the primary grades; the second for the intermediate grades. Within each section, games are arranged alphabetically. Each section is preceded by two charts, one classifying games according to difficulty and type, the other according to special use. A glance at the type-and-difficulty chart for the primary grades will show that introductory circle games such as Cat and Rat, and large group games such as Hill Dill, are easy enough for the first few lessons. Thus, reading across the chart will help the teacher to plan for variety; reading down will guide him in planning the best sequence.

Selecting Games

In selecting a game, it is important that the teacher ask himself whether it is difficult enough to interest his class and ensure some development without being so difficult as to be frustrating. Can the children in his room read and understand the directions? Follow them? Have they developed sufficient motor skill to keep action going well? Will the game help them to develop skills needed for such seasonal games as softball, soccer, and basketball, which they may be playing, in modified form, in the intermediate grades? Useful helps in selecting games will be found by reviewing the section "Materials for Planning" in Chapter 3.

The teacher should ask himself, in addition, whether his class is capable of the kind of group action the game requires, and whether it will provide emotional release without putting undue pressure on children's powers of emotional control. Finally, the children themselves should have a share in choosing the games they want to play. They may understand that certain games help them to run faster, to get stronger, to develop particular skills. Most important to them, however, is the element of enjoyment, which it will reward the teacher to analyze.

Reading Game Descriptions

When a game is chosen before the day on which it is to be played, it is usually possible to have the description duplicated in the principal's or superintendent's office so that each child may have a copy. Any new words appearing in the description should be taught before children are asked to read it; in a surprisingly short time, they will be ready to play. If there are no facilities for duplicating, the class may choose one member to read the description aloud, preferably just before going to the gymnasium. This is a valuable use of the time set aside to practice "reading for meaning"; and because children are eager to play, they listen well. Moreover, as a result of the reading, children seem to accept the game as their own and to assume responsibility for organizing it themselves.

Teaching Different Types of Games

Introductory circle games. The primary value of introductory circle games is that they get a new class accustomed to a group situation and develop a "we" feeling in the group. As each child sees that everyone else is following definite rules, he is helped to make that adjustment himself. The teacher plays with the group to make sure that the rules are understood by all, accepted by all, and obeyed to the best of each child's ability. Forming a circle is the first skill to be learned. The easiest method is to have the children follow the teacher around as he leads into a circle. The game should begin even if the circle is not perfect; it can be improved as they play. After this has been done two or three times, a child may be asked to lead into a circle. Joining hands should be avoided at first, because this is often the occasion for individual push-and-pull contests. Game action should be kept going as rapidly as possible, and stalling or the endless chase should be prevented by having the class count out loud to ten. At that signal the game is stopped, and new runners and chasers are selected. Although every child wants the satisfaction of being "it," the game should not continue until each has had that chance. A better way of giving more chances is to form more groups— several small circles out of one large one.

Small group games. As soon as children can play without direct, continuous help from the teacher, small group games should be used. For example, if thirty-six children have played Cat and Rat in one circle, the teacher may divide them into three circles of twelve. Not only will they get more activity; they will also have more opportunities for direct social interactions. Steps in starting small group play may be summarized as follows:

1. The game is learned in a large group.

2. The teacher divides the large group into several small ones.

3. The teacher designates runners and chasers, and makes clear when the game is to begin.

4. The teacher does not play with any one group, but is ready to help all.

5. Leaders are selected as soon as groups are ready. The leader's function is merely to keep the game going, making changes without delay.

As children become accustomed to working with one another, they also become capable of greater self-direction. They may select their leaders and go to the group of their choice; each group may decide to play a different game. The teacher does not "abdicate," but helps each group to organize its own play and resolve its own difficulties.

Large group games. Even after children have learned to play in both small and large groups the large group games continue to have value. Large groups provide excellent opportunities for teaching beginning strategy, appreciation of skills, and respect for rules, if the teacher brings out these points in the discussion. In Red Light, for example, the teacher's question might be, "Who knows why Jimmie came in first?" (The answer might be that he was able to start and stop quickly, was always ready, obeyed the rules.) After such points have been made, many of the large group games may well be played in small groups.

Simple team games. Simple two-team games, such as Brownies and Fairies, may be used to introduce the idea of "sides" and of group competition. Later, in Trades, the members of each team go into a huddle to decide what occupation they will represent and how they will pantomime it. The teacher reinforces these learnings by speaking of the sides as "teams" and by giving them a chance to talk over their own play. As the team spirit grows, scorekeeping becomes preferable to having children change from one team to another when caught. And as teams and games become more highly organized, the need for team discussion and for definite leadership by captains increases.

Relays. As soon as children can grasp the idea of racing for a team and not as individuals against other individuals, relays, the next step in team development, should be taught. Relay teams are small and often have a permanent membership. If the class is ready, captains may be elected from the whole group and choose their teams from the class list after school. Even in a simple file relay, the captain may use the huddle to discuss how to stand when waiting to be tagged, how to avoid penalties, how to turn quickly and finish at top speed. If it is desired, teacher and class may make up relays, supplementing those described in the text. In the primary grades such simple skills as change of direction and handling balls of different sizes will be called for. In the intermediate grades more advanced skills may be required. For example, shuttle and zigzag relays emphasize weight handling and dodging; a bounce ball relay develops skill in dribbling. As children improve in these skills, a zigzag dribbling relay might be developed. The function of relays is to promote team spirit and add a contest element to skill practice; their use should not be extended beyond this function.

Problems in game skills. An excellent practice device or work session to be used at the beginning of the game lesson is a problem in game skills. The children will soon learn to make their own practice patterns to meet their individual needs, but they will need the teacher's suggestions to make greatest improvement in practice.

Advanced team games. These games are modifications of the seasonal games played later in junior or senior high school: (1) equipment is adapted to the size and strength of fifth- and sixth-grade children; (2) rules and organization are simplified to suit the social and motor development of children in this age group; (3) competition is kept at the children's level rather than having an adult pattern unsuited to the degree of emotional maturity they have achieved. The importance of providing enough experience with the proper sequence of preparatory games has already been pointed out.

Individual games. Deck tennis, tether ball, and other individual games are very important for recreational purposes. They may be taught in a large class by demonstration and practiced in small groups. For example, a class of forty sixth-grade boys and girls may be divided into five squads, each playing a different game:

Squad	Game
1	5–3–1 Basketball
2	Deck Tennis
3	Tether Ball
4	Paddle Ball
5	Four Square

Each squad is responsible for reading about, playing, and demonstrating one of these games. On the first day, the teacher helps to get all the games going well. On the second day, the same game is played by each squad for the first part of the period. Then half the members of each squad continue to play the game they know, demonstrating it. The others move on to the next game in line: Squad 1 to deck tennis, Squad 2 to tether ball, and so on, in order to watch the demonstration of that game. They then try the new game while the other members of their squad move up to watch them. The number of periods that elapse before the next rotation depends upon how well the squads learn the games and how challenging they find them. Other individual games may be added later.

Recreational games. These include many individual and small group games. They should be taught in such a way that they will be played at recess, at home, and on the playground. This involves helping children to become self-directing in their playing, to know how to start games, what equipment is needed, and where to find rules and directions. It may involve their writing about topics such as "My Favorite Game" or "A Good Game for a Party." It will surely involve emphasizing the element of enjoyment.

Focus on purpose in a game situation.

Aggressive action games. Such games are used as a safety valve to help children let off steam while staying within the limits of acceptable conduct. The teacher should take children out of doors or to some place where they will not disturb other classes. Action should be fast, and everyone should be active. Toward the end of the period, mass racing on the field—changing direction at one whistle, stopping at two—repeated often enough, will tire children out and bring them in relaxed.

Primary Games

ANIMAL CHASE

Sometimes, when we are all in a large circle, our teacher holds up a ball. "What Animal is this?" he asks us. We say "Rabbit," or "Dog," or "Kitty." Then he starts it around the circle, and we try to see how fast it can go. Anyone who drops it has to pick it up. When the ball gets back to the teacher, he sends it around again. Then he holds up another ball and says, "Here is a Fox, chasing the Kitty." The Fox goes around the circle, too. Next time around, the teacher starts a Wolf. We help each Animal chase the others. If any Animal catches the one in front of it, the one that is caught is left out of the chase.

If we are good at watching and catching, we do not drop any Animal. Sometimes we have four going around at once.

Notes for the teacher: In the early days of the first grade, this game will give the children a sense of belonging to a large group and of doing just what the rules say. Obviously, it also gives considerable practice in manipulating balls or beanbags, which might be used the first time. The children enjoy this game, but it has a deservedly short life.

BALLOON BATTLE*

This is the most fun. We roll newspapers and make bats. Then we blow up penny balloons. The balloons are tied on our backs. Two boys play it best because they are not afraid of swatting the other boy. When the whistle blows, we start. We try to break the other boy's balloon and he tries to break ours. We have to step lively. When our balloon breaks, we sit down. The last battle of two decides who wins. I like this game. I was the winner.

Notes for the teacher: Obviously this is a party game, or at least should be used only when noise is invited. Better have a penalty for hitting another player's head.

PRIMARY GAMES
Classified According to Difficulty and Special Use

Recreational: Recess, After School, and Home	Aggressive Action	Schoolroom
Follow the Leader		Follow the Leader
Hill Dill		
Birds Fly		Birds Fly
		Busy Bee
Midnight		Bird Catcher
Brownies and Fairies		Queen Dido Is Dead
Uncle Sam		
Trades	Bull in the Pen	
Three Deep		
Halloween Witch		Halloween Witch
	White Bear	Number Relay
Home Run	Old Plug	Tag the Goal Relay
	Free Dodgeball	
	Balloon Battle	
	Jungle Hunt	
	Jump the Shot	
Bat Ball		

PRIMARY GAMES
Classified According to Difficulty* and Type

Introductory Circle	Small Group	Large Group	Two Sides, Mass Play	Simple Team Games
Cat and Rat		Follow the Leader		
Garden Scamp		Hill Dill†		
Duck, Duck, Goose	Jump the Creek	Birds Fly		
Animal Chase	Tiger in the Cage	Busy Bee		
	Midnight	Bird Catcher		
	Center Base	Queen Dido Is Dead	Brownies and Fairies	
		Fire Engine		
	Magic Carpet	Stop the Music	Run, Rabbit, Run	
		Mickey Mouse	Strike and Chase	
		Uncle Sam		
	Bull in the Pen	Three Deep	Trades	
	Chain Tag	Halloween Witch		
		Circle Chase	Fish Net	
		White Bear	Touchdown	Number Relay
	Old Plug			
		Forest Lookout	Home Run	Tag the Goal Relay
	Balloon Battle	Free Dodgeball		Boundary Ball
		Chinese Wall		
		Jungle Hunt		Indian Twirl
		Jump the Shot		Newcomb
				Bat Ball
				Hit, Bounce, and Catch
				First Bounce or Fly

* The easier games appear at the top of each column.
† Variation of Pom, Pom, Pullaway.

BAT BALL*

I think that Bat Ball is the best game ever. It is packed with fun and excitement. I'm sure you would like to know how to play it—here are the directions.

There are two teams of six to eight players, and each team has a captain. One captain arranges his men in the field, putting the best men in the back. The other captain arranges the batting order.

The first man up bats by throwing a soccer ball or playground ball up in the air and hitting it with his hand. If the ball goes over the outside line, it is a strike. Each batter gets three strikes, and each team gets three outs.

A line is drawn across the field 6 feet from the batter's box—the place where the batter stands. If the ball does not go over this line, it is a strike. If it does go over this line, it is a fair ball.

As soon as he has hit a fair ball, the batter runs to the end of the gym, touches the wall, and then tries to run back to home base without being hit by the ball. If he can do this, he scores a point for his team.

The fielding team tries to catch the ball hit by the batter and to throw it at him before he can reach home base. If it hits him below the shoulders, he is out. If it hits him above the shoulders, his team gets a point. The team with the most points wins.

Notes for the teacher: As soon as your class is ready, use basketball rules in fielding the ball: no running with the ball; no taking it away from another player; no holding beyond the count of five. This is an excellent game for developing team passing to head off the runner. Let the class work out this strategy in team huddles.

BIRD CATCHER

A Mother Bird is in her Nest in one corner of the gym. Two or three Bird Catchers stand between the Nest and a Cage, which is marked off in another corner. The rest of us are different kinds of Birds, flying around in the Forest. Some are Robins, some are Bluebirds, some are Wrens, and so on.

When the Mother Bird calls out, "Bluebirds!" all the Bluebirds fly for the Nest, and the Bird Catchers try to tag them before they get there. When a bird is tagged, he goes to the Cage. But if he gets to the Nest before he is tagged, he is safe. After each kind of Bird has been called, the game begins again with a new Mother Bird and new Bird Catchers.

Notes for the teacher: This game provides considerable activity in a small space. It may be played in the schoolroom or playroom as well as in the gymnasium or on the playground. Only three or four kinds of birds should be specified.

BIRDS FLY*

There is a leader in front of the children. He calls out things that can fly and things that cannot fly—for example, "Birds fly," and "Lions fly." When the leader speaks, he *always* raises his hands. If any children raise their hands when the leader names something that cannot fly, those children sit down. The child who stands up longest is the winner.

Things that fly: Chickens fly, turkeys fly, airplanes fly, birds fly, blue jays fly, ducks fly, cardinals fly, clouds fly, butterflies fly, bluebirds fly, mosquitoes fly, flies fly, bees fly, orioles fly, zeppelins fly, catbirds fly, house wrens fly.

Funny things that do not fly: Lions fly, elephants fly, dogs fly, arithmetic flies, trees fly, houses fly, horses fly, pigs fly, cows fly, stars fly, flowers fly, pictures fly, tongues fly, beds fly, desks fly, boys fly, girls fly, teachers fly.

Notes for the teacher: A fine schoolroom game, useful whenever the class seems restless. You may have to be the leader at first, but the children can take over very soon. Sometimes the things they think of will be limited and the game dull, but more often their imagination will give everyone a good time.

BOUNDARY BALL

We play this game with two teams. Each team tries to roll the ball across the other team's goal line. Each time this happens, it counts one point for the team that rolled the ball. The other team tries to stop the ball, run with it to the center line, and roll it across their opponents' goal line. Sometimes we play with two or even four balls, and then you have to look everywhere to stop those balls. Here is a picture of the players and the field:

There are many things to remember:

1. Roll the ball—do not throw it. If it crosses the goal line without touching the ground, it does not count, but is given to the other side to play.

2. Do not let the ball go over the side lines. If it does, the game stops until the nearest player gets it and brings it back. The team that did not send it out gets the ball at the center line.

3. If you stop the ball near your own goal line, you may run up to the center and roll it toward the other goal line. But sometimes it is quicker to pass the ball to one of your players near the center line.

Notes for the teacher: Use a volleyball, utility ball, soccer ball, or any ball that can readily be handled by the children. This game is one of the simplest versions of a team game in which each team shoots at the opponents' goal and defends its own. Its introduction depends on the maturity and experience of the group. Late in the second grade or early in the third is probably a good time to try it. Be sure to get evaluation of skill and strategy from the children, during the game as well as at the end of class.

BROWNIES AND FAIRIES

Two teams play this game. One team is called Brownies, and the other is called Fairies. Each team has the same number of players. One player on each team is chosen as a Lookout. He does not turn his back, but watches the other team.

Each team stands behind a goal line at opposite ends of the gymnasium. First the Fairies turn their backs to the Brownies and cover their eyes with their hands. The Brownies go toward the Fairies on tiptoe. When they are almost there, the Fairy Lookout calls, "Look out for the Brownies!" and then the Fairies chase the Brownies back to their goal line. If any Brownies are caught, they have to go with the Fairies and play on their team.

After this, the Brownies turn their backs, and the Fairies tiptoe toward them. When the game is over, the players on each team are counted. The team with more players wins.

Notes for the teacher: The charm of this game for young children undoubtedly lies in its suspense, followed by the dramatic shout of danger and the sudden chase. Certainly children will play it endlessly if allowed to. The game is useful in developing the concept of two groups playing aganst each other. Play it a few times in class, to teach it, and then let the children play it at recess.

BULL IN THE PEN

We make a circle with one player, the Bull, in the center. We all join hands with a good firm grip, because the Bull is going to try to break the circle by running through it. If he can do this, he runs as fast as he can, and we run as fast as we can right after him. Whoever catches him is the Bull the next time we play.

Notes for the teacher: Be sure that *catching* in this game is understood to be just *tagging*. Perhaps it is the aggressive nature of the game which leads children to grabbing and tackling the fugitive. If this happens, try pointing out that these tactics slow up the game and that all will have more fun if they get back to the circle quickly. Watch for the child who hangs back when the more vigorous children start the chase. Encourage him to run and to head off the Bull if the latter doubles back.

BUSY BEE*

We learned this game last year but we still like it. First you take partners. One boy is the leader. He says, "Face to face," and we face. Then he says, "Back to back," and we turn our backs to each other. He keeps on saying these things. Some leaders try to catch us by saying "Face to face" when we are face to face. Then the leader says, "Busy Bee." We all have to change partners. We take hands with our partners at first and then the game begins again.

It is the most fun when we play with one extra child. There is always some child left out and he has to come to the center. He is the "slowpoke." No one likes to be that, so we try hard to get partners. The teacher keeps track of whether there are more "slowpoke" boys or "slowpoke" girls when we play. That is when it is fun.

> *Notes for the teacher:* For those of you who are interested in words and their derivations, "Busy Bee" is obviously a corruption of "vis-à-vis," but it surely makes more 'sense in our classrooms than the original.

> If you have withdrawn or anxious children in your room who are always a bit slow, and so get labeled "slowpokes," it is better to play this game with even numbers. Join in yourself if they need you.

CAT AND RAT*

We love to play Cat and Rat. In this game everyone joins hands and makes a circle. Two children are chosen. One is the Cat; the other is the Rat. The Cat is outside the circle. The Rat is inside looking out.

The Cat says, "*I* am the *Cat!*" The Rat says, "*I* am the *Rat!*" The Cat says, "I will *catch* you!" The Rat says, "Oh *no, you won't!*" Then the fun begins.

The Cat tries to catch the Rat. We hold up our hands to help the Rat through, but we stoop down when the Cat tries to go under our hands. If the Rat is too quick, we choose two Cats to chase him.

When the Rat is caught, he and the Cat choose two new ones. Then we play again. We never get tired of playing this game.

> *Notes for the teacher:* When there are two Cats—and as soon as the game is learned this is a good variation—give the children a chance to think of offensive strategy. Unless they are helped to think about what the Cats can do, one will trail the other without adding to anything except the noise. But as soon as they perceive that one might go one way while the other heads off the Rat by

going the other way, they have learned the first lesson of strategy. You will have to decide how much noise you want in this game, because the possibilities are limitless. Pointing out that the children are trying to help the Rat, and that if they scream they will frighten it so that it cannot think of how to get away, will help to keep the noise down.

CENTER BASE

For this game we make a circle with one of us in the center, holding a ball. He throws the ball to someone in the circle. As soon as he has thrown it, he starts to run away. The one who catches the ball takes it to the center of the circle, puts it down, and then chases the runner. The runner tries to get back to touch the ball without being tagged. If he does, he may choose the next runner, but if he is tagged, then the catcher does the choosing.

Notes for the teacher: If the children take too long to choose a runner, it may be best to do it yourself. This game does not give much chance for activity, and is used to get first graders accustomed to playing in a group. If it is played in a number of small circles after it has been learned, more children have a chance to be active.

CHAIN TAG

All of us except two chasers are in little chains of three players. We make our chains just by holding hands, but we must hold tight or the chain will be broken. The two players who are not in a chain try to catch the end players in any chain. If this happens, the one who is tagged becomes a chaser, the chaser becomes the middle man of the chain, and the middle man moves to the end. If any chain breaks, the middle man must change places with one of the chasers.

Notes for the teacher: This game will provide a great deal of activity if the chasers are on their toes. If necessary, use more than one chaser. In a very small group, however, one chaser is enough. If the middle player deliberately breaks the chain, show him how he can make the chain stronger by taking a wrist grip. Call time occasionally and let all the players shake their hands to rest them.

CHINESE WALL

We like Chinese Wall because it has so much running in it. The field has two end lines and two other lines, about 10 feet apart, that go across the middle. The space between the two lines in the middle is called the Chinese Wall.

Two players stand on the Wall to defend it. The rest of us are behind one end line. When the whistle blows, we try to cross the Wall and reach the other end line. The players in the middle try to tag us while we are going over the Wall, but they cannot leave the Wall or touch us while we are in free territory outside the Wall. Anyone who is tagged while on the Wall has to become a Defender.

Each runner keeps his own score. He gets one point every time he crosses the Wall and reaches the end line he is running for. He does not have to wait for a whistle to turn and start back across the Wall, but once he leaves the end line he cannot go back to it. When everyone has been caught, the game is over. If there is time, we add up our scores, and the two with the highest score start on the Wall in a new game.

After we knew this game pretty well, we tried playing it with a buddy. At the start we all got partners, and then we played with the partner. We could run together if we wanted to, but we soon found that that made it easier to catch us. If one of us got tagged, the other had to go on the Wall, too. So then we ran separately, and each tried to help his buddy get across. We had the same score as our buddy, which was the lower score of the two. Sometimes we could help our buddy by fooling the Defenders, but we had to think up new ways of doing this all the time. Try it for yourself, and see how you would help *your* partner.

Notes for the teacher: The "buddy" version of this game is very popular, and it encourages strategic play. Let the children make their own choices, observing changes in the social structure of the class. Watch out for those who are rejected, and help the ones who do not find partners.

CIRCLE CHASE

The first thing we do is draw a large circle on the gym floor. Then we all take our places just outside the circle, facing the same way. There should be plenty of space between players, and the spaces should be even. You will see why, in a minute.

When the signal is given, everyone runs around the circle as fast as he can, trying to tag the player ahead of him. When he is tagged, a player must drop out. Be sure to listen while running, because if the whistle blows, everyone turns quickly and runs in the opposite direction.

When the whistle blows twice, the game stops. All the players come back into the circle, and those who have been running all the time get their breath before the next game begins.

Notes for the teacher: It is a good idea to make two or even three circles in order to give the children room to run. Make sure of the spacing before you start. Because timing the whistles is very important, it is better to control this game yourself than to have a child as the leader. Have children change direction once or twice, but do not keep them running too long. During the second game, put all those who were tagged in one circle, and all the faster runners in a second circle.

The following is a good variation for a large group in a single circle: Have the group count off by threes or fours. When the leader calls, "Threes, left!" all having that number run to the left, each trying to tag the player in front of him. The leader can add suspense by calling two numbers at the same time, both running in the same direction, of course; or by changing from one direction to another on successive calls.

DUCK, DUCK, GOOSE

All of us stand in a circle except one player, who is It. He runs around the outside of the circle, touching each player as he goes by. As he touches the other players, he says, "Duck, Duck, Duck," and then, when he wants to, he calls out, "Goose!" The player who is the Goose chases the one who is It around the circle, trying to tag him before he reaches the Goose's empty place.

The winner chooses the new It, but if it takes him too long to decide, the teacher chooses instead.

Notes for the teacher: An introductory circle game, to be used only a few times in one large circle. Then, if it goes well, it can be played in smaller circles of eight or ten children.

FIRE ENGINE

We play this game in teams, with four on a team. Each player has a number: One, Two, Three, or Four. We all stand on a home line, and there is a Fire Line on the opposite side of the playground.

In front of all the players stands a Fire Chief. Watch him, because he may give your signal to run to the Fire Line. First he claps his hands: once, twice, three times, or four times. If he claps his hands twice, and your number is Two, get ready, because when he calls "Fire," you and all the other Twos will run to the Fire Line and back home. The one who gets back first is the next Fire Chief. Sometimes the Fire Chief calls, "General Alarm—Fire!" Then everyone runs to the Fire Line and home, and the fastest runner in the whole class is the next Chief.

Notes for the teacher: This is a good game to use as a transition from individual to team games. Start as described, and then change the reward for winning to scoring for one's team. After the same Fire Chief has called all four numbers, with a general alarm thrown in for good measure, have the teams count up their scores. Then begin the game again, with a new Chief. This may lead to relay races, in which the children do not wait to start with their opposite on the other teams but run as soon as they are touched off. You will have to decide whether a group of children is ready for this transition or not. Let the children have two or three tries at the more advanced group competition. If they accept it easily, they are ready; if they keep reverting to individual races, do not force the new step.

FIRST BOUNCE OR FLY*

Three playground balls and three indoor bats are necessary for this game. There are three sets of players, with nine players in each set. Each player has a number. The first batter has the number One, the catcher Two, the pitcher Three, and the fielders have numbers from Four to Nine.

The fielders scatter on the field. The catcher stands on the foul line and the first batter stands about 3 feet in front of him. The pitcher is 25 feet or less from the catcher.

The object of the game is simply this. The pitcher tosses an underhand pitch to the batter. The batter tries to hit every ball into the field in front of the foul line. The fielders try to catch it on the first bounce or fly. (That is how the game gets its name, I suppose.) When a batter misses a fair pitch (between the shoulder and the knee), or when the catcher or the fielders catch the ball, the batter is through. His score is the number of hits he makes.

Now the batter (One) becomes a fielder (Nine). The catcher (Two) becomes the next batter, and the pitcher (Three) takes the catcher's place. Every child has a chance to play in every position. The boy or girl who has the highest score wins.

> *Notes for the teacher:* In this description three games are going on at once. If there are more than twenty-seven in your class, and if you have enough equipment, it is better to have more games than to increase the size of each group. The batter rotates out to the last fielder's place, while the first fielder (Four) comes in to pitch. This rotation is good preparation for Work Up.

FISH NET

In this game we play on teams. First, each team chooses a captain. One team is the Net, the other is the Fish. At the start, we stand behind our goal lines at opposite ends of the playground, facing each other.

The Net team has its hands joined, and must keep them that way, but the Fish run free.

When the leader says "Go!" both teams run toward the center. The Net tries to catch as many Fish as possible by making a circle around them. The Fish try to get out of the opening before the Net closes. They cannot go through the Net by going under the arms of the players, but if the Net breaks because the players let go of each other's hands, the Fish can go through that opening until the hands are joined again.

The Fish are safe if they get to the opposite goal line without being caught in the circle. When the Net has made its circle, the captain counts the number of Fish inside, and tells the leader the score. The leader adds a point for each Fish that has gone out of the Net by going under the arms of the players.

Then we play again, but this time the teams change. The Fish team is now the Net team, and the team that was the Net is now the Fish. When each side has had a chance to be the Net three times, the game is over, and the leader tells us which team had the highest score for all three times.

Notes for the teacher: Let the children go into a huddle to talk over their play and decide on their strategy. See whether they can figure out that offensive strategy demands that the ends of the Net start running toward each other as soon as they are in motion, and that the Net must vary its direction instead of running straight down the middle each time. Defensive strategy, of course, means running along both side lines at top speed.

FOLLOW THE LEADER*

This game is lots of fun when the leader can think of many stunts to do. We all follow him in a long line, and each of us has to do whatever he does and go wherever he goes. When he does the Duck Walk, we do it, too. Some of the other things we do are walking on tiptoe, walking on all fours, jumping, moving our arms, and walking like Popeye the Sailor Man. Sometimes we have two or three lines and leaders. We even do tricks when the music plays.

Notes for the teacher: This is a good game for trying out some of the things children have invented in movement exploration.

FOREST LOOKOUT

For this game we form a double circle, all facing the Lookout, who stands in the center. Players in the inside circle are Trees, and players on the outside are Fire Fighters.

The Lookout calls, "Fire in the forest, run, run, RUN!" He claps his hands on the last "Run," and all the Fire Fighters run as fast as they can around the outside of the circle. This gives the Lookout a chance to step in front of one of the Trees, who are all standing still. As soon as a Fire Fighter sees him do this, he stops running and steps in front of another Tree. When everyone has stopped running, one Fire Fighter won't have a tree. He goes into the center and is the new Lookout.

Now the Trees are on the outside, and so they are the Fire Fighters in the new game. The Fire Fighters are on the inside, and so they are Trees in the new game. As soon as the circle has moved out from the center, the new Lookout starts the game again.

> *Notes for the teacher:* Start with a large circle, so that the Fire Fighters will have room to run. Moving back each time is necessary for the same reason. This game teaches children to be alert to changes in the general pattern of things. If the Lookout varies the time before he moves into the circle, it makes a more interesting and valuable game for the runners.

FREE DODGEBALL

This is a fine game for throwing and dodging, and no one has to wait for a turn to play.

Our captains take two big bags of balls and all our shoulder bands to the gym. They leave these things in front, and we scatter all over the room. One player puts on a band and takes a ball. When the whistle blows, he throws the ball at anyone near him. We all move about, watching the ball so that we won't get hit. If anyone is hit below the shoulders, he gets a ball and puts on a shoulder band. Then he throws, too. Soon we have lots of balls to watch, and it is hard to keep from getting hit. The last one to be hit starts the next game as the first man with the ball.

Any thrower who hits a dodger above the shoulders has to turn in his ball and shoulder band and sit out the rest of that game. A thrower has to get his ball back after he has thrown it.

> *Notes for the teacher:* This active, aggressive game should be played with soft rubber balls (utility balls) for obvious reasons. Keep a record of the time it takes for everyone to be put out. This is a rough record of improvement in children's skill in handling the ball.

GARDEN SCAMP

For this game we stand in a circle, holding our neighbors' hands. One player is the Scamp, who is inside the circle. Another is the

Gardener, who is outside. The Gardener walks around the circle, then looks up and sees the Scamp. "Who let you into my garden?" says the Gardener. "No one," says the Scamp, and he begins to run, with the Gardener after him.

The Scamp can run anywhere in and out the circle, but he cannot run away from the circle. He does tricks as he runs: sometimes he crawls between a player's feet; sometimes he runs on all fours. The Gardener has to do whatever the Scamp does, and go wherever the Scamp goes. If he catches the Scamp, two new players take their places. If the Gardener does not do everything the Scamp does, the game stops, and the leader selects a new Gardener.

Notes for the teacher: This game is best played in a small group, just large enough to make a circle. If there are more than twelve players, it is better to have two circles. If the Gardener cannot seem to catch the Scamp, have two new players take their places. If choosing players presents a time-consuming problem for the children, it is better to do it yourself.

HALLOWEEN WITCH*

We went to the gym for a Halloween party. One of the boys wore his sister's rain cape and a pointed hat. We sat in a circle. He stood in the middle and said, "I am the Witch and I am going to change you into things when I hit my broom."

The Witch rode as fast as anything and then stopped and pounded "her" broomstick three times. She yelled, "I change you into Cats!" We meowed and ran like cats. Then she pounded her stick again. If we did not get back to the circle fast enough, she pushed our toes with her broomstick. We laughed, and some of the girls squealed.

When the Witch said, "I change you into Pumpkins," we rolled up and whirled around. We played Ghosts and Bats and Mice. We made jack-o'-lantern faces to scare people, and we walked in funny ways. The game was lots of fun, but we were tired after the party.

Notes for the teacher: If there is to be no party for your grade, it is better to change this description, because it will surely create a demand for one. A gymnasium wand makes a good broomstick.

HIT, BOUNCE, AND CATCH

We have played this game with a bouncing ball, but a big baseball is better. First, we measure off 5 feet from a wall and draw a line on the ground. We do not go in front of this line when playing. Then we draw a line on the wall as high as our knees. When the teacher says, "Go!" we begin to play. We hit the wall above the line with a ball, let it bounce *once*, and catch it. We do this as fast as we can for thirty seconds. Each of us has a scorekeeper who counts the number of times we make a correct throw. At the end of thirty seconds, the teacher stops us and we change with our scorekeeper. If we do not drop our balls by being careless, we can win.

> *Notes for the teacher:* A softball should be used, and it will have to be thrown with full force to bounce and be caught well. This game is a good supplement to the informal practice the children will develop in self-testing. If you want to give children a practical problem in ethics, let them keep their own scores when they are capable of doing so.

HOME RUN

There are two teams in this game, batters and fielders. The fielders have a pitcher and a catcher, but the others play anywhere to cover the field. Usually we have from six to ten players on a side.

We play with a rubber ball and have three bases. The batters line up ready to bat in turn. If a batter misses a ball when the pitcher pitches it to him, the catcher gives him the ball; he bounces it and then bats it out into the field. If he misses that ball, too, he takes it and throws it as far into the field as he can. Then he tries to circle the bases before the fielders can put him out. If he does this, he scores one run. The fielders can put him out in two ways. First, they can catch his ball before it hits the ground. Second, they can throw the ball so that it hits the runner below the shoulders before he gets back to home plate.

When three outs have been made, the teams change. The fielders come in to bat, and the batters go out into the field. This game helps us with baseball.

> *Notes for the teacher:* This is one of the first introductory games for baseball. It gives almost everyone a chance to score, whether he can bat or not, but it also gives him two chances to practice batting. Of course, the field is smaller than a regular baseball diamond. Try 30 feet between bases, cutting that distance down if necessary. In this game, the players should first plan the strategy of heading off the runner, either in team huddles or in class discusssion.

INDIAN TWIRL*

One player is the Indian Chief. He starts the game. There are two goal posts. Sometimes children stand as goals. The children form in teams of four. They join hands with the real Indian grip. To do this you curl your fingers up and lock them into the fingers next to you.

The Indian Chief raises his arms like a cross. When he lets them drop, that is the signal to begin twirling.

Two circles race at a time. Both groups twirl like tops, but they keep moving ahead to get around the goals. No one is allowed to run straight ahead. If you learn to pull just right, this game goes fast. The team of four which gets back first wins. The teacher decides that. All the teams have a chance. The winners have another trial to see which is the champion team.

Rules:

If you break hands, you stop and lock them again. If you fall down, you get up and go on. Everyone has to be careful to stay far enough away from the other team. It is not safe to get too close because the teams go so fast.

We learned this real Indian game in the second grade, but we still like it.

Notes for the teacher: Each team of four makes a circle. Use this game after the children have worked together long enough to be able to make a start on the close cooperation necessary. Use a huddle to give them a chance to talk over their problems and improve their techniques.

JUMP THE CREEK

We like to run and we like to jump—that's why we like this game. We stand in rows behind two lines, as in the picture:

C R E E K

x	x	x	x
x	x	x	x
x	x	x	x
x	x	x	x

The lines are the Creek, and we run and try to jump clear across without getting our feet wet. After the first four children have jumped, they go back to the end of the line and the next ones run and jump. Sometimes we make the Creek wider, and then it is really hard to get across.

Notes for the teacher: At first the children will probably do a leap instead of a jump, and this is good training, too. In a leap the child takes off from one foot, lands on the other foot, and goes right on running. In a jump he takes off from one or two feet and lands on two feet. This game is good preparation for the running broad jump, in which the runner takes off from one foot and lands on two. Tell the children to be sure not to fall backwards into the Creek; if they lose their balance, they should try to fall forward.

JUMP THE SHOT

This game keeps us all watching and jumping. We stand in a circle, with one player in the middle. The center player has a long rope, with a small bag of sand tied to one end. This is the Shot. He swings this rope around the circle, close to the floor, and we have to jump over the Shot. This is easy in the beginning, but when the Shot comes faster and faster it is hard to tell just when to jump. If you guess wrong, the rope hits your legs and stops, and then you have to change places with the center player.

Notes for the teacher: Do not use a large or a heavy Shot, since this might hurt bare legs. The game should be played for a short time only, but it is valuable for detecting, and perhaps improving, a sense of timing.

JUNGLE HUNT

This game gives us a chance to show what good shots we are. There are three Hunters. Each one has a Gun, which is a volleyball. The rest of us are Wild Beasts in the Jungle, which is at the other end of the gym.

When our game leader gives the signal, the Hunters begin shooting, and the Beasts begin running and dodging. The Hunters fire their Guns at us as often as they can before time is up. If any of us are hit below the shoulders, we go off to the side lines. But if a Hunter hits anyone above the shoulders, he has to give up his Gun to the player he hit, who then becomes a Hunter.

When time is up, we count the number of Beasts hit by the Hunters. Then the next team of three Hunters begins the game again. We try to play until everyone has had a chance to be a Hunter.

Notes for the teacher: For this game it is best to use either balls that are not fully inflated or utility balls. In the excitement, the Hunters tend to throw the ball hard. Also, plan ahead of time what to do about the Beasts dead on the floor, because that is what happens every time the children play shooting games on their own. Certainly the play space should be kept clear. Perhaps this is a problem the children can solve themselves after the first round.

Although there is a suggestion of teams in this game, it is not necessary to play or score by teams. In fact, it is not necessary to pay much attention to scores, for the action of the game is satisfying enough. Like Bombardment, it is a fine game for expressing aggression on a day when the whole class is a little out of hand.

KICK DODGEBALL*

This game is played with the same rules as Bat Ball, except for one thing. In Bat Ball the ball is batted, and in Kick Dodgeball it is kicked.

Three kinds of kick are used. These are a *place kick*, a *drop kick*, and a *punt*.

Place Kick: The place kick is done like this. The ball is placed on the floor and one boy puts his finger on top to hold it still. The kicker stands back about 6 feet and runs up to the ball to kick it into the field.

Drop Kick: The drop kick is done like this. The kicker drops the ball from his own hands and kicks it immediately *after* the first bounce.

Punt: The punt is done like this. The kicker drops the ball and kicks it *before* it touches the ground.

Players have three chances to kick the ball when their turn comes, and they may use any kick they prefer. The ball must drop first in the field. If it hits the ceiling or walls, or if it rolls along the floor, it is a foul ball and counts as one trial.

Sometimes we use a football in this game, but we have to be good players before we do that because a football is harder to kick and catch than a soccer ball. I like this game better than Bat Ball because I am a pretty good football player.

MAGIC CARPET

For this game we must draw the Magic Carpets on the floor. These are squares or circles, with some space between them. Then we all join hands in a line. When the music starts, the leader of the line starts to skip. We skip after him, keeping our hands joined and watching out for the Carpets on the floor.

When the music stops, everyone must stop still. All those who are caught on a Carpet have to form a second team, with a new leader.

Both lines start when the music starts again, and the leaders have to be careful to keep them away from each other. When the music stops, those on the first team who are caught on a Carpet go to the second team, but those on the second team who are caught must form a third team. Three teams are enough, and after three teams have played this game once we start over again with everybody on one team.

A good leader takes his team right across the Magic Carpets. This makes the game more fun because someone is sure to be caught.

Notes for the teacher: It is not necessary to have music, nor do players have to skip. But if the game is played as described, it will help to develop skipping skill. There is a matter of ethics involved in not breaking the chain in order to dodge a Carpet. If only one player is caught, get two or three volunteers to make a team with him.

MICKEY MOUSE

For this game we stand in a circle, which is a Mousetrap. We put a ball in the center for the Cheese. Then we number around the circle—"One, Two, Three; One, Two, Three"—until everyone has a number. You must be very sure to remember your number and where your place is.

The leader of the game is Mickey Mouse. He calls out a number. If he calls "Two," each child whose number is Two starts to run. He runs fast around the circle and back to his own space, which is empty. It is a hole in the Mousetrap. He runs through his hole to the center. If he is the first, he will get the Cheese. Then he will be Mickey Mouse for a new game.

Notes for the teacher: About twelve players in the circle are enough for this game, unless you are playing it with first-grade children during the first days of school to accustom them to one another and to playing together. If you do use a larger circle, count up to four instead of three.

MIDNIGHT

We start this game with a Fox, who puts on a colored band and goes to his Den in one corner. The rest of us are Sheep in the Sheepfold, which is marked off in the opposite corner.

The Fox goes out of his Den around the field, and the Sheep come out, too. They go as close to the Fox as they dare and ask him, "What time is it?" If he says, "Nine o'clock," or "Two o'clock," or gives any time with a number, they are safe. But when he suddenly says, "Midnight!" the Sheep run for their lives back to the Sheepfold, with the Fox after them. If he catches any Sheep, they become Foxes. They put on shoulder bands, too, and help the old Fox catch more Sheep. But it is only the old Fox who can tell the time.

Notes for the teacher: When about a third of the class are Foxes, it is a good idea to start the game again. Very simple offensive strategy may be developed by the Foxes if they are encouraged to do so. The young Foxes do not have to stay with the old Fox but may go anywhere they like.

NEWCOMB

We play this game in two teams, one on each side of a volleyball net. We play with a volleyball. The object is to throw the ball across the net so that the other team cannot catch it.

The game starts with the captain of one team holding the ball in the center of his field. When the leader says "Go," the captain throws the ball across the net toward an empty space on the other side. The player on the other team who is nearest that space runs toward the ball and catches it (if he can). Then it is his turn to throw it across the net.

The game goes on until someone misses the ball or throws it out of bounds. Then the other team gets a point and gets the ball to start play again.

No player can run with the ball unless he has been running to catch it, and has to take a few steps after he catches it. But he must stop as soon as he can, and then throw it. Before we go back to our room, we count to see which team has the most points.

> *Notes for the teacher:* Newcomb is an easy game, and it can be dull unless children develop the offensive strategy of throwing at an empty space and of watching the ball and moving to meet it when on the defensive. Then the game and the movement of players speed up. Children have to be encouraged to plan ahead of time what they will do with the ball if it comes their way. The game provides good practice in catching and throwing if there are not too many on a team and if a volleyball or a junior basketball is used.
>
> So-called Advanced Newcomb is exactly like the beginning game except that scoring rules are the same as in volleyball (only the serving team scores) and players rotate as in volleyball. It is therefore considered a good preparatory game for volleyball.

NUMBER RELAY*

The players are divided into even teams of seven or eight players. Members of each team are seated one behind the other. Each file is numbered from front to back. There should be a distance of 4 or 5 feet between files and also between members of each team.

The leader calls a number. Those who have that number run *forward*, on the right side, around their own team and then back around the end of their team to their place. The one seated first wins a point for his team. The captains keep score on their fingers.

The game continues, and another number is called. Every time a run is made, all the captains show their scores. The team that has the highest score at the end of the game wins.

Notes for the teacher: It is probably better to have captains use paper and pencil to keep score, although the report may be made on their fingers. As soon as children are ready for simple officiating, let one of the group act as leader and scorekeeper.

OLD PLUG

All of us form a circle except three or four players, who join hands in the center. They are Old Plug, the horse. Old Plug has a Head and a Tail. We try to hit the Tail player with a rubber ball, and Old Plug tries to move so that the Tail will not be hit. If the Tail player is hit, he has to go back to the circle. The child who hit him comes in to be the Head. So now Old Plug has a new Head and a new Tail. Then we start all over again.

We have to remember two rules:

1. We may not hit the Tail player above the shoulders. Anyone who does this may not throw the ball the next time he gets it but must give it to someone else to throw. After that, he may throw it again.

2. Old Plug players have to keep their hands joined. If they let go, they must join hands again and then take the next throw standing still.

Notes for the teacher: This game is best played in small groups, with no more than eight to twelve players in the circle and no more than three or four players in Old Plug. Several circles may play at once, of course. The penalty for letting go of hands is planned to teach the value of dodging as well as of team play.

QUEEN DIDO IS DEAD*

Queen Dido is supposed to be dead. When I get through telling you about her, see if she really was dead.

The class chooses a leader. He or she goes to the front of the class. The leader says, "Queen Dido is dead." The class says, "How did she die?" The leader says, "She died doing this," and starts moving a hand. The class does the same. The leader repeats, "Queen Dido is dead." The class says, "How did she die?" The leader says, "She died doing this," and wiggles his foot. The class does the same. They keep on repeating the lines in this way, each time doing a new movement and keeping all the first ones going too. Soon the leader says, "Stop," and chooses a new leader. The game continues.

Notes for the teacher: Make sure the children understand that they are to keep right on with the old movements during the talk about new ones. Encourage everyone to think up new things to do. This is a good schoolroom or party game, but it does not have enough activity to use in the gymnasium or playground.

RUN, RABBIT, RUN

Half of us are Foxes; the other half are Rabbits. The Rabbits have a Home at one end of the playground, where they are safe. The Foxes are all over the Forest.

Old Mother Rabbit takes her children out for a walk. They tiptoe so that the Foxes will not hear them. When the leader of the Foxes calls out, "Run, Rabbit, run!" all the Rabbits run as fast as they can to their Home, and the Foxes try to catch them before they get there. Any who are caught must become Foxes and try to catch the rest of the Rabbits.

Notes for the teacher: Like Brownies and Fairies, this is a game of suspense, valuable chiefly because it provides opportunities for emotional release and for running. One class period is enough to teach it—then let the children play it to their heart's content at recess and before school.

STOP THE MUSIC*

All the children except two stand in a big circle. One child plays the music. He may play on a drum or on anything that is handy. The other child is the one who is the leader. He says, "Stop the music."

In this game the children may do any kind of funny walk they can think of. They may bend their knees or make their feet toe in. Their arms may go out or up or wiggle in a funny way. They may bend over like old men or walk on their toes. They may dance or walk like a dog on their hands and feet. They may even make faces.

There are only two rules each child must know. He must keep time to the music. That is the first rule.

The other rule is this: Each child must stop right where he is and not move at all when the leader says, "Stop the music." When he says that, the music stops, too.

Then the music begins again and the fun goes on. If the leader is a good one, he plays tricks on the children. He may wait a long time before he says, "Stop the music," or he may say it right away. The children have to do their tricks and listen with both ears, too.

This game is fun to play at school. It is fun to play at parties, too. I like to play it any time because it gives me a chance to be silly.

Notes for the teacher: This is a good rhythm game, to be used as soon as the class is ready to try moving to a uniform rhythm.

STRIKE AND CHASE

Two teams play this game. Each starts behind its own goal line. Every player finds his own place on the line, facing the other team, which is on the other side of the playground. One team is the visiting team, the other is the home team. Each player on the home team stretches out his hand toward the visiting team. When a signal is given, the visiting players leave their goal line and come toward the home team. Each visiting player tries to tag the hand of a home team player and then run back across his own goal line before the player he tagged can catch him. If a visiting player gets back without being tagged, he scores a run for his side.

Then the teams change. The home team becomes the visiting team, and the visiting team becomes the home team. Each team has an inning. Sometimes we play two innings to a game, sometimes four or even six if we have more time. At the end of the game we add up the scores each team has made to see who the winner is.

Notes for the teacher: Make sure that the teams are well spread out on their goal line, so that there will be no traffic mix-ups. There should be the same number of players on both sides. Of course, no home team member should be tagged by more than one visitor. The technique of controlling weight while changing direction can be learned in this game.

THREE DEEP

All except two players make a circle facing in and count off by twos. The Twos step to the right in front of the Ones. One of the extra players is a runner, the other is a chaser. The runner gets a head start and runs around outside the circle, with the chaser after him. To be safe, he must step into the circle in front of two people. That makes "Three Deep." Now the outside player of the three becomes the runner and must get away from the chaser or be tagged. If the runner is tagged, he becomes the chaser.

PARTNER TAG (Variation of Three Deep)

Everyone except a runner and a chaser takes a partner and goes anywhere in the room. The partners lock arms, keeping their other hands on their hips to make a handle. The runner tries to tag the chaser. He is safe if he can hook onto any couple. If he does, that makes three in a row, and the player on the other side has to run or be tagged.

THREE DEEP AND CHANGE (Variation of Three Deep)

We made up this way to play Three Deep. After you learn it you can never play it any other way. Every other child in the circle steps to the right in front of the next player. Two people are chosen for a runner and chaser. The runner goes as fast as he can around the circle and then runs in to stand in front of a pair of children. The chaser tries to tag him before he gets safe. When the runner stands in front of a pair, that makes a row of three. The last one in the old way of playing Three Deep used to be the *runner* but with us he is the *chaser*. Now this is the place you have to think. The chaser has to change himself from the chaser to the runner. He has to make a quick turn and run for a safe place. The game goes on until every child has had a turn.

Notes for the teacher: In the first version of Three Deep, the problem is to have the players change often enough. If they keep on running, it is because they need more activity, which Partner Tag provides. In Partner Tag, try having two sets of runners and chasers.

The third version of Three Deep teaches quick response and change of direction. It deserves to be, and is, a great favorite.

TIGER IN THE CAGE

In this game one of us is the Tiger. His Cage is a large circle on the floor. He may not leave his Cage, but we may go into it or run across it. If anyone is inside the Cage, or even touching it, the Tiger may tag him. If a player is tagged, he has to be the new Tiger, and the old Tiger comes out and plays with the rest of us.

We try to go into the Cage when the Tiger's back is turned. If everyone does this, the Tiger does not know which one to catch, and sometimes he does not catch anyone.

Notes for the teacher: A certain amount of strategy and daring, as well as skill in dodging, are outcomes to be expected from this game. Let the first Tiger be a real leader. If a withdrawn child seems to be languishing in the Cage because of lack of skill, send another Tiger in to help him.

TOUCHDOWN

This game is played with two teams. The teams line up facing each other on opposite sides of the gymnasium. One team has the "ball," which may be any small thing such as a marble, a small stone, or a piece of chalk. The team goes into a huddle to decide who is to carry the "ball" and how each of the others can look as if he were carrying it. Then the members of the team start out for the other goal line, either walking or running, each player carrying his hands as if he had something in them.

The members of the other team try to tag the player with the "ball" before he gets to their goal line. As soon as a player is tagged, he has to open both his hands to show whether he has the "ball." He cannot hide it in his clothes but must keep it in his hands. If the player who has the hidden "ball" gets to the other goal line before anyone tags him, he makes a touchdown. This scores a point for his team, which keeps the ball for another try. But if a member of the other team tags him before he gets to the goal line, there is no score and he must give up the ball. Then the members of the other team take over, go into a huddle, and plan how they can score. When the time is up, each team adds up its score.

Notes for the teacher: This is a good beginning team game, demanding planning and strategy. If the huddle lasts too long and players have difficulty in coming to a decision, it may be wise to elect a captain for each team. To start without a captain and then elect one gives children a good idea of how valuable a captain can be—if he really helps with the team's decisions and does not make them all himself.

TRADES

In this game two teams start on opposite sides of the playground. Each team has the same number of players. One team is the visiting team. This team has to show the home team a trade by doing what people in that trade do.

First the visitors have to decide what trade they will act out. When they are ready, they start toward the home team, coming quite close while the teams chant these words:

> *Visiting team:* "Here we come!"
> *Home team:* "Where from?"
> *Visiting team:* "Washington!"
> *Home team:* "What's your trade?"
> *Visiting team:* "Lemonade!"

Then the visiting team stops, and all the team members go through the same motion to show the other team what their trade is. The members of the home team try to guess the trade, and as soon as a player thinks he knows, he calls it out. When someone guesses the right trade, all the visitors run back to their goal while the home team chases them and tries to catch them before they can get back. The leader counts the number of visitors caught, and that is the home team's score.

Now the home team becomes the visiting team and decides on a trade. At the end of the game, the leader adds up the scores of each team, and the team with the largest total score wins.

Notes for the teacher: If the home team has trouble guessing the correct trade, the visitors may give them the first letter. Encourage, by commendation and evaluation by the children themselves, accurate and original dramatization. Sometimes the visitors will stay back too far to make it possible for the home team to catch them. Let the children work out ways of handling this situation.

UNCLE SAM

We choose one child to be Uncle Sam. He stands in the middle of the playground. The rest of us are all at one end. We all say:

"Uncle Sam, Uncle Sam,
May we cross your ocean dam?"

He answers, "Yes, if you have on the color blue." (Of course, he says a different color each time.) As soon as he tells us the color, all of us who are wearing something of that color may cross to the other end of the playground, and no one may tag us. But the rest of us have to run to the other end, or get there any way we can. If we get tagged, we have to be Uncle Sam's helpers, stand with him in the middle and help him tag children the next time they run. When nearly everyone is helping Uncle Sam, he has to be careful to call out some funny color no one has on.

Notes for the teacher: As well as teaching fast running and good dodging, this game may also give some chance for strategy. Children may try to fool the catchers by running very fast even if they have on the right color, or they may do the opposite: saunter confidently though vulnerable. Of course, they all learn to observe colors.

WHITE BEAR

The old White Bear lives on a piece of Ice in the White Sea. We make a small circle for the Ice and a large circle for the Sea. The rest of us are Fish swimming in the Sea.

The Bear says with a growl, "White Bear is hungry today; he goes fishing." Then he jumps into the Sea and chases the Fish until he catches one. He takes it back to the Ice with him and then does the same thing again.

When he has caught two, he gets lazy and tells the Fish that they are his helpers. Now they must go into the Sea and catch him a Fish while he rests at home. So they join hands, jump into the Sea, and try to catch a Fish by tagging it. Then they take it back to the Bear. He sends them into the Sea for another. As soon as there are two more, they join hands and go fishing also. This goes on until all the Fish but one are caught. He is the next Bear.

Notes for the teacher: This is reputed to be a Russian game. A problem in rules and ethics will come up when the Fish begin to swim outside the boundaries. Perhaps the children will profit from solving this problem themselves.

Intermediate Games

ALLEY SOCCER

This is a good kicking game, because three forwards on each team try to kick a soccer ball over the other team's goal line. The other players on each team are lined up around the side lines and the goal line of their own half of the field. They try to keep the ball from going over their lines by kicking it. No one may touch the ball with his arms or hands.

The field is divided into three long alleys. It looks like this:

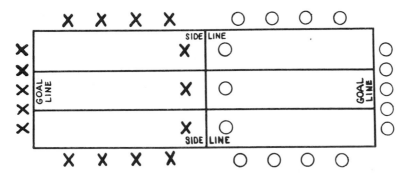

The two center players start the game by saying, "One, two, three," and then trying to kick the ball ahead at an angle to one of their own forwards. Each forward must stay inside his own alley all the time. Whoever gets control of the ball tries to kick it down the field and across the other team's goal line, below the heads of the players. If a player can do this, he scores 2 points for his team.

The center player's own forwards help him. They kick the ball to each other, trying to keep it away from their opponents as they move down the field. If the ball comes toward a player on the side lines or goal lines, he tries to keep the ball in the field by going inside the field to stop it with his feet, then kicking it to one of his forwards. After that he must go back to his place outside the line. If the ball goes over the side line, it is brought inside and kicked by the nearest player of the team that did not send it out.

INTERMEDIATE GAMES
Classified According to Difficulty* and Type

Large Group	Beginning Team	Modified Seasonal Team Games			
		Soccer Football	Softball	Volley-ball	Basket-ball
Pom, Pom, Pullaway				Advanced New-comb†	
Tag Games Red Light					End Ball
Black Wolf	Blue and Gold				
Center Stride Ball	Bombard-ment		Throw It and Run		
	Goal Ball		Long Base		Forwards and Guards
Free and Caught	Relays	Corner Kickball			5–3–1 Basket-ball
Duck on the Rock		Skill Relays	Skill Relays	Skill Relays	Skill Relays
	Club Snatch				
			Work Up		Scramble Basket-ball
	Dodgeball Prisoner's Base	Variations			
	Kick Dodge-ball	Alley Soccer			
	Run, Sheep, Run Soccer Goal Kick	Kickover Football		Volley Tennis	
	Hit Pin Baseball Volley-Base-Basket-ball		Beat Ball	Modified Volleyball	
			Modified Softball		
		Modified Soccer			Boys' Basket-ball
		Flag Foot-ball			Girls' Basket-ball

* The easier games appear at the top of each column.
† Described as a variation of Newcomb.

INTERMEDIATE GAMES
Classified According to Difficulty and Special Use

Recreational: Individual and Group	Aggressive Action	Schoolroom
Pom, Pom, Pullaway	Pom, Pom, Pullaway	
Tag Games		
Red Light		
Black Wolf	Bombardment	
Ante Over		Desk Relays
Four Square		
5–3–1 Basketball	One Against Three	
Duck on the Rock	Duck on the Rock	
Sidewalk Tennis		
Balloon Ball	Keep Away	Balloon Ball
Tether Ball		
Paddle Ball	Dodgeball Variations	
Work Up	Prisoner's Base	
		Shuffleboard
Shuffleboard		
Deck Tennis		
Wastebasket Ball		Wastebasket Ball
Paddle Tennis		

Remember these rules:

1. No one may touch the ball with his arms or hands.

2. The ball may not be kicked higher than a player's head.

3. Only a forward may score goals.

4. No pushing, tripping, or other rough play is allowed.

5. A line player or guard may go into the field only to stop the ball and kick it to a forward. He must then return to his place.

6. No one may try to block a free kick.

7. Each forward must stay inside his own alley.

Breaking any of these rules is a *foul*.

The penalty for a foul is a free kick for the other team from the center of the field. If this goes over the goal line, no higher than a player's head, it counts as 1 point.

Whenever a goal is made, either from a free kick or from play, all players rotate as if they were moving with the hands of a clock. First the three forwards face inward, so that each team makes a big square. Then every player moves over three places to his left. This puts all the old forwards on the side lines as guards, and brings three new forwards into the field from guard positions.

Notes for the teacher: This game prepares for modified soccer by having six players instead of twenty try to advance the ball.

The strategy of offense and defense is obvious, but should be mentioned to the class nevertheless. Players should also learn to keep their position in relation to one another.

Be very careful about enforcing the rule preventing rough play, since soccer can be very rough unless it is begun properly. If you have separate classes for boys and girls at the fifth- and sixth-grade levels, this game and modified soccer make good games for the boys. They are all right for either sex or for mixed classes, but when boys play by themselves they are more likely to get the kind of vigorous activity they need.

ANTE OVER

This is a good game to play at home, or any place where there is a small building, such as a garage, to throw the ball over. At school we play it at recess, over the tool shed or the handball board. The ball we usually play with is an old tennis ball, but we could use a soft rubber ball instead. A hard ball cannot be used.

One team is one one side of the garage or other small building, and the other stands on the other side. Neither team can see the other, but players can hear each other. One player has the ball. He tries to throw it over the roof, shouting "Ante-ante-over!" just before he throws it. If it does not go over, he shouts "Pig's tail!" and then throws again, first shouting "Ante-ante-over!" The players on the other team try to catch the ball before it hits the ground. If they cannot catch it they throw it back, just as the first team did, shouting the same signals.

But if anyone catches the ball, something different happens. The players on the team that caught it run as fast as they can around the building, and the players on the other team scatter as soon as they see them coming. The player with the ball tries to throw it so as to hit an opponent with it. If he hits him, then that player joins the thrower's team. If he misses, the thrower has to go over to the other team. Then each team goes back to its own side and the game begins again. Teams take turns making the first throw.

Notes for the teacher: Although this is primarily a recreational game, it can be used in class when you have a number of small group games going on at once. Any number from one to four on a side can play it.

AUTOMOBILE TUBE RELAY*

Make three or four lines of players. Have the same number in each one. Chairs should be put about 30 feet from each leader. These are goals. The automobile tubes are rolled like hoops around the goals.

They are easy to roll if they are blown up at the gas station. If they are soft, they will not roll where you want them to go.

The way to play the game is for each captain to take a tube. When the whistle blows, they roll the tubes around the goal and back to their places. The next one does this. Every child has a turn. The line which finishes first wins. When we play this, the captain holds the tube up when the race is over. There is one rule to watch. Children must not lift it around the goal. It takes time to learn to steer it straight. It is fun to do and I like to watch it because the game is never the same.

Notes for the teacher: Any hoop may be substituted for tubes.

BALLOON BALL

When we want to have fun without working very hard, we play Balloon Ball. It is played just like volleyball except that we use a balloon and we do not have many rules.

Because nobody can tell where the balloon will go, we say that any number on one side can hit it before it goes over the net as long as no player hits it twice. It cannot be caught, carried, or hit with the fist, and there is no use in trying to hit it hard, because it will not go fast. When we play on the playground or in the gym, we play across a volleyball net. Sometimes we play in our own classroom or even at home, and then we use a heavy string or a rope, and fasten pieces of paper to it so that we can see it better.

One side serves, and the serving side scores 1 point if the receivers do not get the balloon back across the net before it touches the ground. If they do get it back, we try to keep it going back and forth. When the servers do not get the balloon back, they lose the serve but there is no score against them. A game is 5 points. Two games out of three make a set.

When we play in the classroom, nothing is out of bounds. We keep on hitting the balloon even if it bounces off the wall.

The following are fouls:
1. Hitting the balloon with the fist.
2. Stepping on or over the service line when serving.
3. One player hitting the balloon twice before it has been returned.
4. Catching or carrying the balloon instead of hitting it.

If the serving side fouls, the serve goes to the other side. If the receiving side fouls, the servers score a point.

Notes for the teacher: This is a fine game when the class is sluggish or on edge and cannot get into the gymnasium. It is fun, will be noisy, but will not permit players to let off steam as a more vigorous game will. It does not develop skill, but it does keep players alert and laughing.

BOYS' BASKETBALL

Basketball, which was invented in the United States, is now played by thousands of people in this country and in other countries, too. Although most of us have seen it and know how to play it, it is a good idea to have the important rules down in black and white.

The purpose of the game is to throw a basketball through your own team's basket. There are five players on a team: two forwards, two guards, and one center. When the game begins, our forwards are near the basket we are shooting into; our center is in the center circle; our guards are between the other team's forwards and the basket they are shooting into. Our opponents are in corresponding positions, ready to move toward their basket.

The referee puts the ball in play by tossing it up between the two centers. They jump in order to tap it at the highest point they can reach. Each tries, of course, to tap it to one of his own teammates. Whichever team gets the ball passes it among its players as they move down the court toward their goal. When a player is in good position, he shoots for the basket. If he makes the basket, 2 points are scored for his team. The ball is then given to a player on the other team who stands out of bounds at the end of the court where the basket was made. He throws it in to one of his own team, and the game goes on.

Basketball has many rules. Breaking a rule is a *foul*, if it is serious like pushing; if it is something smaller, like stepping over a line, it is called a *violation*. The penalty for a foul is a free throw for the other side; for a violation it is to give the ball to the other side, out of bounds. If the free throw goes through the basket, a point is scored for the team that made it.

Fouls: Personal fouls are blocking—that is, moving in to prevent the progress of an opponent, pushing, holding, tripping, and charging. *Technical fouls* are delaying the game, unsportsmanlike conduct, illegal substitution, and leaving the game without reporting to an official. Five personal fouls put a player out of the game.

Violations: Stepping over the line on a free throw, sending the ball out of bounds, running with the ball or kicking it, and beginning a second dribble before shooting or passing, are *violations*. "Running with the ball" means moving both feet while holding the ball.

Held Ball: When two or more opposing players have a firm hold of the ball with one or both hands, the referee tosses the ball up between them as at the start of the game.

Time of game: A game consists of six-minute quarters, with two minutes of rest between, and a ten-minute rest between halves.

Notes for the teacher: These rules are a simplified form of official basketball rules. The ball as well as the court should be smaller than in regulation basketball. The basket should be lower, not more than 9 feet from the floor. Boys and girls should play basketball, as well as any other games involving bodily contact, in separate classes. At the elementary level, competition in basketball should be limited to intramural games.

GIRLS' BASKETBALL

Girls have their own rules in basketball, as they do in many other team games. In general, girls play better when they use their own rules, because these rules emphasize clever play rather than skill in running.

There are six players on a team: three forwards and three guards. The forwards of one team and the guards of the other team stay in one half of the court, separated by a center line from the other forwards and guards. The forwards are responsible for scoring by throwing the ball through their own team's basket. The guards are responsible for defense; that is, they try to keep the opposing forwards from scoring.

The game begins with the referee's throwing the ball to a forward in the center circle after the teams have tossed to see who receives this first throw. The forward passes the ball to a player on her own team, who must pass it again before anyone can shoot for a basket. The forwards try to get into a good position to shoot while passing the ball among themselves. The guards on the other team try to get the ball without rough play, by being quicker and better at jumping and catching the ball than their opponents.

There are many rules for this game because so many things can happen. The players have to have rules to keep the play clean and open and to give everyone a fair chance. To break an important rule, such as the one against pushing, is called a *foul.* The penalty for a foul is a free throw into the basket for the other team. Breaking a less important rule, such as the one against stepping over a line, is called a *violation.* The penalty for a violation is giving the ball to a player on the other team, who throws it in from out of bounds.

Fouls: Individual fouls are holding, pushing, tripping, charging, and any other unnecessary roughness; obstructing the player who has the ball or blocking the progress of a player who does not have a ball; overguarding the ball by putting hands on it after the opponent has secured it; "boxing up" the player with the ball between two opponents; waving hands in front of the face of the player who has the ball; and delaying the game. A player with five fouls has to leave the game. The penalty for a foul is a free throw for the other team. But if an opponent fouls a forward as she is shooting for a basket, the forward gets two free throws.

Violations: Stepping over a boundary line, holding the ball more than five seconds before throwing it, running with the ball, bouncing the ball more than twice before passing it, and kicking the ball, are violations. For any of these offenses, the penalty is giving the ball to a member of the other team to throw in from out of bounds.

Starting the game: The center throw already described is used to start the game, after a basket has been made, and at the beginning of each quarter. The referee throws the ball alternately to each team at the beginning of the quarters, but after a basket has been made by one team, the other gets the center throw.

Out of bounds: Whenever the ball goes out of bounds, the opponent of the player who touched it last throws it in to her team.

Tie ball: When two players put one or both hands on the ball at the same time, the referee blows his whistle and tosses the ball up between them. Each one jumps as high as she can to try to tap the ball to a player on her own side.

Time of game: A game consists of six-minute quarters, with two minutes of rest between, and a ten-minute rest between halves.

Notes for the teacher: Have boys and girls play separately, with different rules. Intramural competition is preferable to interschool competition at the elementary level.

BEAT BALL

Beat Ball helps us in playing softball. We use a softball, but not a bat, and we play on the softball diamond. There are two teams, one in the field, the other running bases.

When the game begins, the first runner stands at home plate holding the ball. He throws the ball anywhere he wants to inside the first and third base lines, and then starts right away to run around the bases. The fielders try to catch the ball before it hits the ground. If they do catch it, the runner is out. If they do not catch it, they field it to first base, then to second base, third base, and home. If the ball beats the runner to home plate, the runner is out. If the runner beats the ball, he scores a point for his team.

After all the players on the running team have had their turn they change places with the fielding team. After both teams have had their turn at running, the inning is over. We play as many innings as we have time for.

Notes for the teacher: This game provides excellent practice in throwing and catching. If your school has a batting tee, the next step in development is to have the runner bat the ball off the tee instead of throwing it.

BLACK WOLF

Black Wolf is a game for a big playground or a neighborhood where there are open spaces and good hiding places. One player is the Black Wolf, who goes out to hide. The others stay at home and blind-fold their eyes, and one of them counts up to any number that gives the Wolf time to hide. We count to one thousand—not "One, two, three," but "One hundred, two hundred," and so on, quite slowly.

When the counter gets to one thousand, he shouts it out so that the Wolf knows we are leaving home. Then we spread out to wander around and enjoy ourselves, but we keep an eye out for the Wolf. As soon as anyone sees the Wolf, he shouts out as loud as he can, "Black Wolf" and everyone runs for home. The Wolf has to run, too, and he tries to catch as many of us as he can before we get home. Those who are caught become Wolves, too. Five Wolves are enough, and then we begin the game again. The last Wolf caught starts out as the first Wolf in the new game.

BLUE AND GOLD

Half the players are on the Blue team and the other half on the Gold team. Each team lines up on its own line, about 3 feet away from the other team's line. Both lines are drawn across the middle of the field. At each end of the field is a goal line.

Our game leader has a big, round piece of heavy cardboard, painted blue on one side and gold on the other. He stands in the middle and spins or tosses this disk so that no one can tell which way it is going to land. If it lands with the blue side up, the Blue players run as fast as they can toward their own goal line, with the Golds after them. But if it lands with the gold side up, then the Golds must run away from the Blues. Anyone who is caught must go over to the other side. The side with the most players at the end of the game wins. In our school everyone wants to be on the Gold team, because gold is our school color. But we play it just as hard for the Blues, if we are on that team, because no one would have any fun if we did not.

Notes for the teacher: The game leader may be one of the children. Unless he is handicapped or otherwise restricted in activity, change leaders after two or three games.

BOMBARDMENT

This is a good game because it is exciting.

Bombardment is played with two teams. Each team tries to do two things: first, we want to knock down the other team's clubs with balls;

second, we want to defend our own clubs and keep them standing up. Usually we have a club for every player, and four balls. Each team keeps its clubs spread out at the back of its own space. The players are between a line in front of their own clubs and the center line.

Here is a picture of the way we start:

At the beginning of the game each captain has a ball, and so does another player on his team. They are up near the center line. When the umpire blows the whistle, they throw the balls across the line at the other team's clubs. Of course, the defenders on the other team try to catch the balls and pass them to their own players near the front. Then these players throw them across at the other team's clubs.

When a club is knocked down, it cannot be touched or set up again. After a short time, the whistle blows for the end of the inning and the umpire counts the clubs that are still standing up. Each one standing counts 2 for that side.

There are five fouls in this game:

1. Going over the center line into the other team's space.
2. Running with the ball or dribbling it. You must pass it to some other player on your team if you are outside or too far back to throw it yourself.
3. Throwing at a club from outside the side lines.
4. Holding the ball instead of throwing it.
5. Touching one of your clubs that has been knocked down.

Every foul counts a point for the other side, so that each team has a club score plus a foul score, made for it by the other team.

The scores are added up after each inning. Five innings make a game.

Notes for the teacher: This is a fine game for letting off steam on a bad day. It also permits the teams to develop strategy if they are given time for a huddle after each inning. For example, they will soon see the advantage of having some of their team play defensively, standing a little in front of the goal line, and some play an offensive game, standing just behind the center line, with those in between playing either an offensive or a defensive game. Later, players may change places, so that all get a chance to score. The captain should place his team.

Children may act as umpires in this game. If their activity is not restricted for some reason, however, they should also take turns at playing.

The dimensions of the playing area should be about 40 by 20 feet. The length of an inning depends somewhat on the children's skill. Try two minutes at first. If they knock all the clubs down, shorten the time. If the game seems to go slowly, use more balls. If it seems to confuse the children, try fewer balls, but remember to give them as much activity as they can take.

If scoring on fouls breeds too much hostility, try a free-throw penalty—that is, give the captain a chance to knock down a club without having his throw blocked.

BOUNCE BALL RELAY

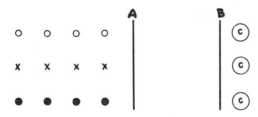

Several teams with an equal number of players line up behind Line A, as shown in the diagram. The first runner in each team has a tennis ball. At the signal he runs forward, bouncing and catching the ball while running between Lines A and B, and then again in Circle C. There is one circle for each team. He then runs back to his team, at the same time passing the ball by one long bounce to the second runner in his line, who starts as soon as he catches the ball. The first runner takes his place at the end of the line, moving up one as each player runs. A team finishes when the first runner catches the ball bounced to him by the last player.

Notes for the teacher: As soon as players have enough skill, the first bounce should be taken while running at top speed. At C, however, the bounce should be vertical, so that it can be controlled without overrunning the mark. The bounce to the next player should be long, but not too hard to be caught. Give the teams a chance to huddle and work out some of these problems themselves. Keep the teams small, with not more than four or five players on each. The distance between lines should be increased as the children develop skill. Try 20 feet at first.

CENTER STRIDE BALL

We play this game in a circle, which we make by putting our feet apart and standing close enough to our neighbors so that our feet touch. One player stands in the center with a volleyball, which he tries to throw outside the circle below our shoulders. We try to keep the ball in the circle by batting it or catching and throwing it away from the center player. If the ball goes out of the circle between our feet or on our right side, we have to get it and change places with the center player. While the ball is in the circle, we are not allowed to move our feet. No one may kick the ball.

Notes for the teacher: Sometimes a player is left in the center for a long time because of his own lack of skill. This may do no harm to a well-accepted youngster, but it may be undesirable for one who is rejected by the group. To avoid such a situation, or to speed up the game, try having two center players. When either ball goes out, let both players change places with someone in the circle.

CHASE*

This game is like Three Deep. The difference is that we play it in our room.

We have a chaser and a runner. The runner may save himself from being caught by sitting with someone. That person is the new runner. We cannot run in the room because we might slip on the floor or hit a seat or a table, so we walk very fast instead.

No player is allowed to cut through a row of chairs. He must go up and down the aisles.

Sometimes we say that a girl must sit with a boy or a boy with a girl, because if we did not do that only girls or only boys would be playing.

Runners should make quick changes so that everyone has a chance to play.

Notes for the teacher: Only your ingenuity will keep the same runner from going on forever. Ask the children how the game could be improved, and they will tell you that the runners should change more often. If you can make it appear that the runner has outsmarted the others by changing, you may provide a stimulus for him to do so. Or, you might use the tried device of having the class chant the count up to ten. If there has been no change by then, both the runner and the chaser must give way to two other players.

CLUB SNATCH

Two teams line up facing each other. A goal line is drawn in front of each team. Every player has a number, and the teams line up in order behind their own goal line. A wastebasket with a colored shoulder band on top of it is placed in the center, an equal distance from each team.

When the leader says, "Ones . . . go!" the Number One player on each team goes toward the basket. Each tries to snatch the band and get back to his own goal line without being tagged by the other. Whoever succeeds scores a point for his side. Then the leader calls out another number. The game goes on until all the numbers have been called.

This is a very tricky game, because sometimes each player waits to see what the other one is going to do. If they wait too long, we all start to count, and if no one has snatched the band before we get to five, they must both go back to their team without a score.

Notes for the teacher: Tricky games such as this one are good for developing quick thinking and the ability to outguess an opponent. Give the children a chance to analyze the points of good play. Keep the teams small; five on a side is enough, and several sets can be playing at once. The object snatched was originally an Indian club, and if that is available, use it without the wastebasket.

CORNER KICKBALL

When we play this game, each team lines up inside the end zone in its own half of the field. The end zone is marked off by a line 6 feet from the end line and parallel to it.

A soccer ball is placed exactly in the center of the field. When the whistle blows, the two corner players from each team run toward it to play it. They play as forwards and try to kick the ball over the end zone of the other team. The players in the end zone try to stop the ball and to kick it back to their own forwards.

If the ball does go over the end lines or the side lines, the four forwards go back to their own team. They go to the center of the line, and the other players move toward the ends. Then the next four corner players get ready to run in at the whistle.

No player may touch the ball with his hands or arms, nor may he trip, push, or hold any other player. These are fouls, and count 1 point for the other side. Whenever a ball is kicked clear across the end zone, 2 points are scored for the side that kicked it. Each team's score has two parts: the fouls made by the other team, and the goals made by the team itself.

The game is over when every player on each side has had a chance as a forward.

> *Notes for the teacher:* All players except the four forwards must stay inside the end zone. If there is difficulty in enforcing this rule, add it to the list of fouls. This game provides good preparation for soccer.

DECK TENNIS

When we play this game we have four, five, or six on a side, but if the court is small the game may be played with three, two, or even one on a side. Sometimes it is played on big ships, in a small space on the deck. Then there are never more than two on a side.

In our front yard we have a court big enough for two on a side. It is 40 feet long and 18 feet wide, with a net across the middle. The top of the net is 4 feet 8 inches from the ground. We play with a rubber ring about 6 inches in diameter, called a *tenikoit*. At school, when we play with six on a side, we use the volleyball court so that we will all have room.

The game starts with the server on one side standing behind the end line. He throws the ring underhand so that it goes over the net. It must be caught with one hand, and thrown back over the net with a continuous motion of the same hand.

The game is scored like volleyball. When the receiving side does not return the ring correctly, the servers get a point and go on serving. But when the serving side fails, either in serving or in returning, the serve goes to the other side with no score. Players rotate as they do in volleyball.

> *Notes for the teacher:* The net is always the same height, no matter how large the court. On official courts there is a restraining line 3 feet on either side of the net. All serves must go beyond that line, which is not used at any other time. All throws must be upward in motion as they leave the hand. The continuous movement from catching to throwing requires a little practice. However, it is similar to all good technique in throwing after catching, and is good training for the relaxed "give" with the ball so important in any ball game.

DOUBLE DODGEBALL*

For this game, we make a large circle with one team and draw a circle in front of our feet with chalk. The other team stands inside the circle. Those on the outside try to hit the center players with a large bouncing ball. Each time a center player is hit, the other team scores a point.

No player in the outer circle may step over the line except to get the ball. The ball must be thrown low, so that no one will be hit on the head. The players in the center try to duck the ball so that they will not be hit.

When the whistle blows, we change sides. The team that hits more center players wins. We use the chest throw, the underarm throw, and the shoulder throw in this game. We throw with both hands.

Notes for the teacher: A utility ball is a good ball to use in this game. The description emphasizes "ducking" the ball, but all the arts of dodging should be encouraged. The length of time one team remains in the center depends on the skill of the group. Three minutes may be necessary at the beginning.

TRIPLE DODGEBALL*

For this game we need three courts of the same size. Each court is about 15 feet wide and 30 feet long. We play with a large bouncing ball.

There are three teams and three captains. Each team has a court. The two end teams play against the center team, trying to hit the center players as many times as possible. Every time a center player is hit by a fair ball, his team gets a black mark. A fair ball is a direct hit on the person and not a bounce from the floor.

To score, a player must stand *behind* the line of his court when he throws at a center player. He may not hit a center player above the shoulders. If he does, he is asked to sit on the side lines and think about it for a while.

After each team has been in the center court for three minutes, the scores are counted. The team with the lowest score wins.

Notes for the teacher: A variation of this game, called Double-team Dodgeball, is described in Chapter 4, in the section "Four Lessons." Double-team Dodgeball is a good game for a large group and for a class that has progressed beyond Triple Dodgeball. As soon as the children are ready, emphasize the element of team play between the two end teams. A basketball is used for Triple Dodgeball. Two balls should be used as soon as the class is familiar with the game.

QUADRUPLE DODGEBALL*

In this game there are four courts but only two teams. The teams are divided into hitters and dodgers, as in this picture.

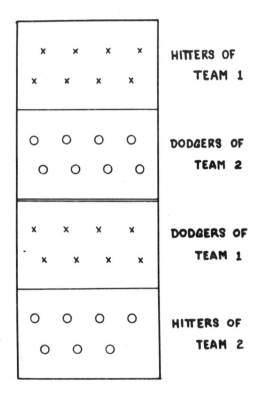

A soccer ball is used in this game. Teams wear colored bands to help the referee.

The object of the game is for the hitters to hit as many of the opposite team's dodgers as they can. They score 1 point for each hit. It is not fair to step over the line to throw, or to hit a player above the shoulder. Such hits do not count. The team with the highest score wins the game.

The game starts with a center jump. The referee tosses the ball up between the two captains, who try to bat it with one hand toward their own hitters. The captain who bats it toward his hitters gets the ball for his team to begin the game.

The hitters try to hit the dodgers. After the ball is "dead" (on the floor), the dodgers pick it up and try to return it to their own hitters. The opposite dodgers block this play if they can and try to give the ball to *their* hitters instead. No player is allowed to step out of his court to get the ball. If he does, he must give the ball to the players in the next court.

We play for five minutes and then the hitters and dodgers change places. Running with the ball is allowed with IV B's but not with IV A's. This is a fine game for the fourth grade.

> *Notes for the teacher:* "IV B's" here are the first half year of the fourth grade. Progress toward this "IV A" rule when your class is ready.

DUCK ON THE ROCK

This is our family's favorite game when we go on a picnic. Everyone can play.

First each of us must find a Duck, which is a stone just the right size to throw at another Duck. Usually we choose one a little bigger than a hard baseball. Then we find a big rock with a flat top.

One player is It. He starts with his Duck on the rock, and he stands at the side, but fairly near the rock. The rest of us line up behind a line that my Dad draws, just within easy throwing distance of the rock.

The first player throws his Duck underhand at the Duck on the rock, trying to knock it off. If he misses, he goes to where his Duck has landed and stands next to it. If he knocks the Duck off the rock, he runs quickly after his own Duck, and tries to bring it back home before It can replace *his* Duck and tag the runner.

Soon there are three or four of us standing close to our Ducks, waiting for someone to make a good shot and knock the Duck off the rock. If this happens, we all grab our Ducks and try to make it back to the home base line. Once you have touched your Duck, you have to pick it up and run for home, hoping you can run faster or dodge better than It.

When his Duck is knocked off the rock, or even if it falls off, the player who is It must put it back before he can tag anyone. When he does tag another player, It changes places with the player he has tagged.

Sometimes everyone is in the field standing by his Duck and there is no one left to throw. Then two or three players will pick up their Ducks at the same time, to get It mixed up so that he will not know which one to tag. It is fun to make a pass at your Duck but not really touch it. Then someone else slips home with his Duck while It is watching you.

One day in school we decided to try this game in the gym, with shuffleboard disks for Ducks and a "rock" marked on the floor. We used the shuffleboard pushers instead of throwing the disks, and it worked pretty well. This is a good game for a rainy day, but I like it better played out of doors with real rocks.

Notes for the teacher: If yours is a well-cared-for playground, it probably affords no opportunities for picking up rocks. In that case teach the indoor version and let the children make the transfer to the outdoor situation. Of course, if you are fortunate enough to have outings or camping as a regular part of the school program, use Duck on the Rock in its outdoor setting. A point of ethics that seems important to the authors is self-regulation in running if a child touches his Duck.

END BALL

The object of this game is to throw the ball so that our "point catchers" at the other end of the field can catch it on the fly without moving out of the end zone. The field is marked as shown in the drawing.

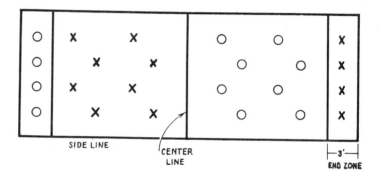

There are two end zones, in which the point catchers must stay. These end zones are only 3 feet wide, and each point catcher must watch his step to keep inside the lines. The passers have the rest of the field on the other side of the center line. They have to stay inside their boundary lines, too.

When we first learned this game we played with one ball, but as soon as we had learned it we used two balls, which made it more exciting. If there is only one ball, the game is started by tossing it up between two players, a passer from each side. When there are two balls, a passer on each side has one. When a passer near the center gets the ball, he tries to throw it all the way to a point catcher on his side, over the heads of the passers on the other team. If a passer who is back near the end zone catches the ball, he passes it quickly to another passer on his team who is near the center line and so has a better chance to score.

Sometimes the ball goes out of bounds. When it does, it goes to the nearest player on the team that did *not* send it out. He takes it outside the side line and throws it in to one of his passers. If the ball goes over the end line, one of the passers on the other team throws it in from the side line. The passers try to be very quick in getting the ball, bringing it to the side line, and throwing it in.

A point is scored whenever a point catcher catches the ball while it is in the air, before it hits the floor or goes over the boundary lines. If he drops it after catching it there is no score.

There are four fouls in this game:

1. Going over any line into the other team's space.
2. Running with the ball or dribbling it, unless a player goes outside the boundary line to get it. Then he runs with it to the sideline to pass it in.
3. Holding the ball instead of passing it.
4. Pushing, holding, or trying to take the ball away from another player.

Whenever a player fouls, the ball is given to the nearest passer on the other team.

We usually play five-minute halves, and take time for a huddle between halves to discuss our play so that we can score more points the second half. Sometimes we play two games in one day.

> *Notes for the teacher:* The huddle is important, since children should be encouraged to evaluate their play. Do not change positions between halves, but if another game is played, let the point catchers take their turn at being passers. Try to get the children to see the advantage of distributing the play: that is, of passing to all the players.

ERASER RELAY

This game is played in the classroom. The desks must be placed in rows, with the same number of desks in each row. The captain sits in the front seat, and has an eraser on his desk. At a signal he *passes* the eraser over his head to the next player, who passes it to the one behind him, and so on to the end of the row. When the last man gets it, he stands up on the *right* side of his seat and runs to the front seat. All the other players do as the captain does. They get out on the *left* side to avoid bumping other players, and move back one seat.

The game continues without stopping. Each time the last man in a row gets the eraser, he runs forward. When the captain is back in his own place, he holds the eraser high so that the leader can see who the winner is.

This is a fast game, and you have to know right from left in order to play it well. Sometimes we put a row out of the race if a player makes a mistake in changing seats. It does not take long to learn to play the game right.

Notes for the teacher: Needless to say, in a modern school the supply of erasers may not be equal to the demands of this game. Beanbags, or anything else that will not break when dropped or hurt when grabbed, may be used instead of erasers. Balls are too elusive.

5–3–1 BASKETBALL*

I like Basketball Throw because I like to throw for the basket and get it in. Sometimes I catch it on a fly or first bounce. Basketball Throw is lots of fun. Sometimes we just practice, and sometimes we play a game with Basketball Throw. We call it 5–3–1.

When we play 5–3–1, each one has three tries. We get 5 points if we make the first basket. Then we get 3 points when we try again. The last one counts 1 point. We add these points ourselves. The teacher adds them if we play in teams. Once I made 8 points. When we make a basket, we make so much noise we have to close the doors. Basketball is very easy and thrilling. When the other team wins, be a sport about it. I like it very much. You will like it, too.

Notes for the teacher: This is a good game to begin developing the skill of throwing for baskets, if the ball is small, and the basket lower than regulation. A soccer ball will be thrown at an 8-foot basket with fairly good technique by a 9- or 10-year-old. Have three on a team, two teams using one basket, with the shooter following up his own throw and giving the ball to the other side after the third try.

FLAG FOOTBALL

This game is *almost* like regular football. The most important difference is that we do not tackle each other. Each of us carries two flags, which hang over the side seams of our pants. At least half of the flag should be hanging on the outside. When you want to stop an opponent who is running with the ball, you take his flag and he has to stop on the spot.

Usually we have nine on a side: a center, four other linesmen, and four backs. We start the game by having the captains toss. The one who wins may choose either which goal his team will defend or whether his team will kick off or receive the ball. If he decides to receive, his team scatters over its half of the field. The other team puts the ball at the center of the zone line closest to its goal, spreads out along that line, and kicks the ball to the receivers.

The receiver nearest the ball tries to catch it and run it back toward the opponents' goal. Or he may pass it sideways (not forward) to a teammate who has a better chance of running it back. The object of the game is to advance the ball over the opponents' goal line and touch it down. If the runner has a flag pulled, play stops, then starts again with the ball on the spot where the runner was tagged. The center bends over the ball with two linesmen crouched on either side of him (an imaginary line across the field at the center of the ball is called the "line of scrimmage"). The backs are behind the center. The opposing team is spread out facing them, 3 yards away from the ball. The center passes the ball between his legs to one of the backs, who may kick, pass ahead, or run with the ball until he is flagged. The team with the ball has four chances (downs) to advance the ball into the next zone. If it fails to do this or if the opposing team catches a pass or a kick, the ball is awarded to the opposing team, where it was caught, in case of a pass or punt, or where it was put in play on the fourth down, in case of a running play. Then the opposing team tries to advance in the opposite direction.

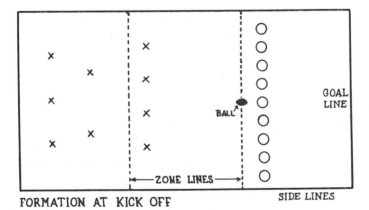

FORMATION AT KICK OFF

When a team makes a touchdown, it scores 6 points. Right after the touchdown has been made, the same team gets one chance to score an extra point. The ball is placed 5 yards out from the opponents' goal line. If the team is able to advance the ball over the goal line in one play it scores an extra point. Whether it makes the extra point or not, the team that has scored takes the ball back to the zone line nearest their goal and kicks off.

Remember these things:
1. No tackling or holding is allowed.

2. Blocking (or getting in the way of an opponent so he cannot go forward) must be done with your arms next to your body and your feet on the ground.

3. No player may move over the line of scrimmage before the center snaps the ball. This is offside.

4. If a team kicks the ball and the receiving team does not catch it, the receiving team gets the ball and plays it from the spot to which it rolled, unless it goes over the goal line. If it does roll over the goal line, it is brought out 20 yards and put into play by the receiving team.

5. If a forward pass is not caught, the ball is dead and put into play at the line of scrimmage, on the spot where the ball was at the beginning of the play. This counts as a down for the team with the ball.

Penalties:

1. Offside—5 yards.

2. Illegal tackling, blocking, holding, or rough play—15 yards.

Notes for the teacher: Boys love to play sand-lot football on their own. Because they have no supervision and almost no rules, this can be a very dangerous game, as statistics of severe accidents prove. If they can have fun with Flag Football at school, and if the coach tells them that it teaches them agility in dodging as well as the basic speed and footwork necessary for open-field running, they may play it recreationally. But be sure not to tell them that they are too young for tackle football. It is perfectly true, but also perfectly unacceptable to the youngsters. They should play with a junior regulation football.

FORWARDS AND GUARDS

Players are scattered in pairs over the playground. One of each pair is a forward; the other a guard. At a signal, the forwards try to dodge away from the guards, who follow them closely but may not touch them until the next whistle. When the whistle blows, both players stop still. Each guard then tries to touch his opposing forward. Neither one may move his feet. Then players reverse positions and start again.

Notes for the teacher: This game is good preparation for Keep Away or any other modified basketball game. Players will have to be cautioned about sharing space and watching out for other pairs to avoid collision.

FOUR SQUARE

Almost any time we can get there, you will find four of us on the playground or in the gym playing Four Square. It is one of the games we like best.

First we mark out a big square, 12 by 12 feet, and then we divide it into four squares by center lines running each way. Each of us plays in one of the squares, and each square has a number. The object of the game is to get to Square Number One and stay there as long as you can. We play with a soft rubber ball, but the older boys and girls, who like this game as much as we do, play it with a tennis ball. Our square looks like this:

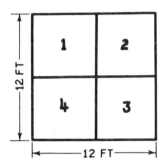

Number One player starts the game by letting the ball bounce in his own square, and then hitting it underhand so that it bounces in any of the other squares. If it goes into Square Number Three, the player in that square must hit it underhand, on the first bounce, into some other square. The player in that square tries to hit it into another. We go on playing until someone misses, hits the ball the wrong way, or hits it out of bounds. When that happens, he goes to Square Number Four and the others move up one.

If other boys and girls want to play, each one gets a number, starting with five. When someone misses, he goes to the end of the line instead of to Square Number Four, and Number Five moves into Square Number Four when the others move up.

We must remember two rules:

1. The ball is always hit on the first bounce, and must be hit underhand.

2. If the ball lands on an outside line, it is good. If it lands on one of the inside lines, it is good, and must be returned by the player in the lowest-numbered square whose line is hit.

Notes for the teacher: This is a favorite recreational game, and should by all means be taught if your grade does not already know it. It may well be included in a lesson on small group games, when each squad is playing a different game. If there are as many as eight in a squad, it it better to play with partners. Partners alternate inside and outside the square. As soon as the partner inside has played the ball, he changes places with the player waiting outside, and the game goes on without interruption. This is a good game for teaching both offensive strategy (try to get the opponents off balance) and defensive strategy (keep on toes, in far corner of court, facing center, with eye on ball).

FREE AND CAUGHT

We like to play this game with two or three catchers, who have bands over their shoulders. They try to tag as many players as they can. Whenever a player is caught, he has to stand still. But if a "free" player comes along and touches him, he is free to run around again. The catchers try to get everyone caught and standing still, while the rest try to keep everyone free.

Notes for the teacher: If the catchers are having a very difficult time, use more than two or three. There are some elements of strategy that the catchers can use, and it is desirable to stop the game occasionally to ask how they might work together to keep the caught children from being freed. Shoulder bands are very useful in all games. Each room should have a supply, one for every child.

FREEZE IT

For this game we need one ball—a tennis ball, rubber ball, or volleyball. Ten or fifteen children may play at one time, either on the playground or in the gymnasium. The object of the game is to keep from being a Ghost.

One player has the ball and starts the game by throwing it high in the air as he calls the name of another player in the group. This second player catches the ball, if he can, or fields it quickly while all the other players scatter. As soon as he has a good hold on the ball he calls, "Freeze it!" Every other player must then stand still.

The one with the ball throws it at someone who is near enough to make a good target; he must hit him below the shoulders. The player who is the target may not move except to try to catch the ball. If he catches the ball, is hit above the shoulders, or is missed, the thrower is out. If he is hit below the shoulders, or if he catches but then drops the ball, he is out. Whichever player is out must start the game again by throwing the ball in the air and calling out the name of another player.

A player with three outs is a Ghost. He may play, but no one may call his name or throw the ball at him. Any player who forgets and does so gets an out.

Notes for the teacher: Occasionally an aggressive child will try to become a Ghost so that he may tease the other children. If this does not increase his rejection by the class, let the situation work itself out. If tension approaches the danger point, start a different game, or a repeat, with all outs and Ghosts canceled.

GOAL BALL

This game is played with two goals, one at each end of the field. One volleyball or soccer ball is needed. Any open space, either on the playground or in the gymnasium, which is at least 50 by 30 feet, may be used. The field may be as large as 80 by 50 feet. The goals may be Indian clubs, tin cans, or any improvised marker. A circle with a radius of 3 feet is drawn around each goal.

There are two teams of six to twelve players. One member of each team is a goalkeeper, who stands close to the goal circle his team is defending and tries to keep the goal from being hit. The others are guards and forwards. The forwards play up near the opponents' goal and try to hit it with the ball. The guards play back near their own goal and try to prevent the opponents' forwards from scoring. The object of the game is to hit the opponents' goal with the ball.

At the beginning of the game the ball is tossed up between two opposing players. It is then passed among members of one team until one of them is close enough to hit the goal with the ball. If he does, he scores a point for his side, and the game is started again in the center. If he misses and the ball goes out, a guard on the other side gets the ball, brings it to the side lines, and throws it in to one of his own players. If two players have both hands on the ball at the same time, it is called a "jump ball" and is thrown up between them.

Fouls:
1. Running with the ball.
2. Rough play or personal contact.
3. Holding the ball more than five seconds.
4. Entering the goal circle.

In case of a foul, the other side gets a free throw from the spot where the foul was made.

HIT PIN BASEBALL

We like to play this game in the gymnasium, but on a warm day we can play it outdoors on the softball field. It is very much like softball, with nine players in softball positions. What is different is that we kick a soccer ball when it is pitched to us instead of batting a softball, and we have to make a home run to score. Another thing that is different is the way of putting a runner out. There is an Indian club, called a pin, on every base. After he has kicked a fair ball, the runner tries to circle the bases, touching each one before the fielders can throw the ball around the bases. Both the ball and the runner have to go around the bases in the right order: first, second, third, and home. If the ball gets ahead of the runner and the baseman knocks down an Indian club with the ball, which he is holding, before the runner touches that base, the runner is out. The runner is also out if he does not touch each base; if he accidentally knocks down a pin, either with his foot or with the ball he has kicked; if he kicks a fly ball which is caught; or if the pitcher knocks down the home base pin with a pitched ball. When a team has three outs, its players go out into the field and the fielding team comes in to kick.

Notes for the teacher: This is a good fast game. It is satisfying to the poor batters in the class because they can almost always kick a fair ball even if they cannot bat one. The rules prevent the strategy of heading off the runner, so important in softball as well as in Bat Ball and in other modified forms of baseball. It is therefore important to emphasize the fact that the ball follows the runner only in *this* game, and not in others that do not have the rule.

HOP SCOTCH

This game is so old that there are many ways of playing it. The way we like best is played like this:

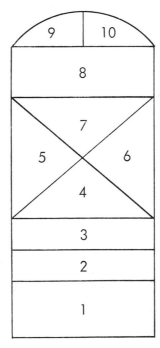

First we make the diagram or the "Scotch" as they used to call it. Then each player gets a small stone. When it is his turn he tosses his stone so that it lands in box Number 1. Then he hops on one foot into that box, picks up his stone, and hops on one foot into boxes Numbers 2, 3, and 4 in turn. He then hops and lands on two feet, right foot in Number 6, left foot in Number 5. From there he hops on one foot to Numbers 7, 8, 9, 10, and back the way he came to Number 1, then outside, landing on two feet. If he does all this without touching a line or dropping his stone, on his next turn he throws his stone into Number 2, and repeats the whole thing. But if he makes a mistake, he loses the rest of his turn and has to begin again by throwing his stone into that same box. The player who completes all ten rounds first wins.

This game takes endurance and skill. If we do not have much time we play one of the shorter versions. Of course we make enough "Scotches" so that there are only two or three players at each one.

The following are some of the variations of Hop Scotch.

5
4
3
2
1

Game:

Throw stone into box Number 1.

Hop from Number 1 to Number 5 and back.

Pick up stone and throw into Number 2.

Proceed successively.

After having thrown into Number 5, reverse by throwing stone into Number 1 while standing on one foot in Number 5. Pick up stone and return to 5 holding stone on thumb.

Throw from Number 5 into Number 2.

Return with stone in eye.

Throw from Number 5 into Number 3.

Return with stone in palm (hand open).

Throw from Number 5 into Number 4.

Return with stone on head.

Throw from Number 5 into Number 5.
Return to Number 1 with stone on back of neck.

Each time on returning to goal without dropping the stone, throw it up and catch it as it falls.

Dropping the stone, missing on the throw, and hopping on a line puts a player out.

Part I

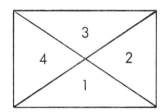

Game:

Throw stone into Number 1. Pick it up.
Hop, not touching lines from Number 1 to Number 4 and "out."
Throw stone into Number 2 and repeat as before.
Same into Number 3 and Number 4.

Part I

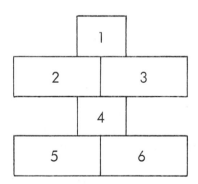

Game:

Throw stone into Number 1.
Hop into Number 1 and pick up stone.
Hop, having one foot in Number 2 and the other in Number 3.
Hop into Number 4 on one foot.
Hop, having one foot in Number 5 and the other in Number 6.
Jump turning around, one foot in Number 5 and the other in Number 6.

Return to Number 1 as you came.

Each time Number 1 is reached step out and toss or **drop stone** catching it as it falls.

Part I

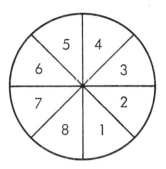

Game:

Throw stone into Number 1.

Pick it up.

Hop from Number 1 through to Number 8 without touching lines.

Repeat throwing into Number 2 and so on.

Part II

Walk into Number 1 with stone on foot and out through Number 8.

Kick up stone and catch it.

Same with stone on hand, toss it up, and catch it.

Same with stone on back, straighten up and let stone slide into hand.

HOT POTATO

This is a lively game played in a circle, with one player in the center. The others try to keep a Hot Potato out of his reach by passing it quickly around, or across, the circle. Of course the Hot Potato is only a ball, or a beanbag, or sometimes a towel tied in a knot. But if it comes your way, you will want to pass it on fast, because if the center player touches it while you are holding it or just after you have touched or held it, then he takes your place in the circle and you have to go inside.

The game is more fun when the circle is small than when it is large. If there are more than twelve players, we make another circle. Sometimes we have two or three center players instead of one.

Notes for the teacher: When an overanxious or a withdrawing child, or any child rejected by the others, is in the center, make sure that he does not stay there very long. If possible, do not let the game begin with such a situation—call for a volunteer, or select a leader to go in. If a relatively unskilled child does get hold of the Hot Potato, give him some word of commendation for his success.

KEEP AWAY*

Use a soccer ball for this game. Choose three people and practice passing the ball. Three more children practice at the other end of the gymnasium. Then we play.

We try to keep the ball in our team by tossing it to each other. We also try to *keep* it *away* from the other team. That is why the game is called by that name, I guess. The players on the other team try to get the ball. They cannot grab it from us. They can get it if we drop it or if we throw it low enough for them to catch it. When the players on the other team have the ball, we try to stop their passes.

This is one of the best games we have. It is a very fast game. Sometimes we count the number of times we catch the ball without dropping it. The other team does that, too. Then we know which group is the best. We wear colored bands over our shoulders so that we can see our own players.

Notes for the teacher: The number of practice groups depends on the number of balls available. When it is time to play, divide into sets of teams so that no teams will be watching. There should be from three to five or six on a team. This is the best game for teaching the essentials of guarding: keeping between your opponent and the ball, but close enough to him to intercept a high ball. Later, the essentials of getting free of your guard—moving fast and changing direction—may be thought out and practiced.

KICKOVER FOOTBALL

In this game we try to kick the ball better than the other team so that we can score by a drop kick over the opponents' goal line.

One team starts play by punting out from its own goal line. The best punter holds the ball, and the rest of his teammates have to be "onside"; that is, on the goal line, even with the ball. Players of the other team are all over the field, waiting for the kick. Any one of them can try to catch the ball, and no one can interfere with him while he is trying. If he catches it, he punts back from the place he caught it. If he misses it, anyone else may try to field it and punt it back from the place he first picked it up. Whenever anyone kicks, the rest of his team must get onside, or even with the ball.

Whenever the player who is going to kick the ball thinks that he is near enough to the other team's goal line to drop kick the ball over the goal line he tries that, because that is the way a score is made. If the ball goes over the goal line in the air, as high as a player's head, his team scores a point. Then the other side gets the ball and starts again at its goal line. Any defending player may try to catch the ball before it goes over the goal line.

If you have gone to football games, or have seen games on television, probably you know the difference between a punt and a drop kick. It is just this: In each kind of kick, you drop the ball toward the ground. When you punt, you kick the ball *before* it touches the ground; when you drop kick, you kick the ball just *after* it has touched the ground.

> *Notes for the teacher:* Since this game affords practice in kicking but not much activity, use it for only part of a period, preferably after the children have evaluated their need for training in kicking. If they have trouble with the drop kick, try to get an older boy to come in and demonstrate it to the class. Use a soccer ball at first, then a football.

LONG BASE

Long Base is played on a field that has a home base line, a pitcher's box, and a goal line. The goal line is 40 feet from home base. A playground ball and bat are used.

There are fielders, a pitcher, and a catcher on each team. Only five or six players are needed for each team. When the game starts, the catcher is behind home base and the pitcher is 25 feet in front of him. The batter stands a safe distance from the catcher, with his side turned to the pitcher.

The pitcher throws an underhand throw to the batter. The batter tries to bat the ball beyond the home base line into the field. He has to stay at bat until he hits a ball. When he does that he drops his bat and runs to the goal. The players on the other team try to put him out. They can do this in several ways. If they catch the ball on the fly he is out. If they tag the goal or home line before he gets there, he is out. He can put himself out by slinging his bat.

If he goes from home to goal and back again without having any of these things happen to him, he scores a point. He may stay at the goal if he is afraid of being caught. Several batters can be on goal at the same time, and then run home in turn. If they leave the goal, they have to run home. When there are three outs, the teams change places.

> *Notes for the teacher:* Long Base provides an opportunity for practice of fundamentals in a simply organized game. It is excellent batting practice for beginners, as the fear of striking out is eliminated by the rule permitting the batter to stay up until he hits the ball (foul, tip, or fair). The small number of players re-

quired for a team enables several games to be organized in the average class group, thereby encouraging more practice for all players.

ONE AGAINST THREE

You have to move fast and dodge well to win in this game. We start by counting off in fours, and we play in these groups of four. Numbers Two, Three, and Four make a triangle by joining hands. Number One is outside, opposite Number Four. Number One tries to tag Number Four while the others try to keep him from doing this. If he succeeds, he scores a point and starts again opposite Number Three, trying to tag this player. The three players in the triangle must keep hands joined. If the triangle is broken, the tagger gets a point.

When the whistle blows, all the groups stop. Then they make a new triangle, with Number Two outside, and the game begins again. After everyone has had a turn at being the tagger, the game is over, and it is time to add up your score.

Notes for the teacher: This game presents certain problems of adjustment the first time it is played. It may be advisable to take a quick look at the groups of four before blowing the whistle to begin. If a well-accepted child is Number One—the first to be "against" the group—no harm will be done. But if the most rejected of the four starts in that position, his feeling of rejection is likely to be increased. In such a situation it would be advisable to ask the child to change with Number Three or Four in the group. Taking his turn later, when it has become obvious that this is something everyone does, will be less difficult for him.

Whether or not much is made of individual scores depends on the philosophy of competition prevailing in a particular school. Certainly the children will enjoy this game regardless of scores, and usually it is a good idea to let scores be added but not to give them any further emphasis.

PADDLE BALL

We like to play this game before school or during recess. Sometimes we play it in class, when several different kinds of games are going on at the same time. The object of the game is to keep the ball going, as in tennis, but we play against a wall, as in handball. We can play singles, with one on a side, or doubles, with two.

We play with a tennis ball and hit it with the same kind of paddle we use for paddle tennis. We play on a handball court, or anyplace, indoors or out, where there is a wall at least 18 feet high and 18 feet wide and a hard-surfaced court about 26 feet long and 18 feet wide. A line is drawn across the wall 2 feet above the ground. Across the court, a service line is drawn 13 feet from the wall.

The server starts, standing anywhere between the wall and the service line. To be good, the ball must hit the wall above the 2-foot line and then land inside the court. The receiver waits until it has bounced once and then hits it back against the wall. Server and receiver take turns hitting the ball against the wall until one misses. A player "misses" when his ball does not hit the wall above the 2-foot line and then bounce back to land inside the court, or when he does not return the ball on the first bounce. If the server misses, the receiver gets the serve. If the receiver misses, the server scores a point and goes on serving. Whoever gets 11 points first, wins. When we play doubles, we like to make the game 21 points if we have time.

Notes for the teacher: This is a good game to teach when there are several different small groups or individual games going on at once. It is a good introduction to paddle tennis. A tennis backboard, the side of a building, or an unobstructed wall space in the gymnasium or playroom may be used. Groups can umpire their own games as they play.

PADDLE TENNIS

We play paddle tennis on the paved part of the playground when only two or four of us want to play. Sometimes, on rainy days, we play it in the gym. It is played like tennis, but the court is smaller, the ball is made of sponge rubber, and we use wooden paddles instead of rackets. If two play, we call it singles; if four play, we call it doubles.

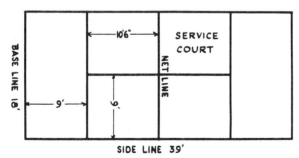

The server stands behind the base line on the right-hand side of his court. He tries to hit the ball with the paddle so that it first bounces in his court and then goes over the net into the service court diagonally across from him. The receiver returns it by hitting it with his paddle after it has bounced once on his side. Then each side hits the ball in turn, either in the air before it bounces or after it has bounced once. If one side does not get it back across the net, inside the court boundaries, the other side scores a point. The same player serves throughout a whole game, but from alternate sides of his court.

Paddle tennis is scored like tennis. If one side made 4 points in a row, the score would be 15, 30, 40, and game. But if both sides have won 3 points, the score is called *deuce*, and then one side or the other has to score 2 points in succession in order to win the game. Zero is called *love*. The server's score is always mentioned first.

This is how the score in a game might go:

First point for server: *15–love*
Next point for receiver: *15 all*
Next point for receiver: *15–30*
Next point for server: *30 all*
Next point for receiver: *30–40*
Next point for server: *deuce*

Next point for server: *advantage in*
Next point for receiver: *deuce*
Next point for receiver: *advantage out*
Next point for receiver: *game*

After each game, the service goes to the other side. If four are playing, one of the partners serves straight through a game, and then when the service comes to that side again, the other partner serves throughout the game. The side winning six games first wins a *set*. But if both sides win five games, the set score is *deuce* and then one side or the other has to win two games in succession in order to win the set.

> *Notes for the teacher:* This game is good preparation for tennis. Players should learn elementary strategy, such as returning to the center of the court after play and trying to place the ball out of their opponent's reach. They should also learn such elements of good form as a free arm swing, with wrist firm. Footwork is also important: moving sideways with a kind of slide-and-slide step (called *chassé* in dance) in order to cover the court and watch the ball, then turning the body when hitting the ball in order to swing the arm from the shoulder and follow through. It is important to prevent footfaulting (stepping on or over the line when serving). Since this loses points, it may readily develop into a costly habit.

POM, POM, PULLAWAY*

I love to run; that is why this is my favorite game. We play it like this. We choose one child to be It. He stands in the middle of the playground. The rest of us stand on one side, back of a line we have scraped with our heels. The one who is It says:

> Pom, Pom, Pullaway,
> Come away or I will
> *Fetch* you away!

When he says this, we have to run past him to the other end of the playground. We are allowed to dodge. The one who is It tries to tag us. If we are tagged, we are in the middle, too. We help him tag the rest.

The next time, we face the other way. The one who is It says the verse again. If the players do not run *right away*, we can go right after them and tag them.

We play until there are no more players to catch. The best dodgers and the best runners are usually the last ones caught.

> *Notes for the teacher:* The old way of playing this game required the chaser to tag the runner three times on the back. It can easily be seen that this invited tackles and an imitation of football tactics by no means harmless.

Hill Dill, listed in the chart of primary games, is played like Pom, Pom, Pullaway, except that the following verse is used:

> Hill Dill, come over the hill
> Or else we'll catch you
> Standing still.

The game is listed under both names because although children like both verses, they enjoy the more threatening tone of Pullaway in the intermediate grades.

PRISONERS' BASE

For this game we need a very large space, because it is a game that has lots of running back and forth. The playground is divided by a line in the middle, and the players are divided into two equal teams. Each team has half the playground for its own space and marks off an end line at the back, with a Prison about 4 by 4 feet in one corner. A player is safe anywhere in his own space, but when he crosses over into the enemy's territory he can be tagged and put into Prison.

The object of the game is to run through the other team's space to its Prison without being tagged. If you can do this when the Prison is empty, you score a point for your side. But if you are tagged before you get there, you must go to the enemy's Prison and stay inside it until you are rescued. If someone on your team is fast enough to get through and touch you without being tagged himself, you are rescued, and both of you can go back safely. Only one Prisoner can be taken back by a Rescuer.

At the end of the game each team adds the number of points it has made to the number of Prisoners in its Prison for the total team score.

Before we start, we get together to decide what players are to guard our Prisoners. Sometimes we even have a Lookout, who tells us when to try to get through. But most of the time we watch and run ourselves, because the enemy is always on the move.

> *Notes for the teacher:* Running, dodging, and, above all, strategy are to be learned from this game. It is a good test of temperament, also, for it distinguishes good judgment from sheer rash-

ness. Of course the children—especially those who tend to be withdrawn—should be encouraged to make sorties into the other team's territory. Withdrawn children are likely to be made Prison guards, but they should not be kept in that position during the whole game. To avoid this, you might suggest a general change on both teams: "Let's give someone else a chance to defend the Prison!" Teams need captains to organize both offense and defense. This is a fine opportunity to point out that all games are like Prisoners' Base in having offensive play and defensive play, both of which must be planned.

RED LIGHT*

First, two goals are decided upon. We all stand behind one of these goals. One child, who is chosen to be It, stands halfway between the goals. He turns his back to the others and shuts his eyes tight. He may count to ten slowly and say "Red Light!" or he may say this verse:

> No moving,
> No talking,
> No laughing,
> Red light!

While he is saying the words or counting to ten, we run for the other goal. When the one who is It yells "Red Light!" he turns around. We must stop running and become still as statues. If the one who is It sees anyone take a step or move after he has turned around, that child must go back to the goal he started from. Then the one who is It repeats the verse or counts to ten again. The first one to get to the other goal is It for the next game.

Notes for the teacher: This game affords fine training in ethics. To call violations honestly means that It must be fair; to accept his call takes honesty and a sense of responsibility as well. The game also provides good training in control of momentum—the children must learn to lean back and take a wide stance immediately in order to keep their balance when they stop.

RELAYS*

When we have relay races there are about six on each team. If the teams are uneven, some children run twice. All the teams stand behind a line so that they will have the same distance to run.

When the leader says "On your mark," and "Get set," we get ready. When he yells "Go!" the first person in each team runs to the fence and back. He tags the hand of the next person. We keep on doing that until everyone has had a turn. The first team to finish, wins.

Rules:

We must stay *behind* the line until we are tagged. It is a foul against our team if we do not obey this rule. Each foul counts 1 point against us. The team that finishes first gets 5 points. The next one gets 4 points, and so on. Fouls take away points, so a careful team may finish last and still be the winner.

OTHER RELAYS

Backward relay

We carry a scarf. When we get back to the line, we give it to the next player. We *walk* backward to the goal and *run* back to the line.

Bounce ball relay

We bounce a ball with one hand to the goal and back.

Obstacle relay

We do funny things. We run around a chair, do a somersault on the mat, go under a table, tag the wall, and hop back to our places.

Twin relay

We take partners in two double lines and hold our partner's hand. Two pairs run at a time. They have to stop running and join hands again if they let go. This is a tricky relay.

> *Notes for the teacher:* There are endless varieties of relays, and they have their uses. Skill relays may be used to teach skills of various seasonal sports when the group is not yet ready for drills. Often the children and the teacher together can make up such relays. Six on a team is too many for efficient practice, however.
>
> The relay should be introduced as soon as children are ready to function as a team, with each player running when tagged without waiting to run an individual race with his opposite in another line. The starting rule of the relay should be strictly enforced. It is an excellent introduction to the appreciation of rules as giving everyone an equal chance. Other relays are listed on the charts for primary and intermediate grades.

SCRAMBLE BASKETBALL

We play this game with six on a side, using half the basketball court. Usually there are two games going on at once.

Players on each team are numbered, and line up by number on opposite side lines. The umpire stands in the center circle, holding a basketball. He calls out three numbers, and at the same time rolls or bounces the ball into the court. The three players on each side who have the numbers he called run onto the court, try to get the ball, and, with the help of their teammates, try to make a basket. As soon as a team makes a basket, 2 points are added to its score. Then the ball goes back to the umpire, and the players go back to the side lines. The next time the umpire calls three different numbers.

We play with basketball rules; that is, no rough play, no touching the ball when another player has two hands on it, no running with the ball. We may not hold the ball longer than three seconds nor dribble it more than twice. If anyone fouls, the ball is given to the other side.

When we first learned this game, we could score by hitting the backboard. But as we learned how to shoot baskets, we made the rules harder. Now we score only if the ball goes through the basket.

Notes for the teacher: Sometimes it is advisable to have only two numbers called, giving four players a chance to play at one time. Children can umpire this game readily enough, and you can keep an eye on both games. If you try to have a class of twenty-five or thirty playing in one set, too much time is spent in watching. After all players have had two chances, give the teams time for a huddle so that they may evaluate their own play.

SHUFFLEBOARD

One of the girls in our room played this game on an ocean liner last summer. She liked it so much and talked so much about it that we asked our teacher for the equipment so that we could play it. He and the principal agreed that if we wanted to make the cues and the disks, they would have a couple of courts marked out in the gym. Our shop teacher helped us to make eight disks and four cues.

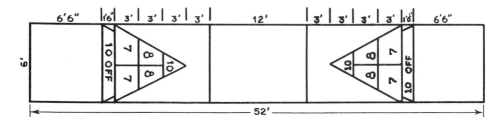

The purpose of the game is to push your disks along the court with a cue so that they land where they will score as many points as possible. To score 10 points, for example, your disk must come to rest inside the Number 10 zone, not touching the boundary lines, after you have given it a push. The same is true of all the other zones except the 10 Off zone at the end of the court. If your disk lands in that zone, or if it touches any of its boundaries, 10 points are taken off your score.

When we play doubles, there are two Reds and two Blacks. Each side plays from its own side of the court with four disks of its own color. That means that one Red and one Black player stand side by side at each end. Each places his four disks in the 10 Off zone. Red plays first, then Black, and they continue alternately until each has played four disks. In pushing his disk, a player may knock any other disk already on the court so that it lands to his own advantage.

After the Red and the Black players at one end have played eight disks, their scores are counted. Then the other two players, the Red and the Black at the other end of the court, play their eight disks from the 10 Off zone, Red leading. A game may be 50, 75, or 100 points, depending on what has been decided before the game begins.

Singles in shuffleboard is played like doubles, except that each player moves from one end of the court to the other after having played four disks.

Rules:

1. Disks must be played from the player's half of the 10 Off zone. Penalty: 5 points.

2. Players may not step into the 10 Off zone while pushing a disk, or even touch the line. Penalty: 5 points.

3. No player may interfere with another player, or touch any "live" disk except by pushing it with his own disk.

4. "Dead" disks are those that (*a*) do not go past the farthest "dead" line, (*b*) strike some object other than another disk, (*c*) come in from another court, (*d*) go beyond the base line. Dead disks must be removed.

> *Notes for the teacher:* Although this is a good recreational game, the disks and cues are expensive if bought. The game obviously provides no exercise, but it does hold the interest of older boys and girls.

SHUTTLE RELAY

As in any relay, each player runs in turn when he is touched off by the teammate ahead of him. Teams are divided into two equal files standing opposite each other, anywhere from 25 to 50 feet apart. At the signal, Number One in each file runs across the space, touches off Number Two, and then goes to the end of the file, which moves up one. Number Two does the same thing, running in the opposite direction and touching off Number Three.

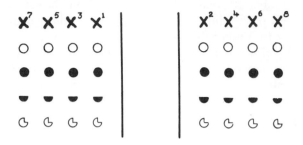

The team that finishes first wins, every player having run in turn; that is, when Number Eight player crosses Line A. If teams are uneven, it is better to have some players run twice than to have any drop out.

> *Notes for the teacher:* This formation speeds up activity because each player runs a shorter distance than in the usual relay. Keep each team small, with six to eight players on a team and three or four at each end. Variations such as hopping and skipping may be introduced.
>
> Make sure that players respect the restraining lines. This is one of the most direct ways of teaching observance of rules as giving a fair chance to all. Ask the first and second runners to watch the line after they have run themselves. If their reports, followed by commendation for the teams that did not foul, do not have the desired effect, try working the fouls into a scoring system, as follows. Give 5 points to the team finishing first; 3 to that finishing second; 1 to that finishing third. At the end of play, add the scores; then subtract 1 point for every foul.

SIDEWALK TENNIS

We like to play this game at home on the sidewalk or patio, or on any smooth hard surface that is large enough. There are four squares in a row, each square 6 feet wide and long. At first we use a playground ball, throwing and catching it. As soon as we learn the game that way we try it with a tennis ball, batting it with our hands.

The rules are like tennis except we do not have rackets or a net. If two play, we call it singles; if four play, we call it doubles.

The server stands with the ball behind the back line of his court and tries to throw the ball so it lands in the receiving square (the first square) on the other side. The receiver returns it by letting it bounce once, catching it and then throwing it to any place on the other courts. Then each side catches and throws the ball in turn, either in the air before it bounces or after it has bounced once. If one side does not get it back inside the court boundaries, the other side scores a point. The same player serves throughout the game, but if we are playing doubles we change off when our side gets the service again.

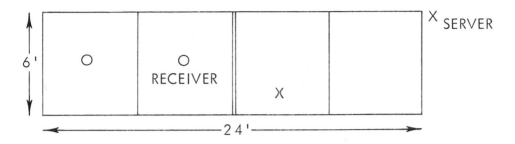

At first we score points, and the first side that wins 4 points wins the game. Then the serve goes to the other side. When we play with a tennis ball, we keep score like tennis, which is much harder. It is explained in this book under the rules for Paddle Tennis.

> *Notes for the teacher:* This game is simpler than paddle tennis, and more available, since it does not require a net or as much space. It works well as an individual game for squad play.

MODIFIED SOCCER

This is a very good team game because everyone is playing, and no one is waiting for a turn. We play on a big field with boundaries marked and goal markers at each end. There are two restraining lines, one on each side of the center. Here is a diagram showing the field and players at the beginning of a game. Each team has eleven players: a center and four other forwards, three halfbacks, two fullbacks, and a goalie.

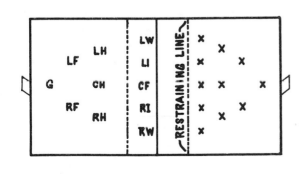

LW - LEFT WING
LI - LEFT INNER
CF - CENTER FORWARD
RI - RIGHT INNER
RW - RIGHT WING
LH - LEFT HALFBACK
CH - CENTER HALFBACK
RH - RIGHT HALFBACK
LF - LEFT FULLBACK
RF - RIGHT FULLBACK
G - GOALIE

Of course, we can play on a smaller field if we have fewer players. But it is no fun to play on a field so small that we get in one another's way.

The object of the game is to try to kick the ball through your opponents' goal. The game begins with one team in possession of the ball on the center line and the other team behind its restraining line. The center with the ball must kick the ball forward. His teammates try to get the ball and kick it on down the field until they can kick it through the other team's goal, not above the goalie's head. A goal counts 2 points.

Soccer is a game in which your feet must be very skillful, because you are not allowed to touch the ball with your hands or arms. You have to count on your feet to move both you and the ball. This takes good balance. The goalie is the only exception to the rule. Because he is the last hope of his team, and *must* keep the ball from going through the goal, he is allowed to use his hands and arms to catch the ball. Then he may throw or kick it down the field, but he may not run with the ball.

Fouls in soccer are tripping, rough play, shoving, holding another player, or using hands on the ball. The penalty for a foul is a free kick for the other side. This is a kick from the ground at the spot where the foul occurred, and no other player may be within 3 yards of the ball.

Whenever the ball goes out of bounds, the team that did not send it out may kick it in from the side line. This should be done at the spot where the ball went out of bounds.

We usually play quarters, and take time for a huddle between quarters as well as between halves to talk about our play.

Notes for the teacher: It is important to give players an opportunity for the huddle so that they may become accustomed to evaluating their own play and improve their strategy. Be available during a huddle so that you can answer questions and ask them, too. Also give direct advice. In playing a modified version of more highly organized team games keep the rules simple but insist that they be obeyed. If the rules seem unworkable, let the class revise them by discussion and vote; after they have been accepted, they should be observed. Do not play this version of soccer until the class has become fairly adept at managing the ball with the feet, as in the preliminary games of Corner Kickball, Alley Soccer, and others.

SOCCER GOAL KICK

This game helps us develop skills we need for soccer, but it reminds me of baseball, too. The object of the game is to have each player on the kicking team score a run when it is his turn. To do this, he kicks a soccer ball out into the field and then tries to run around a post at the opposite end of the field and back home before the team in the field can kick the ball back over the home goal. If the runner can do this, he scores a point.

After everyone on the running team has had a chance to kick, the teams change. When both teams have taken a turn at kicking and fielding, the inning is over. Sometimes we play two innings, but if we have time we play more. When we play a team from another room, we like to play four innings.

We tell the runner to remember these things:

1. Be sure to go all the way *around* the post and *through* the goal when you come back.

2. Do not touch the ball while you are running. If you forget either of these two things, your run does not count.

When we are fielders we remember these things:

1. To kick the ball, not to touch it with our hands or arms. If a player does touch the ball with his hands or arms, he must raise both arms and shout "Safe!" Then the runner scores whether he gets home ahead of the ball or not.

2. To kick the ball to a teammate if we are far out in the field, instead of trying to kick it home ourselves, because the ball gets back much more quickly that way. But if we are near enough, we try to kick the ball through the goal ourselves.

Notes for the teacher: The goal may be marked with Indian clubs, stones, or any clear markers. The space between markers should be 6 to 10 feet.

MODIFIED SOFTBALL

In the spring this is our favorite game. After we have played many other games that help us with softball and have had enough practice, we know the positions we like best and can play best. We also know how to play, and we are ready to form our teams and have regular games.

Each softball team has nine players. Look at the diagram to find out where they play when they are in the field and what their positions are called. The other team comes up to bat in a definite order, which is decided at the beginning of the game and does not change during the game.

The game begins with the pitcher's throwing an underhand ball to the batter, who tries to hit it out into the field, between the first and third base lines. If he hits the ball, he runs to first base, trying to get

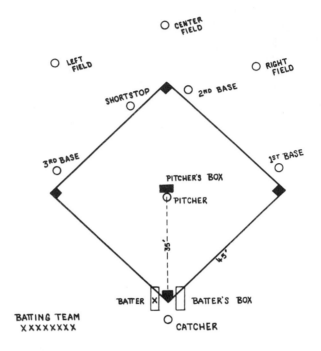

there before the ball is fielded and thrown to the player on first base. If he succeeds, he is safe, and is then called a *runner*. Of course, if he hits a long ball, he may get further.

If he is on first base when the next batter is up and hits a fair ball, the runner must get to second base before the ball is thrown to the second baseman. In this way, he tries to get to third base and then home without being put out. When he has safely crossed home plate, he has scored a run for his team.

Of course, the fielders try to put batters out before they become runners, and try to put runners out before they can get home and score. When they have put out three of the players of the team that is at bat, sides change and the fielding team comes in to bat.

A batter may be put out in the following ways:

1. By striking him out. If a batter swings at the ball and misses it, that is a strike. If he swings and misses three times, he is out. If he decides not to try to hit a ball, and the ball crosses any part of home plate between his knees and his shoulders, it counts as a strike. If he hits a foul ball (outside the base lines), it counts as a strike unless he already has two strikes. But if he just tips a ball and the catcher catches it, that counts as a strike even if it is the third strike.

2. By catching a foul hit before it touches the ground.

A runner may be put out in the following ways:

1. By fielding the ball to the first baseman before the runner gets there. The baseman must hold on to the ball while touching the base. Whenever the runner is forced to run to another base, he may be put out in the same way.

2. By tagging him with the ball when he is off base, without dropping the ball.

3. By catching a fair ball before it has hit the ground.

4. If the runner has left his base before a fly was caught, the fielder may throw the ball to that base. If the ball gets to the baseman before the runner can get back, he is out.

There are four ways a batter can get to first base besides hitting a fair ball:

1. If the pitcher pitches four "balls." A ball is a pitch that goes outside the plate, or higher than the batter's shoulders or lower than his knees.

2. If a pitched ball hits a batter, unless he did not try to get out of the way.

3. If the catcher interferes with the batter.

4. If the pitcher does not follow rules when he pitches. That is, if he does not start his pitch with both feet touching the pitcher's plate, if he takes more than one step forward, or if he does not pitch underhand.

There are two ways a base runner can get to the next base besides running on a fair hit:

1. If the pitcher has pitched four balls and runners are forced to move on to make room for the runners behind them.

2. If a pitched ball reaches or passes the catcher, the runner may "steal" if he wants to take a chance. He may not move off his base or start to run with the pitch, but he may start when the ball gets to the catcher or goes by him on a wild pitch.

You can see that there are many rules and many fine points to the game. There are two rules of safety that every batter should remember. One is to hold the bat with the trademark up. The bat is made so that it will not crack if it is held that way. The other rule is *never throw your bat,* because, of course, it will hit and hurt anyone in its path.

We need a good umpire to call strikes and balls, and to decide when the runner is safe. We also need a captain to help decide our batting order and to call plays, if we use them.

Notes for the teacher: Softball has additional rules, but you will probably agree that these are enough to begin with. Official rules may be found in the *Official Softball Guide,* published each year. When the older boys begin to talk about the fine points of the game, get the office to order a copy and let them study it.

STRIDE BALL RELAY*

To play this game, we make four teams. Each team lines up in front of a low basket in the gymnasium, and the first one in each row gets a ball.

When the whistle blows, everyone stands with his legs apart. Then the first one in each line—the leader—rolls the ball between the legs of each player on his team. When the ball reaches the last one in line, he picks it up, runs to the basket, and throws it in. If he misses, he does not try again but gets the ball, runs to the front of the line, and rolls the ball back, between the other players' legs just as the leader did. Everyone else moves back one place. The game continues until the leader has thrown the ball into the basket and is back at the front of the line.

When all the teams have finished, each player who has made a basket raises his hand. Each basket counts 1 point. The team that finished first gets an extra point.

Suggestions: Practice throwing the ball into the basket. Do not *bounce* the ball back; *roll* it.

Notes for the teacher: A utility ball or a junior basketball may be used for this game. If there are no baskets in your playroom, a good game may be played without the basket shooting. In a gymnasium with baskets, use both ends of the room in order to keep the teams small. A problem of spacing is sure to arise, which you may wish either to avoid or to let the children solve themselves. It is, of course, highly advantageous for a team to crowd up to the front so that the file is shortened as the ball is passed between the players' legs. If nothing is said about this, watch to see which team thinks up the device. One will, if the teams are given a chance to huddle occasionally. Then watch for complaints or imitation from the other teams. If they begin to crowd enough to spoil their play, it may be advisable to agree on a front and back boundary line for each team.

SUITCASE RELAY*

The Suitcase Relay is the funniest game I know. There are four teams, four captains, four goals, and four suitcases. There is a long space between the captains and the goals, and the suitcase is put in the middle of this space. Every suitcase has several kinds of hats, a pocketbook, and a big pair of galoshes inside. We trim the hats with old flowers and ribbons.

The object of the game is to have each captain open the suitcase and put on one hat and the galoshes. He has to take the pocketbook, too, and then close the suitcase. After he has run around the goal at the end of the gymnasium, he hurries back to the suitcase, takes off what he has put on, and shuts everything out of sight. Then he runs back to his team and tags the next player, who does the same thing.

Sometimes the galoshes are hard to keep on and we almost fall down. It is funny to see a boy with a girl's hat on or a girl in big galoshes. We laugh and laugh when we play this game.

Notes for the teacher: This is another party game enjoyed by children of all ages up to 60. Eight- and nine-year-olds will have fun getting into long skirts, in addition to the articles mentioned.

TAG*

Tag is the game I like to play. The person who is It tries to tag someone else. All the others try to get away. There are so many different kinds of tag that it is hard to name them all. To be safe in Wood Tag, you must touch wood. In Stork Tag, you stand on one foot; in Statue Tag, you kneel with your arms stretched out.

I like plain tag best. One rule we have is that we must not grab the clothes of any players we are tagging. If we touch them with the flat part of our hand, we do not make this mistake. We try not to run into each other.

Bronco Tag is fun, too. We choose partners and stand one behind the other. The one who is It tries to tag the player in back. If he does, that one must take his place.

TETHER BALL

This game can be played on the playground, in the gym, or in your own backyard if your parents will let you have the standard, the paddle, and the ball.

The standard is a strong pole 10 feet tall. It should be set in a cement base in the ground. The ball can be an old tennis ball, a sponge rubber ball, or a volley ball. It is fastened to the end of a 6-foot rope, which is attached to the top of the standard. If you play with a tennis ball or a sponge rubber ball, each player needs a paddle for hitting it. If you play with a volleyball, just use your hands.

A white line is painted on the standard about 6 feet up from the ground. Around the base of the standard, on the ground, there is a circle 6 feet across. A boundary line 20 feet long goes through the center of the circle, dividing the space in half.

Two players stand on opposite sides of the standard, outside the circle, and hit the ball in opposite directions. One player starts the game by serving. That is, he gives the ball a hard hit in the direction he wants it to go. The other player hits it as soon as he can in the other direction. Each player tries to hit the ball hard enough, or often enough, to wind it up in his direction above the marker on the pole. If he can do this, he scores 1 point. Then the game begins again with the receiver serving first.

The following are fouls in this game:

1. Stepping inside the circle or across the boundary line into your opponent's field.

2. Reaching over into your opponent's field.

3. Touching the pole with hands or paddle.

4. Letting the ball wind up around your hand or your paddle.

Whenever one player fouls, the other may have a free hit. If the ball is wound around the pole, he may unwind it one turn before hitting it.

Notes for the teacher: This individual game is well suited for recess or after-school play. It may also be used during class periods when the children are divided into small groups for individual sports. Although sometimes played with four players—two on a side, the partners taking turns hitting the ball—it does not work very well that way. It is a good game to suggest to parents who want to put some play apparatus in the yard for 10- to 11-year-olds.

THROW IT AND RUN

We can play Throw It and Run on the softball field or in the playground. It is a good softball game for playing in our yard at home, too, because we do not bat the ball. We use a softball or playground ball and need a home plate and first base marked on the field. There are fielders and a pitcher and catcher on each team.

The pitcher of the team in field tosses an underhand throw to the first player up. This player must catch the ball, throw it as hard as he can into the field, then run to first base and back to home plate. Any player on the team in field who recovers the ball throws it to the catcher as fast as he can. If the runner beats the ball back to home plate, he scores a point. If the ball is in the catcher's hand, and the catcher has one foot on home plate, the runner is out. We must remember these rules:

1. The player up does not have to try for a badly pitched ball. However, if he tries for the ball and misses it, a strike is counted. Three strikes and he is out.

2. Three outs and the teams change places.

3. If a ball thrown by the player up is caught by any member of the team in field before it touches the ground, the player up is out.

Notes for the teacher: By eliminating the batting element, the game encourages practice in throwing and catching skills essential for active play in the softball type games. It is an excellent preparation for modified softball and is an active, appealing game for early intermediate grade children.

MODIFIED VOLLEYBALL

Two teams with an equal number of players stand on opposite sides of the volleyball net, which is 7 feet high. Players on each team have a number and take up positions according to their number, as the diagram shows. The arrows indicate the direction in which players move when they "rotate." Rotation will be explained in a moment.

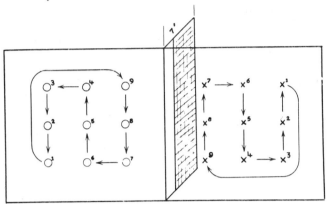

The Number One player of the serving side takes the ball, stands behind his end line, and tries to hit the ball over the net. In serving, he holds the ball in one hand and uses an underhand motion to hit the ball with the palm of the other hand. If his serve does not go all the way over the net, another player may hit it to help it along. This is called an "assist."

The players on the other side try to bat the ball back, and so it goes back and forth across the net until it strikes the floor or goes out of bounds. If the receiving side does not return it correctly, the serving side scores 1 point, and the same player serves again. But if the serving side fails to return the ball, it goes to the receiving side, which now has a chance to serve and to score.

As soon as the service changes, the players on the side that has lost the serve change places, or rotate. Number Two goes to Number One's place, and all the others move in the direction of the arrows on the diagram. Number One goes to the spot left vacant when Number Nine moved over to Number Eight's spot. Always remember that you take the place of the player with the next lower number, unless you are Number One. Here are some other things to remember:

1. Only the serving side scores. When the receivers win a play, they win the ball and become servers.

2. Only one assist is allowed on a serve.

3. On a return, any number of players on the same side may hit the ball before it goes back over the net.

4. However, the same player may hit the ball only twice in succession.

5. Players must hit the ball—not catch, hold, or throw it.

6. The server must keep both feet behind the end line in serving.

7. A player may hit a ball that has gone into the net, provided he does not touch the net.

8. No player may reach over the net.

If the serving side "faults" by breaking any of these rules or by not returning the ball properly, the side is out and the receivers become servers. If the receivers fault, the servers get a point and the same player continues to serve. Game score is 15 points.

> *Notes for the teacher:* This game is like volleyball except in permitting assists and repeated playing of the ball by the same side. It should be played in preparation for volleyball. If lack of skill prevents the game from going well, let the players discuss their weak points and work on either serving or volleying techniques in special practice sessions. This is a comparatively easy game for pupils to officiate.

VOLLEY-BASE-BASKETBALL

This game combines three of our favorite games. We call it VBB for short.

Two teams with an equal number of players take turns batting a volleyball into a basketball court which has a small baseball diamond drawn in one half. Here is a diagram of the playing area. The X players are at bat, and the O players are in the field.

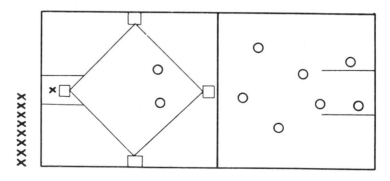

When a player comes up to "bat," he hits the volleyball with his hand as if he were serving in a volleyball game. If it is a fair hit he runs, circling the bases in order, touching each one and trying to make a home run before being put out. The players in the field can put him out by fielding the ball, making three passes to teammates, and then trying to shoot a basket. If the ball goes through the basket before the runner gets around all the bases and home, the runner is out. If the ball misses the basket, the forwards keep on shooting until someone makes a basket, but this gives the runner a good chance to get home first and score a run.

If we have time, we let one side bat until each player has had a turn. If we do not have that much time, we play three-minute or five-minute innings.

VOLLEY TENNIS

Two teams with an equal number of players play this game with a volleyball, on the volleyball court, with the net 4 feet high. Number One of the serving team starts, standing behind the end line. He hits the ball with his hand so that it bounces on his side of the net, and someone on his team hits it again so that it goes over the net. The other team tries to send it back by hitting it either after it bounces or on the fly.

The ball is sent back and forth over the net until someone sends it out or it falls to the floor. If the serving side fails to return it, the receiving side gets the serve. If the receiving side fails to return it, the serving side scores a point. Game score is 15 points.

Remember these things:

1. Each player serves in turn, when his number comes up.

2. Both on the serve and on the return, the ball may bounce on the floor only once before it is sent across the net.

3. The ball may be volleyed—that is, hit on the fly—any number of times before being sent across the net to the other side.

4. The ball is out of bounds when it hits any object outside the boundary lines.

5. No player may touch or reach over the net.

6. The ball must be hit—not caught, held, or thrown.

Notes for the teacher: This is an easier form of volleyball than modified volleyball, and may well be used if the children in your class are too short to get the ball over a higher net. For this game the net may be lowered to 3 feet at first, but a height of 4 feet is preferable. When the children are familiar with the game, they may wish to start rotation. They may also get an idea of the smash from this game. The smash is, of course, the best form of offense in volleyball, badminton, and tennis. It is based on the same principle in all games: hitting the ball from as great a height as possible, near the net, at a sharp angle down to the court on the other side, with as much speed or force as possible. If well done, it is very difficult to return.

WASTEBASKET BALL

This is a fine game to play at home in any room big enough to let you move around fast. Of course, it is a good game for school, too. You need a wastebasket, a tennis ball, and a tennis racket or paddle for each player. We play singles (one on a side) or doubles (two on a side). The object of the game is to hit the ball, after it has bounced once, into the wastebasket. Every time you succeed in doing that, you score 1 point for your side.

Before you start, move the furniture out of the way and draw a circle on the floor around the basket 2 feet from it. No player may go inside this circle. Opponents stand on opposite sides of the basket, outside the circle. The server drops the ball anywhere on his side, outside the circle, lets it bounce once, and then tries to hit it so that it will go into the basket. If he succeeds, he gets a point and another serve. If he misses, the ball is in play, and his opponent lets the ball bounce once and then tries to hit it into the basket. If the server is so good that he serves 3 points in succession, the serve goes to the other side. If the opponent returns the ball into the basket, then he gets a point as well as the serve. If the basket is missed, the ball is played alternately by each side until someone makes a basket or the ball lands foul. A foul ball is one that lands where it really cannot be played. The person who hit it calls "Foul!" and loses his serve to his opponent. Usually we play an 11-point game.

Remember these rules:

1. Both server and receiver may score, but only by hitting the ball into the basket after it has bounced once.

2. If a player fails to keep the ball in play, or hits it so that it lands foul, his opponent gets the serve.

3. If the server makes 3 points in succession on his serve, the service changes.

4. A foul ball is one that lands so that it really cannot be played on the first bounce. It may be too close to the basket, or it may have hit the wall or some other object and then rolled instead of bouncing.

Notes for the teacher: This is a good game to teach when several different small group games are going on simultaneously. When playing it in the gymnasium or playroom, it is advisable to have a circle with a 20-foot radius from the basket as an outer boundary. Any ball landing outside the outer circle is a foul ball. Do not expect children to get along without arguments about what is really a foul ball unless they receive some good instruction from you. First, let them talk about why they have so many arguments. They may want to try having the receiver instead of the one who hit the ball call fouls. Usually, however, the other method is preferable, and they may be able to figure out why. Sometimes sixth graders play this game without paddles or rackets, but it works better with them. One of the skills developed by the game is the ability to change one's pace; that is, to move quickly toward the ball and then hit it very gently and accurately in order to get it into the basket.

WORK UP

This game is like softball and can be played on any softball field. We use softballs and softball bats, and follow softball rules about batting, outs, and scoring runs. Any number from four to twelve or fourteen can play. If you have more than fourteen, you might as well play softball with teams.

The object of this game is to work your way up from fielder to batter and to score as many runs as you can before being put out. There are no teams, but all the players in the field play as a team to get the batter out. When we have to stop playing, we count to see who has scored the most runs.

When we play this game at school, we decide who will play what position by drawing a number before going out to the playground. If there are fourteen players, here is what the numbers mean:

1—first batter
2—second batter
3—third batter
4—fourth batter
5—catcher
6—pitcher
7—umpire
8—first baseman
9—second baseman
10—third baseman
11—shortstop
12—left fielder
13—center fielder
14—right fielder

If there are fewer than fourteen, we do not use the higher-numbered positions. But when we get down to ten players, we have only three batters. Then all the other positions have a different number, although they stay in the same order:

1—first batter
2—second batter
3—third batter

> 4—catcher
> 5—pitcher
> 6—umpire
> 7—first baseman
> 8—second baseman
> 9—third baseman
> 10—shortstop

When we play by ourselves, we just call out the position we want, and whoever calls "First bat!" first, gets it. Sometimes it is hard to tell who called out first, but we have to be fair or we spend too much time quarreling and not enough time playing. If there are only four of us, we have only one batter and one base, but if there are as many as seven we can have two batters and two bases. If someone wants to play after the game has started, he can come in as a fielder and work his way up.

To begin the game, each player goes to his own position. The umpire makes sure that everyone is in the right place and then says, "Play ball!" The pitcher pitches underhand, and the batter can be put out according to softball rules—that is, by striking him out, by catching a fly ball, or by fielding a ball to first base before he gets there. Once he gets to first base, he is a base runner. Then he can be put out if he is tagged with the ball if he is off base, or if he has to run to a base and the ball is fielded there ahead of him. If there is no batter left at home plate, the runner nearest home has to get there before the ball is thrown home. If he does not, he is out.

When a player is put out, he goes to right field and everyone else moves up one position. This makes the catcher the fourth batter. The player who was put out works up to being batter again by playing every position in turn.

Notes for the teacher: This is an excellent game for small groups during the softball season. It is about as difficult as softball, but puts less pressure on individual players. However, if an unskilled player comes along to pitch and slows up the game, adapt the rules in any way necessary to keep the game going. Dimensions for the field depend on the skill of the players. For sixth graders, bases should be 35 feet apart and the pitcher's box 35 feet from home plate.

Umpiring is good practice for everyone, but some exceptions to the rule of having players move into that position in turn may seem advisable. First, it may be a very good spot for the handicapped child who cannot participate more actively. Second, it may be a very bad spot for the child who is overanxious and already somewhat isolated. If this child wants to try umpiring and does it well, it may be excellent therapy for him. If, on the other hand, he does it badly, it may be a near-disaster.

ZIGZAG RELAY

This relay is like Shuttle Relay except that the runners dodge around three Indian clubs or other markers. The markers are set up about 5 or 6 feet apart in the lanes between the two sets of players on each team. The dotted line in the diagram shows where the runner goes:

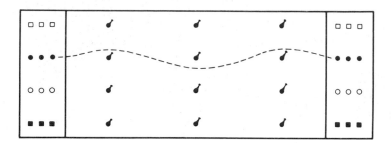

If the runner goes to the right of the first club, he must go to the left of the second and to the right of the third. It does not matter to which side of the first club he goes, but he does have to zigzag in his run. This relay helps us improve our broken-field running in football.

The team whose last runner crosses the finish line ahead of the others wins.

> *Notes for the teacher:* This relay provides good training in footwork, changing direction, and maintaining balance. Try varying the space between clubs. Give the teams a chance to huddle between runs and work out themselves the best ways of swerving at different intervals.

Selected References

AAHPER, *How We Do It Game Book,* 2d ed. Washington, D.C., 1959.

Ashton, Dudley, *Physical Education for Nebraska Elementary Schools.* Lincoln, Nebraska: State Division of Supervision and Curriculum, 1957, Chap. 6.

Hartley, Ruth, and Robert M. Goldman, *The Complete Book of Children's Play.* New York: Thomas Y. Crowell Company, 1957.

Latchaw, Marjorie, *A Pocket Book of Games and Rhythms.* Englewood Cliffs, N.J.: Prentice-Hall, Inc., 1956.

Radler, D. H., and Newell C. Kephart, *Success Through Play,* Part II. New York: Harper & Row, Publishers, 1960.

CHAPTER 12

Dance

DANCE IN THE ELEMENTARY SCHOOL PROGRAM comprises two main divisions: creative dance and the social forms of dance. The latter includes folk, square, round, and social dances. In the primary years, creative dance is given priority in the program. In the intermediate grades, the social forms of dance receive increasing emphasis because they contribute to the recreational interests and cultural understanding of the children. The two divisions should receive approximately equal time during the intermediate years.

In creative dance the teacher encourages and guides children in the use of rhythmic movement as a means of expressing and communicating ideas that are of real importance to them. In the social forms of dance the teacher hands on to children dance forms that are their cultural heritage. Nevertheless, a common approach is possible in teaching all forms of dance. This approach includes (1) the creative development of movement and rhythm skills basic to all dance forms, (2) an encouraging, permissive atmosphere, which contributes to all creative endeavor, and (3) carefully planned dance activities that grow out of the daily experiences and immediate needs and interests of children.

Developmental experiences in movement and rhythm lead to confidence in dance and help children maintain and enhance the spontaneous pleasure in dancing that most of them bring along when they come to school. The teaching approach emphasized in the chapter on movement exploration aids in the development of free, expressive movement. Further suggestions for the development of dance steps and rhythm skills basic to both creative dance and the social forms of dance are presented in this chapter. Such developmental activities comprise an essential part of the dance program and provide a basis for planning appropriate experiences in both creative and social dance forms. They provide continuity and progression in the total dance program. Charts illustrating the sequence and interrelatedness of dance experiences for primary and intermediate grades appear on the next two pages.

Fun with Music—Musical Games

Introductory activities in a dance program are chosen to help children have a satisfying experience immediately. Satisfying introductory experiences are important at all age levels, and they are particularly important if there have been gaps in the children's dance education or if the boys have been conditioned to think of dance as a "sissy" activity. The following games are useful beyond the purpose of providing fun, however. They require that children pay careful attention to the music—that they start, stop, and move with the music. While they are enjoying the games, the teacher can concentrate on ascertaining their level of development in dance skills. Do they move freely, without self-consciousness? How is their skill in movement? In rhythm?

MAGIC CARPET (See pages 298–299)

STOP THE MUSIC (See page 302)

STOOP

The children move freely with the music and stoop when the music stops. The last person to stoop is It and helps the teacher determine who stoops last the next time the music stops. The game helps children to develop balance—to move in space without touching one another and to stop quickly.

DANCE EXPERIENCES ARRANGED IN DEVELOPMENTAL SEQUENCE

Primary Grades

Movement Skills	Rhythm Skills	Creative Dance	Social Forms of Dance
Use movement exploration to develop: Free use of body and parts of body (see Chapter 9)	Use games with musical accompaniment, and rhythm games, to develop rhythmic movement and response to: Pulse (beat)	Create movement sequence to express familiar ideas	Singing games without partner, substituting walk for skip in beginning
		Dance to various forms of accompaniment (free expression)	Singing games with partner
Simple dance steps, variations, and combinations: Walk Run Hop Jump	Accent Successive beats of different time intervals—moderate, fast, slow	Create individual dances, using themes from everyday experience, such as pets, toys, seasonal activities	Singing games using skip and slide
			Folk dances without partner; with partner using simple dance steps
Complex dance steps, variations: Skip Gallop Slide	Phrases Rhythmic patterns	Create small group dances, using a central theme—familiar song, story, poem	Folk dances using skip, gallop, slide
Combinations of simple and complex steps, dance steps, and body movements	Create rhythmic patterns	Create dances using original rhythmic patterns and movement sequences; work out accompaniment	Play-party games in circle and longways formation

DANCE EXPERIENCES ARRANGED IN DEVELOPMENTAL SEQUENCE

Intermediate Grades

Movement Skills	Rhythm Skills	Creative Dance	Social Forms
Use movement exploration to develop free use of body and parts of body	Use advanced problems (see "Rhythm Skills," in this chapter) to develop response to rhythmic patterns	In small groups, create dances using central theme related to group interests and experiences	Learn "mixer" dances with singing accompaniment
Develop complex dance steps: Step-hop and schottische; experiment with dance positions, turns, directions	Play accompaniment for complex dance steps as developed; read and write note patterns showing time structure	In groups of three, four, or more, create dances using schottische and step-hop	Learn dances based on walk, run, hop, skip; longways, quadrille, and circle formations
Polka; use open and semiclosed (two hands joined) dance positions	Develop movement sequence for jingles, commercials, rounds	Create dances using polka and variations	Learn dances based on schottische
Two-step; develop "top" turns, use semiclosed dance position			Learn dances based on polka
Shuffle, buzz step, square dance figures	Develop rhythmic movement and response to phrases	Create dances using two-step to popular music	Learn dances based on two-step; Learn square dances with singing calls; simple figures
Waltz run, waltz, waltz balance; use closed dance positon		Arrange and call square dances	Learn dances based on waltz
Fox trot, swing fox trot; use closed, open, and conversation dance positions	Develop rhythmic movement and response to regular and syncopated accents	Arrange "mixer" dances using waltz music	Ballroom dancing

FISH IN THE OCEAN

Children form in groups of four kinds of Fish, previously named by them. These Schools of Fish establish a base (a circle) in each corner of the play area. The Fisherman moves freely in space with the music, and as he passes a School of Fish, he beckons them to follow in single file. The Fish must follow the movements of the Fisherman, who skips, leaps, or spins as the music may suggest. The Fisherman lures as many Fish as he can before the music stops, then catches as many as he can while the Fish run to base. Those who are caught form a line behind the Fisherman as his helpers, and another round is played. The group may decide the number of times a Fisherman leads off before another takes his place. The winning Fisherman is the one who catches the largest number of Fish.

MOUSE TRAP

The group moves freely in a circle with the music, passing under the Mouse Trap, which is an arch formed by the joined hands of two children. When the music stops, the Mouse Trap comes down, catching any prey that happens to be passing through. The child who is caught goes to the center of the circle and waits for another victim. These two form another Trap. The game continues until the last Mouse is caught. It is well to permit the children who made the first Trap to join the circle after other Traps have been formed.

MAGIC SPOT

The group moves freely in space with the music while the leader stands with his back to the group and decides on a Magic Spot. This may be *any* spot—the phonograph, a light switch, a marking on the floor, a child in the group. When the music stops, the child standing nearest the Magic Spot is caught and becomes the leader for the next round. Use music with a variety of rhythmic patterns and encourage appropriate response.

COME ALONG

The group stands in a large circle with left hands outstretched. The child who is It travels along the inside of the circle to the right, moving with the music (walking, skipping, skating, galloping). He joins hands with his neighbor to the right, taking him along; the neighbor takes the hand of the person to his right, and so on. The line continues to grow until the music stops. Then each person races back to home position. The last person back has one "penalty" and starts the game again. If one person gets three penalties, he may be asked to pay a forfeit decided on by the group.

Suggested Recordings for Musical Games

The Rhythm Program	RCA Victor: 78 RPM E71–E76; 45 RPM WE 71–WE 76
Adventures in Music	RCA Victor: 33⅓ RPM LE 1000–1009; 45 EP EED 100–109
Boston Pops Picnic	RCA Victor: LM 1985
Jungle Drums	RCA Victor: LSC 1994
Pops Christmas Party	RCA Victor: LSC 2329

Rhythm Skills

Rhythm is one aspect of movement. The development of movement skills and of rhythm skills progress hand in hand. As stated in the chapter on movement exploration, children should have the opportunity to develop their natural rhythm in any movement pattern before being held to an imposed rhythm. However, in planning developmental experiences in dance, the teacher gives priority now to one skill, now to the other. The rhythm of the movement or the rhythm of the accompaniment may provide the focus of purpose for a particular lesson or part of a lesson. Suggestions for the development of basic rhythm skills follow in this section.

Rhythm is described as the time structure of movement. All movement has rhythm. In dance, rhythm is of regular occurrence and ordered sequence. The development of rhythm in dance is dependent upon many factors, including body structure and motor proficiency, the kinesthetic sense, concentration, and the ability to synchronize movement and accompaniment.

All children have a sense of rhythm, though they differ widely in the extent to which it is developed. The lack of ability to move in time with a group or conform to a set pattern does not mean that a child is deficient in this respect. Many children appear deficient in rhythmic ability because they do not listen to the accompaniment. Others are restrained in movement due to self-consciousness. These deficiencies may be overcome by interesting and motivating experiences.

Experiences to help children develop the skills of rhythm should be of short duration and satisfying in themselves. Rhythm games such as Follow the Beats provide practice for children in the primary grades, and they are fun. Children in the intermediate grades continue to enjoy rhythm games, but they are challenged by the mathematical relationships of rhythm, as in music. They enjoy the problems for the sake of solving them.

Time Structure of Movement

The time structure of movement is similar to that of music. Both have *pulsation*, which is the underlying beat; and *accent*, which gives order to what would otherwise be an undifferentiated series of movements or beats. The *measure* comprises the particular number of pulsations between accents. Complex dance steps such as the skip and the two-step, like the melody of a song, are based on a *rhythmic pattern* consisting of a sequence of beats. A *movement phrase*, like a musical phrase, is composed of a thematic sequence of movements (or measures), which can be compared to the expression of an idea in a sentence. Because of this basic similarity, the terminology and notation of music are used to describe the rhythm of dance movement.

The Use of Musical Symbols

The use of note values is the most efficient way of describing the timing of a series of movements. The teacher will find it helpful to be able to read and write simple rhythmic patterns in note values. Ability to play the piano is an asset, but it is not a prerequisite for teaching dance. In today's music classes, children become familiar with the reading of music at an early age. This knowledge is reinforced as it is used to describe the rhythm of dance movement. A kinesthetic feeling for time structure in music and in movement develops through well-planned experiences for the growth of rhythm skills.

The following analysis includes symbols commonly used in elementary school music and dance. The moderate value of the quarter note and the walk are used as a point of reference.

Through exploration, other movements will be found that can be performed in moderate, fast, or slow tempo.

Symbol	Note	Note Value	Movement
♩	Quarter	Moderate	Walk
♪	Eighth	Twice as fast	Run
♩	Half	Half as fast	Slow walk
o	Whole	One fourth as fast	Sustained walk
♫♩	Triplet	Three times as fast	Very fast run
♩♪	Quarter and eighth	A 2:1 relationship	The uneven step-hop of the skip, or the step-run of the gallop

Duple time means that there are two beats or some multiple of two to a measure. *Triple time* means that each measure contains three beats or some multiple of three. The time signature designates the relative value of the notes in a measure.

Duple Time

2/4 Signifies two beats to a measure, with each quarter note receiving one beat.

4/4 Signifies four beats to a measure, with each quarter note receiving one beat.

4/4

6/8 Signifies six beats to a measure, with each eighth note receiving one beat. In fast moving music, each group of three eighth notes receives one beat.

6/8

Triple Time

3/4 Signifies three beats, or some multiple of three, to a measure, with each quarter note receiving one beat.

3/4

6/4 Signifies six beats to a measure, with each quarter note receiving one beat.

6/4

Teaching Suggestions

An overview of developmental steps includes the following experiences:

1. Exploring the movement—finding the natural rhythm of the movement skill. Performing the movement naturally and with variations and combinations.

2. Accompanying the movement—following the natural rhythm of the movement; clapping; using percussion instruments.[1] Reading the rhythmic pattern from the chalkboard.

3. Responding to accompaniment of different tempos; to accompaniment accelerating and decelerating in tempo.

4. Creating movement patterns; working out accompaniment.

5. Creating a dance. As children work out original patterns, these can be written on the chalkboard. Individual patterns can be combined to make a short dance, just as the group combines efforts to compose a song or a poem.

Suggestions follow for the development of specific rhythm skills through games or problem-solving situations. These skills include the following:

1. The ability to express pulsation, accents, rhythmic patterns, and phrases in movement.

2. The ability to listen and respond to pulsation, accents, rhythmic patterns, and phrases in an accompaniment through movement.

---

[1] Elizabeth Waterman, *The Rhythm Book*. New York: A. S. Barnes & Company, Inc., 1937. Contains excellent material on making percussion instruments and for integrating rhythm and art.

3. The ability to recognize and use the symbols of musical notation to describe the rhythm of movement patterns. (Intermediate grades)

Pulsation

FOLLOW THE BEATS[2]

The leader beats the tom-tom as the group responds. Change leaders frequently. Play in a large group at the beginning, with the teacher as leader. Then play in small groups with several leaders.

1. Beats of *moderate* intervals. Class responds with appropriate locomotor movements: walk, hop, jump, and body movements, moving parts of body and whole body over axis.

2. Beats of *short* intervals. Class responds with movements such as the run, hop, bounce, and with body movements such as jabbing, flicking, and punching.

3. Beats of *long* intervals. Class responds with locomotor movements such as slow walk and jump, and with body movements such as pulling, slashing, twisting, bending, and swinging.

4. Successive beats of *moderate, short,* and *long* intervals. It is well to start with the moderate beat and return to it after each change. An understanding of and kinesthetic feeling for the mathematical relationship should be developed.

2:1 relationship:	3:1 relationship:	
4 moderate,	A triplet run of eighth	
8 short,	notes is three times as	
2 long	fast as a quarter note.	

Use familiar music. Respond to pulsation.

[2] Ruth Lovell Murray, *Dance in Elementary Education.* New York: Harper & Row, Publishers, 1963.

Accent

FOLLOW THE ACCENT[3]

The leader arranges beats of an established interval, accenting the first of each series. Repeat each series for the group to let children get the "feel" of it, and have them clap the rhythm before moving. Encourage use of locomotor and body movements.

1. Respond to the accented beats only.
2. Respond to a series of beats with a strong movement on the accents, or a change of level or direction on the accents.
3. Respond to the unaccented beats only. A syncopated movement quality results.
4. Work with partner: Number One responds to the accent; Number Two responds to the succeeding beats.

GROUP PATTERNS

Two groups work in opposition, with one group showing accented movements, the other responding to the succeeding beats.

BAND CONDUCTORS

The class works out movements for leading the band, using a downbeat of the hands for each accented beat. Try walking and conducting. This requires advanced coordination of hands and feet. Use various meters.

Rhythmic Patterns

MAKE SIMPLE RHYTHMIC PATTERNS

Begin with patterns of two speeds. Combine moderate and fast intervals or moderate and slow intervals; then make patterns of three speeds.

Note: Letters signifying fundamental locomotor movements are used in the illustrative rhythmic patterns on page 374. However, children should use other locomotor and body movements freely.

W............Walk
S............Slow walk
R............Run

[3] *Ibid.*

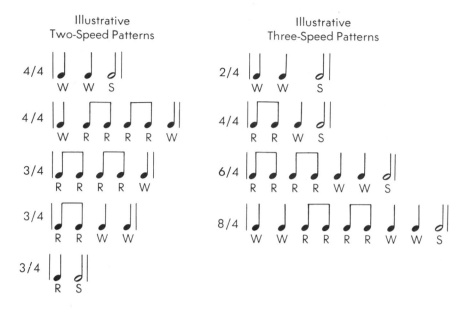

MOVEMENT PATTERNS FOR NAMES

The use of nursery rhymes, jingles, and radio and television commercials will stimulate the creation of a sequence of movement patterns and provide an excellent opportunity for beginning creative work. It is also fun to perform rounds in movement. The group decides on the movement pattern for a familiar round, then divides into parts and dances as a round.

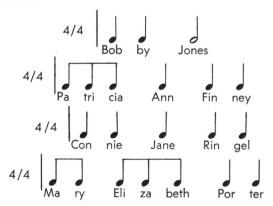

Phrases

The concept of a *phrase* (which usually consists of four or eight measures in simple music) can be established by questioning the children:

What is a sentence? Yes, a sentence expresses a thought in words. How do we express a thought in music? Can *you* express a thought in movement? Let's listen to some familiar music and show the beginning and ending of the phrase by extending and lowering our hands. Now our whole bodies.

TRAFFIC COP[4]

The Cop faces the group, which should be scattered over the play space. He establishes hand signals for directions—forward, backward, sideways, turning in place, and so on. The Cop signals the group to change direction with each musical phrase, and the group follows his signals.

FOLLOW THE LEADER

The leader changes direction on each phrase and the group follows.

The leader changes movement on each phrase and the group follows.

QUESTIONS AND ANSWERS

The group divides into partners. Number One asks a question through movement on the first phrase; Number Two answers on the second phrase.

Suggested Recordings for Rhythm Skills

Childhood Rhythm Records Series I, II, III	Ruth Evans 326 Forest Park Ave. Springfield, Mass.
Music for Rhythms and Dance	Freda Miller 8 Tudor City Place New York 19, N.Y.
Rhythmic Play	Sally Tobin Dietrich Electro-Vox Recording 5547 Melrose Hollywood, Calif.
The Rhythm Program (short selections from	RCA Victor Albums 78 RPM E71–E76;

[4] *Ibid.*, p. 8.

well-known classical and romantic composers)	45 RPM WE 71–WE 76
Toy Shop and Other Rhythms for Little Folks	Estamae Rhythm Records 2401 Grand Avenue Pueblo, Colo.
Basic Rhythms for Primary Grades	R.R. 1 David McKay Company, Inc. 119 West 40th Street New York 18, N.Y.

Movement Skills of Dance

Through movement exploration children develop movement skills and a vocabulary of movement that enable them to enjoy dancing readily. They will feel comfortable when they are encouraged to express their imaginative and creative drives through *creative dance*. They will have developed control of locomotor movements essential to successful performance of *social forms of dance*. Further suggestions for techniques useful in developing movement skills of dance are given in this section followed by an analysis of complex dance steps.

Developing Fundamental Dance Steps

Most children come to school with the fundamental dance steps developed or in the process of emerging. They can walk, run, hop, and jump with varying degrees of grace and dexterity. These steps are termed *fundamental* since they require only one kind of locomotor movement and, when performed naturally, an even tempo. The following sequence may be followed in developing fundamental dance steps:

1. Proceed first without accompaniment, permitting each child to find his own rhythm in the fundamental steps and to explore variations.

2. Encourage children to provide their own accompaniment by clapping and using percussion instruments. This may be done in either small or large groups according to the maturity of the group.

3. As children develop competence, have them conform to

an imposed rhythm, as in rhythm games, which are described in this chapter.

4. Provide an opportunity for children to learn and to create dances based on the fundamental dance steps.

5. Have the class create combinations of the fundamental dance steps—for example, walking and running, running and hopping, hopping and jumping. Encourage each child to work out his own accompaniment to original patterns and permit these to be shared with the class. Complex dance steps are often discovered in this process.

Developing Complex Dance Steps: Beginning Experiences

The simplest of the complex (traditional) dance steps are the skip, gallop, and slide. The *skip* is a step and a hop; the *gallop* is a step and a run; both are performed in an uneven rhythm. The *slide* is like a gallop performed sideways. Some children can skip, gallop, and slide by the time they enter school, having developed these steps naturally through play experiences. For many children, the steps emerge during the primary years. All children need stimulating practice in order to develop the control and quality of movement demanded for successful performance of the social forms of dance. Such practice might include:

1. Playing rhythm games involving the skip, gallop, and slide.

2. Learning to accompany small and large groups with percussion instruments. Begin by clapping hands or beating floor.

3. Learning and creating dances based on the skip, gallop, and slide.

Developing Complex Dance Steps: Advanced Experiences

Among the more complex traditional dance steps are the step-hop, schottische, polka, two-step, and waltz. General suggestions for developing these steps are given first, followed by an analysis of each together with specific teaching suggestions. The steps are presented in order of difficulty, as are the specific developmental experiences under each one. Dancing comfortably with a partner in closed dance position requires not only mastery of the step but also a high degree of social maturity, and the teacher may want to defer this experience until junior high school.

General Suggestions for Developing Complex Dance Steps

1. Listen to the music, clapping out the rhythmic pattern and establishing the desired movement quality.

2. Perform the step pattern in place, then in all directions.

3. Dance with partner in open dance position. In this position, partners face in same direction; inside hands are joined and total body movement is achieved by swinging the arms forward and backward on consecutive steps. If partners begin on outside foot, a face-to-face and back-to-back swing results. Find ways of turning and other ways of joining hands.

4. Explore variations of each step, changing level, dimension of steps, force, tempo.

5. Learn folk dance based on step.

6. Create a dance based on the step learned, using traditional or popular music. Popular music adds interest.

7. Dance with partner using closed dance position. Preliminary to this experience it is good for the class to practice spinning turns individually. With the children facing in the same direction, have them turn continuously in one direction like a top. The first step of each step pattern is taken with a half turn, turning left if beginning with the left foot and right if beginning with the right foot. Now the entire group should be facing in the opposite direction. The second step pattern completes the turn. Continue turning in the same direction.

Analysis of Complex Dance Steps

DANCE STEP	STEP PATTERN	RHYTHMIC PATTERN
Skip	Step and hop	Uneven
		6/8 ♩ ♪ ♩ ♪
		walk hop walk hop
Gallop	Step and run	Uneven
		6/8 ♩ ♪ ♩ ♪
		walk run walk run
Slide	Step and run performed sideways	Uneven
		6/8 ♩ ♪ ♩ ♪

Step-hop   Step and hop   Even

2/4   walk hop

As children step in place and hop on the same foot, have them try swinging the free leg in a different position each time. Continue, alternating feet. Perform in even timing.[5]

Try rocking forward and backward on each step-hop like a rocking horse.

Play accompaniment for small group, using percussion instruments.

Try step-hop in different directions, in small circles.

Make or learn a dance based on step-hop.

Schottische   Three lilting walks   Even
                    and a hop

4/4   walk walk walk hop

Try combining two schottische steps and four step-hops; move in all directions.

Try pattern above with partner, using open dance position. See how many ways partners can turn each other or around each other on the step-hops.

Emphasize principles of movement that lead to the lightness characteristic of the schottische.

Learn or create a dance based on the schottische and step-hop.

Polka   A hop and three   Uneven
                springy walks; the
                hop precedes the
                accented beat of
                each measure

2/4   hop walk walk walk hop

The polka is easily developed from the slide performed in lilting fashion with lightness and upbeat accentuated. Have children do eight slides in a circle, leading with the left foot; then, facing out, eight with

[5] These suggestions supplement the general suggestions starting at the beginning of this section, "Movement Skills of Dance." Do not omit the developmental steps listed there.

the right foot while continuing in the same direction. Practice this pattern until changes in the leading foot are made smoothly and rhythmically, then change the pattern to four steps and finally to two. As the pattern of two slides with alternate feet leading is repeated continuously, the polka rhythm and step pattern become established. Supplement polka music with an accented beat on the tom-tom to help children feel changes. When polka rhythm is well established, try dancing with partner, using open dance position and then semiclosed position.

Two-step   **Walk, walk, walk**   **Uneven**

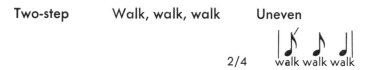

The two-step is sometimes called "a polka without a hop." The step pattern of the two-step may be simpler than that of the polka, but because of its smoother, more restrained quality it seems more appropriate to introduce it after the polka.

Clap rhythmic pattern and then perform in place, first with tomtom, then with music.

Diagram floor pattern of the two-step:

1. Moving forward or backward, the first step is taken diagonally left, the second step is placed behind the heel of the left, the third and slow step is taken diagonally left. Repeat, alternating direction. Try individually and then with partner in open dance position.

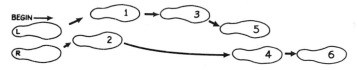

2. In the two-step box, the left foot is placed to the side; the right foot closes to the left; the left foot (slow step) is taken forward. Complete the box by stepping back (slow step) right. Try individually, then with partner in closed dance position.

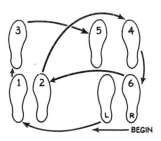

Waltz   Walk, walk, walk   Even

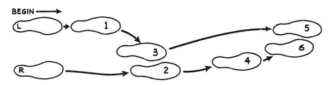

3/4   walk walk walk

Perform step pattern in place, responding to the accent of the music with slight bend of the knee.

Move forward and diagonally to the left, with left foot leading on the first three steps, then diagonally to the right, with right foot leading. Respond to the accent with slight knee bend on leading step.

Diagram floor pattern of the waltz:

Repeat the pattern above, closing the third step of the pattern: step diagonally left, right, and close left foot to the heel of the right; step diagonally right, left, close right foot.

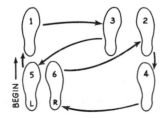

Try the same pattern with partner, using open dance position.

Try reverse arm swing: A pleasing "swish" is given the waltz by reversing the arm swing used in the face-to-face and back-to-back swing described previously. This is accomplished by swinging joined inside hands forward as partners take the first waltz step with outside foot; then swinging joined hands back as the step is taken with the inside foot. This swing is commonly used in folk and round dancing.

Try box waltz: This requires two waltz steps, as follows:

Step forward with left foot; move right foot to the right of the left foot; close left.

Complete the "box" by stepping back on right, moving left foot to the left of the right foot; closing right foot to left.

Dance with partner in closed dance position.

Develop waltz balance: Step forward with the left foot; bring right foot up to left; step left in place; then step back with the right foot, close left, and step right in place. A down-up motion is desired with this step and is achieved by rising on toes on the second and third steps of each pattern.

Develop spinning turns.

Waltz with partner, using combination of steps and turns.

Creative Dance

Creative dance experiences should grow out of the immediate interests and daily experiences of the children. A study of Indian life, a favorite story, seasonal music, or a unit in social studies may provide a theme for the movement and rhythm problems described in the previous sections. Such experiences become sources of ideas for *dancing* and for *creating a dance* as well. Murray[6] defines *dancing* as "the act of moving rhythmically and expressively to an accompaniment"; and *a dance* as "movement organized in time and structured in space." It is apparent that both of these experiences have an important place in the dance program. Suggestions for creative dance experiences are discussed in this chapter.

Primary Grades

In the primary grades, children enjoy dancing to various forms of accompaniment—instrumental music, songs, percussion instruments, nonsense rhymes, and jingles. They enjoy telling a story or expressing ideas in movement. They have only minor concern for the organization and structure demanded in creating a dance that can be repeated again in exactly the same manner. Their enjoyment is in the doing, and while they will want to "play it again," new and more exciting ways of moving will be discovered each time it is repeated.

As in self-testing, the teacher sets the stage for "dancing." Setting the stage, however, involves more than suggesting that the children "dance the way the music makes them feel," or "dance like the wind or a fairy or a clown." It involves structuring the situation so that children not only accept the purpose, but know *how* they are going to proceed and *what* is to be expressed. At the same time, reference as to *what to do* is avoided so that each child is free to express or interpret the idea or mood in his own manner.

[6] Murray, *op. cit.*, p. 7.

Presentation of the theme (story, idea, musical selection) is followed by a planning session. If a musical selection is the theme, the teacher asks questions concerning the mood, quality, and rhythm and stimulates discussion of how it sounds and how it makes them feel. She helps them identify the form of the music— the contrasting parts and phrases. Or she helps children decide on the parts of a story or poem that has been presented as the theme. What characters are involved? What characteristics of movement do they have? She encourages use of large, rhythmic body movements that express the mood or characteristics rather than the use of literal, imitative actions. If all children are to have the opportunity to move freely without interference from others, the discussion must likewise include the use of space and relationship with others. In a class of thirty youngsters, thirty individual, unique performances result.

Illustrative Lessons

THE CANDY STORE

A dramatic theme involving a sequence of events which children portray through movement.

Presentation: The children have been invited to a candy store. They happily accept the invitation and are immediately on their way. When they arrive they find shelf after shelf of candy. Some of it is behind cartons, some under the counter, and some of it is coming right out of the kettle. Before they have explored every nook and cranny in their search for candy, their mothers call them home. Oh, how unhappy they are! How dejectedly they leave! How slowly they make their journey home!

Discussion and Preparation: What parts of the story shall we show? What type (quality) of movement shall we use for each part? What accompaniment shall we use for each part? (Each child may select a percussion instrument for self-accompaniment *or* the children may want the teacher to provide the accompaniment, suggesting that happy, light, fast music is best for part 1; quiet, mysterious music, for part 2; slow, heavy, sad music, for part 3.) If the latter choice is made, the music should be played at this time. Agreement on relationships are established: children to store, home, and so forth.

Dancing: Children tell the story in movement. They may want to work further on specific parts; then repeat the whole.

Evaluation: Half of the class may be selected to perform for the other half in turn, or smaller groups may be selected. The teacher guides the evaluative session that follows each performance, basing her questions on the specific points discussed in the planning session.

THE STORY OF DANDELIONS

A dramatic theme involving personification of characters in movement.

Presentation: A cobbler is busily working in his shoe shop. All the money he makes is hidden in large sacks under the floor. One night the cobbler falls asleep while counting his money. Through an open window crawl four robbers. They quietly pick up the sacks of money and steal away into the night! The cobbler awakens and is heartsick to find his money gone. A good fairy appears and tells the cobbler that she will help him. The fairy finds a trail of gold pieces leading through the woods to a cave. The sacks of money had little holes in the bottom of them and out dropped the coins. The good fairy captures the robbers and returns the gold to the cobbler. But as the fairy walks through the woods she touches some of the gold pieces with her wand. As soon as a gold piece is touched, it turns into a beautiful dandelion. And, that is why we have all those dandelions in our yard every spring!

Discussion and Preparation: What characters appear in the story? What are the movement characteristics of each? Answers may be written on the chalkboard for review as experimentation with movement patterns for the various roles follows. Accompaniment is then decided for each character.

Dancing: On first presentation all the children may perform each part. Then characters may be selected for each role when a second presentation is given. Children will enjoy dancing the story at frequent intervals, exchanging roles freely.

Evaluation: Guided evaluation by the teacher will bring forth appropriate suggestions for improvement and should follow each presentation.

THE STORM

A seasonal theme growing out of the science lesson.

Presentation: Since children are familiar with the ideas to be expressed, questioning by the teacher concerning the specific elements they would like to personify is a first step in presentation of the theme. She writes on the chalkboard the list in the order suggested, noting with considerable satisfaction that the voluble difference of opinion which occurred during the science lesson on which comes first—the lightning or the clap of thunder—had been resolved.

Discussion and Preparation: What type of movement shall we use to express the fierceness and destructiveness of the wind? Ideas involving abstract characterizations such as the elements call for considerable guidance, if random movements depending heavily on sound effects for communication are to be avoided. Children should be helped to develop a pattern of movement and repeat it in the original configuration and quality until they evolve a rhythmic pattern that satisfactorily expresses their ideas. Then they may work out variations for emphasis and interest. The responses to the question are listed on the chalkboard, together with suggestions from children for effective use of space and relationships. The work session follows with intermittent evaluation and discussion to improve individual patterns, during which time the children decide on and practice with the accompaniment. The entire process is repeated for each of the ideas, completion of which requires several lessons.

Dancing: In the first presentation, all of the children perform all of the roles, except those who have been selected to provide the accompaniment with percussion instruments.

Evaluation: Small groups are invited to perform for the class in turn, with an evaluation following each performance. Children are then given the opportunity to select a favorite role and practice in small groups at the next lesson.

The satisfaction expressed by the children after their finished performance is often sufficient to cause the teacher to suggest a special performance with another grade as guests.

Suggestions for Themes:
Primary Grades

Children in the primary grades identify themselves readily with anything in their immediate environment. They like to be inanimate objects as well as animals, people, or fictional characters. As their horizons widen during the first years of school, dancing becomes a means of expression and a source of enrichment for other areas of the school program. Examples of themes for creative dance experiences follow. These may lead the teacher to think of many other subjects in the child's real or imaginary world that lend themselves to rhythmic movement expression.

Immediate Environment

Animals, pets, insects
Play activities
Seasons, holidays, special days
Occupations
Transportation
Community helpers

Storybook Character, Fables

Land of make-believe: fairies, goblins, witches, brownies
Fables: The Hare and the Tortoise, The Dog and the Bone
Characters: Pied Piper, Lone Ranger
Nursery rhymes

Suggested References for Movement Skills of Dance

Anthologies and Poetry Books
The following are among those that contain many poems suitable for movement expression and accompaniment:

Stevenson, Robert Louis, *A Child's Garden of Verses*. New York: Charles Scribner's Sons, 1947.

Brown, Helen A., and Harry J. Heltman, eds., *Let's-Read-Together Poems: An Anthology of Verse for Choral Reading*. New York: Harper & Row, Publishers, 1949.

Library Committee of the Association for Childhood Education, *Sing under the Silver Umbrella*. New York: The Macmillan Company, 1946.

Field, Rachel, *Taxis and Toadstools*. New York: Doubleday & Company, Inc., 1944.

Untermeyer, Louis, ed., *This Singing World*. New York: Harcourt, Brace & World, Inc., 1926.

Songs and Music

Songs: action and folk songs (see school music series)
Instrumental Music: Sleigh Ride, Waltzing Cat, Waltz of the Dolls, March of the Toys, Circus Music, Carnival of the Animals, Jungle Drums
Recordings (especially for children):

Creepy the Crawly Caterpillar, The Merry Toy Shop, and many other Record Guild Selections	Children's Record Guild 27 Thompson Street New York 13, N.Y.
Shoemaker and the Elves, Johnny Appleseed, Music of American Indians, etc.	RCA Victor Records for Children

Songs to Grow On	Folkways 117 West 47th Street New York, N.Y.
Themes for Children's Rhythms	Emma Hayden 1804 Hermosa Nashville, Tenn.
Animal Rhythms	R.R. 2 Educational Record Album David McKay Company, Inc. 119 West 40th Street New York 18, N.Y.

Intermediate Grades

Procedures for guiding intermediate grade children in creative dance experiences differ in only a few respects from those previously described for primary grades. The differences grow out of the changing characteristics and interests of children 9 to 12 years of age. These differences and the implications for planning dance experiences are summarized below:

Characteristics	*Implications*
Less interest in activity for its own sake; more interest in moving to achieve a specific goal.	Focus on purpose.
Characteristic interest in rhythmic and dramatic activity may be concealed or submerged due to: (1) lack of previous opportunity; (2) early specialization as in sports only; (3) lack of understanding that dance is a vigorous, masculine activity.	Motivation often needed, especially for boys in a class. Create a dance for a program or demonstration.
A growing awareness of themselves as persons—unwillingness to *be* inanimate objects; some reluctance to make-believe roles and stout refusal to be placed in a situation considered "childish" or effeminate.	Plan themes that give boys an opportunity to show their masculine strength; that give both sexes an opportunity to put to work their vivid imaginations and altruistic interests; that enable them to portray their hero or heroine of the day.
A "we" feeling as opposed to the "I-me-mine" of primary children. Display of an eagerness to participate in group projects; assumption of responsibility for leadership and other group roles.	Provide opportunity for work in small groups; delegate responsibility; release the power of the group to work for agreement on movement patterns that express their mutual purpose; help them organize and structure their patterns into *a dance* completely their own.

The subject matter listed below is illustrative of themes for creative dance that appeal to this age group.

Occupational groups

Construction crews
Explorers
Assembly line workers
Circus performers

Sports of seasonal interest

Performers
Spectators

Characters

Fantastic characters: visitors from outer space
Historical characters: Lewis and Clark, Vikings, Marco Polo, Astronauts
Fictional characters: Pinocchio, Paul Bunyan, Huckleberry Finn
Film, radio, television, and comic-strip characters

Suggested Songs and Music for Creative Dance

Songs: folk songs, ballads, work songs, rounds, cowboys' songs, sea chanteys (see Music Series).

Recordings:

Adventures in Music	RCA Victor 1006, 1009
Brass and Percussion	RCA Victor 2080
Chisholm Trail	YPR 407
Dance-a-Long	Folkways
Going West	YPR 301
Jump Up Calypso	RCA Victor 2388
Lure of the West	RCA Victor 2356
Mark Twain and Other Folk Favorites	RCA Victor 1022
Music of American Indians	RCA Victor E 89
Peter and the Wolf	RCA Victor 1803
Rodeo	RCA Victor 2195
Train Whistle Blues	RCA Victor 1640

Movement exploration is transformed into creative dance.

Steps in Creating a Dance

Deciding on an idea. Purpose is essential to success in any creative enterprise. A prerequisite for creating a dance is a felt need or desire on the part of the pupils to express and communicate an idea through movement. The goal of performing expressive movement per se, as discussed before, is modified or expanded to include the desire to organize and structure the movement. In the elementary school, this desire develops with growth in social maturity and in movement and rhythm skills. It depends also on the teacher's skill in helping children adopt goals that are meaningful to them. Purposes in creating a dance may include the wish to present dances as a part of an afternoon tea for mothers; interest in a "sharing program" with children of another grade; the desire to make a dance as part of a social studies unit, showing how people of another time or place work or play or fight; the need to plan entertainment for a party. As children achieve satisfaction in such objective experiences, creating a dance may become the end rather than the means. The first step in creating a dance consists of deciding to make a dance and selecting the theme for it.

Planning the dance. The number of ideas to be expressed in the dance will determine the number of parts to be included. Once this is decided, the creative process begins. This consists of experimenting, sharing, evaluating, and, finally, selecting the movement patterns to be used in each part. In a group dance, the members decide jointly on the most appropriate patterns and then work together on modifications and variations and on the sequence to be followed.

Deciding on the floor pattern or design of the dance. The decision to use symmetrical lines, circles, closely knit groups working in opposition, and the like may be influenced by the sequence of movement patterns and by the variations agreed on in the previous steps. Or, the design may be decided on first and the number and sequence of movement patterns determined by it.

Watching . . . then dancing . . . then understanding, may become the basis for accepting a classmate who has a very different background.

Deciding on accompaniment. If children have access to a variety of percussion instruments, they will be able to decide on and provide their own accompaniment. If the idea for the dance originated with the accompaniment, the time and structure of the dance will be ordered by it and the accompaniment will have to be played throughout the composition period. If an accompanist adept at improvisation is available, the final performance may take on more flavor.

Performing and evaluating the dance. As the dance is performed for class members, pupils should be guided in evaluating it and helped to make constructive criticism. The teacher can help the class prepare a list of evaluative criteria and apply them to the final performance.

Social Forms of Dance

Social forms of dance include the traditional singing games and play-party games, square and round dances, international folk dances, and contemporary social dance. Social forms of dance are in reality "folk dances" because they are those which "evolve from the people—those which are danced and enjoyed by the people."[7] As in all art forms, only the tried and true survive. Folk dances of all nations contain basic patterns, themes, and steps that are a common heritage from primitive times. Folk dances of this country can be traced directly to those of other nations, but they have evolved distinctive characteristics and types. Our unique contributions to folk dance culture are play-party games, pioneer or western-type square dances, and fox trot and swing dance steps. Because square and social dance require a special vocabulary, teaching suggestions for these forms are listed separately.

Folk Dance

Folk dance is an integral part of the folklore of our country. United States history, which constitutes an important part of the elementary school curriculum, comes alive as children have an opportunity to participate in period dances and traditional singing games.

[7] Anne Schley Duggan, Jeanette Schlottmann, and Abbie Rutledge, *The Teaching of Folk Dance.* New York: A. S. Barnes & Company, Inc., 1948.

The revival of interest in square and round dance forms, as well as the more recent interest in international folk dances, is reflected in increased emphasis on these activities in the school program. Learning and performing folk dances fosters pride in local ethnic groups and is an excellent means of increasing children's understanding of other countries and other cultures. Folk dancing is an excellent form of adult recreation, providing opportunity for desirable social interaction and satisfying, vigorous activity. Folk dancing has comparable values for children, if the dances taught are appropriate to their stage of development and if they are taught in a permissive but stimulating atmosphere.

Folk dances can be quickly learned and enjoyed through the use of the whole-part-whole method of teaching, provided the necessary skills have already been acquired in previous dance experience. The following steps facilitate learning and enjoyment of the dances:

1. Give something of the origin, characteristics, and significance of the dance. Interest in the dance should be an outgrowth of teacher-pupil planning.

Folk dancing is fun.

2. Demonstrate or give an idea of the whole dance; that is, its feeling, rhythm, formation, and basic steps.

3. Listen to the music, identify parts, "feel" the phrases, clap the rhythm.

4. Try the whole dance, or parts of the dance, depending on its complexity and on the maturity of the group.

5. Brush up on rough spots; help individuals or groups who are having trouble.

6. Repeat the entire dance. Give children an opportunity to review it frequently, so that it can be thoroughly learned and enjoyed.

Class organization is also important to the feeling of satisfaction children derive from dancing. Such dancing is essentially a social activity, and desirable social interaction is achieved through careful planning by the teacher. Getting the group into the necessary formation should be done quickly and efficiently. The importance of "choosing a partner" should be minimized, and this procedure should probably be eliminated with beginning groups. If partners are changed frequently throughout each dance and during the class period, pupils will place less importance on the first choice. The "extra" child should not be allowed to retire to the sidelines but should be given a place of importance during the dance, and everyone should take a turn in this position. The use of the grand march and circle mixers facilitates organization. Folk dancing provides an excellent opportunity for practice in manners and for desirable social relations within the group.

Basic Dance Formations[8]

RING

Two or more dancers join hands to form a circle. If partners are required in the dance, the boy stands to the left of his partner. The line of direction is clockwise unless otherwise specified.

DOUBLE CIRCLE

Partners Facing. Boys stand with their back to the inside of the circle; girls face the center.

[8] In the diagrams accompanying the descriptions of formations, X is used to designate boys; O for girls.

Couples Facing Counterclockwise. This is the usual line of direction for the promenade figure and for round dances which are performed in this formation.

Lines. Separate lines of boys and girls. The girls are always to the right of the boys and both files face front.

SETS

Circle Dances. Two couples face each other to form a set. Boys stand to the left of partners. Boy and girl of the facing couples are termed *opposites.* All sets are arranged in a circle.

Quadrilles. Four couples are arranged in a square. Couples with backs to the music or facing the music are designated as *heads;* the remaining two couples are designated as *sides.* Boys and girls who stand adjacent to each other but are not partners are designated as *corners.*

Squares. In American square dancing, squares are arranged as above, except that the couple whose back is to the music is designated as *couple one;* the remaining couples are numbered consecutively in counterclockwise order.

Contra or *Longways Sets.* These sets vary in the number of couples involved. Usually four to six couples face each other in separate lines. The couple facing the music is the *head couple;* the one last in line is the *foot couple.*

Basic Dance Figures

PROMENADE

Couples dance around circle in counterclockwise direction unless otherwise specified.

BOW

The curtsy and formal bow are used in American period dances and international folk dances. *Honor* is the comparable square-dance term.

TURNING WITH PARTNER

Right or *Left Elbows Joined* or *Both Hands Clasped.* Used as couples walk, skip, and so on, around each other as experienced in the different forms of dance.

Hungarian Turn. Couples stand in "banjo position"; that is, with right sides together and with right arms around each other's waist. The opposite arm is usually held curved above the head.

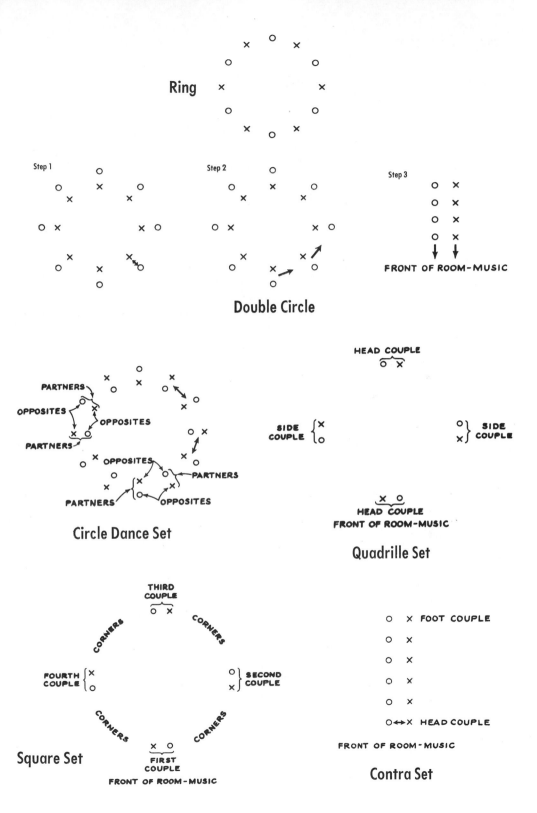

Ring

Step 1   Step 2   Step 3

FRONT OF ROOM—MUSIC

Double Circle

PARTNERS

OPPOSITES   OPPOSITES

PARTNERS

OPPOSITES   PARTNERS

PARTNERS   OPPOSITES

Circle Dance Set

HEAD COUPLE

SIDE COUPLE   SIDE COUPLE

HEAD COUPLE
FRONT OF ROOM—MUSIC

Quadrille Set

THIRD COUPLE

CORNERS   CORNERS

FOURTH COUPLE   SECOND COUPLE

CORNERS   CORNERS

FIRST COUPLE
FRONT OF ROOM—MUSIC

Square Set

FOOT COUPLE

HEAD COUPLE

FRONT OF ROOM—MUSIC

Contra Set

CHAIN FIGURES (Weaving or figure-eight patterns)

Right and Left Through. Two couples face each other with each boy standing to the left of his partner. The boys and girls of the facing couples are termed opposites. Each person changes places with his opposite, clasping right hands in passing; then changes places with partner, clasping left hands in passing. During this last change, the boy places his right hand on his partner's waist and helps turn her around. This completes the figure. In most instances, there is an immediate repetition of the figure, during which time the dancers return to starting position.

Ladies Chain. Two couples face each other with each boy standing to the left of his partner. The boy and girl of the facing couples are termed opposites. Each girl crosses over to the opposite boy, clasping right hands in passing; then extends her left hand to the opposite boy who clasps her hand with his left and places his right hand on her waist, helping to turn her around. The same pattern is repeated as girls return to original position.

Four Ladies Chain. This figure involves four couples arranged in quadrille or square formation. Each boy stands to the left of his partner. The boys and girls of facing couples are termed opposites. All four ladies extend right hands to the center, forming a "star" as they walk clockwise halfway around the square to the opposite boy. Each girl extends her left hand to the opposite boy, who clasps her hand with his left and places his right hand on her waist, helping to turn her around. Then the girls continue the star formation, each walking clockwise to original position where her partner turns her about, thus completing the figure.

Grand Right and Left. This figure involves four or more couples arranged in quadrille or square formation or in a circle, with all couples facing each other to begin the figure. In the performance of this weaving figure, all dancers move around the circle in the direction they are originally facing. In passing, each one clasps right hands with partners so that right shoulders are adjacent; then clasps left hands with the next person and passes with the left shoulders adjacent. All the dancers continue alternating hands as they make their way around the circle.

Reel. A common figure in contra dances, in which the active couple turns around each other with a right-elbow swing; then each turns around the opposite with a left elbow swing; and then repeats the right elbow swing with the partner, continuing down the set according to the calls of the particular dance.

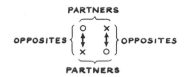

Right and Left Through Chain

Ladies Chain

Four Ladies Chain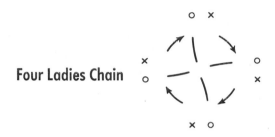

Dance Positions

OPEN

Inside hands of partners are joined or crossed as in skating.

VARSOUVIENNE

The boy stands slightly behind and to the left of his partner. He holds the girl's upraised right hand in his right; her left hand, which is only slightly raised, in his left.

CLOSED

Partners face each other with shoulders parallel and toes directly pointed to each other. The boy places his right hand just below the girl's left shoulder blade; the girl's left hand rests lightly on the boy's right shoulder. The boy holds the palm of the girl's right hand in his upraised left hand. Note: This position requires advanced coordination and social maturity. It is advisable to select dances using open position, or to substitute open position, until the latter part of the intermediate grades.

Dance Steps

In addition to the dance steps included in the section, "Movement Skills of Dance," the steps below are commonly referred to in folk dance instructions.

BLEKING

A hop step, in which the free foot is extended forward with heel touching the floor. Alternate hopping and extending the opposite foot.

BUZZ

A swinging step performed as though one were riding a scooter. The free foot pushes as the other foot bears the weight. Most commonly used in the square dance "swing," it is also found in European folk dances.

DRAW

A sideways walking step; the first step is taken to the side and the other foot is then "drawn" alongside the first. Usually performed with a bend of the body in the direction of the first step.

GRAPEVINE

A series of walking steps taken to either side; for example, step left foot to the side, step right foot behind left, step left foot to the side, step right foot in front of left, and so on. Bending the knees slightly facilitates placing the weight on the balls of the feet while stepping.

Planning the Program: Selecting Folk Dances

The dances included in a developmental dance program should be carefully selected to fit the needs and abilities of a particular group. Only the teacher can know the past experiences and present interests of his group, and whether these will contribute to success in learning a particular dance. This means that the teacher must tailor the choices to the group rather than adopt without modification a list prepared by someone outside.

A dance with singing accompaniment is easier for children to learn than one with instrumental accompaniment. The words help children to remember the parts, whether or not they direct the action. They give children independence of action by enabling them to provide their own accompaniment and "calls." Because of the gaiety and simplicity of the traditional singing games and play-party games, they are excellent mixers and lead-ups for more adult forms of folk dance.

Materials for teaching folk dance are virtually unlimited. The teacher has only to select wisely from the wealth of materials on the market. Record companies are supplying an increasing number of recordings of authentic folk music for the elementary school. Directions are usually included with each record or album. The following criteria should guide the teacher in the selection of dances and dance materials for his group:

1. Is the dance suited to the ability of the group? Does it give children an opportunity to use movement and rhythm skills already developed? Do they know the basic steps? Can it be learned quickly and joyously? Does it provide the vigorous activity they need?

2. Is the dance suited to the social maturity of the group? Will it be enjoyed and used outside of school hours now or in the next stage of development? (If the junior high school has school dances, the sixth grade may be the place to begin ballroom dancing.)

3. Does the dance enrich children's interest in, and understanding and appreciation of, people of other lands and times? Is the dance program correlated with other areas of the school program? (If fifth-grade children are studying about colonial days in social studies, they will want to learn the minuet or dance a quadrille. But if these dances are imposed on them as a regular prescribed activity in physical education, the formality of the patterns will seem stuffy to this age group, and they may become prejudiced against all dance as a "sissy" activity.)

The material that follows is organized to help the teacher select dances for a developmental and integrated dance program. It includes (1) a resumé of the development of dance in this country, with references and descriptions of period dances; (2) references and descriptions of selected folk dances that have been enjoyed by many children in the elementary school. These are arranged in approximate order of difficulty within each type or form of dance.

Periods of Dance in the United States[9]

NORTH AMERICAN INDIAN DANCES

Ceremonial and tribal dances present excellent possibilities for an understanding of the North American Indian culture and of the ethnological characteristics of the many tribes. The source materials for these intricate rituals are given at the end of this chapter. Children in the primary grades enjoy dramatizations portraying Indian life and dances. In the intermediate grades they are interested in working out authentic steps. In *Rhythm of the Redman*, Buttree presents characteristic dance steps. A few basic ones are described here.

Side Step (2/4 rhythm): Step sideways right, drag left along ground to right. Repeat as long as desired in bouncing rhythm.

Trot Step (2/4 rhythm): Front trot is performed with a jump onto the right foot, lifting the left knee high in front, followed by a jump onto the left foot, lifting right knee high. May be performed in even rhythm, or the knee may be held high for one or two counts. A variation, the back trot, is performed with free foot lifted high in back.

Toe Flat (slow 2/4 rhythm): Step forward on ball of left foot, drop left heel in place; repeat, stepping forward on right foot, dropping right heel in place. A good resting step. A variation, the heel flat, is performed by stepping on the heel first and dropping the toe.

Tap Flat (slow 2/4 rhythm): Similar to toe flat, except that the ball of the foot is tapped three times before the heel is dropped.

Jump Step (2/4 rhythm): A small jump landing with both feet flat is followed by another jump with one foot slightly raised and ahead of the other. Jumps are repeated, with alternate feet raised every other jump.

Scare Step (slow 2/4 rhythm): Walk in crouched position to the left by crossing right foot in front of left. Continue walking left in this crossed position, with knees bent, head turned right, and hands extended right with palms out, as if warding off danger. Change hand direction when traveling right, and keep left foot crossed in front of right.

Sneak Step (2/4 rhythm): Travel in grapevine fashion, with knees slightly bent; that is, step right with right toe; step left with left toe crossing in front of right; step right with right toe uncrossing; step left with left toe crossing in back.

[9] Classification as arranged by Dudley Ashton, "Syllabus of American Rhythms." Iowa City, Iowa: Department of Publications, State University of Iowa.

COLONIAL DANCES

The dances of this period were brought here by the aristocrats and adventurers from England and France who settled in the middle and southern colonies. These pattern dances were popular in the European courts, and consisted of interesting figures performed in circle, contra, and quadrille formations. They were performed with comparable dignity and style in this country, whether in the governor's mansion or in the stockade. These "old-time" dances have been revived in recent years under the leadership of Mr. and Mrs. Henry Ford. They have sponsored both research and dance groups, the influence of which has stimulated group dancing throughout the country. The Dearborn group remains active today, performing colonial dances in authentic style.

Circles. These are composed of sets of two couples, arranged in a circle. All the sets perform the same series of figures; then couples progress in opposite directions to form new sets. The dance continues until the same couples meet again. "Prompting calls" may be given.

Circle Dances

Portland Fancy	Folkraft 1131
	Ford 114
Sicilian Circle	Folkraft 1140
	RCA Victor 541-6203
Spanish Circle	World of Fun M105
	RCA Victor EPA 4131

Quadrilles. As danced in colonial days, they were direct descendants of the French court quadrille. However, this form was popular in the peasant dances of most European countries as well, and is the basis of many current European and American folk dances today. The formal colonial quadrille consisted of five parts, but these dances are usually condensed to three parts today.

Quadrilles

Plain Quadrille	Ford 101
Standard Club Quadrille	Ford 102
Standard Lancers	Ford 104
Wearing of the Green	Folkraft 1094

The Minuet. Of French origin, the Minuet was commonly used to "open the ball" in colonial days. It consisted of sedate walking and balance steps or "points," interspersed with formal bows and posturing, as befitted the attire of the day. The minuet began with a processional and progressed through contra, circle, and quadrille patterns.

Minuet

Minuet   Burns and Wheeler, Album A
                                          Victor EPA–4132

Contra Dances. Performed in longways formation with partners in opposite lines facing one another, contras usually consist of two parts. The first is made up of figures peculiar to the dance; the second part consists of "casting off," a progressive figure which enables the couples to dance with different people each time the figure is repeated. The contras have remained popular in England and the mountain regions of the United States since colonial times. Interest in them has spread throughout the country since World War II.

Contra Dances

Money Musk   Victor 20447
Virginia Reel   Folkraft 1141
                                          Victor EPA–4138

PIONEER DANCES

Two new forms of dance, distinctly American in character, developed during the westward movement before the Civil War. These reflect the rugged life of the frontier and the individualism and inventiveness of the pioneer.

Square Dances. These dances were patterned after the old quadrille. Songs, chants—and, with good fortune, a fiddle—were used for accompaniment. The formal dance steps were superseded by a shuffle or tricky jig step, and a "caller" endeavored to keep the dancers going and the groups together. The basic figures of the pattern dances were arranged extemporaneously. A study of the "calls" of this period reveals much about the dangers and joys of pioneer days. Lloyd Shaw's book, *Cowboy Dances,* is an excellent source of calls handed down from pioneer days.

Note: See the special section, "The Square Dance."

Play-Party Games. Performers furnish their own accompaniment by hardy singing and clapping. "Games with singing" were tolerated in localities where there was an aversion to dancing and the fiddle was considered an instrument of the devil. Play parties continue to be a popular form of recreation in many communities today. Some of the play-party games are patterned after the folk games of Europe. Others were invented in this period, and, like the square dance calls, are rich in the folklore of that day. Lynn Rohrbough's *Handy Play Party Book* is an excellent source of play-party games. These dances are easily learned and greatly enjoyed by children. They are excellent "mixer" dances and good lead-ups for the more adult contras and square dances. Play-party games are listed with "Dances with Singing Accompaniment," on pages 406–407.

Play-Party Games

Bluebird, Jump Jim Jo	Folkraft 1180
Paw Paw Patch, Turn the Glasses Over	Folkraft 1181
Bingo, Bow Belinda	Folkraft 1189

DANCES OF THE "GAY NINETIES"

The group dances of the former periods declined in popularity as the new couple dances were imported in quick succession from Europe during the nineteenth century. The waltz, the polka, and the two-step were enthusiastically taken up in turn. The schottische and the varsouvienne were danced also, though these are considered to be revived versions of steps appearing in the peasant dances of many countries. The couple dances were considered exciting and somewhat daring, since the closed dance position was introduced for the first time with the waltz. The dances of this period were performed in a "lilting" style, and movement was restricted by the dress of the day.

Round Dances. These are couple dances performed in a double circle with couples progressing in a counterclockwise direction, performing the same sequence throughout the dance. In *The Round Dance Book*, Lloyd Shaw gives an interesting account of the derivation of the couple dances and the origin of the round dances.

Mixers. These are variations of the round dance. A progression of partners is made after each completion of the dance pattern.

Note: The following are suggested recordings of popular dances of the "Gay Nineties."

Title	Dance Type	Recording
The Military Schottische	Schottische	Ford 117B
		Folkraft 1166
The Badger Gavotte	Two-Step	Folkraft 1094
Laces and Graces	Two-Step	Shaw 105
		Folkraft 1047
Susan's Gavotte	Two-Step	Folkraft 1047
		MacGregor 1010
Veleta Waltz	Waltz	Shaw 145
Black Hawk Waltz	Waltz	Imperial 1006B
		Shaw 145
Varsouvienne (Mazurka and Waltz)	Waltz	Shaw 103
		Decca 3131A
Jennie Lind Polka	Polka	Folkraft 1071
Cotton-Eyed Joe	Polka	Folkraft 1035
		Imperial 1045B

CONTEMPORARY DANCES

Since 1900, standard ballroom dance steps have included the fox trot, waltz, two-step, and tango. The fox trot is the only one of these of American origin. Its name was derived from Harry Fox, of musical comedy fame, who introduced the step in a Ziegfeld show.[10] The step was refined and standardized for ballroom dancing by Vernon and Irene Castle. The fox trot was first performed to ragtime music, and changes style as style in music changes.

Jitterbug and swing fox trot version were similarly refined for ballroom usage. The Latin influence is second only to swing in influencing contemporary social dancing. The tango, rumba, samba, cha cha, and meringue have each achieved an important place in the American dance scene.

Fleeting fads in dancing have included the turkey trot, camel walk, grizzly bear and flea hop. The big apple, Charleston, bunny hop and shag were destined for more lasting interest. Only time will tell whether or not interest in bop, stomp, twist, push, roach and goulash will survive sufficiently long for them to be classed as "folk dance" fifty years hence.

[10] Lawrence Hostetler, *Walk Your Way to Better Dancing*. New York: A. S. Barnes & Company, Inc., 1942.

Music References and Descriptions of Selected Folk Dances

Primary Grades — Dances with Singing Accompaniment

1. *Danced in a ring without partners—involve dramatic action*

Title	Dance Type	Recording
Muffin Man	English Singing Game	Folkraft 1188
Round and Round the Village	English Singing Game	Folkraft 1191
Looby Loo	English Singing Game	Folkraft 1181
Farmer in the Dell	English Singing Game	Folkraft 1182
Bluebird	American Song Play	Folkraft 1184
Did You Ever See a Lassie	Scottish Song Play	Folkraft 1183
Rig-a-Jig-Jig	American Song Play	Folkraft 1188
Chimes of Dunkirk	French Song Play	Victor 45: 6176

Note: If young children have difficulty in maintaining a circle, it may be advisable to substitute the walk for the skip or slide specified.

2. *Danced in a ring with partners*

Title	Dance Type	Recording
Oats, Peas, Beans (dramatic action)	English Singing Game	Folkraft 1182
On the Bridge of Avignon (dramatic action)	French Song Play	Folkraft 1191
Jump Jim Jo (dramatic action)	American Song Play	Folkraft 1180
How Do You Do My Partner (skipping, running)	Swedish Song Play	Folkraft 1190 Estamae 202
Let Your Feet Go Tap (dramatic action)	German Song Play	Folkraft 1184
Shoo Fly (walking, swing)	American Play-Party	Folkraft 1185 Windsor A751
Skip to My Lou (skipping, introductory square dance figures)	American Play-Party	Folkraft 1192 Estamae 204
Carrousel (slow to very fast sliding—difficult to keep from "breaking down")	English Singing Game	Folkraft 1183 Victor 45-6179

3. *Danced in longways (contra) formation with partners*

Title	Dance Type	Recording
Paw Paw Patch (skipping, dramatic action)	American Play-Party	Folkraft 1181
A-Hunting We Will Go (sliding, skipping)	English Song Play	Estamae 203 Folkraft 1191
Pop Goes the Weasel (skipping, dramatic action)	American Play-Party	Victor 45: 6180 Methodist 104

Beginning Folk Dances

1. *Danced in a ring without partners*

Title	Dance Type	Recording
Nixie Polka (skipping and bleking step; dramatic action)	Danish Folk Dance	Burns and Wheeler Album E

2. *Danced in a ring with partners*

Title	Dance Type	Recording
Shoemaker's Dance (skipping, dramatic action)	Danish Folk Dance	Folkraft 1187 Victor 45: 6171
Dance of Greeting (skipping, clapping, swing)	Danish Folk Dance	Folkraft 1187 Victor 45: 6183
Children's Polka	German Folk Dance	Folkraft 1187 Victor 45: 6172
Bleking (skipping and bleking step, swing)	Swedish Folk Dance	Folkraft 1188 Victor 45: 6169
Seven Steps (run with quick turns, schottische)	German Folk Dance	Victor 45: 6172 Methodist 101

Intermediate Grades — Dances with Singing Accompaniment

1. *Danced in a ring without partners*

Title	Dance Type	Recording
Skating Away Steps: Skip Figures: Right- and left-hand star	American Play-Party	Victor 45: 541-6201

2. *Danced in a ring with partners*

Title	Dance Type	Recording

Jolly Is the Miller
  Steps: Step-hop
  Figures: Circle prome-
    nade
  (Mixer type; involves
    extra person and pro-
    gression of partners)
	English Song Game	Folkraft 1192
		Victor 20214

Turn the Glasses Over
  Steps: Walk
  Figures: Promenade,
    reverse lines
  (Mixer type; involves
    extra person)
	English Song Game	Folkraft 1181

Bingo
  Steps: Walk, skip
  Figures: Promenade,
    grand right and left
  (Excellent mixer type)
	English Song Game	Folkraft 1189
		Victor 45: 6172

Oh Susanna
  Steps: Walk
  Figures: Ladies to cen-
    ter, men to center,
    grand right and left,
    promenade
	American Play-Party	Folkraft 1186

Brown-Eyed Mary
  Steps: Walk or skip
  Figures: Promenade,
    turning partner and
    opposite
  (A lead to "allemande"
    in square dance)
	American Play-Party	Folkraft 1186

3. *Danced in longways formation*

Title	Dance Type	Recording

Bow Belinda
  Steps: Walk, skip
  Figures: Forward and
    back, elbow swing,
    dos-a-dos, cast-off
  (A good lead-up to the
    Virginia Reel)
	American Play-Party	Folkraft 1189

4. *Danced in circle with groups of three*

Title	Dance Type	Recording
Come Let Us Be Joyful	English Folk Dance	Victor 45: 6177

Steps: Walk
Figures: Circle prome-
   nade, center person
   turns side person in
   turn
(A good choice when
   one sex outnumbers
   the other in a group)

Intermediate Folk Dances

1. *Dances based on the walk*

Title	Dance Type	Recording
Yankee Doodle	United States Folk Dance	Windsor A-7S1

Steps: Walk, skip
Figures: Promenade,
   right- and left-hand
   turns
Formation: Sets of
   three dancers, facing
   line of direction, in
   circle

Circassian Circle	United States Folk Dance	Windsor A-7S3

Steps: Walk, skip
Figures: In and out of
   circle, swing, prome-
   nade
Formation: Ring with
   partner

Noriu Miego	Lithuanian Folk Dance	Folkraft 1050

Steps: Walk, bleking
Figures: Star
Formation: Groups of
   four scattered with
   or without partners
(Music gets progres-
   sively faster)

Glow Worm	American Mixer	Imperial 1044

Steps: Dance walk

Title	Dance Type	Recording

Figures: Partners separate, move one place to the right, promenade
Formation: Double circle

2. Dance based on the leap and jump

Title	Dance Type	Recording
Tinikling	Philippine Folk Dance	Victor EPA-4126

Steps: Leap, jump, waltz
Figures: steps in, out, and around two bamboo poles
Formation: partners facing in center of poles; two persons at each end of pole beat the rhythm.

3. Dances based on the skip, slide, or gallop

Title	Dance Type	Recording
Gustaf's Skoal	Swedish Folk Dance	Victor 45: 6170

Steps: Walk, skip
Figures: Forward and back, skipping through arches
Formation: Quadrille

Virginia Reel	American Contra	Victor 45: 6180

Steps: Walk, skip
Figures: Partners, cast-off, reel
Formation: Contra

Csebogar	Hungarian Folk Dance	Victor 45: 6182

Steps: Slide, walk
Figures: Forward and back, Hungarian turn
Formation: Single ring

Title	Dance Type	Recording
Ribbon Dance	English Folk Dance	Victor 45: 6175

Ribbon Dance
  Steps: Walk, skip
  Figures: Weaving with
    ribbons, casting off
  Formation: Lines

| La Raspa | American Mixer | Folkraft 1119 |

La Raspa
  Steps: Shuffle (similar
    to bleking), skipping
    or two-step turn
  Figures: Circle, right
    and left turns
  Formation: Double
    circle

| Patty Cake Polka | American Mixer | Folkraft 1124 |

Patty Cake Polka
  Steps: Heel-toe and
    slides, skip
  Figures: Circle, hand-
    claps, right and left
    turns
  Formation: Double
    circle

| Sextur | Danish Folk Dance | Folk Dancer 1021 |

Sextur
  Steps: Skip
  Figures: Alternate
    couples in and out of
    circle, grand right
    and left
  Formation: Six couples
    in a ring

4. Dances based on run

Title	Dance Type	Recording
Troika	Russian Folk Dance	Methodist 105

Troika
  Steps: Run
  Figures: Side person
    runs under arch
    made by other two
  Formation: Groups of
    three
  (*Troika* means "three
    horses abreast")

| Mountain March | Danish Folk Dance | Victor 45: 6173 |

Mountain March
  Steps: ¾ run

Title	Dance Type	Recording
Figures: Sides follow leader, turn under arch made by other two		
Formation: Groups of three		
(Imitates action of guide taking travelers up the mountain)		
Mayim	Israeli Folk Dance	Folkraft 1108
Steps: Grapevine run, fast toe touch and clap		
Figures: In and out of circle, circle left		
Formation: Ring without partners		
(*Mayim* means "water"; movements express joy at finding water in arid land)		

5. *Dances based on step-hop*

Title	Dance Type	Recording
Crested Hen	Danish Folk Dance	Victor 45: 6176
Steps: Step-hop		
Figures: Circle, outside person turning under arches made by other two		
Formation: Groups of three		
(The men of Denmark wear red stocking caps with a tassel representing the hen's crest. Dance imitates action of the girls trying to snatch the cap off while passing through arch, so that they become the crested hen)		

Title	Dance Type	Recording
Seven Jumps	Danish Folk Dance	Methodist 108
		Victor 45: 6172

Seven Jumps
Steps: The "jumps"
consist of accumula-
tive balance acts,
such as balance on
one foot, one knee,
and so on
Figures: Circle left and
right, "jumps"
Formation: Ring with-
out partners
(In Denmark, the
dance is performed
by men; the one los-
ing his balance treats
the crowd)

Tropanka	Bulgarian Folk Dance	Michel Herman
		1020

Tropanka
Steps: Run, step-swing,
stamping
Figures: Circle left and
right
Formation: Ring with-
out partners
(Commonly called the
"stamping dance"; it
is an excellent ice-
breaker)

6. Dances based on schottische

Title	Dance Type	Recording
Highland Schottische	Scottish Folk Dance	Victor 45: 6179

Highland Schottische
Steps: Toe touch and
lift of the Highland
Fling; link-arm turns
Figures: Circle left and
right, right and left
turns
Formation: Double
circle

Rheinlander Schottische	German Folk Dance	Imperial 1037

Rheinlander Schottische
Steps: Schottische, run,
step-hop

Title	Dance Type	Recording
Figures: Diagonal steps forward left and right, arches, forward and turns, backward and turns		
Formation: Sets of three dancers, facing line of direction in circle		
Horah	Israeli Folk Dance	Folkraft 1110
Steps: Sideways schottische, step-hop		
Figures: Open ring moves left throughout dance		
Formation: Open ring without partners		
(The Horah is the Jewish national dance. There are many Horah tunes—the dance begins slowly and accelerates to a very fast tempo)		

7. Dances based on polka

Title	Dance Type	Recording
Clap Dance (Klappdans)	Swedish Folk Dance	Victor 45: 6171
Steps: Heel-toe polka, schottische		
Figures: Circle, honor, clapping, turning in place		
Formation: Double circle		
Hop Mother Annika (Hopp Mor Annika)	Swedish Folk Dance	Victor EPA-4142 Burns Album F 774
Steps: Walk, skip face-to-face, back-to-back polka		
Figures: Honor, circle, clapping, stamping		

Title	Dance Type	Recording
Formation: Double circle		
Tantoli	Swedish Folk Dance	Victor 45: 6183
Steps: Heel-toe polka, step-hop		
Figures: Circle left and right, turning partner		
Formation: Double circle		
Kalvelis	Lithuanian Folk Dance	Folkraft 1051
Steps: Polka, clapping and linked-arm turns		
Figures: Circle, forward and back, weaving		
Formation: Ring with partners		
(*Kalvelis* means "the little smith"; the clapping suggests the hammer and the anvil)		

8. *Dances based on two-step*

Title	Dance Type	Recording
Czardas	Hungarian Folk Dance	Burns Album B 344
Steps: Draw, Hungarian turn		
Figures: In and out of circle, right and left turns		
Formation: Ring with partners		
(The national dance of Hungary)		
The Roberts	Scottish Folk Dance	Folkraft 1161
Steps: Draw, heel-toe, two-step		
Figures: Couples facing in circle dance in open and closed position		

Title	Dance Type	Recording
Wrangler's Two-Step	American Round	Windsor 7621

Steps: Walk forward, grapevine, balance, twirl

Figures: Round dance in open dance position

Formation: Double circle

Title	Dance Type	Recording
Teton Mountain Stomp	American Round	Western Jubilee 725
		Windsor A–7S3

Steps: Side, close, stomp, walk

Figures: Circle in open and reverse open dance position

Formation: Double circle

9. *Dances based on waltz*

Title	Dance Type	Recording
Dance of the Bells	American Round	Windsor A–7S4

Steps: Waltz balance, walk, draw

Figures: Balance forward, backward, right- and left-hand star, circle

Formation: Double circle

Title	Dance Type	Recording
Little Man in a Fix	Danish Folk Dance	Victor 20449

Steps: Run, waltz

Figures: Wheel formation

Formation: Groups of four

(The name signifies the predicament of the man who fails to find a place with a new group before the dance begins again)

Title	Dance Type	Recording
To Ting	Danish Folk Dance	Folk Dancer 1018

To Ting
   Steps: Waltz, walk,
     pivot turn
   Figures: Circle in open
     dance position, turn
     with partner in
     closed position
   Formation: Double
     circle
     (*To Ting* means "two
     things," and refers to
     the two rhythms of
     the dance)

Mexican Waltz   Southwestern United   Folkraft 1093
   Steps: Step-swing,   States Folk Dance
     waltz balance, waltz
   Figures: Couples facing
     in circle, circle
     counterclockwise
   Formation: Double
     circle

The Square Dance

Social groups again begin to include members of both sexes when children reach 11 or 12 years of age. Their desire to be together in a large group increases and is accompanied by the continued drive for vigorous activities—to be on the move and to do things. Ability to square dance becomes an important recreational skill during these years.

Children should have an opportunity to learn dances they can manage "on their own" after school hours. For this reason, dances with singing calls or simple patterns should be selected. Experiences in square dance should include the opportunity for interested members of the group to practice "calling."

Square formation. Squares are arranged with the girl to the right of her partner, so that the first couple has its back to the music. Couples are numbered counterclockwise around the square. The beginning position is *home* for each couple throughout the dance. The first and third couples are the *head couples;* the second and fourth couples are the *side couples.* The girl to the left of each boy is the *corner girl;* the girl in the couple to the right is the *right-hand girl;* the girl directly across the set is the *opposite girl.*

Parts of the square dance. There are usually four parts to a square dance. Introductory figures, breaks, and endings are used interchangeably. The parts are:

1. Introduction
2. The main figure (usually the name of the dance)
3. Breaks (trimmings, fill-ins, or chorus)
4. Ending

These are selected and arranged at random by an expert caller.

Basic steps and figures. The shuffle step is most commonly used in square dancing, though variations are popular in different sections of the country, and the nature of square dancing encourages improvisation. The shuffle consists of an easy, light step with the feet maintaining light contact with the floor. The two-step is interspersed frequently with the shuffle.

Practice in the shuffle step and basic figures used for introductions, breaks, and endings is efficiently provided through a "Paul Jones"—a dance performed in a circle but using square dance figures, selected at random by the caller. In this formation, the teacher can keep the entire group together and actively engaged. It is well to include "everybody home" as one of the calls in the beginning stages. This serves to establish this important position, and is preferable to stopping the dance and starting it all over again when confusion arises—something which is bound to happen! After the group is arranged and home, corners, and so on, are established, children should walk through and then dance some of the basic figures, using the shuffle step. Some suggestions are:

Call	Figure	Beat
Honor your partner	Bow or curtsy.	4 counts
Honor your corner		4 counts
Join hands and circle left		16 counts
The other way back on the same old track		16 counts
Everybody balance and swing	*Balance*—Take two steps away from partner and curtsy with inside hands joined; then back to partner and swing (elbow swing for this age).	8 counts

The square dance teaches old figures and calls to new dancers as they enter the intermediate grades.

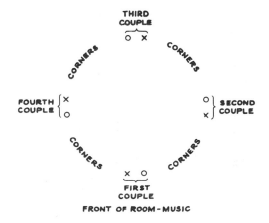

Call	Figure	Beat
Sashay round your cor-ner	*Sashay*—Move around each other with sliding steps, facing the center throughout. Boy go to the left and behind the girl.	8 counts
See-saw round your own	Reverse direction and move around partner.	8 counts
Face your partner—grand right and left	Pause after "partner" until everyone is facing correctly; then proceed with weaving figure.	16 counts
When you meet your partner, promenade home	When couples meet partners halfway around the circle, extend right hands; boy turn the girl about (girl turns under her partner's hand); and walk or shuffle back to home position in skating or varsouvienne position.	16 counts

When the group can perform these figures easily, others should be added. Avoid giving them in the same order. The following arrangement introduces new figures and provides a review of the grand right and left.

Call	Figure	Beat
All join hands, go forward	Take four steps to the inside of the circle.	8 counts
And back—	Take four steps back.	
Dos-a-dos the corner	Face corner and move around each other, passing by right shoulders until back-to-back; then walk backward to home position.	8 counts
Dos-a-dos your own	Face partner; move as above.	8 counts
Allemande left your cor-ner	Face corner, clasp left hands and walk around each other, and back to home position.	8 counts
Allemande right your partner	Face partner, clasp right hands and walk around each other, and back to home position.	8 counts
Allemande left your cor-ner		8 counts

Call	Figure	Beat
Face your partner and— Grand right and left		16 counts
Meet your partner and promenade home		16 counts

Figures for visiting-couple dances. The simplest arrangement of a square dance is that in which each couple in turn visits around the set. Figures used for this type can easily be taught in a double circle, with two couples facing each other. When children are familiar with the main figure, they should form sets and try the dance. An example of a visiting-couple dance is given below:

TAKE A PEEK

Call	Figure	Beat
Introduction		
All join hands and circle left		8 counts
The other way back, you're going wrong		8 counts
Dos-a-dos your corner girl		8 counts
Dos-a-dos your own		8 counts
And promenade, O promenade		16 counts
Main Figure		
First couple out to the couple on your right	First couple walks over to face second couple.	4 counts
Around that couple, take a peek	First couple separates, boy walks to the left of girl of second couple and peeks behind and across her to look at his partner, who has walked to the right of boy of second couple at the same time and is peeking in the same way.	4 counts

Call	Figure	Beat
Back to the center and swing your sweet	First couple return to the center of the set and swing.	8 counts
Around that couple and peek once more	First couple repeat action of peeking around second couple.	4 counts
And back to the center and swing all four	First couple return to the center of the set; both couples swing.	8 counts
On to the next couple on your right, and so on	(Calls and figure are repeated twice more for first couple to visit third and fourth couple then.)	
Home you go and everybody swing		8 counts
Break		
Allemande left with your hand		8 counts
Right to your partner and right and left grand		16 counts
Meet your partner, promenade home		16 counts
Main Figure and Break Ending	Repeat three more times for second, third, and fourth couples.	
Bow to your partner		4 counts
And corners all—		4 counts
Honor your partner across the hall		4 counts
And, that is all!		

The following figures are useful in visiting-couple dances:

STAR BY THE RIGHT

Call	Figure	Beat
First couple out to the couple on the right		4 counts
Form a star with the right hand crossed	First couple walk to second couple; all four extend right hands, touching fingers to form a star, while walking to the left around the circle.	8 counts

Call	Figure	Beat
Back by the left and don't get lost	Reverse direction, touching left fingers to form star.	8 counts
Turn the opposite with the right hand 'round	Boy of first couple turns girl of second couple, while boy of second couple, turns girl of first couple.	8 counts
Turn your partner with the left hand 'round	Each boy turn his own partner around once.	8 counts
And on to the next— and so on		

DIVE FOR THE OYSTER

Call	Figure	Beat
First couple out to the couple on the right	First couple walk over to face second couple.	4 counts
Circle four go half way 'round	All four join hands and circle half way around to the left.	4 counts
Dive for the oyster, dive	First couple walk under the joined hands of second couple, then back out.	4 counts
Dig for the clam, dig	Second couple walk under the joined hands of first couple then back out.	4 counts
Dive for the sardine and take a full can	First couple dive under the joined hands of second couple; then, releasing hands of second couple, continue walking to the next (third) couple.	8 counts
On to the next, and so on		

BIRDIE IN THE CAGE

Call	Figure	Beat
First couple out to the couple on the right	First couple walk over to face second couple.	4 counts
Circle four hands 'round	All four join hands and circle once around to the left.	8 counts
Birdie in the cage and three hands 'round	Girl of the visiting couple go to the inside of the ring, while her partner and the opposite couple circle around her.	8 counts

Call	Figure	Beat
Birdie hop out and the crow hop in	Boy of the visiting couple go to the inside as his partner joins the circle (*tweet*'s and *caw*'s usually accompany these figures).	8 counts
Crow hop out and circle four	All four circle once around.	8 counts
On to the next—		

Teaching aids. For the teacher who feels her experience does not qualify her for teaching the fundamentals of square dancing, the square dance album, *Honor Your Partner*, Album I, contains clear-cut directions and beginning dances. Many excellent recordings are available, with calls by professional callers. It is advisable to listen to each one carefully before purchasing it to make sure that it is within the ability range of the group and to determine whether the calls can be clearly understood.

Square Dance Music

Honor Your Partner, Ed Durlacher, caller, Square Dance Associates, Freeport, New York.
  Album I: Formation of set, Susanna, Honolulu Baby, Two Head Ladies Cross Over, Do-si-do Swing, Around the Outside and Swing.
  Albums II–VI: Contain square and round dances progressing in difficulty.
  This series gives basic instructions on one side of the record; the music and calls on the reverse side.
Let's Square Dance, Dick Kraus, caller, RCA Victor EEB 3001–3004.
  Album I: Shoo Fly, Duck for the Oyster, Red River Valley, Girls to the Center, Take a Peek, Hinky-Dinky Parlez-vous, Divide the Ring, The Noble Duke of York, Little Brown Jug (without calls).
  Album II: Skating Away, Life on the Ocean Wave, Swing at the Wall, Nellie Gray, Form an Arch, Uptown and Downtown, Double Sashay, Bow Belinda, Angleworm Wiggle (without calls).
  Both albums are excellent for intermediate grades. Album III is recommended for junior high youngsters.

Records With Singing Calls

Oh Johnny	MacGregor 652
Hot Time in the Old Town	MacGregor 652

Buffalo Girls	Folkraft 1135
Hinky Dinky Parley Vous	Folkraft 1023
Pop goes the Weasel	Folkraft 1014
Alabama Jubilee	Folkraft 1136
Red River Valley	Folkraft 1053

RECORD COMPANIES

Burns Record Co., 755 Chickadee Lane, Stratford, Conn.

Columbia Records, 1473 Barnum Ave., Bridgeport, Conn.

Educational Record Albums, David McKay Company, Inc., 119 West 40th St., New York 18, N.Y.

Estamae Rhythm Records, 2401 Grand Ave., Pueblo, Colo.

Folk Dancer, Box 201, Flushing, Long Island, N.Y.

Folkraft Records, 1159 Broad St., Newark, N.J.

Imperial Records, 137 North Western Ave., Los Angeles, Calif.

MacGregor (World of Fun Records), 729 South Western Ave., Hollywood, Calif.

Methodist Publishing House, 150 Fifth Ave., New York, N.Y.

Shaw, Lloyd, Recording Co., Box 203, Colorado Springs, Colo.

Victor Records, Radio Corporation of America, Camden, N.J.

Windsor Records, 5528 North Rosemead Blvd., Temple City, Calif.

Selected References

Andrews, Gladys, *Creative Rhythm Movement for Children*. Englewood Cliffs, N.J.: Prentice-Hall, Inc., 1954.

Beliajus, Finadar, *Dance and Be Merry*. Evanston, Ill.: Summy-Birchard Publishing Company, 1940.

Buttree, Julia M., *The Rhythm of the Redman*. New York: A. S. Barnes & Company, Inc., 1930.

Duggan, Anne Schley, Jeanette Schlottmann, and Abbie Rutledge, *The Folk Dance Library*. New York: A. S. Barnes & Company, Inc., 1948.

Geri, Frank, *Illustrated Games, Rhythms and Stunts for Children*, Vols. I and II. Englewood Cliffs, N.J.: Prentice-Hall, Inc., 1957.

Hunt, W. Ben, *The Golden Book of Indian Crafts and Lore*. New York: Golden Press, 1954.

Kraus, Richard, *Square Dancing of Today*. New York: A. S. Barnes & Company, Inc., 1950.

LaSalle, Dorothy, *Rhythms and Dances for Elementary Schools*, rev. ed. New York: A. S. Barnes & Company, Inc., 1951.

Lovett, Benjamin, *Good Morning*, Music, Calls and Directions for Old-Time Dancing as Revised by Mr. and Mrs. Henry Ford. Dearborn, Michigan: Edison Institute, 1943.

Mason, Bernard S., *Dances and Stories of the American Indian*. New York: A. S. Barnes & Company, Inc., 1944.

Murray, Ruth Lovell, *Dance in Elementary Education*. New York: Harper & Row, Publishers, 1963.

Piper, Ralph, and Zora Piper, *Developing the Creative Square Dance Caller*. Minneapolis, Minnesota: 132 Orlen Ave. S. E., 1956.

Rohrbough, Lynn, *Handy Play Party Book*. Delaware, Ohio: Cooperative Recreation Service, 1946.

Sehon, Elizabeth, and Emma Lou O'Brien, *Rhythms in Elementary Education*. New York: A. S. Barnes & Company, Inc., 1951.

Shaw, Lloyd, *Cowboy Dances*. Caldwell, Idaho: Caxton Printers, Ltd., 1940.

Shaw, Lloyd, *The Round Dance Book*. Caldwell, Idaho: Caxton Printers, Ltd., 1948.

Stuart, Frances R., and John S. Ludlam, *Rhythmic Activities*, Minneapolis, Minnesota: Burgess Publishing Company, 1956.

Tolentino, Francissa Reyes, *Philippine National Dances*. Morristown, N.J.: Silver Burdett Company, 1955.

Waterman, Elizabeth, *The Rhythm Book*. New York: A. S. Barnes & Company, Inc., 1937.

APPENDIXES

Appendix A

COMMITTEE ON SCHOOL HEALTH

The American Academy of Pediatrics
Competitive Athletics[1]
A Statement of Policy

COMPETITIVE ATHLETICS for children is an important subject; it is also a controversial one. It is generally agreed that athletic programs for children of all ages are a necessary part of their education and recreation. There are differences of opinion as to the time in a child's life at which games requiring considerable co-ordination should be introduced and the extent to which such games should be organized on a competitive basis. Because of this, educators, community leaders in recreation, and particularly parents, often turn to physicians, especially pediatricians, for guidance and direction when they consider the development of athletic programs. To aid physicians in this advisory role, the Committee on School Health of the American Academy of Pediatrics has summarized its study of the subject.

A considerable fund of information as to extent of organized competitive athletic programs among children and as to the effects of these programs has been accumulated from the experience and investigation of recognized leaders in the fields of education and recreation, who have collaborated with interested and informed physicians. Those concerned with sports programs for children should give careful consideration to the opinions repeatedly expressed by these groups. Many of these opinions are contained in the appended reference list. The American Academy of Pediatrics definitely encourages and promotes continuing research to establish sound policies.

The Committee on School Health has considered the subject under the following headings:

Age

We are concerned in this statement with the question of competitive athletics for children 12 years of age and under. In discussing or planning programs for this age group, great care must be taken to avoid thinking interchangeably in terms of the older high school or college age activities. Many well-intentioned sports leaders and parents fall into this trap.

Sex

Published statements heretofore have made little mention of athletics for girls who constitute about a half of our ele-

[1] Reprinted by permission from *Pediatrics*, Vol. 18, No. 4, October 1956.

mentary school population. A proper program of games and sports is equally essential for girls and boys. The problems of growth and development are even more evident among girls as some begin normally to mature before the age of 12 years. Fortunately, in most communities highly organized competitive sports are not available for girls. More often there is no sports program of any kind, implying that girls are being encouraged to be spectators only. Sports programs which include calisthenics, folk dancing, kickball, baseball, swimming, skating, tennis, golf, archery and similar activities should be encouraged for both sexes. The difference in interests of boys and girls at various ages should be considered in planning programs.

Competition

Competition has been defined as a contest between two or more individuals striving for the same objectives, but it may also be thought of as an attempt to surpass previous accomplishment, singly or collectively. Competition is a natural, healthy process and is in no way being denied. The young child competes with his associates, with himself, or with his environment. Vying with one another is not only part of our society, but, as defined here, it is an inherent part of the growing, developing child. This inherent competitive drive should be understood and aided to develop normally, not suppressed nor overstimulated. It can be developed to better advantage when correlated with the child's physical and emotional growth and development. Competitive drives should be so directed that when children mature they will have devel-

oped a perspective in which competition and co-operation are properly balanced. Athletics become highly competitive and undesirable when the main emphasis is placed on winning; when emotional pressures are applied by teachers, parents and others; and when parental interest goes to the point of expressing concern over winning or losing.

Athletics

Under consideration here are the in-school and extracurricular programs for preteen-age children. Athletics are defined as physical activities in the form of competitive and noncompetitive sports and play activities. Developmental needs of elementary school children are best met if physical activities are informal and not highly competitive. Athletic competition should be gradually introduced with simple games involving few participants; five small groups are better than one large one. This plan will allow the child to develop early a sense of belonging as well as giving him the experience of pride in his accomplishment.

Children in this age group are particularly susceptible to bone and joint injury because the growing ends of the long bones have not yet calcified, and because they do not possess the protection of adult musculature. Such injury may result in interference with normal bone growth. For this reason body-contact sports, particularly wrestling, tackle football, and boxing should be avoided in the sports program. Baseball, a good game in itself, often becomes highly competitive, a tendency that must be guarded against in this age group.

Programs

At present competitive athletic programs consist of the following: 1) those that are part of the regular school curriculum; 2) those outside the school curriculum, but under the community recreation programs; 3) those organized under independent, special interests related to various sports, and 4) unorganized, haphazard activities.

Provision of a program of suitable games for children of elementary school age requires professionally trained personnel who understand the needs and interests of children. Active community-wide interest and participation is needed. Particularly important is the close co-operation of parents, teachers, recreation leaders and qualified medical advisors. Schools and communities must recognize the dangers of exploitation of programs at any level. They must be alert to recognize the undue motivating pressures of advertising and commercialism in any form. The pressures which a highly organized competitive sports program place on children far outweigh any possible advantages which such programs may seem to offer.

Physical Aspects

Boys and girls are children and not "little men" or "little women" and in Nature's own way and time they gradually grow up. With understanding guidance they can reach healthy physical and emotional maturity. The physical maturation process does not have the same chronological curve in all children. Bone, joint, and muscle development shows individual variation during the preadolescent and adolescent years. Chronic fatigue has long been recognized as a factor which can interfere with healthy growth. Differentiation between healthy, transient fatigue and exhaustion which leads to chronic fatigue and other ill effects may not be readily discernible. Exhaustion may lead to physical injury which may be acute and apparent, or nonapparent, but likely to manifest itself at a later time. Ill effects may result from its insidious interference with optimal body functions and so predispose to illness.

Good medical care assumes regular medical examinations, and any additional examinations which may be indicated in the course of the sports or physical education program. One objective of good medical care should be to detect any ill effects of sports upon the elementary school age child. Another aim should be to detect evidences of need for encouraging participation in these activities. Careful and continuing health observation by coaches and teachers is an important part of a good health program.

Physical fitness is not attained solely by participation in competitive athletics, nor can it be said that physical fitness is necessarily related to degrees of strength and flexibility of certain posture muscles. The comparison of results of muscle testing in groups of children from different countries, likewise, is not a valid estimate of physical fitness or whether they are "healthy" school children. These comparisons fail to take into account the many factors which may be involved, such as heredity, rapidity of maturation, local customs pertaining to physical activities and the general interests of children of comparable age groups. In grade school children physical fitness can best be achieved not by greatly ballyhooed interscholastic or interleague competition, but by a program of intramural sports and play activities in which children of both sexes with varying abilities and capacities have an opportunity and are encouraged to participate freely. It is important that the various competitive sports are appropriate to the individual differences in children's capacities at successive developmental levels.

Emotional Aspects

All growing children need some regular exercise. This should be a satisfying experience, not a routine chore imposed upon them by unimaginative adult leadership. Too often, however, a satisfying experience is denied children because they fail to "make the team." This may lead to the development of unwholesome attitudes toward both competition and athletics. Other children may be so highly motivated by the prestige of "wearing the uniform" or "winning the game" that their scale of values becomes warped in the process. All children need a sense of belonging, of being wanted, and their acceptance by playmates or adults should not be dependent solely upon success in competitive athletics.

Athletic competition among children produces strong emotional reactions in adults—parents, teachers, leaders, coaches, and even spectators. These reactions in the adults such as undue stress on "winning the game," undue adulation of the skilled athlete, coercion of the child beyond his ability or interests, all of these may be reflected in the children.

Physicians and educators should be interested in the growth and development, physically and emotionally, of all children. They should help children learn to play for the fun of playing. At the elementary school level programs of physical education should contain

many noncompetitive, nonathletic activities such as games, stunts, hiking, nature study, etc., as well as team sports in which all children participate. The adult may then experience pride and satisfaction not only in the children's achievements, but in his own participation in and observation of their over-all physical, emotional, and social development.

The emotional and social needs of those children who for any reason are unable to participate in competitive athletics may often be met through opportunities for activities associated with sports programs.

Underlying emotional difficulties of various kinds may account for failure of a child to participate willingly in group activities or to gain satisfaction from any sport. After recognition of these emotional problems further medical, social or other studies may be necessary.

Leadership

Proper leadership places the interest and welfare of children first. Guidance within the school program and in recreation programs outside of school activities is of basic importance. Supervision should be through individuals who understand the desires, needs and limitations of growing children. Such leadership will promote wholesome attitudes, encourage good health standards, and play an important role in the planning of proper programs.

Conclusions and Recommendations

1. All children should have opportunities to develop skill in a variety of activities.

2. All such activities should take into account the age and developmental level of the child.

3. a. Athletic activities of elementary school children should be part of an over-all school program. Competent medical supervision of each child should be ensured.

b. Health observation by teachers and others should be encouraged and help given by the physician.

4. Athletic activities outside of the school program should be on an entirely voluntary basis without undue emphasis on any special program or sport, and without undue emphasis upon winning. These programs should also include competent medical supervision.

5. Competitive programs organized on school, neighborhood and community levels will meet the needs of children 12 years of age and under. State, regional and national tournaments, bowl, charity and exhibition games are not recommended for this age group. Commercial exploitation in any form is unequivocally condemned.

6. Body-contact sports, particularly tackle football and boxing, are considered to have no place in programs for children of this age.

7. Competition is an inherent characteristic of growing, developing children. Properly guided it is beneficial and not harmful to their development.

8. Schools and communities as a whole must be made aware of the needs for personnel, facilities, equipment, and supplies which will assure an adequate program for children in this age group.

9. All competitive athletic programs should be organized with the co-operation of interested medical groups who will ensure adequate medical care before and during such programs. This should include thorough physical examinations at specified intervals, teaching of health observation to teachers and coaches, as well as attention to factors such as: a) injury; b) response to fatigue; c) individual emotional needs, and d) the risks of undue emotional strains.

10. Muscle testing is not, per se, a valid estimate of physical fitness, or of good health.

11. Participation in group activities is expected of every child. When there is a failure to do so, or lack of interest, underlying physical or emotional causes should be sought.

12. Leadership for young children should be such that highly organized, highly competitive programs would be avoided. The primary consideration should be a diversity of wholesome childhood experience which will aid in the proper physical and emotional development of the child into a secure and well integrated adult.

COMMITTEE ON SCHOOL HEALTH

John Lester Reichert, M.D., Chairman
Ernest L. Glasscock, M.D.
George B. Logan, M.D.
George Maksim, M.D.
E. Earl Moody, M.D.
Thomas E. Shaffer, M.D.
Harold C. Stuart, M.D.
Alfred Yankauer, M.D.

SELECTED BIBLIOGRAPHY

School Athletics—Problems and Policies. Educational Policies Commission, National Education Association of the United States, Washington, D.C., 1954.

Children in Focus—Their Health and Activity. 1954 Yearbook, American Association for Health, Physical Education and Recreation, Washington, D.C.

Report of the Committee on Athletics for Pupils of Junior High and Elementary School Age. Minnesota State High School League Bulletin, Volume XXIX, Oct. 1954.

Editorial—Accidents in children. J.A.M.A. January 2, 1954.

Parmalee, Arthur H.: Fatigue in relation to growth and development. J. Health Educ., Volume 16: No. 3, February 1953.

Desirable Athletic Competition for Children. Report of the Joint Committee on Athletic Competition for Children of Elementary and Junior High School Age, American Association for Health, Physical Education and Recreation, Washington, D.C., 1952

McNeely, Simon A.: Of "mouse" and men. J. Am. A. Health, Phys. Ed. & Rec., December 1952.

Sports Illustrated: Summit meeting for sport, July 15, 1955; Report that shocked the President, August 15, 1955; 19th hole—The readers take over, August 29, 1955.

Phillips, Marjorie: How fit are our American children? J. Am. A. Health, Phys. Ed. & Rec., p. 14, September 1955.

Krogman, Wilton M.: Child growth and football. *Ibid.*, p. 12, September 1955.

Appendix B

PRESIDENT'S COUNCIL ON YOUTH FITNESS

Policy Statement on School Health and Physical Education

AMERICAN YOUNG PEOPLE, while fundamentally healthy, often lack the vigor and physical well-being basic to the full development and use of their inherent capacities. Our schools must recognize and accept their share of the responsibility for the physical development of every girl and boy.

Therefore, one of the primary roles of the President's Council on Youth Fitness is to explain the need for—and to motivate parents, citizens, and school administrators to provide—quality programs of health and physical education in all schools.

The Council believes the following elements are basic to instruction in health and physical education:

1. Full recognition by physical educators, health educators, parents, citizens, and school administrators that the attainment and maintenance of physical fitness is a basic responsibility of physical education and health education.

2. A daily class period allotted to physical education, grades K through twelve.

3. During this period, every girl and boy participates in sufficient vigorous activity to insure the benefits which result from exercise. This is the unique function of physical education.

4. Every physical education class should be conducted to provide proper warm-up, sequence of activities, progressive development of strength, endurance, and other physical attributes.

5. Teachers must, themselves, project the image of fitness. They always should endeavor to be examples through personal appearance, enthusiasm, and participation.

6. In addition to the period allotted for

physical education, sufficient curriculum time should be provided to adequately teach healthful and safe living, which includes an understanding of the effects of inactivity and the role of exercise in the development and maintenance of good health.

In order of priority, the Council's objectives include:

1. To encourage all elementary and secondary schools to provide a physical education program which includes the four basic concepts of the "Blue Book,"[1] which are:

   a. Every child should have a medical examination, with proper follow-through, upon entrance to school, and periodically thereafter at least three additional times in his school career.
   b. Use of a screening test to identify the physically underdeveloped child, and provision of a developmental program to meet individual needs.
   c. A daily physical education period

which conforms to items 2 and 3 above.

   d. Use of a comprehensive testing program to evaluate pupil progress and to motivate improvement.

2. To encourage elementary and secondary schools to work toward quality programs, encompassing the administrative standards set forth in the "Blue Book" (pp. 10–13).

3. To develop basic recommendations for health education similar to those relating to physical education in Part II of the "Blue Book," and to work for the implementation of the recommendations.

4. To establish suggested guide lines for health education and physical education at various grade levels to encourage progressively developmental programs in school systems throughout the country. (Because of the increasing mobility and urbanization of the American population, such guide lines are recommended to encourage equalized opportunities for all our children and youth.)

5. To develop basic recommendations to insure the physical fitness of college students.

---

[1] President's Council on Youth Fitness: *Youth Physical Fitness—Suggested Elements of a School-Centered Program*. Washington 25, D.C.: U.S. Government Printing Office, Supt. of Documents, 1961.

Index of Games, Dances, and Stunts[*]

General Index

Abdominals, testing strength of, 230
Accent, 369, 373
Acceptance, by adults, 30
　by peers, 30, 38, 39
Accidents, prevention of, 108
　See also Safety
Accompaniment, creative dance, 391
　singing, dances with, 405–408
Adjustment, *see* Social adjustment
Adults, acceptance by, 30
After-school play, 71–72, 163, 282
Aggression, expression of, in dramatic play, 40
　intermediate grades, 40, 41
　preschool period, 24
　See also Overaggression
Aggressive action games, 282, 309
　teaching, 281
Aldrich, Anita, 13
Allen, Frederick Lewis, 15
Allen, Ross L., 103, 115
American Academy of Pediatrics, Policy Statement on Competitive Athletics, 428–433
American Association for Health, Physical Education, and Recreation, 13, 46, 74, 94, 114, 160, 169, 271, 361
American Medical Association, 156
Amylong, Tora, 272
Anderson, Harold H., 217
Andrews, Gladys, 169, 217, 424
Anger, in intermediate grades, 38
　in preschool period, 22, 23
　in primary grades, 30
　See also Aggression; Hostility
Apparatus, films demonstrating use of, 255
　intermediate grades, 37, 65
　preschool period, 21, 56–57
　primary grades, 26, 27, 28, 60
　safety and, 108
　self-testing program and, 222, 255–265
　swinging, 262
　See also Equipment; Facilities
Appraisal, health, 103–104

See also Evaluation
Arithmetic, integration with physical education, 146
Arms, testing strength of, 228, 231
Art, integration with physical education, 147–148
Ashton, Dudley, 142, 361, 400
Association for Childhood Education, International, 128
Athletics, competitive, Policy Statement of American Academy of Pediatrics on, 428–433

Baker, Gertrude M., 74, 95
Baker, Harry J., 114
Balance, in square dance, 417
　testing, 229, 230
Balance beams, 256–257
Balancing, 26, 27
Baldwin, A. L., 46
Baller, Warren, 46
Ball handling, intermediate grades, 35, 36
　preschool period, 20, 21, 24
　primary grades, 26
Ballroom dance steps, 404
Balls, contests involving, 248
　for intermediate grades, 37
　for preschool period, 21
　for primary grades, 26, 28
　games played with, 248
　self-testing and, 247–248
　teacher-directed problems involving, 247–248
Band conductors, 373
Bands, color, *see* Color bands
　rhythm, 141
Bars, doorway, 262
　horizontal, 262
　parallel, 262
　use of, preschool period, 20
　　primary grades, 26, 27
Bats, 35, 36, 37
Beams, 262
Beanbags, use of, 248–249